W9-BRF-445

Larousse
Treasury
of
Country
Cooking

LAROUSSE
Treasury of Country
Cooking

CROWN PUBLISHERS, INC. NEW YORK

Most of the recipes in *Larousse Treasury of Country Cooking* have been adapted from

    Les cuisines régionales by Marie Maronne and Rose Montigny
and *Cuisine à travers le monde* by Rose Montigny

Translated by the Translation Company of America

The English-language edition was prepared by Leone Botwinick, Pres Bowles, Marion Burge, Julia C. Colmore, Judy de Rubini, Regina Hersey, Matthew Kangas, Ljuba Lefebre, Albert Rice Leventhal, Jeanette Mall, Robert Myer, Patricia Read, Phyllis Stoller, Natalie Ting, Marjorie Tippie, Pilar Turner, Margaret L. Wiener, José Wilson, and Shirley Wohl.

Published by CROWN PUBLISHERS, Inc.
419 Park Avenue South, New York, New York 10016

An original work created and produced by
Vineyard Books, Inc.
159 East 64th Street
New York, New York 10021

© Copyright Librairie Larousse 1968, 1975
English translation © Vineyard Books, Inc. 1975

All rights reserved. No part of this book may be reproduced or utilized in any form or by any means, electronic or mechanical, including photocopying, recording, or by any information storage retrieval system, without permission in writing from the Publisher. Inquiries should be addressed to Vineyard Books, Inc.

Printed in the United States of America
Published simultaneously in Canada by General Publishing Company Limited

Library of Congress Cataloging in Publication Data
Main entry under title:

Larousse treasury of country cooking.

   "A Vineyard book."
   "Most of the recipes . . . have been adapted from Les cuisines régionales, by Marie Maronne and Rose Montigny and Cuisine à travers le monde, by Rose Montigny. Translated by the Translation Company of America."
   1. Cookery, International.   I. Maronne, Marie. Les cuisines régionales. II. Montigny, Rose. Cuisine à travers le monde. III. Larousse, firm, publishers, Paris.
TX725.A1L27   641.5'9   75-4175

ISBN 0-517-52101-6

CONTENTS

The discovery of a new dish does more for the happiness of mankind than the discovery of a star.

—JEAN-ANTHELME BRILLAT-SAVARIN,
The Philosopher in the Kitchen

Preface

Gathered together in this book are hundreds of regional recipes, evolved over the centuries in country kitchens of many lands by ingenious, painstaking and imaginative cooks.

Provincial cookery, using fresh, low-cost, locally available ingredients, is the cornerstone of any great cuisine. It is on these simple and sensible recipes that the elaborate, heavily sauced dishes one orders at astronomical prices in gourmet restaurants have been built. But in today's fast-paced world most people no longer care to indulge in pretentious five-course dinners. For reasons of health, vitality, weight and even boredom, the trend in contemporary life style is toward simplicity. Informal entertaining and a worldwide move back to the basics are reasons for a renewed interest in simple foods, simply prepared.

This widely varied collection of recipes has been assembled with four specific goals in mind. First, the element of cost. Second, the availability of the ingredients. Third, the preferences and biases of Anglo-American cooks and consumers. Finally, ease of preparation.

The editors are quick to admit that "cost" is an elusive term, dependent on season and geography. Some ingredients—leeks and cauliflower, for example—may be low-priced in London and relatively expensive in New York. There are even wide variations in the price of a given item between New Orleans and Denver, Oxford and Glasgow, Melbourne and Perth. In most cases, however, this book lives up to its purpose and shows the average cook how to make a little go a long way (stews and casseroles); how to make inexpensive cuts hugely tasteful (marinades and slow cooking); how to use every part of the animal (fat for cooking oil, bones for stock); how to devise dozens of variations for daily staples (fish in France, pasta in Italy). Where cost *is* ignored is in the few instances where a specific ingredient, while abundant in its native land, may be expensive or rarely found on our own shores. A few such recipes *were* kept for the festive occasions when one might want to splurge in order to reproduce a recipe that would not be authentic without the use of, let's say, truffles or pâté de foie gras.

Wherever possible the editors offer acceptable substitutes for items that are unavailable or prohibitively expensive in the English-speaking world. By way of example, white mushrooms are suggested in lieu of cèpes and chanterelles, shellfish for langoustine, olive oil for goose fat.

Another significant change resulted from the fact that the original Larousse recipes were generalized and often non-specific—a clear tribute to the expertise and inventiveness of French cooks. Since English-speaking readers prefer step-by-step instructions in preparing dishes, the editors meticulously adhered to the content and intent of the Larousse recipes while adapting them for kitchens in America and the British Commonwealth. With each recipe the home chef is told how much time is needed to prepare a given dish and how much time it will take to cook. A "Fundamentals" chapter at the end of the volume explains cookery terms, and recipes are given for such basics as Hollandaise and Béchamel sauces, which are used again and again with various recipes in the book.

Since France has admittedly been headquarters for brilliant provincial cooking for centuries, more than half of the recipes in this book originated in Gallic kitchens. All of the historic provinces are represented—Normandy and Brittany, Alsace and Lorraine, Provence and Île de France, along with dozens of others.

Almost an equal number of culinary gems included are indigenous to over fifty other nations. There are Spring Rolls and Steamed Ground Pork plus a score of others from China. Baked Clams Oregano and Brisket of Beef with Fruit partially represent Italy and Israel. Baked Lamb with Cracked Wheat comes from Lebanon, Tongue with Almond Sauce from Argentina plus nearly 200 others, ranging all the way from Germany's renowned chocolate cake (Schokoladentorte) to the humble American meat loaf.

The *Larousse Treasury of Country Cooking* makes no pretense of being an encyclopedic work. It is highly selective, hugely diversified. Many but not all of the foreign recipes will appeal on first glance to the English or American palate (the editors assume, for instance, that the reader will be more inclined to try the Hungarian recipe for Chicken Paprika than the Peanut Soup from Ghana). An effort has been made to make this collection truly international in scope and at the same time appeal to the armchair traveler. Ideas abound from all corners of the earth for every occasion—twosomes and family meals; buffets and dinner parties; teas, cold suppers and brunches.

More than anything else, this is a Discovery Cookbook. It contains the unexpected and the unique. It is down to earth and totally specific. It should be a boon to the family budget and a delight to all those whose taste buds are receptive to new dishes in their day-to-day menus.

Appetizers and
Hors D'Oeuvres

AVOCADO DIP *(guacamole)*

Mexico

Preparation time: 10 minutes
Ingredients

2   avocados, peeled and
    pitted
    Juice of 1 lemon
1   onion, minced
1   to 2 cloves garlic,
    minced
1   hot green jalapeño
    pepper, minced

Salt
1   tomato, peeled, seeded
    and chopped
    Mayonnaise for coating
    guacamole

1. In a non-metallic bowl lightly mash the avocados to chunky consistency.

2. Add the lemon juice, minced onion, minced garlic and *jalapeño* pepper. Mix thoroughly, then season to taste with salt.

3. Stir in the chopped tomato, then transfer to a serving bowl.

4. Using a broad spatula, spread a very thin layer of mayonnaise over the *guacamole*, cover the bowl with foil and refrigerate until needed.

Serves 6

CAULIFLOWER AND TURNIP DIP
(tsvetnya kapysta i brukva)

Preparation time: 20 minutes

Cooking time: 5 minutes
Refrigeration time: 1 hour

USSR

Ingredients

1 head cauliflower, broken into flowerets

6 young turnips, scraped and cut into sticks

Russian Mayonnaise:

3 egg yolks, hard-boiled

1 teaspoon dry mustard

1 pint sour cream

5 tablespoons olive oil

2 tablespoons vinegar
Salt
Freshly ground pepper

3 tablespoons capers, chopped

1 tablespoon fresh parsley, chopped

1. Parboil the cauliflower and turnips in separate saucepans of boiling salted water until barely tender. (This will take about 5 minutes.) Refresh under cold running water, drain and reserve.

2. Push the egg yolks through a strainer into a mixing bowl. Add the dry mustard and beat in the sour cream. Drop by drop, gradually beat in the oil and then stir in the vinegar.

3. Add the chopped capers and parsley. Season to taste with salt and pepper. Scrape into a serving bowl.

4. Place the serving bowl in the center of a platter and surround with the cooled cauliflower and turnips. Chill for at least an hour before serving.

Serves 6 to 8

CHICK-PEA APPETIZER *(humous)*

Preparation time: 15 minutes

Israel

Ingredients

A   20-ounce can chick-peas
Salt
½   cup tahini (sesame-seed paste)

1   clove garlic, pressed
Juice of 1 lemon
Cayenne pepper
Chopped fresh parsley for garnish

1. Drain the chick-peas and reserve the liquid. Purée the chick-peas in a food mill or blender, using as much of the liquid as needed to make a smooth paste.

2. In a bowl, combine the chick-pea purée and the *tahini*. Blend thoroughly, then season to taste with pressed garlic, lemon juice and cayenne pepper.

3. Transfer *humous* to a serving dish and garnish with chopped parsley. Serve at room temperature as a dip or a spread with crackers, *pita* bread (page 374) or bite-sized raw vegetables.

Serves 8 to 10

EGGPLANT DIP *(baba ghanoúj)*

Preparation time: 15 minutes **Baking time:** 40 minutes

Lebanon

Ingredients

1 *large eggplant*
¼ *cup tahini*
   (sesame-seed paste)
1 *clove garlic, pressed*
2 *tablespoons lemon juice*

2 *tablespoons olive oil*
   Salt
   Chopped fresh parsley
   for garnish

1. Set oven at 400°.

2. Bake the eggplant until tender, about 40 minutes.

3. Allow the baked eggplant to cool enough to be handled, then peel. Discard skin.

4. Place the eggplant pulp in a mixing bowl and mash with a fork.

5. Add the *tahini*, garlic, lemon juice and olive oil to the mashed pulp. Mix thoroughly, then season to taste with salt.

6. Cover bowl and store in the refrigerator until needed.

7. Before serving, stir dip thoroughly, then transfer to a serving bowl and garnish with chopped fresh parsley. Serve at room temperature.

Serves 6

Serve as a salad or as a spread with pita bread (page 374) and bite-sized raw vegetables.

NIÇOISE "CAVIAR" *(tapénade)*

Preparation time: 10 minutes

France

Ingredients

6 anchovy fillets	3 tablespoons olive oil
2 cups dry oil-cured Mediterranean or Greek olives, pitted	Freshly ground pepper
½ cup tuna fish packed in olive oil	2 to 4 garlic cloves, pressed

1. Rinse the anchovy fillets under running cold water. Pat dry.

2. Put the olives, anchovy fillets and tuna fish through a food mill or blender. Beat in the olive oil. Season to taste with freshly ground pepper and garlic.

3. Serve in a small earthenware crock with fresh French bread or toast.

Serves 4 to 8

VARIATION: *Blend hard-cooked egg yolks in during Step 2. Stuff the tapénade mixture into the egg whites.*

ARTICHOKES WITH GREEN VINAIGRETTE *(artichauts vinaigrette)*

Preparation time: 20 minutes   **Cooking time:** 40 minutes   *France*

Ingredients

- 4 artichokes
- 1 lemon, cut in half
- 4 peppercorns

Green Vinaigrette Sauce:

- ⅓ cup red wine vinegar
- 3 cloves garlic, pressed
- 1 tablespoon dry mustard

- 1 teaspoon salt
- 1 teaspoon freshly ground pepper
- 1 cup olive oil
- 8 tablespoons fresh minced herbs (parsley, tarragon, basil)

1. In a large pot bring 5 quarts of salted water to a rapid boil.

2. Cut off the stems of the artichokes, remove the tough bottom leaves and rub the base of each artichoke with lemon. Put the artichokes into the water with the lemon and peppercorns and bring back to a boil. Partially cover and boil gently until a center artichoke leaf pulls out easily, about 40 minutes.

3. When the artichokes are done, remove them from pot and place upside down to drain.

4. Make the vinaigrette sauce, combining the vinegar, garlic, mustard, salt and pepper and blending well, then adding the oil and the minced herbs.

5. Serve the artichokes at room temperature with the green vinaigrette sauce on the side.

Serves 4

GRATED CARROT HORS D'OEUVRES *(carottes râpées)*

France

Preparation time: 15 minutes   **Marination time:** 2 hours

Ingredients

½   *pound carrots, peeled*
2   *shallots, minced*
⅓   *cup olive oil*
     Juice of ½ lemon

Lettuce leaves for garnish
Chopped parsley for garnish

1. Grate the carrots into a glass bowl.

2. Combine the carrots with the shallots, olive oil and lemon juice. Marinate for 2 hours.

3. To serve, arrange on a bed of lettuce and sprinkle with chopped parsley.

Serves 4

CELERY-ROOT RÉMOULADE
(céleri-rave rémoulade)

Preparation time: 30 minutes   **Refrigeration time:** overnight   *France*

Ingredients

1   *celeriac (root or knob celery), peeled, washed and cut in julienne strips*

1   *teaspoon salt*

1   *tablespoon vinegar*

Mustard Mayonnaise:

½   *cup mayonnaise*

2   *tablespoons dry mustard*

2   *tablespoons lemon juice*

1. Place the celeriac strips in a glass bowl. To prevent discoloring, cover with cold water and add the salt and vinegar. Allow to stand for 15 minutes, then drain.

2. Blanch the celeriac strips in boiling water for 30 seconds. Drain, refresh under cold running water, then pat dry.

3. Prepare the mustard mayonnaise by combining the three ingredients.

4. Place the celeriac strips in a glass bowl and toss gently with the mustard mayonnaise. Cover and refrigerate overnight.

Serves 4

EGGPLANT FAREED *(batinjan)*

Lebanon

Preparation time: 10 minutes
Eggplant stands—30 minutes

Cooking time: 6 minutes
Prepared dish chills—3 hours

Ingredients

2	*small eggplants, peeled and cubed*
	Salt
6	*tablespoons olive oil*
1	*clove garlic, minced*
¼	*medium onion, minced*
	Juice of 1 lemon

2	*tablespoons fresh parsley, chopped*
½	*pint yoghurt*
	Chopped fresh mint for garnish
	Thinly sliced black bread

1. Put the eggplant cubes in a non-metallic colander. Salt cubes lightly, then cover colander with a cloth and rest over a plate (or in the sink) for 30 minutes.

2. Drain eggplant thoroughly and dry on absorbent paper.

3. Heat ½ the oil in a frying pan. Add the eggplant and sauté over moderate heat until tender, about 6 minutes. Remove from heat.

4. In a mixing bowl, combine the sautéed eggplant, garlic, onion, lemon juice and remaining olive oil. Toss until well mixed.

5. Stir in the parsley and yoghurt. Adjust seasonings.

6. Transfer the eggplant to a serving bowl, cover and refrigerate for at least 3 hours.

7. Serve at room temperature, garnished with chopped fresh mint and accompanied by thinly sliced black bread.

Serves 6

FENNEL ANTIPASTO
(insalata di finocchi)

Preparation time: 10 minutes   **Marination time:** 2 hours   *Italy*

Ingredients

1 *fennel bulb, trimmed and thinly sliced*	*Juice of ½ lemon*
½ *cup olive oil*	*Salt*
	Freshly ground pepper

1. Place the fennel in a glass bowl. Coat the fennel with the olive oil and the lemon juice. Add salt and pepper to taste.

2. Cover and let stand at room temperature for at least 2 hours. Stir occasionally.

3. Serve as part of an antipasto or as part of a green salad, using the marinade as the base for the salad dressing.

Serves 2 to 4

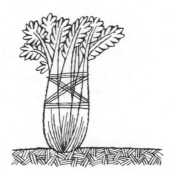

CRACKED-WHEAT SALAD *(tabooley)*

Syria

Preparation time: 10 minutes
Bulgar soaks—15 minutes

Ingredients

1 cup bulgar (cracked wheat)	¼ cup olive oil
6 scallions, chopped	¼ cup lemon juice
½ cup fresh parsley, finely chopped	Salt
5 tablespoons fresh mint, finely chopped, or 3 tablespoons dried crushed mint	Freshly ground pepper
	Lettuce for garnish
	Sliced cucumbers for garnish
3 large tomatoes, peeled and finely chopped	Black olives for garnish

1. Soak the bulgar in a bowl of water for 15 minutes. Drain and squeeze dry.

2. Transfer the bulgar to a mixing bowl. Add the remaining ingredients, except for the garnishes, and mix well.

3. Line a serving platter with lettuce leaves. Heap the salad in the center of the platter and garnish with cucumber slices and black olives.

Serves 6

KIDNEY BEAN SALAD
(ensalada de habichuelas)

Preparation time: 10 minutes   **Marination time:** 12 hours   *Cuba*

Ingredients

- 1 pound canned red kidney beans, drained
- 1 white onion, finely chopped
- 1 clove garlic, pressed
- 1 tablespoon olive oil
- 1 tablespoon red wine vinegar
- ¼ teaspoon dry mustard
- ¼ teaspoon salt
- ⅛ teaspoon curry powder

1. Combine all of the above ingredients in a glass bowl. Mix well.

2. Cover bowl tightly with plastic wrap. Allow mixture to marinate at room temperature for at least 12 hours.

Serves 4

MARINATED LEEKS WITH RICE
(salade de poireaux et de riz)

France

Preparation time: 10 minutes

Cooking time: 20 minutes
Refrigeration time: 1 hour

Ingredients

3 to 4   leeks
  ½   cup water
  2   tablespoons olive oil
  1   tablespoon rice

  ¼   tablespoon salt
Juice of ½ lemon
Lemon wedges for garnish

1. Cut off the roots and the upper thirds of the green part of the leeks. Pull off tough outer leaves. Wash thoroughly to remove all traces of sand.

2. Cut the leeks into 1-inch pieces. Rinse again.

3. Place the leeks in a saucepan. Add the water, oil, rice and salt. Bring to a boil, then cover and simmer over low heat for 20 minutes.

4. With a slotted spoon, transfer leeks and rice to a serving dish. Sprinkle with lemon juice and refrigerate for at least 1 hour. When ready to serve, garnish with lemon wedges.

Serves 2 to 4

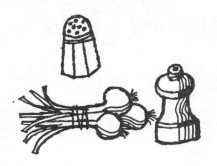

MUSHROOMS ÎLE DE FRANCE
(cassolettes aux champignons)

Preparation time: 25 minutes   **Cooking time:** 30 minutes

France

Ingredients

1 *pound firm white mushrooms, minced*	2 *tablespoons lemon juice*
1 *onion, minced*	2 *teaspoons salt*
1 *cup water*	*Freshly ground pepper*
Herb bouquet (thyme, basil, oregano)	4 *eggs*
	½ *cup cream*

1. Set oven at 400°.

2. In a saucepan, combine the mushrooms, onion, water, herb bouquet, 1 tablespoon lemon juice, salt and pepper. Cook rapidly until the water has evaporated, about 10 minutes. Remove herb bouquet.

3. In a bowl, beat the eggs and the cream.

4. Remove the mushroom mixture from the heat and add the remaining lemon juice. Taste and correct seasoning.

5. Add the mushroom mixture to the cream and egg mixture.

6. Ladle the mixture into an ovenproof ramekin. Place in a shallow pan of hot water and bake until set, about 20 minutes.

7. Serve warm as a first course or chilled as a spread with hot buttered toast.

Serves 4

CREAMED MUSHROOMS WITH CHEESE *(croûtes comtoises)*

France

Preparation time: 20 minutes   **Cooking time:** 20 minutes

Ingredients

1 pound morels (wild mushrooms) or small white mushrooms, cleaned and sliced	Salt Freshly ground pepper
7 tablespoons butter	¼ cup heavy cream
¼ teaspoon grated nutmeg	½ cup Gruyère or other Swiss cheese, grated
	8 one-inch slices French bread

1. Preheat oven to 400°.

2. Melt the butter in a large skillet and cook mushrooms rapidly over a high heat until they begin to give off steam, about 5 to 8 minutes.

3. Lower heat and add nutmeg, salt and pepper to taste and stir in cream.

4. Arrange the slices of bread on a baking pan. Make a slight hollow in the middle of each slice.

5. Spoon the creamed mushrooms over the slices and sprinkle with the grated cheese.

6. Bake until golden, about 10 minutes, and serve.

Serves 4 to 8

BROILED STUFFED MUSHROOM
CAPS *(funghi alla parmigiana)*

Preparation time: 20 minutes   **Baking time:** 25 minutes   *Italy*

Ingredients

12	large white mushrooms
1	clove garlic, minced
3	shallots, minced
3	tablespoons butter
4	tablespoons olive oil
½	cup bread crumbs

½	cup Parmesan cheese, grated
1	teaspoon basil
3	tablespoons parsley, chopped
	Salt
	Freshly ground pepper

1. Wipe the mushrooms with a damp cloth. Remove the stems and chop them finely and squeeze dry in absorbent paper.

2. Preheat oven to 350°.

3. In a small saucepan, sauté the garlic and shallots in 2 tablespoons of the butter and 1 tablespoon of the olive oil. Add the chopped mushroom stems and stir over moderate heat until mushroom liquid has evaporated, about 5 minutes. Remove from heat.

4. Mix the remaining ingredients into the mushroom-stem mixture. Taste and correct seasoning.

5. Stuff the mushroom caps with the mixture. Top each cap with a dot of the remaining butter.

6. Arrange the caps in a shallow well-oiled ovenproof dish and bake about 25 minutes. Serve hot.

Serves 2 to 4

GREEN PEPPERS GABOR

(töltött zöldpaprika Gyor)

Hungary

Preparation time: 20 minutes

Ingredients

8 ounces cottage cheese	Freshly ground pepper
8 anchovy fillets, finely chopped	6 small green peppers, halved and seeded
3 tablespoons capers	3 eggs, hard-boiled and quartered
4 medium onions, finely chopped	6 slices black bread, buttered and quartered
Salt	

1. In a large bowl, combine the cottage cheese, anchovies, capers and onions. Season to taste with salt and pepper.

2. Fill the peppers with the cottage-cheese mixture.

3. Arrange the stuffed peppers and hard-boiled eggs on a platter. Garnish with the slices of buttered black bread.

Serves 6 to 8

ANTIPASTO OF STUFFED PEPPERS *(peperoni alla Piemontese)*

Preparation time: 20 minutes

Baking time: 30 minutes

Italy

Ingredients

2 to 4 cloves garlic, minced	3 tablespoons olive oil
3 firm ripe tomatoes, peeled, seeded and chopped	6 sweet peppers, seeded and quartered
12 anchovy fillets, coarsely chopped	4 tablespoons butter

1. Set oven at 350°.

2. In a bowl, mix the garlic, tomatoes and anchovy fillets with the olive oil.

3. Stuff each pepper section with some of the mixture and dot with the butter.

4. Arrange the peppers on an oiled cookie sheet. Bake for 30 minutes. Remove cookie sheet from oven and allow peppers to cool to room temperature.

5. Serve accompanied by cruets of olive oil and vinegar.

Serves 4 to 6

A combination of red and green sweet peppers makes an attractive presentation.

CRISP VEGETABLE BITS *(samosas)*

India

Preparation time: 1 hour

Cooking time: 3 minutes per batch

Ingredients

1	*cup whole wheat flour*
½	*cup vegetable oil*
½	*teaspoon salt*
½	*cup water*
3	*potatoes, peeled*
½	*teaspoon each ground cumin, coriander and garam masala (optional)*
2	*onions, chopped*
1	*clove garlic, minced*
¼	*teaspoon ground turmeric*
2	*teaspoons lemon juice*
	Vegetable oil for frying
1	*green pepper, chopped*
1	*cauliflower, broken into flowerets*
1	*cup spinach, chopped*
2	*tomatoes, chopped*
4	*carrots, peeled and chopped*

1. In a large mixing bowl, combine the flour, ¼ teaspoon salt and 4 tablespoons of oil. Add the water, a little at a time, to form a stiff dough. Knead until smooth, about 10 minutes. Roll into a ball, brush lightly with oil and reserve.

2. Boil the potatoes in salted water until tender, about 15 minutes. Mash lightly. Heat 4 tablespoons of oil. Add the cumin, coriander, half the chopped onions, the garlic and turmeric. Cook until the onions are tender, about 5 minutes. Add the potatoes, ¼ teaspoon salt, the garam masala and lemon juice. Cook for 5 minutes. Remove from heat.

3. Roll out the dough to ¼-inch thickness. Cut the dough into 2-inch rounds. Place a spoonful of the potato mixture in the center of each round. Fold into crescents and pinch to seal.

4. Pour the vegetable oil to a depth of 3 inches in a wok or 12-inch skillet. Heat to sizzling, then reduce heat to moderate. Fry a few samosas at a time until golden brown, about 3 minutes. Drain. Place the samosas in a serving dish, accompanied by bowls of the chopped vegetables.

Yields about 3 dozen samosas

CHEESE TRUFFLES *(Kaastruffels)*

Preparation time: 20 minutes

Ingredients

¼ pound unsalted butter, at room temperature

⅓ cup Gouda or Cheddar cheese, grated

Salt

Freshly ground pepper

Paprika

4 slices stale pumpernickel bread (without crusts), very finely crumbled

The Netherlands

1. In a mixing bowl, cream the butter well with a wooden spoon.

2. Gradually blend in the grated cheese, then season with salt, freshly ground pepper and paprika. Reserve.

3. Using a spoonful of the cheese mixture at a time, shape the mixture into small balls. Reserve.

4. Spread the bread crumbs out on greaseproof paper. Season with freshly ground pepper.

5. Roll the cheese truffles in the seasoned bread crumbs until well coated, then transfer the truffles to a serving plate. Chill until needed.

Yields about 3 dozen truffles

BURGUNDY CHEESE RING (gougère)

Preparation time: 20 minutes   **Cooking time:** 35 minutes

France

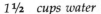

Ingredients

1½ cups water
9   tablespoons butter
2   teaspoons salt
1½ cups sifted flour

6   eggs, beaten
2   cups Gruyère or other
    Swiss cheese, grated
1   egg, beaten, for glazing

1. Set oven at 400°.

2. Bring the water, butter and salt to a boil in a saucepan. When the butter has melted, remove the pan from heat and vigorously beat in all the flour at once. Continue beating until flour is totally incorporated.

3. Return saucepan to moderate heat. Beat constantly with a wooden spoon until the dough forms a ball and comes away from the sides of the pan (about 2 to 4 minutes).

4. Remove saucepan from the heat. Beat in the eggs a little bit at a time, making sure each addition is well incorporated before adding the next. Gradually beat in the grated cheese.

5. With moist hands, form the dough into a sausage roll and twist the roll into a ring.

6. Place on a greased cookie sheet, make a few slits on the surface of the dough with a knife and, to glaze, brush with the beaten egg.

7. Bake 30 to 35 minutes, until the cheese pastry is golden brown on the outside and has puffed up. (Do not open the oven door during baking.) Slice and serve immediately as an appetizer.

Serves 4 to 6

MELTED CHEESE APPETIZERS
LORRAINE *(croûtes à la bière)*

Preparation time: 35 minutes   **Broiling time:** 5 minutes   *France*

Ingredients

    8   *slices white bread*
       Butter
1½   *cups beer*
 ½   *pound Gruyère or*
       other Swiss cheese,
       grated

    Dash cayenne pepper
3   *tablespoons butter*
4   *slices ham*

1. Preheat broiler to 400°.

2. Lightly toast the bread and butter it.

3. In a saucepan reduce the beer by half over moderate heat. Add the grated cheese, stirring until the mixture has the consistency of paste. Season with cayenne pepper.

4. In a skillet melt the 3 tablespoons of butter and pan-fry the slices of ham over moderately high heat. Place the ham slices on toast, cover with the cheese mixture and top with the remaining toast, butter side up.

5. Put the sandwiches on a baking sheet and run under the broiler until the toast is golden, about 5 minutes.

6. Serve very hot, accompanied by cold beer at lunch, or cut into quarters as an appetizer.

Yields 4 sandwiches

LITTLE UKRAINIAN PIES *(piroshki)*

Preparation time: 30 minutes   **Baking time:** 15 to 20 minutes
Sour cream pastry chills—1 hour

USSR

Ingredients

Sour Cream Pastry:

3½	cups flour
1	teaspoon baking powder
½	teaspoon salt
½	cup butter, chilled
2	eggs, lightly beaten
½	pint sour cream

Mushroom Filling:

6	scallions, minced
¾	pound mushrooms, chopped

4	tablespoons butter
1	tablespoon flour
3	tablespoons sour cream
3	tablespoons fresh dill
	Pinch allspice
	Salt
	Freshly ground pepper
2	hard-boiled eggs, chopped

Beaten egg for glazing

1. Prepare the pastry: Sift the flour, baking powder and salt into a large bowl. Cut the butter into the flour until it is the consistency of cornmeal. In another bowl, combine the eggs and the sour cream until smooth, then blend in the flour mixture. Knead the dough on a floured board until smooth. Shape into a ball, cover and chill for 1 hour.

2. Sauté the scallions and mushrooms in the butter until golden. Remove and reserve. Sprinkle in the flour and stir over moderate heat for 1 minute. Blend in the sour cream and remove from heat. Return the scallions and mushrooms to the pan. Mix thoroughly, then add the dill, allspice, salt and pepper. Add the chopped eggs, mixing well.

3. Preheat the oven to 400°. Roll out the dough to ¼-inch thickness on a lightly floured board. Cut into 3½-inch rounds. Place a heaping tablespoon of filling in the center of each round. Fold into crescents and pinch the edges to seal. Place on a buttered baking sheet. Brush with the egg and bake until golden, about 15 to 20 minutes.

Yields 3 dozen piroshkis

VEAL AND CHIVE TURNOVERS
(petits pâtés à la ciboulette)

Preparation time: 20 minutes
Refrigeration: pastry—1½ hours
               filling—1 hour

Baking time: 20 minutes

France

Ingredients

Flaky Pastry:

- 2½ cups flour
- 12 tablespoons butter
- ½ cup ice water
- ½ teaspoon salt

Filling:

- 10 ounces ground veal
  (shoulder or rump)

- 2 teaspoons salt
- Freshly ground pepper
- ⅛ teaspoon nutmeg
- 2 eggs, whole
- 1 egg, separated
- ¾ cup heavy cream
- 2 tablespoons chopped
  chives

1. Prepare flaky pastry (page 474) and chill for about 1½ hours.

2. Place the ground veal in a bowl. Add the seasonings and beat in the whole eggs. Beat the extra egg white until stiff and fold into the veal. Refrigerate mixture for 1 hour.

3. Set oven at 425°.

4. Beat the cream until stiff and fold into veal. Add the chives.

5. Roll out 1/3 of the pastry to ¼-inch thickness and cut into 3-inch circles. Roll out the remaining pastry and cut into 4-inch circles.

6. Put a tablespoon of the filling onto each small circle. Moisten the edges of the circles with water, cover with the larger circles and seal. Slit tops of turnovers, then transfer to a buttered baking sheet. Beat the remaining egg yolk with a little water and brush onto the pastry. Bake for 20 minutes. Serve hot.

Yields about 24 individual turnovers

SPRING ROLLS *(chun chuan)*

Preparation time: 1¼ hours
Canned sprouts chill—2 hours

Cooking time:
Filling—12 minutes
Spring rolls—4 minutes
per batch

China

Ingredients
Filling:

½   pound lean boneless pork, cut into julienne strips

1   teaspoon cornstarch

1   pound fresh mung bean sprouts or 1 two-pound can bean sprouts

5   tablespoons vegetable oil

3 to 4   thick slices fresh ginger root, peeled

½   pound small shrimp, shelled, deveined and halved

1½   teaspoons salt

1   tablespoon Chinese rice wine or dry sherry

10   small white mushrooms, sliced

2   leeks (white parts only), chopped

1   tablespoon soy sauce

3   eight-ounce packages spring-roll wrappers (6-inch squares)

1   egg, lightly beaten

4   cups vegetable oil for deep-frying

1. Toss the pork with the cornstarch in a bowl. Cover and reserve.

2. Prepare the bean sprouts: Rinse fresh sprouts well, discard husks, drain, pat dry and reserve. (If canned sprouts are used, drain, cover with cold water and refrigerate for 2 hours; rinse, drain and pat dry.)

3. Place a wok or frying pan over moderately high heat for 1 minute. Add 1 tablespoon of the oil. Wait ½ minute, then add the ginger. Stir-fry for 1 minute.

4. Raise heat and add the shrimp. Briskly stir in ¼ teaspoon of the salt and the rice wine (or sherry). Stirring constantly,

cook until the shrimp are pink, about 1 minute. Remove shrimp with a slotted spoon and reserve on a heated platter.

5. Add another 2 tablespoons of the oil to the pan. Heat a few seconds, then briskly stir in the pork strips. Stir-fry for 2 minutes, then lower heat, add mushrooms and stir-fry for another 1½ minutes. Remove with a slotted spoon and add to the shrimp.

6. Add the remaining oil to the pan. Raise heat and add the leeks and the sprouts. Stir-fry for 1 minute.

7. Return the shrimp mixture to the pan. Stir briefly over high heat, then add the soy sauce and the remaining salt. Remove pan from heat.

8. Using a slotted spoon, transfer filling to absorbent paper. Drain well. Place in a bowl, cover and cool to room temperature. (Filling may be prepared in advance and stored in the refrigerator.)

9. To fill spring rolls: a) Place 3 to 4 tablespoons of filling in the center of a wrapper; b) mold filling into a 4-inch-long sausage shape, running diagonally across wrapper; c) wrap one of the large triangular sections of wrapper around filling; d) fold the 2 shorter sections of wrapper over the filling, pushing corners down to secure them; e) lightly brush surface of the remaining wrapper section with egg; f) roll into a compact cylinder. Repeat until all the filling is used.

10. In a wok or heavy saucepan, heat the 4 cups of oil to 375°.

11. Gently lower 4 to 6 spring rolls at a time into the oil and fry until crisp and golden, about 4 minutes. Remove with a slotted spoon, drain on absorbent paper and keep warm in a slow oven. Repeat until all the spring rolls have been fried.

Yields about 2 dozen

Spring rolls may be assembled in advance and frozen. Defrost to room temperature and deep-fry as directed.

China

ANCHOVY CANAPÉS *(anchoïade)*

Preparation time: 15 minutes

France

Ingredients

2	*two-ounce cans anchovy fillets, drained and chopped*
2 to 3	*cloves garlic, minced*
1⅓	*tablespoons olive oil*
1	*tablespoon vinegar*
6	*shallots, minced*
¼	*cup fresh parsley, chopped*

4   *tomatoes, peeled, seeded and chopped*
Freshly ground pepper
Thinly sliced French bread, rubbed with garlic and fried on one side in olive oil

1. Set oven at 400°.
2. In a mortar combine the garlic and anchovies. Grind mixture to a paste, then transfer to a mixing bowl.

3. Gradually beat the olive oil into the anchovy-garlic mixture. Continue beating until oil is thoroughly incorporated, then beat in the vinegar.

4. Add the shallots, parsley and tomatoes. Blend thoroughly, then season to taste with freshly ground pepper. Reserve.

5. Arrange the thinly sliced bread (fried side down) on a baking sheet. Make a slight depression in the unfried side of each slice of bread and spread the anchovy mixture on top.

6. Before serving, place baking sheet in oven until canapés are heated through, about 3 minutes, then arrange the hot anchovy canapés on a platter and serve hot.

Serves 4

SMOKED FISH ROE DIP *(taramasalata)*

Preparation time: 20 minutes

Ingredients

Greece

1	three-ounce jar tarama or smoked cod roe	¼	medium onion, grated
3	slices white bread, crusts trimmed	6	tablespoons olive oil
	Milk or water for soaking bread	3 to 4	tablespoons lemon juice
1 to 2	cloves garlic, pressed		Toasted white bread
			Black olives

1. Soak the bread in a little milk or water. Squeeze out excess liquid.

2. Crush the roe in a mortar and add the bread a bit at a time. Then crush in the pressed garlic and grated onion. Blend thoroughly.

3. Beating vigorously, as for a mayonnaise, gradually add the olive oil and the lemon juice, a tablespoon at a time. Taste as you go along until the flavor seems right.

4. Serve on toast accompanied by black olives.

Serves 4

Tarama is the dried, salted roe of the gray mullet. It is a favorite appetizer, in one form or another, throughout the Middle East.

CHRISTMAS PICKLED HERRING
(sild)

Denmark

Preparation time: 20 minutes
Herring soaks—overnight

Marination time: 4 days

Ingredients

16	*herring fillets*
4	*onions, thinly sliced*
1¼	*ounces pickling spice mixture**

Marinade:

4	*cups white vinegar*
4	*cups water*
¼	*cup brown sugar*

1. Soak the herring fillets overnight in cold water.

2. Drain the fillets and, if necessary, remove the black membranes. Cut fillets into bite-sized pieces.

3. Place a layer of herring in a large earthenware crock. Cover with a layer of sliced onions and a generous sprinkling of pickling spices. Continue layering and seasoning until crock is ¾ full.

4. In a non-metallic bowl, combine the marinade ingredients. Mix thoroughly, then add to the crock.

5. Cover crock tightly and marinate herring in a cool place or refrigerator for 3 days. Gently stir herring with a wooden spoon, then re-cover crock and marinate for at least 1 more day.

Yields 12 to 16 servings

Although sild *is delicious all year round, traditionally it is a Christmas-season favorite. Since the herring "gathers virtue" with prolonged marination, a large batch is often prepared at the end of November so that it will be at its best for the holidays.*

*Packaged pickling spice mixtures usually contain cassia, allspice, coriander, mustard seed, bay leaves, ginger, cloves, chilies, black peppercorns, mace and cardamom.

MARINATED HERRING WITH 3 DRESSINGS *(suolasilli)*

Preparation time: 30 minutes
Raw herring marinates—3 hours

Cooking time: 3 minutes

Finland

Ingredients

¼ cup salt
2 cups water
1 cup vinegar
5 pounds herring fillets
1 cup dry white wine
2 tablespoons sugar

2 onions, thinly sliced
2 lemons, thinly sliced
2 teaspoons peppercorns
½ teaspoon dried chili peppers, crushed
2 bay leaves, crushed

Cream Cheese Dressing:

3 ounces cream cheese
½ cup light cream
1 tablespoon lemon juice
2 tablespoons chives

Mustard Mayonnaise:

2 tablespoons mustard
1 cup mayonnaise
2 tablespoons herring marinade

Dill Dressing:

½ pint sour cream
1 small onion, minced
¼ cup vinegar
½ cup fresh dill, chopped

1. Combine the salt, water and vinegar. Add the fillets and marinate for 3 hours. Drain the fillets and reserve.

2. Pour the marinade into a small saucepan. Add the wine and sugar. Boil rapidly for 2 minutes, remove from heat and cool.

3. Roll up the herring fillets. Layer the fillets in 3 glass pickling jars, covering each layer of herring with a layer of the onions, lemon, and spices. Pour in the marinade. Cover and refrigerate for 24 hours.

4. Prepare the three dressings in separate bowls, blending the ingredients listed above for each. To serve, drain the fillets and cut into bite-sized pieces. Add ⅓ of the fillets to each dressing and mix gently.

Yields 12 servings

MARINATED FISH *(ceviche)*

Mexico

Preparation time: 15 minutes

Refrigeration time: 3 hours

Ingredients

½ *pound halibut fillets or other firm white fish, diced*

½ *pound bay scallops*

Juice of 2 limes

1 *ripe avocado*

½ *pound tomatoes, peeled, seeded and chopped*

½ *green pepper, seeded and diced*

4 *tablespoons olive oil*

4 *tablespoons parsley, chopped*

2 to 4 *scallions, white part only, diced*

Pinch of cayenne

Salt

Freshly ground pepper

1. Put the fish and scallops in a glass bowl, toss with lime juice, cover and refrigerate for 2 hours, stirring occasionally.

2. Peel and dice the avocado.

3. Add the avocado and the remaining ingredients to the fish. Toss and correct seasoning. Refrigerate for at least 1 hour.

4. Serve on a bed of lettuce or in individual chilled glass bowls.

Serves 4

SALMON WITH DILL SAUCE
(gravlax med dillsås)

Preparation time: 1 hour   **Marination time:** 2 to 7 days   *Sweden*

Ingredients

A   2½-pound salmon, cleaned

3   tablespoons coarse salt

2   tablespoons sugar

1   tablespoon pepper

1   tablespoon vegetable oil

1   tablespoon cognac or other brandy

1   large bunch fresh dill

Dill Sauce:

3   tablespoons Dijon or dark mustard

1   tablespoon sugar

2   tablespoons white vinegar

½   cup vegetable oil

½   cup fresh dill, chopped

Salt and pepper

1. Cut the salmon in half lengthwise. Bone. Pat dry and reserve.

2. In a small bowl, combine the salt, sugar and pepper.

3. Rub both sides of the salmon with oil and brandy, then season with ½ the sugar, salt and pepper mixture.

4. Spread ⅓ of the dill in a shallow baking dish. Place 1 piece of fish (skin side down) on top. Sprinkle on half the remaining dill. Cover with the second piece of fish (skin side up), then sprinkle on the remaining dill.

5. Cover with a double thickness of aluminum foil, place a plate on top and weight. Refrigerate for 2 to 7 days, turning and basting the fish every 12 hours.

6. Prepare sauce: Combine mustard, sugar and vinegar in small bowl. Using a wire whisk, beat in the oil, as for a mayonnaise (page 476), then add the dill, salt and pepper.

8. Slice the cured salmon in long, thin strips and serve with the dill sauce, lemon wedges and black bread or toast.

Serves 6 to 8

SHRIMP MARINATED WITH DILL
(marinerad räkor med dill)

Sweden

Preparation time: 25 minutes

Marination time: 3 hours

Ingredients

Court Bouillon:

1	onion, chopped
1	stalk celery
4	cups water
2	bay leaves
6	peppercorns
½	tablespoon salt

—

2½	dozen shrimp
1	cup tarragon vinegar
4	bay leaves, crushed
6	peppercorns
¼	cup fresh dill, chopped

1. In a large saucepan, combine the court-bouillon ingredients listed above. Boil rapidly for 15 minutes.

2. Add the shrimp to the court bouillon. Return to a boil, then lower heat and simmer until shells of shrimp turn pink, about 3 to 5 minutes.

3. Remove shrimp with a slotted spoon, shell and devein, then chop coarsely.

4. In a non-metallic bowl, combine the chopped shrimp, vinegar, bay leaves, peppercorns and dill. Mix gently, then cover and let stand at least 3 hours.

5. Before serving, drain well, then transfer to a serving bowl and surround with thinly sliced black bread.

Serves 4 to 6

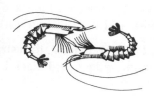

POTTED SHRIMP

Preparation time: 20 minutes   **Cooking time:** 5 minutes
Prepared dish chills—30 minutes

Great Britain

Ingredients

1 pound tiny shrimp	½ teaspoon ground mace
Herb bouquet (bay leaf, parsley, 5 peppercorns, thyme)	Pinch cayenne pepper
	Salt
½ pound butter, at room temperature	Freshly ground black pepper
1 tablespoon lemon juice	Fresh toast triangles

1. Drop the shrimp and the herb bouquet into a pot of lightly salted boiling water. Reduce heat to moderate and cook shrimp until firm and pink, about 5 minutes. Remove from heat, drain and allow to cool to room temperature.

2. Shell and devein the shrimp. Finely chop half the shrimp and reserve.

3. Place the remaining shrimp in a blender or mortar. Add half the butter and the lemon juice. Purée mixture to a paste.

4. Mix the reserved chopped shrimp into the paste. Add the mace and cayenne pepper, then season to taste with salt and black pepper.

5. Press the shrimp mixture into a 3-cup mold or ramekin.

6. Melt the remaining butter in a small saucepan and pour it into the mold. Refrigerate mold until the butter is firm, about 30 minutes.

7. Present the potted shrimp in the mold or unmold and serve as a spread on hot buttered toast triangles.

Serves 6

STUFFED MUSSELS *(moules farcies)*

France

Preparation time: 1 hour

Cooking time: 10 minutes

Ingredients

2   quarts mussels

¼   cup water or dry white wine

12 tablespoons lightly salted butter, at room temperature

2   cloves garlic, finely minced

4   teaspoons fresh parsley, finely chopped

1. Wash the mussels thoroughly, using a stiff brush to scrub the shells. Discard any that are open. Rinse with cold running water until there is no trace of sand.

2. Put them in a large covered pot with the water (or white wine). Cover and steam over high heat until shells open (about 5 minutes).

3. Set oven at 475°.

4. Transfer mussels to a cookie sheet and discard one shell from each mussel. Do not use mussels that have not opened.

5. Cream the butter in a bowl with the minced garlic and parsley. Stuff each mussel with ½ teaspoon of the mixture.

6. Bake until butter mixture bubbles, a few minutes. Serve piping hot.

Serves 4

BAKED CLAMS OREGANO
(vongole reganata)

Preparation time: 20 minutes   **Baking time:** 5 minutes   *Italy*

Ingredients

24 clams in their shells	¼ cup fresh bread crumbs
2 tablespoons minced Italian parsley	1½ teaspoons oregano
1 clove garlic, minced	3 tablespoons olive oil
2 shallots, minced	Freshly ground pepper
4 tablespoons grated Parmesan cheese	

1. Rinse the clams under cold running water until no trace of sand remains. Using a stiff brush, scrub the clam shells thoroughly. Discard any clams with shells that remain open.

2. Put the clams in a large kettle. Cover kettle and steam over high heat until shells open, about 5 to 10 minutes. Remove from heat immediately.

3. Preheat oven to 400°.

4. Discard any clams whose shells have not opened. Remove and discard top shells from the remaining clams, then arrange the clams in their half shells on a baking sheet.

5. In a small bowl combine the parsley, garlic, shallots, Parmesan, bread crumbs, oregano, olive oil and freshly ground pepper. Mix well.

6. Spoon a teaspoon of the mixture onto each clam.

7. Bake for 5 minutes. Serve immediately.

Serves 4

SNAILS WITH GARLIC BUTTER
(escargots de Bourgogne)

France

Preparation time: 10 minutes   **Cooking time:** 6 to 7 minutes

Ingredients

4   dozen canned snails (and shells)

Snail Butter:

12   tablespoons butter, at room temperature

4   cloves garlic, minced

4   shallots, minced

2   tablespoons finely chopped parsley

Salt

Freshly ground pepper

1. Set oven at 425°.

2. Cream the butter and blend in the garlic, shallots and parsley. Season with salt and pepper.

3. Put one snail into each shell. Fill each shell opening with the butter mixture.

4. Arrange the snails on individual ovenproof snail plates. Bake for 6 to 7 minutes and serve immediately.

Serves 4

SALT COD WITH GARLIC MAYONNAISE AND GARNISHES

(aïoli garni)

France

Preparation time: 20 minutes   **Cooking time:** 45 minutes
Salt cod soaks—10 hours

Ingredients

1½	*pounds salt cod*
8	*new potatoes*
8	*small carrots, diced*
4	*white turnips, diced*
4	*small artichokes*
2	*dozen canned snails*

Garlic Mayonnaise (aïoli):

8	*cloves garlic, peeled*
3	*egg yolks*
⅛	*teaspoon salt*
2	*cups olive oil*
	Juice of ½ lemon
	Freshly ground pepper

1. Soak the cod in cold water for 10 hours to remove the salt. Change the water 3 or 4 times.

2. Cook vegetables in separate pots of boiling salted water until tender, about 45 minutes. Drain and reserve.

3. While the vegetables are cooking, prepare the *aïoli*: a) Crush the garlic; b) add the yolks and salt and beat thoroughly; c) add the oil drop by drop, beating constantly, as for a mayonnaise (page 476); d) when thickened, add the lemon juice, salt and pepper.

4. Rinse the cod a final time, place in a saucepan and cover with cold water. Bring to a boil, then reduce heat and poach fish until it flakes when tested with a fork, about 10 minutes. Drain and cut into serving pieces.

5. Arrange the cod, vegetables and snails on separate serving platters. Serve the *aïoli* in a bowl as an accompaniment.

Serves 4

Aïoli, *the "butter of Provence," is also served as a sauce for hearts of palm, eggs, tomatoes, green peppers and meats.*

BEAN AND TUNA FISH
ANTIPASTO *(insalata di fagioli e tonno)*

Italy

Preparation time: 15 minutes
Beans soak—overnight

Cooking time: 2½ hours

Ingredients

 2 cups dry white beans
 1 Spanish onion, sliced
    thinly
 ⅔ cup olive oil
 2 tablespoons wine
    vinegar

 Freshly ground pepper
 Salt
 2 *cans tuna fish packed
    in olive oil, broken into
    chunks*
 *Chopped Italian
 parsley for garnish*

1. Put the beans in a bowl and add enough cold water to reach 3 inches above level of the beans. Let beans soak at room temperature overnight. Drain.

2. Put the beans in a saucepan and add enough cold water to cover. Bring rapidly to a boil. Lower heat, cover and simmer until tender, about 2½ hours. Remove from heat and drain.

3. In a bowl, combine the beans with the onion, olive oil, vinegar, freshly ground pepper and a little salt. Cover and let the mixture cool to room temperature.

4. Add the tuna fish and toss briefly. Sprinkle with the parsley before serving.

Serves 4 to 6

SMOKED FISH MOUSSE

Preparation time: 35 minutes   **Refrigeration time:** 1 hour

Great Britain

Ingredients

¾ *pound fillet of haddock or other fish*

   Herb bouquet (bay leaf, parsley, peppercorns)

3 *ounces smoked trout*

4 *tablespoons butter, creamed*

¼ *cup dry white wine*

1 *tablespoon unflavored gelatin*

¼ *cup water, boiling*

1¼ *cups mayonnaise*

¼ *medium onion, grated*

½ *cup heavy cream*

   Salt

   Freshly ground pepper

Horseradish Cream:

1 *cup heavy cream*

1 *tablespoon fresh horseradish, grated*

   Salt

1. Place the fillets and herb bouquet in a saucepan. Cover with water. Bring to a boil, then lower heat, cover and simmer until fish flakes when tested with a fork, about 10 minutes. Remove pan from heat and cool fish in its liquid.

2. Drain the fillets and transfer to a large mortar or bowl. Add the smoked trout. Mash the fish to a paste with a pestle or wooden spoon. Add the paste to the butter. Mix thoroughly.

3. Pour the wine into another bowl. Sprinkle in the gelatin, then pour in boiling water. Blend in mayonnaise and onion. Add to the fish mixture. Mix well.

4. In a small bowl, beat the cream until stiff. Fold the cream into the fish mixture and season to taste. Pour into an oiled mold. Refrigerate until set, about 1 hour.

5. Whip the cream until stiff. Fold in the horseradish and adjust seasoning. Unmold the mousse and serve with the bowl of horseradish cream.

Serves 6 to 8

CHICKEN TERIYAKI

Japan

Preparation time: 15 minutes   **Cooking time:** 6 to 8 minutes
Chicken marinates—4 to 6 hours

Ingredients

Teriyaki Marinade:

6   tablespoons soy sauce

6   tablespoons sake or
pale dry sherry

2   teaspoons peeled fresh
ginger root, minced

½   pound chicken livers,
halved

1   pound chicken breasts,
skinned, boned and cut
in cubes

Fresh watercress

1. In a cup, combine the marinade ingredients listed above. Reserve.

2. Place the chicken livers and chicken breast cubes in a non-metallic bowl. Pour in the marinade. Stir gently until meat is thoroughly coated, then cover and let stand at room temperature for 4 to 6 hours.

3. Thread the marinated chicken and chicken liver pieces onto small bamboo skewers. (Alternate chicken pieces with chicken liver pieces when threading.) Reserve marinade.

4. Brush the *teriyaki* with the marinade and then broil over charcoal (or under the broiler) for 3 minutes.

5. Turn skewers and brush *teriyaki* with the marinade, then continue broiling until chicken is tender, about 4 minutes.

6. When the *teriyaki* is done, arrange on a heated platter, garnish with fresh watercress and serve immediately.

Serves 2

VARIATION: *Prepare a beef* teriyaki. *Substitute 1 pound sirloin steak cut in 1-inch cubes for the chicken and chicken livers. Proceed as above and serve hot, garnished with raw mushroom slices.*

FIVE SPICED COLD BEEF
(wu shiang new ru)

Preparation time: 10 minutes   **Cooking time:** 1 hour   *China*
                                          Standing time: 1 hour

Ingredients

A	1-pound piece stewing beef
4	tablespoons soy sauce
1	tablespoon Chinese rice wine or dry sherry
1	teaspoon sugar
3	half-inch cubes fresh ginger root, peeled

1	whole star anise or 8 sections star anise
3½	cups cold water
4	hard-boiled eggs, thinly sliced
½	pound Smithfield ham, Westphalian ham or prosciutto, thinly sliced

1. In a heavy pot, combine the beef, soy sauce, rice wine (or sherry), sugar, ginger, star anise and cold water.

2. Bring to a boil, then lower heat. Simmer for 1 hour, turning meat frequently. Remove from heat.

3. Remove meat from pot and cut into very fine slices.

4. Return sliced meat to pot. Allow liquid to cool to room temperature, then remove meat slices and reserve.

5. To serve, arrange the slices of beef in the center of a serving platter and surround with the eggs and ham.

Serves 4 to 6

ROAST SPARERIBS *(tas sow py kua)*

China

Preparation time: 5 minutes
Ribs marinate—2 hours

Cooking time: 40 minutes

Ingredients

A   2-pound strip
spareribs, trimmed but
uncut

Marinade:

4   tablespoons soy sauce

1   teaspoon sugar

3   tablespoons Chinese
rice wine or dry sherry

1   tablespoon star anise
powder or hoisin sauce

2   teaspoons honey

1. Combine marinade ingredients in a small bowl.

2. Place ribs in a shallow pan. Pour on marinade, spoon over
ribs several times to coat evenly, then let stand at room
temperature for at least 2 hours. Baste occasionally.

3. Preheat oven to 475°.

4. Transfer ribs to a rack placed in a roasting pan and roast for 20
minutes, basting occasionally with the marinade.

5. Lower heat to 375°.

6. Turn ribs over and baste well. Continue roasting until crisp,
about 20 minutes. Remove pan from oven.

7. Carve strip into individual ribs with a knife or cleaver.

8. Serve hot or cold.

Serves 4 to 6

CALVES' BRAINS VINAIGRETTE
(cervelles vinaigrette)

Preparation time: 20 minutes
Calves' brains soak—2 hours

Cooking time: 25 minutes
Prepared dish chills—2 hours

France

Ingredients

1 to 2	pair calves' brains
¾	cup white vinegar
1	leek, chopped
1	onion, chopped
2	carrots, peeled and chopped
	Herb bouquet (bay leaf, thyme, parsley)
5	peppercorns
2	teaspoons lemon juice
1	teaspoon salt

Vinaigrette:

½	cup olive oil
3	tablespoons red wine vinegar
1	teaspoon dry mustard
	Salt
	Freshly ground pepper
2	tablespoons fresh parsley, chopped
2	tablespoons chives, chopped

1. Rinse the brains under cold running water and place in a large non-metallic bowl. Cover with cold water and add ¼ cup of the white vinegar. Soak brains for 40 minutes, then drain. Repeat soaking process 2 more times and drain.

2. Place the brains in a large saucepan. Cover with cold water and add the leek, onions, carrots, lemon juice and seasonings. Cover and simmer for 25 minutes. Using a slotted spoon, plunge the brains in a bowl of iced water. Drain, pat dry and reserve.

3. Prepare the vinaigrette sauce (page 482). Pour the vinaigrette sauce over the brains and refrigerate for 2 hours.

4. To serve: Cut the brains into even slices and arrange on a bed of Bibb lettuce. Spoon remaining vinaigrette over the slices.

Serves 2 to 4

JELLIED CALVES' FEET *(kholodietz)*

Preparation time: 30 minutes   **Cooking time:** 4 hours
                                          Refrigeration time: 2 hours

USSR   **Ingredients**

4 *calves' feet, split*	2 *teaspoons salt*
1 *veal knuckle*	¼ to ⅓ *cup vinegar*
1 *stalk celery*	5 *hard-boiled eggs, sliced*
2 *carrots*	*Bibb lettuce*
2 *onions*	*Parsley sprigs and*
2 *garlic cloves, minced*	*lemon wedges for*
Herb bouquet (bay leaf,	*garnish*
peppercorns, parsley)	

1. Drop the calves' feet into a large pot of boiling water. Blanch for 2 minutes, drain and rinse.

2. In a soup kettle cover the calves' feet, veal knuckle, celery, carrots, onions, garlic and herb bouquet generously with cold water. Bring to a boil and skim until liquid clears. Lower heat, cover and simmer until the meat is tender, about 3 hours.

3. Skim the fat, then remove the calves' feet and veal knuckle. Cut the meat from the bones and reserve. Return the bones to the kettle. Return the stock to a rapid boil, then lower heat, cover and simmer for 1 more hour.

4. Skim the fat again. Discard the herb bouquet and bones. Strain the stock into a large bowl. Pour ¼ cup of vinegar into the stock. Adjust seasonings and add more vinegar, if necessary. Let stand 15 minutes.

5. Arrange the eggs and the meat in an oiled mold. Pour in the stock. Cover and refrigerate until set, about 2 hours. To serve, unmold onto a bed of Bibb lettuce and garnish with parsley sprigs and lemon wedges.

Serves 8

Traditionally, jellied calves' feet are served with a side dish of sour cream that has been seasoned with freshly grated horseradish and salt.

COUNTRY PÂTÉ
(terrine de campagne)

Preparation time: 30 minutes

Cooking time: 1½ hours

France

Ingredients

¾	*pound fresh pork fat*
½	*pound pork loin*
½	*pound boneless veal*
½	*pound ham*
½	*pound pork livers or chicken livers*
2	*cloves garlic, crushed*
2	*eggs*

¼	*cup dry white wine*
2	*tablespoons cognac*
2	*teaspoons salt*
1	*teaspoon pepper*
¼	*teaspoon allspice*
	Pinch thyme
	Pinch ground bay leaf

1. Set oven at 350°.

2. Grind together ⅓ of the pork fat, the pork loin and the veal. Finely dice the ham and half the remaining pork fat. In a blender, purée the pork (or chicken) livers, garlic, eggs, wine, cognac and seasonings.

3. In a large bowl, combine the purée, the ground ingredients and the diced ingredients. Mix thoroughly.

4. Slice the remaining pork fat. Line a 1½-quart terrine or baking dish, reserving a few slices to cover the pâté. Fill the terrine with the pâté. Arrange the pork fat on top, then cover tightly with a double thickness of aluminum foil.

5. Set the terrine in a pan of water and bake in oven until pâté comes away from the sides of the terrine, about 1½ hours.

6. Remove terrine from the oven and cover with a board or lid that fits inside the terrine. Weight the board and cool to room temperature. (The excess fat will overflow as the pâté cools and firms.) Remove weights and chill. Present the pâté in the terrine, or warm terrine slightly, unmold and transfer to a platter. Slice thinly and serve.

Serves 10 to 12

CHICKEN LIVER PÂTÉ

Canada

Preparation time: 20 minutes
Pâté chills—2 hours

Cooking time: 15 minutes

Ingredients

1 onion, minced	⅛ teaspoon nutmeg
1 clove garlic, minced	½ teaspoon basil
2 tablespoons chicken fat or bacon drippings	¼ teaspoon marjoram
1 pound chicken livers, trimmed	¼ teaspoon thyme
½ cup butter	3 tablespoons cognac
¼ teaspoon salt	3 tablespoons heavy cream
Freshly ground pepper	1 egg, hard-cooked
	Chopped chives

1. Sauté the onion and garlic until translucent in the chicken fat. Add the chicken livers, cover and cook over low heat for 10 minutes. Cool slightly, then purée in a food mill or blender.

2. Melt the butter in the same casserole. Add the seasonings, cognac and cream. When heated through, add to the chicken purée and blend until the consistency of whipped cream.

3. Pour the purée into a lightly oiled mold and chill, covered, for 2 hours or more. To serve, unmold the pâté onto a serving plate. Garnish with the sieved yolk of the egg and the chives. Surround the base of the pâté with finely minced egg white.

Serves 4

Soups

CHERRY SOUP *(soupe aux cerises)*

France

Preparation time: 20 minutes   **Cooking time:** 25 minutes

Ingredients

1½	pounds sour cherries
3	tablespoons butter
4	teaspoons flour
5	cups boiling water
2	tablespoons sugar

⅓	cup kirsch
1	piece lemon peel
1	cup cold water
6	slices French bread, sautéed in butter

1. Wash the cherries and remove pits. Reserve the pits.

2. Melt the butter in a large saucepan. Stir in the flour and continue stirring for 1 minute. Do not let the flour brown.

3. Stirring constantly, slowly pour in the boiling water. Add the cherries, sugar, kirsch and lemon peel. Bring to a boil, then lower heat, cover and simmer for 20 minutes. Discard peel.

4. Combine the reserved cherry pits and the cup of cold water in a small saucepan. Cook over moderate heat for 15 minutes.

5. Line a heated soup tureen with the sautéed bread. Strain the cherry-pit liquid into the tureen, then pour in the cherry soup. Serve immediately.

Serves 4

COCONUT SOUP *(soupe au miti ha'ari)*

Preparation time: 25 minutes   **Cooking time:** 10 minutes
Coconut bakes—25 minutes

Tahiti

Ingredients

2 coconuts	4 cups chicken broth
⅛ teaspoon nutmeg	Cayenne pepper

1. Puncture the "eyes" of the coconuts and drain, reserving the milk.

2. Split the coconuts. Remove the meat, paring the brown skin. Finely dice enough meat to make 1 cup. Grate the remaining meat.

3. Toast the diced coconut in a slow oven until light brown, about 25 minutes.

4. In a heavy saucepan, combine the reserved coconut milk, grated meat, nutmeg and chicken broth. Season to taste with cayenne pepper. Simmer over low heat for 10 minutes.

5. Strain soup, then return to saucepan and reheat gently.

6. Serve accompanied by the toasted diced coconut.

Serves 4

COLD CUCUMBER-YOGHURT
SOUP *(tarator)*

Turkey

Preparation time: 15 minutes
Cucumbers stand—20 minutes

Refrigeration time: 1 hour

Ingredients

4   *cucumbers, peeled,
    seeded and chopped
    Salt*
4   *cloves garlic, peeled*
¼   *cup olive oil*
5   *cups yoghurt*

1   *cup light cream*
2   *tablespoons fresh
    parsley, chopped
    White pepper
    Chopped fresh mint for
    garnish*

1. Put the chopped cucumbers in a glass bowl. Salt lightly and toss. Cover bowl and let stand at room temperature for 20 minutes. Drain cucumbers, pat dry and reserve.

2. In a large glass bowl, crush the garlic. Add 1 teaspoon salt, then gradually beat in the olive oil.

3. Add the reserved cucumbers, yoghurt, cream and parsley. Mix thoroughly, then cover and refrigerate for at least 1 hour.

4. Before serving, season to taste with salt and white pepper and garnish with fresh chopped mint.

Serves 6

GAZPACHO ANDALUZ

Preparation time: 20 minutes

Refrigeration time: 2 hours

Spain

Ingredients

2 slices dry white bread, crumbled

4 tablespoons olive oil

2 tablespoons wine vinegar

3 cups chicken broth

2 cloves garlic

2 pounds large ripe tomatoes, peeled, seeded and chopped

4 large scallions, chopped

1 cucumber, chopped

1 green pepper, chopped

¼ teaspoon cumin

Pinch of cayenne

Salt

Freshly ground pepper

Chopped fresh parsley (or other chopped fresh herbs: basil, dill, tarragon, chervil) for garnish

1. In a non-metallic bowl, combine the crumbled bread with the olive oil, vinegar and chicken broth. With a press, crush the garlic into the mixture.

2. Add the tomatoes, scallions, cucumber, green pepper, cumin and cayenne. Blend well.

3. Add salt and pepper to taste (remember that when chilled, the soup will taste less salty). Refrigerate for a minimum of 2 hours. Serve in chilled soup cups with a sprinkling of chopped parsley or other fresh herbs.

Serves 4

There are as many variations of gazpacho as there are cities in Spain. Some cooks make gazpacho in a blender and offer bowls of croutons, chopped cucumber, green pepper, celery, onions or chives to sprinkle over the soup.

BORSCHT

Poland

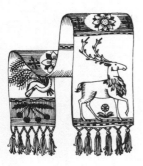

Preparation time: 25 minutes

Cooking time: 2¾ hours

Ingredients

4	tablespoons butter
2	pounds raw beets, scraped and grated
2	celery stalks, diced
3	leeks, chopped
½	head cabbage, shredded
2	carrots, shredded
2	onions, chopped
1	clove garlic, chopped
1	pound brisket of beef, cut in ½-inch cubes

2	quarts water
1	tablespoon salt
	Herb bouquet (bay leaf, peppercorns, parsley, 2 cloves)
2	egg yolks
½	pint sour cream
	Chopped fresh dill for garnish
	Sour cream for garnish

1. Melt the butter in a large saucepan and sauté the beets, celery, leeks, cabbage, carrots, onions and garlic until the green vegetables are slightly limp.

2. Add the beef, water, salt and herb bouquet. Bring to a boil and skim the surface. Cover and simmer over low heat for 2½ hours, skimming occasionally. Discard herb bouquet.

3. Just before serving, beat the egg yolks in a bowl with the ½ pint sour cream. Add some soup, a spoonful at a time, to the egg mixture, then gently stir the mixture into the remaining soup, taking care not to let it boil.

4. Serve in warmed soup bowls topped with a sprinkling of dill and a spoonful of sour cream.

Serves 6

VARIATION: *For a clear chilled borscht, proceed through Step 2. Strain the soup, pour into individual cups and refrigerate. Serve garnished with cucumber slices, fresh dill and sour cream.*

SHREDDED CABBAGE SOUP
(caldo verde)

Preparation time: 20 minutes   **Cooking time:** 25 minutes   *Portugal*

Ingredients

½ medium cabbage	3 medium potatoes
2 tablespoons olive oil	Salt
1 onion, thinly sliced	Freshly ground pepper
3 cups chicken stock	

1. Shred the cabbage as finely as possible. (The strands should be almost threadlike.) Reserve.

2. In a large saucepan, heat the oil and gently sauté the sliced onion until translucent, about 5 minutes.

3. Add the stock, potatoes, salt and pepper. Bring to a boil, then lower heat and simmer until potatoes are tender, about 15 minutes. Remove from heat.

4. In a food mill or blender, purée the soup to the consistency of cream.

5. Return soup to saucepan, add the reserved cabbage and boil, uncovered, for 3 minutes. Remove from heat.

6. Taste and correct seasoning, if necessary. Serve piping hot.

Serves 4

GARLIC BROTH PROVENÇAL
(soupe à l'aïgo bouïdo)

France

Preparation time: 5 minutes   **Cooking time:** 10 minutes

Ingredients

6 *cups water*	1 *small sprig thyme or 1*
1½ *teaspoons salt*	*teaspoon dried thyme*
6 *cloves garlic, crushed*	1 *egg*
1 *sprig sage or 1*	*Salt*
teaspoon dried sage	*Freshly ground pepper*
½ *bay leaf*	4 to 6 *slices French bread,*
	sautéed in olive oil

1. Bring the salted water to a boil in a large kettle. Add the crushed garlic and herbs. Boil for an additional 8 minutes, then remove from heat.

2. Beat the egg in a large bowl.

3. Beating well, gradually strain the broth into the bowl. Add salt and pepper to taste.

4. Serve in soup bowls garnished with the sautéed French bread.

Serves 4 to 6

BEER SOUP *(Biersuppe)*

Preparation time: 5 minutes **Cooking time:** 25 minutes

Germany

Ingredients

4	tablespoons butter
2	tablespoons flour
4	cups beer
	Pinch salt
	Pinch nutmeg
	Pinch ginger

Pinch cinnamon
4 egg yolks
1 tablespoon sugar
1 cup dry white wine
Grated peel of 1 lemon

1. Melt the butter in a large saucepan. Stirring constantly to avoid lumps, gradually blend in the flour and cook over moderately low heat until the flour is golden.

2. Still stirring, slowly pour in the beer. Add the salt, nutmeg, ginger and cinnamon. Simmer gently for 20 minutes.

3. While the beer is simmering, beat the egg yolks well in a bowl. Add the sugar, then beat in the white wine and the grated lemon peel.

4. Drop by drop, beat ¼ cup of the hot beer into the egg mixture.

5. Gently stir the egg and beer mixture into the remaining hot beer. Heat through, making sure the soup remains below the simmering point. Taste and correct seasoning, if necessary.

Serves 4

EGG AND LEMON SOUP
(avgolemono)

Greece   **Preparation time:** 10 minutes   **Cooking time:** 30 minutes

Ingredients

2   *quarts strong chicken stock*
⅓   *cup rice*
3 to 4   *eggs*

Juice of 2 lemons
Chopped fresh parsley or chives for garnish

1. In a saucepan, bring the stock to a boil. Add the rice, cover and cook over low heat until the rice is tender, about 20 minutes.

2. Just before serving, bring the broth to a boil. Remove from heat.

3. Beat the eggs in a bowl until light and frothy. Add the lemon juice. Beating constantly, gradually add a cup of the hot broth to the egg and lemon mixture in the bowl. When thoroughly mixed, beat in another cup of the broth.

4. Return the saucepan with broth to low heat. Slowly ladle in the egg and lemon mixture, stirring constantly to prevent curdling. Heat through, but do not allow the soup to simmer.

5. Serve immediately, garnished with parsley or chives.

Serves 6 to 8

BLACK BREAD SOUP *(svartbrødsoppa)*

Preparation time: 5 minutes   **Cooking time:** 10 minutes

Norway

Ingredients

4	cups chicken broth	¼	cup brown sugar
1	teaspoon grated lemon peel	2	cups dark beer
	Pinch nutmeg	4	slices black bread
	Pinch cinnamon	1	cup sour cream for garnish

1. In a large saucepan, combine the broth, lemon peel, nutmeg, cinnamon, brown sugar and beer. Bring to a boil, then lower heat and simmer for 10 minutes.

2. Line a warmed soup tureen with the slices of black bread. Pour in the soup.

3. Serve with the sour cream on the side.

Serves 4

HOT AND SOUR SOUP

(shran la tong)

China

Preparation time: 45 minutes   **Cooking time:** 20 minutes

Ingredients

5	dried Chinese mushrooms
1	tablespoon dried shrimp
¼	pound lean pork
¼	pound chicken breast
½	cup bamboo shoots
2	bean-curd cakes
6	cups chicken stock
A	1-inch cube ginger root, smashed

1	scallion, minced
½	teaspoon salt
2	tablespoons vinegar
	Freshly ground pepper
2	teaspoons soy sauce
2	tablespoons cornstarch mixed with ¼ cup cold water
1	egg, beaten
	Minced scallions
	Seasame-seed oil

1. Soak the mushrooms and shrimp in separate bowls of warm water for 30 minutes. Drain the mushrooms and slice into julienne strips. Reserve 1 cup of the liquid. Drain and rinse the shrimp. Slice the next 4 ingredients into julienne strips.

2. In a large saucepan, combine the chicken stock and the mushroom liquid. Bring to a boil, then add the mushrooms, pork, chicken, bamboo shoots and ginger. Return to a boil, then lower heat, cover and simmer for 10 minutes.

3. Add the bean curd and scallion. Re-cover and simmer for 3 more minutes. Season the soup with the salt, vinegar, pepper and soy sauce, then gently stir in the cornstarch paste. Continue stirring until soup thickens, about 2 minutes. Slowly dribble in the egg, remove from heat and garnish with scallions and sprinkle with a few drops of sesame-seed oil.

Serves 4 to 6

WONTON SOUP *(won ton)*

Preparation time: 2 hours

Cooking time: 10 minutes

Ingredients

Wonton Wrappers:

1½   cups flour

¾   teaspoon salt

1   egg, lightly beaten

3 to 4   tablespoons water

Filling:

1   pound pork, ground

6   scallions, minced

1   green pepper, minced

4   thick slices ginger root, peeled and minced

½   teaspoon salt

1   tablespoon soy sauce

½   cup shrimp, diced

1   egg, lightly beaten

8   cups chicken broth

1   tablespoon sesame-seed oil

½   teaspoon soy sauce
    Minced scallions

China

1. Sift the flour and salt. Incorporate the egg and just enough water to form a stiff dough. Knead until smooth, cover and refrigerate for 45 minutes. Knead, then roll out to a ¹⁄₁₆-inch thickness. Cut into 3-inch squares.

2. Combine the filling ingredients and let stand at room temperature for 30 minutes.

3. To assemble the wonton, place 1 tablespoon of filling in the center of each wrapper, then fold one corner over the filling, tucking the tip under the filling to secure. Fold the 2 small sections of the wrapper toward the center, pressing down the edges to seal, then brush the remaining section with the egg and roll up the wonton.

4. Drop the wontons into a pot of rapidly boiling water and simmer until tender, about 10 minutes. Drain and reserve.

5. Pour the chicken broth into the pot and bring to a boil. Add the sesame-seed oil and soy sauce, then pour over the wontons. Garnish with minced scallions and serve immediately.

Serves 6 to 8

SPRING VEGETABLE SOUP
(kesäkeitto)

Finland

Preparation time: 20 minutes

Cooking time: 30 minutes

Ingredients

1	small cauliflower
1	pound fresh green peas, shelled
½	pound fresh string beans, snapped in half
6	small carrots, sliced
2	new potatoes, sliced
4	radishes, halved
2	quarts water
2	teaspoons salt

¼	pound fresh spinach
2	tablespoons butter
2	tablespoons flour
1	cup milk
1	egg yolk
¼	cup cream
½	pound shrimp, deveined (optional)
	Salt and pepper
	Chopped fresh parsley

1. In a large soup kettle, combine the cauliflower, peas, string beans, carrots, potatoes, radishes, water and salt. Bring to a boil and cook until vegetables are barely tender, about 5 minutes. Add the spinach and cook for 5 more minutes. Strain broth into a bowl. Reserve vegetables in another bowl.

2. Melt the butter in the soup kettle. Stirring constantly over moderate heat, blend in the flour and cook for 1 minute. Pour in the broth. Beat vigorously until well blended, then cook over moderate heat for 10 minutes. Stir in the milk.

3. Beat the egg yolk and cream together. Stirring vigorously, gradually add 1 cup of the hot soup. When well mixed, stir back into the remainder of the soup.

4. Add the reserved vegetables (and shrimp) to the soup. Heat just to the simmering point, then remove from heat. Season with salt and white pepper. Pour soup into a heated tureen, garnish with parsley and serve.

Serves 6

CHICKEN VEGETABLE SOUP
(satsuma jiru)

Preparation time: 15 minutes   **Cooking time:** 25 minutes   *Japan*

Ingredients

1 tablespoon peanut oil	2 tablespoons soy sauce
1 large carrot, peeled and diced	6 cups chicken broth
1 medium potato, peeled and diced	2 tablespoons soy sauce
½ cup daikon (Japanese radish), diced	1 tablespoon sake or dry sherry
½ pound canned bamboo shoots, diced	1 teaspoon fresh ginger root, peeled and minced
1 whole chicken breast, boned, skinned and diced	1 tablespoon cornstarch, dissolved in 2 tablespoons water
6 cups chicken broth	3 scallions, chopped

1. Heat the oil in a soup kettle. Add the carrot, potato, *daikon*, and bamboo shoots. Stir briskly over moderately high heat for 2 minutes.

2. Add the diced chicken and continue stirring over high heat until the chicken pieces turn color, about 2 or 3 minutes.

3. Add the chicken broth, soy sauce, *sake* (or sherry) and ginger. Bring to a boil, then lower heat and simmer gently until the vegetables are barely tender, about 15 minutes.

4. Briefly stir ¼ cup of the hot broth into the cornstarch, then stir it into the soup. Simmer for another 5 minutes.

5. Pour soup into a heated tureen, add the chopped scallions and serve.

Serves 6

CHICKEN SOUP WITH CLAMS AND SPINACH *(dak kook)*

Korea

Preparation time: 15 minutes

Cooking time: 15 minutes

Ingredients

16   *clams or mussels*

1   *tablespoon peanut oil or other flavorless vegetable oil*

1½   *teaspoons fresh ginger root, minced*

1   *clove garlic, minced*

3   *scallions, chopped*

1   *chicken breast, skinned, boned and shredded*

4   *cups chicken stock*

¾   *pound fresh spinach, washed and chopped*

1   *teaspoon sesame-seed oil*

1. Using a stiff brush, scrub the clam (or mussel) shells and rinse thoroughly in cold water until no sand remains.

2. Heat the oil in a soup kettle. Add the ginger, garlic, scallions and chicken. Stir-fry over high heat for 30 seconds.

3. Add the chicken stock and bring to a boil. Lower heat and simmer for 5 minutes.

4. Add the clams. Bring broth to a simmer, cover and steam clams until shells open, about 8 minutes. Discard any clams with unopened shells.

5. Add the spinach to the soup, stir briefly, then remove kettle from heat.

6. Stir in the sesame-seed oil and serve immediately.

Serves 4

CHEESE AND VEGETABLE SOUP
(Kaas en Groetnesoep)

The
Netherlands

Preparation time: 20 minutes
Beans soak—overnight

Cooking time: 3¼ hours

Ingredients

1	cup dry white haricot beans (preferably Great Northern)
7	tablespoons butter
6	cups chicken broth
4	leeks, thinly sliced
4	stalks celery, thinly sliced
2	onions, thinly sliced

½	pound cabbage, shredded
1	tablespoon fresh parsley, chopped
1	tablespoon cream
1½	cups Edam cheese, grated
	Salt
	Freshly ground pepper

1. Soak the beans overnight in cold water.

2. Drain the beans, transfer to a saucepan and cover with cold water. Bring to a boil, then lower heat, cover and simmer until tender, about 2½ hours. Drain.

3. Mash the beans or run them through a food mill or blender to make a purée. Reserve.

4. Melt the butter in a large saucepan. Add the leeks, celery, onions and cabbage. Sauté until the vegetables are tender but not browned.

5. Add the bean puree and the chicken broth. Simmer for 25 minutes.

6. Add the parsley, grated cheese and cream. Season to taste with salt and pepper. Heat through and serve.

Serves 4

TOMATO AND CHEESE SOUP
(tourin Périgourdin)

France

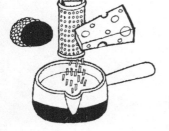

Preparation time: 15 minutes   **Cooking time:** 1 hour

Ingredients

2   *large onions, sliced*
1   *tablespoon olive oil or*
    goose fat
1   *clove garlic, minced*
1   *pound tomatoes,*
    peeled, seeded and
    chopped
6   *cups water*

Salt
Freshly ground pepper
¾   *cup Gruyère or other*
    Swiss cheese, grated
8   *slices French bread,*
    sautéed in olive oil or
    goose fat

1. Heat the oil in an enameled cast-iron casserole and gently cook the onions for 10 minutes over moderate heat. Do not let them brown.

2. Add the garlic, tomatoes and water. Season with salt and pepper. Bring to a boil, then lower heat and simmer for 45 minutes. Taste and correct seasoning, if necessary.

3. Preheat broiler to 425°.

4. Put half the sautéed bread slices at the bottom of an oven-proof tureen and sprinkle with half the grated cheese. Strain the stock into the tureen. Top with the remaining sautéed bread slices and cheese.

5. Place under the broiler for about 5 minutes to brown the cheese. Serve immediately.

Serves 4

ONION SOUP LYONNAISE
(soupe à l'oignon gratinée)

Preparation time: 10 minutes   **Cooking time:** 1 hour   *France*

Ingredients

2	tablespoons butter	12	slices French bread, toasted
2	tablespoons oil	1½	cups Gruyère or other Swiss cheese, grated
5	large onions, sliced		
8	cups beef bouillon		
	Freshly ground pepper		

1. Heat the butter and the oil in an enameled cast-iron casserole. Add the onions and cook over low heat until translucent, about 20 minutes. Do not allow onions to brown.

2. Add the bouillon and season to taste with pepper. Bring quickly to a boil. Boil rapidly for 5 minutes, then lower heat and simmer for 25 minutes. Taste and correct seasoning, if necessary.

3. Set broiler to 425°.

4. Place half the toasted bread slices in an ovenproof tureen. Cover with half the grated cheese and then pour in the soup. Add the remaining slices of bread and top with the balance of the cheese.

5. Put the tureen under the broiler until the top is browned, about 3 to 5 minutes.

Serves 6

PYRENEES HAM AND ONION SOUP *(tourin español)*

Spain

Preparation time: 20 minutes   **Cooking time:** 30 minutes

Ingredients

6   tablespoons olive oil
5   onions, thinly sliced
¼   pound smoked ham,
    cut into julienne strips
1   bay leaf
1   teaspoon thyme

Freshly ground pepper
6   cups chicken broth
4   egg yolks
4 to 8   slices French bread
    fried in oil and rubbed
    with garlic

1. In a large saucepan, heat the olive oil. Add the onions and sauté over low heat until limp, about 10 minutes.

2. Add the ham, bay leaf and thyme. Season with pepper. Pour in the broth and bring to a boil, then lower heat and simmer for 25 minutes.

3. Beat the egg yolks well in a bowl. Beat in 1 cup of the hot broth, a little at a time, then gently stir mixture into the remainder of the soup. Quickly heat through, but do not allow soup to come to a boil.

4. Place the fried bread slices in a warmed soup tureen. Pour in the hot soup and serve immediately.

Serves 4

CREAM OF ONION SOUP ÎLE DE FRANCE

(tourin de l'Île de France)

France

Preparation time: 10 minutes   **Cooking time:** 45 minutes

Ingredients

½ *pound onions, thinly sliced*

2 *tablespoons butter*

2 *tablespoons flour*

6 *cups hot milk*

Salt

Freshly ground pepper

4 *egg yolks*

1½ *cups light cream*

4 to 6 *slices French bread, sautéed in butter (optional)*

1. Melt the butter in a large saucepan and sauté the onions until they become translucent. Do not let them brown.

2. Stir in the flour and mix thoroughly. Add the hot milk, salt and pepper. Cook for 30 minutes, stirring frequently to prevent lumps. Remove sauce from heat.

3. In a bowl, beat the egg yolks and cream. Beating constantly, very slowly drip 1 cup of soup into the egg mixture. Beat this mixture into the saucepan, then heat to thicken slightly. Do not boil.

4. Pour soup into a warmed tureen and garnish with the sautéed bread, if desired.

Serves 4 to 6

PEANUT SOUP *(shorba)*

Ghana

Preparation time: 20 minutes

Cooking time: 1 hour

Ingredients

1	*pound shelled roasted peanuts*
2	*tablespoons butter*
1	*onion, minced*
2	*stalks celery, chopped finely*
6	*cups beef broth*
1	*tablespoon cornstarch*

1	*cup milk*
1	*cup cream*
	Salt
	Cayenne pepper
	Chopped parsley for garnish
	Chopped peanuts for garnish

1. In a blender or food chopper, grind the peanuts to a fine consistency.

2. Heat the butter in a large, heavy saucepan and gently sauté the onion and celery until translucent. Do not brown.

3. Add the ground peanuts and 5¾ cups of the broth. Bring to a boil, then lower heat and simmer for 30 minutes. Remove from heat.

4. Mix the cornstarch with the remaining broth and stir into the soup.

5. Return soup to low heat. Add the milk and cream. Season to taste with salt and cayenne pepper (the soup should be spicy). Cover and simmer very gently for 30 minutes.

6. Serve garnished with chopped parsley and peanuts.

Serves 6 to 8

In South Africa this soup is laced with liberal amounts of cayenne. It is even better made in advance and reheated a day later.

BLACK BEAN SOUP

Preparation time: 20 minutes
Beans soak—overnight

Cooking time: 3 hours

USA

Ingredients

¾	pound dry black beans	¼	teaspoon pepper
1	ham bone, cracked	2	tablespoons butter
3	quarts cold water or beef stock	2	onions, chopped
	Herb bouquet (bay leaf, parsley, 3 cloves)	2	stalks celery, chopped
		2	carrots, chopped
1	tablespoon salt	½	cup dry sherry
		1	lemon, thinly sliced

1. Soak beans overnight in cold water.

2. Discard any beans floating on top of the water. Drain the remaining beans and transfer to a soup kettle. Add the ham bone and the 3 quarts cold water (or beef stock). Bring rapidly to a boil. Skim the surface, then add the herb bouquet, salt and pepper. Lower heat, cover tightly and simmer until beans are tender, about 2½ hours.

3. While the beans are cooking, heat the butter in a skillet and sauté the vegetables until the onions are translucent but not brown. Remove from heat and reserve.

4. When the beans are tender, add the sautéed vegetables to the kettle. Return to a boil, then lower heat, re-cover and simmer for another ½ hour. Remove from heat. Skim the soup, then discard the ham bone and herb bouquet.

5. Purée the soup in a food mill. Taste and adjust seasoning.

6. Return soup to the kettle and heat through. Stir in the sherry. Serve in a warmed tureen, topped with the lemon slices and serve immediately.

Serves 8

SPLIT PEA SOUP

Canada

Preparation time: 15 minutes
Split peas soak—overnight

Cooking time: 3 hours

Ingredients

1   *pound dry green or yellow split peas*

3   *quarts cold water*

½   *pound salt pork, diced*

2   *medium onions, chopped*

3   *carrots, chopped*

¼   *teaspoon powdered savory*

Herb bouquet (bay leaf, 2 sprigs parsley, 3 cloves)

Freshly ground pepper

Salt

French bread, diced and sautéed in butter for croutons

1. Soak the split peas overnight in cold water.

2. Drain the peas and transfer to a soup kettle. Pour in the 3 quarts of cold water and bring rapidly to a boil.

3. Skim the surface, then add the salt pork, onions, carrots, savory and herb bouquet. Season with pepper and a little salt (remembering the pork is salted).

4. Return to a boil, then lower heat, cover and simmer for 3 hours.

5. Remove herb bouquet and correct seasoning. Pour into a heated soup tureen and serve garnished with the croutons.

Serves 6

SOUP WITH LIVER MEATBALLS
(Leberklössesuppe)

Preparation time: 20 minutes   **Cooking time:** 15 minutes   *Austria*

Ingredients

2	slices stale bread, soaked in milk
½	pound pork liver, ground
4	tablespoons butter
1	medium onion, chopped
1	clove garlic, minced

2	eggs, well beaten
	Pinch powdered marjoram
	Salt
	Freshly ground pepper
6	cups beef broth
	Chopped fresh parsley for garnish

1. Squeeze the milk from the bread, then crumble in a large bowl. Add the ground liver and mix well. Reserve.

2. Heat 1 tablespoon of the butter in a skillet. Add the onion and garlic. Sauté over low heat until the onion is limp, about 5 minutes. Transfer to the liver and bread mixture.

3. Bind the mixture with the beaten eggs, then season with the marjoram, salt and pepper. Mix thoroughly, then shape into small meatballs.

4. In a large skillet, heat the remaining butter and sauté the meatballs until nicely browned. Remove from heat.

5. In a large saucepan, bring the beef broth to a boil. Add the meatballs. Lower heat and simmer for 5 minutes.

6. Pour into a heated soup tureen, garnish with chopped parsley and serve.

Serves 6

TYROLEAN BEEF SOUP *(Rindsuppe)*

Preparation time: 20 minutes   **Cooking time:** 1½ hours

Austria   **Ingredients**

5 onions, minced	1 pound shoulder of beef, diced
3 ounces lard or oil	Salt
2 cloves garlic	Freshly ground pepper
1 teaspoon cumin seed	3 tablespoons flour
1 teaspoon marjoram	1 pound potatoes, peeled and diced
1 teaspoon paprika	
8 cups beef broth	

1. In a large heavy saucepan, sauté the onions in the lard (or oil) until translucent but not brown.

2. While the onions are cooking, crush the garlic, cumin seed and marjoram together in a mortar. Reserve.

3. Sprinkle the onions with paprika and stir in 7 cups of the broth. Bring to a boil and add the diced beef. Return to a boil, then lower heat and simmer gently for 20 minutes.

4. Add the crushed garlic, cumin seed and marjoram to the soup. Season with salt and pepper, then cover and simmer for 45 minutes over low heat.

5. Gradually stir the remaining cold broth into the flour. Stirring constantly to avoid lumps, slowly pour the mixture into the hot soup.

6. Add the potatoes to the soup and continue simmering until the potatoes are done, about 15 minutes.

7. Pour into a heated soup tureen and serve.

Serves 4 to 6

VEGETABLE SOUP PROVENÇAL
(soupe au pistou)

Preparation time: 25 minutes
White beans soak—overnight

Cooking time: 1½ hours

France

Ingredients

- 1   *pound dry white beans*
- 2   *quarts water*
- 2   *teaspoons salt*
- ¼   *pound green beans, sliced*
- 3   *large potatoes, peeled and diced*
- 2   *zucchini, sliced*
- 3   *carrots, sliced*
- ¼   *pound kidney beans*
- ⅛   *pound vermicelli*
- ½   *teaspoon pepper*

Pistou:

- 4   *cloves garlic, mashed*
- ¼   *cup fresh basil, chopped, or 2 tablespoons dried basil*
- 4   *large tomatoes, peeled, seeded and chopped*
- ¼   *cup olive oil*

- 1   *cup grated Gruyère cheese for garnish*

1. Soak the white beans overnight. Drain and reserve.

2. Bring the water to a boil in a large casserole. Add the salt, vegetables and white beans. Lower heat and simmer gently for 1¼ hours. Add the kidney beans, vermicelli and pepper. Cook an additional 15 minutes.

3. Make the pistou: Place the garlic, basil and tomatoes in a mortar and crush to a paste. Add the olive oil, drop by drop, as for a mayonnaise.

4. Stirring well, add the pistou to the soup. Bring back to a boil and immediately remove from heat. Adjust seasoning. Serve with a dish of grated cheese.

Serves 6

BASQUE BEAN AND CABBAGE SOUP *(elzekaria)*

Spain

Preparation time: 20 minutes
Beans soak—overnight

Cooking time: 3 hours

Ingredients

10 ounces navy or Great Northern beans

2 medium onions, sliced

3 cloves garlic, minced

4 tablespoons lard or olive oil

1 white cabbage, shredded

Salt

Freshly ground pepper

3 quarts water

½ soup spoon red wine vinegar per person (optional)

1. Soak beans overnight. Drain and reserve.

2. In a large soup kettle, brown the onions and garlic in the lard (or olive oil).

3. Add the cabbage, beans, salt, pepper and water.

4. Bring soup to a boil. Lower heat, cover and simmer for 3 hours. Taste and adjust seasoning if necessary.

Serves 8 to 10

The Basques traditionally add a touch of vinegar to their soup plates.

SCOTCH BROTH

Preparation time: 30 minutes

Cooking time: 2½ hours

Scotland

Ingredients

½ pound breast of lamb, cut into pieces

½ pound neck of lamb, chopped

2 quarts water

½ cup pearl barley

4 tablespoons butter

3 carrots, peeled and diced

2 turnips, peeled and diced

2 onions, chopped

2 leeks, chopped

2 stalks celery, chopped

Herb bouquet (thyme, bay leaf, parsley)

Salt

Freshly ground pepper

Chopped fresh parsley

1. In a soup kettle, combine the meats and 6 cups of the water. Bring to a boil and skim off any foam that appears. Lower heat, cover and simmer for 20 minutes.

2. In a small saucepan, bring the remaining water to a boil. Stir in the barley and cook, uncovered, over high heat for 10 minutes. Drain barley and reserve.

3. Melt the butter in a skillet. Add the carrots, turnips, onions, leeks and celery. Sauté until the onions are golden.

4. Add the vegetables, reserved barley and herb bouquet to the soup. Simmer for 2 hours, skimming off foam occasionally.

5. Discard the herb bouquet. Remove the bones from the soup. Cut any meat remaining on the bones into small pieces and return it to the broth. Discard the bones. Skim off any fat on the surface of the soup, then season to taste with salt and pepper. Garnish with chopped fresh parsley and serve immediately.

Serves 4

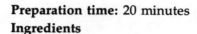

LAMB AND VEGETABLE SOUP
WITH VERMICELLI *(cherbah)*

North Africa

Preparation time: 20 minutes   **Cooking time:** 2¾ hours

Ingredients

1½	pounds lean lamb
2	lamb bones, cracked
2	quarts cold water
	Salt
	Freshly ground pepper
	Pinch cayenne pepper
¼	pound dried apricots
4	tablespoons oil
4	onions, coarsely chopped

4	tomatoes, peeled, seeded and chopped
3	green peppers, seeded and coarsely chopped
1 to 2	tablespoons fresh mint leaves, chopped
¼	pound large vermicelli
1	tablespoon lemon juice
	Chopped fresh parsley and mint for garnish

1. Put the meat and bones in a large heavy pot and cover with the cold water. Add salt, pepper and cayenne. Bring to a boil and skim the surface. Add the apricots, then lower heat, cover and simmer for 1½ hours.

2. Heat the oil in a frying pan. Add the onions, peppers and mint leaves and cook until the onions are limp.

3. Add the onions, tomatoes, peppers and mint leaves to the soup. Continue simmering for 1 hour.

4. Remove the meat and bones from the soup. Discard bones and cut the meat into bite-size chunks. Return meat to soup.

5. Adjust seasoning, then bring to a boil. Add the vermicelli and cook for 5 minutes, or to desired tenderness.

6. Pour into a heated soup tureen, stir in the lemon juice and garnish with chopped parsley and mint.

Serves 4 to 6

MINESTRONE

Preparation time: 20 minutes
Beans soak—overnight

Cooking time: 3 hours

Italy

Ingredients

½ pound dry white
     haricot beans

½ cup olive oil

4 onions, chopped

2 leeks, chopped

1 clove garlic, minced

2 stalks celery, diced

½ pound fresh green
     beans, snapped

2 zucchini, diced

½ pound potatoes, peeled
     and diced

2 ripe tomatoes, diced

9 cups beef broth

¼ pound macaroni

½ tablespoon fresh sage,
     chopped

½ tablespoon fresh basil,
     chopped

½ tablespoon fresh
     parsley, chopped

   Salt

   Freshly ground pepper

   Freshly grated
   Parmesan cheese

1. Soak the white beans overnight in cold water.

2. Drain the white beans and transfer to a saucepan. Cover with cold water. Bring to a boil, then lower heat, cover and simmer until nearly tender, about 2 hours. Drain and reserve.

3. Heat the olive oil in a soup kettle and stir in the onions, leeks, garlic and celery. Sauté until the onions are translucent but not browned.

4. Add the reserved white beans, the remaining vegetables and the broth. Cover and simmer for 40 minutes.

5. Uncover and turn up heat. When the soup comes to a boil, add the macaroni, chopped herbs, salt and pepper. Cook uncovered for 20 minutes. Pour into a tureen and serve with freshly grated Parmesan.

Serves 4

MAIN-COURSE CABBAGE AND BEAN SOUP BÉARNAIS *(garbure)*

France

Preparation time: 15 minutes
Beans soak—overnight

Cooking time: 2½ hours

Ingredients

1¼ cups dry white beans	3 quarts water
1 pound boiling potatoes, peeled and quartered	2½ pounds green cabbage, coarsely chopped
A 1½-pound piece smoked pork butt	2 carrots, peeled and quartered
4 cloves garlic, crushed	1 leg preserved goose (optional, page 477)
Herb bouquet (bay leaf, parsley, thyme, 8 peppercorns)	Freshly ground pepper
	Salt

1. Soak beans overnight. Drain and reserve.

2. Put the potatoes, smoked pork, garlic, herb bouquet and water in a large enameled cast-iron casserole. Bring to a boil. Lower heat, cover and simmer for 1 hour.

3. Add the beans, cabbage and carrots (and goose). Cover partially and simmer for 1½ hours.

4. Salt and pepper to taste.

5. Before serving, remove the meats, cut into serving pieces and return to the casserole.

Serves 6

GRISONS-STYLE BEEF AND BEAN SOUP *(Rindfleisch und Bohnensuppe)*

Preparation time: 25 minutes
Beans soak—overnight

Cooking time: 3¼ hours

Switzerland

Ingredients

½ *pound dry white beans* *Soup bones*	1 *pound cabbage,* *coarsley chopped*
½ *pound smoked beef*	2 *stalks celery*
½ *pound beef round, cut* *into strips*	*Salt* *Freshly ground pepper*
2 *quarts cold water*	¾ *cup cream*
1½ *cups barley*	1 *tablespoon cornstarch*
3 *medium potatoes,* *peeled and quartered*	*Chopped fresh parsley* *for garnish*

1. Soak the beans overnight. Drain and reserve.

2. Combine the beans, soup bones, meats and water in a soup kettle. Bring to a boil, then lower heat and simmer, uncovered, for 2 hours.

3. Add the barley, potatoes, cabbage and celery. Season with salt and pepper. Cover and simmer over low heat for 1 hour. Remove soup bones.

4. Five minutes before serving, blend the cream and cornstarch together in a bowl. Stirring constantly, add the mixture to the soup and cook very gently for a few minutes. Do not let the soup boil.

5. Sprinkle with parsley and serve.

Serves 4

ALBIGEOIS MAIN-COURSE SOUP
(potée Albigeoise)

France

Preparation time: 30 minutes
Beans soak—overnight

Cooking time: 3½ hours

Ingredients

1	*pound dry white beans*
4	*quarts water*
1	*veal knuckle*
1	*soup bone*
2	*pounds beef shin*
1	*pound ham*
6	*carrots, peeled and quartered*
6	*leeks, white parts only*
4	*cloves garlic, crushed*
	Herb bouquet (bay leaves, parsley, thyme, peppercorns)

1	*onion, stuck with 4 or 5 cloves*
1	*tablespoon salt*
2	*teaspoons freshly ground pepper*
1	*cabbage, cut into quarters*
2	*pounds garlic sausage or Italian cotechino*
¼	*preserved goose (optional, page 477)*
16	*slices French bread (optional)*

1. Soak beans overnight. Drain and reserve.

2. Put the water in a very large soup kettle. Add the veal knuckle, soup bone, beef shin, ham, carrots, leeks, garlic, herb bouquet, onion, salt and pepper. Bring to a boil and skim off the foam. Cover and simmer for 2½ hours.

3. Blanch the cabbage and the beans for 2 minutes in a separate large pot of rapidly boiling water. Drain and refresh.

4. Add the cabbage, beans, sausage (and goose) to the soup. Simmer, uncovered, for another hour. Taste and correct seasoning. Discard herb bouquet.

5. Using a slotted spoon, arrange the meats, vegetables and beans on a heated platter. Pour the broth into a warmed tureen and serve at the same time.

Serves 8

MAIN-COURSE PORK SOUP
(potée Lorraine)

Preparation time: 30 minutes   **Cooking time:** 2 hours   *France*
Pork soaks—4 hours

Ingredients

A   *3-pound piece breast of salt pork*

2½ *quarts water*

8   *leeks, trimmed*

8   *carrots, peeled and quartered*

1   *onion stuck with 4 cloves*

4   *shallots, chopped*

Herb bouquet (parsley, bay leaf, garlic clove)

1   *celeriac (celery root), quartered*

Freshly ground pepper

1   *small cabbage, quartered*

½   *pound string beans*

1   *pound green peas*

8   *slices French bread, toasted*

1. Soak the salt pork in cold water for 4 hours, changing the water twice.

2. Put the salt pork in a soup kettle with the water, leeks, carrots, onion, shallots, herb bouquet and celeriac. Season with pepper. Bring to a boil and skim the foam off. Reduce heat, cover and simmer for 1½ hours.

3. Blanch the cabbage and string beans in salted boiling water for 5 minutes. Drain and refresh. Add the cabbage to the soup kettle and cook for an additional 20 minutes.

4. Add the beans and peas to the soup and cook until they are tender, about 10 minutes. Discard the herb bouquet.

5. Transfer the pork and vegetables to a platter. Arrange the bread in a warmed tureen and add the broth. Serve the soup immediately and follow with the meat and vegetables as a main course.

Serves 8

MAIN-COURSE PORK AND VEGETABLE SOUP *(potée Champenoise)*

France

Preparation time: 30 minutes

Cooking time: 3 hours

Ingredients

A   ½-pound piece lean bacon

1   pound pork shoulder butt

3   quarts water

3   carrots, peeled and quartered

5   small white turnips, peeled and quartered

1   small cabbage, quartered

Freshly ground pepper

4   potatoes, peeled and quartered

4   fresh sausages

8   thin slices French bread, toasted

1. Cut the bacon into chunks and blanch in boiling water for 10 minutes to remove the salt. Drain.

2. Put the bacon and the pork shoulder butt into a large soup kettle. Pour in the water. Bring to a boil and skim.

3. Add the carrots, turnips and cabbage. Season with pepper. Simmer for 2½ hours.

4. Add the potatoes and the sausages which have been pricked with a fork. Simmer for an additional 30 minutes.

5. Remove the vegetables and meat and arrange them on a heated platter. Keep warm.

6. Pour stock into a tureen lined with the bread slices. Serve immediately. The meat and vegetables are served separately.

Serves 4

VEAL KIDNEY SOUP *(Nier Soep)*

Preparation time: 20 minutes   **Cooking time:** 30 minutes

The Netherlands

Ingredients

1	*pair veal kidneys*	1	*pound mushrooms, chopped*
4	*cups chicken stock*		
1	*onion, minced*	3	*tablespoons Madeira*
4	*tablespoons butter*		*Juice of ½ lemon*
4	*tablespoons flour*	2	*tablespoons fresh parsley, chopped*
1	*cup heavy cream*		

1. Prepare the kidneys: Remove the outer membrane and split in half lengthwise. Discard the core of fat and the white veins, then dice the kidneys.

2. In a large saucepan, combine the chicken stock and the kidneys. Bring to a boil, then lower heat, cover and simmer until tender, about 15 minutes.

3. While the kidneys cook, melt the butter in another saucepan and sauté the onions until tender, about 5 minutes.

4. Off the heat, stir the flour into the onion mixture. Return to low heat and stir for 5 minutes. Do not let the flour brown. Add the hot stock, a little at a time, to the flour, stirring constantly to avoid lumps. Cook until thickened.

5. Add the kidneys, cream and chopped mushrooms and heat through but do not boil. Simmer for 5 minutes. Just before serving, stir in the Madeira, lemon juice and the chopped parsley.

Serves 4

VOLGA-STYLE FISH CONSOMMÉ
(uhka)

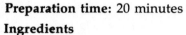

USSR

Preparation time: 20 minutes   **Cooking time:** 2 hours

Ingredients

2	*pounds white-fleshed fish (cod, whiting or haddock), cleaned*
1	*small eel, cleaned*
2	*quarts water*
2	*onions, chopped*
3	*stalks celery, chopped*
1	*carrot, peeled and chopped*

¼	*cup fresh parsley, chopped*
1	*bay leaf*
1	*teaspoon salt*
6	*peppercorns*
	Pinch nutmeg
½	*cup dry white wine*
	Chopped fresh dill for garnish

1. In a soup kettle, combine the fish, water, vegetables, herbs, salt, peppercorns and nutmeg.

2. Bring to a boil, then lower heat, cover and simmer for 2 hours.

3. Using a fine sieve lined with cheesecloth, strain broth into a large saucepan.

4. Bring strained broth to a simmer. Stir in the wine and heat through.

5. Pour into a warmed tureen, garnish with freshly chopped dill and serve immediately.

Serves 6

FLEMISH FISH SOUP
(waterzooï de poissons)

Preparation time: 20 minutes   **Cooking time:** 25 minutes   *Belgium*

Ingredients

8	tablespoons butter
2	leeks, chopped
2	onions, chopped
2	carrots, sliced
2	pounds assorted fish (perch, small carp, sea eel), cut into chunks
2	cups dry white wine

2 cups fish stock or water
Salt
Freshly ground pepper
Herb bouquet (bay leaf, thyme, sage)
Chopped parsley for garnish

1. Melt 6 tablespoons of the butter in a large saucepan. Add the leeks, onions and carrots; sauté until the onions are translucent but not browned.

2. Add the remaining butter and the fish. Pour in the wine and fish stock (or water). Salt and pepper lightly and add the herb bouquet.

3. Bring soup to a boil, then cover, lower heat and simmer for about 20 minutes, or until all the fish chunks flake easily when tested with a fork.

4. Discard the herb bouquet, correct seasoning and serve piping hot, sprinkled with parsley.

Serves 4

According to **The World Atlas of Food,** *this soup originated in Ghent. Waterzooï may also be made with chicken and thickened with egg and cream.*

BASQUE FISH AND ONION SOUP *(ttoro)*

France

Preparation time: 10 minutes   **Cooking time:** 1¼ hours

Ingredients

4 *medium onions, sliced*	*Freshly ground pepper*
½ *cup olive oil*	4 *thick pieces hake, cod*
2 *quarts water*	*or haddock, boned*
Herb bouquet (thyme,	4 *slices French bread*
parsley, bay leaf,	2 *cloves garlic, peeled*
oregano)	*and cut in half*
1 *teaspoon salt*	

1. In a large heavy pot, sauté the onions in half the olive oil until lightly browned.

2. Add the water, herb bouquet, salt and pepper. Bring to a boil, then cover and cook over moderate heat for 15 minutes.

3. Add the fish, re-cover and simmer over low heat for 1 hour.

4. While the fish is cooking, fry the bread in the remaining olive oil and rub each slice with half a clove of garlic.

5. To serve, carefully remove the fish from the pot with a slotted spoon and arrange in a warmed deep dish. Top each piece of fish with a slice of fried bread. Taste broth and adjust seasoning, if necessary, then pour over the fish. Serve immediately.

Serves 4

BAHIA FISH SOUP *(bouquet do mar)*

Preparation time: 15 minutes   **Cooking time:** 35 minutes

Ingredients

Brazil

2 tablespoons olive oil	¾ pound shrimp, shelled, deveined and halved
3 cloves garlic, minced	
6 onions, chopped	5 cups chicken broth
3 tomatoes, peeled, seeded and chopped	Salt
	½ teaspoon cayenne pepper
3 green peppers, seeded and chopped	1 teaspoon marjoram
1 pound fish fillets, cut into chunks	

1. In a large saucepan, heat the olive oil with the garlic and sauté the onions until translucent, about 5 minutes.

2. Stir in the tomatoes and green peppers. Cook for 1 minute over moderately high heat, then add the fish and the shrimp.

3. Pour in the chicken broth; season with salt, cayenne pepper and marjoram.

4. Bring soup to a boil, then lower heat, cover and simmer until the fish chunks flake easily when tested with a fork, about 20 minutes. Correct seasoning and serve piping hot.

Serves 4

ANGOUMOIS FISH CHOWDER
(chaudrée)

France

Preparation time: 20 minutes   **Cooking time:** 30 minutes

Ingredients

7	*tablespoons butter*
4	*medium onions, sliced*
	Herb bouquet (bay leaf, 3 cloves, parsley, dill)
1	*clove garlic, minced*
1	*teaspoon salt*
	Freshly ground pepper

4	*cups dry white wine, or half wine, half water*
3	*pounds white fish fillets (sole, whiting, flounder), cut in chunks*

1. Melt the butter in a large heavy pot and sauté the onions for 5 minutes.

2. Add the herb bouquet, garlic, salt and pepper. Cover with the white wine and simmer for 15 minutes.

3. Add the fish to the pot, cover and simmer until the fish is tender, about 15 minutes.

4. Using a slotted spoon, transfer the fish to a heated tureen and keep warm.

5. Reduce stock by half and pour over fish.

Serves 4 to 6

VARIATION: *Add small whole potatoes to the* chaudrée *at Step 2.*

NEW ENGLAND CLAM CHOWDER

Preparation time: 30 minutes   **Cooking time:** 1 hour   *USA*

Ingredients

4 dozen clams	3 medium potatoes, peeled and cubed
2 cups water	Salt
A 2-inch cube salt pork or 3 slices bacon, chopped	Freshly ground pepper
1 medium onion, chopped	2 cups milk
	1 cup cream
	3 tablespoons butter

1. Wash the clams thoroughly. Place them in a deep pot and add the water. Cover closely and bring to a boil. Lower heat and simmer until the shells open, about 10 minutes. Discard any clams that do not open.

2. Drain the clams, reserving the broth. Remove the clams from their shells and chop them finely.

3. Sauté the salt pork (or bacon) pieces until crisp and drain. Add the onion to the fat and cook until transparent. Add the clam broth and potatoes. Season with salt and pepper. Cover and simmer until the potatoes are tender, about 30 minutes. Remove from heat.

4. Stir in the milk, cream and butter. Return to heat. When the broth simmers, add the clams and pork bits and simmer for about 3 minutes. (Do not let soup boil.) Correct seasoning. Pour into warm soup plates and serve immediately.

Serves 6

PURÉE OF SHELLFISH SOUP
(soupe aux écrevisses)

France

Preparation time: 20 minutes   **Cooking time:** 1 hour

Ingredients

1 cup dry white wine	8 cups boiling water
8 crayfish, deveined, or 8 jumbo shrimp	Herb bouquet (parsley, thyme, rosemary, lemon peel)
3 tablespoons olive oil	
1 leek, sliced	1 tablespoon salt
2 onions, sliced	Freshly ground pepper
1 carrot, sliced	1 egg yolk, beaten
1 tablespoon flour	Chopped parsley

1. Bring the wine to a boil in a saucepan. Add the shellfish, cover and simmer for 10 minutes. Drain, reserving the wine.

2. Heat the oil in a large saucepan. Add the leeks, onions and carrot. Cook over moderate heat for 5 minutes.

3. Sprinkle the flour over the vegetables. Stir for 1 minute, then slowly pour in the wine and the water. Add the herb bouquet, salt and pepper. Bring soup to a slow boil and reduce to 5 cups. (This will take about 30 minutes.)

4. While the soup is reducing, grind the shellfish in a food mill or blender. Reserve.

5. Strain the soup back into the saucepan. Add the shellfish. Bring to a boil, lower heat, cover and simmer for 15 minutes.

6. Just before serving, combine ½ cup of soup with the egg yolk, then gently stir the mixture back into the soup. Heat through, but do not bring to a boil. Pour the soup into a warmed tureen and sprinkle with parsley.

Serves 4

FISHERMAN'S BOUILLABAISSE
(bouillabaisse du pêcheur)

Preparation time: 20 minutes   **Cooking time:** 15 minutes   *France*
Fish marinates—1 hour

Ingredients

3 pounds assorted white fish (halibut, red snapper, whiting, bass, haddock)	Herb bouquet (fennel, bay leaf, savory, parsley)
4 cloves garlic, crushed	½ cup olive oil
4 tomatoes, peeled, seeded and chopped	12 slices French bread
2 onions, sliced	2 quarts boiling water
1 tablespoon salt	½ teaspoon saffron
Freshly ground pepper	Chopped fresh parsley

1. Wash the fish and cut into 2-inch chunks.

2. Put the fish in a large pot. Add the garlic, tomatoes, onions, salt, pepper, herb bouquet and olive oil. Marinate at room temperature for 1 hour, stirring occasionally.

3. While the fish is marinating, dry (but do not brown) the slices of French bread in a slow oven. Sprinkle each slice with olive oil and rub with a clove of garlic.

4. Remove the fish chunks and reserve. Add the boiling water and the saffron to the pot and cook over high heat for 6 minutes. Return the fish to the pot and boil rapidly until the fish flakes easily, about 5 minutes.

5. Remove the fish and arrange on a platter. Sprinkle with the chopped parsley. Place the toasted bread slices in a warm tureen, pour in the stock and serve with the fish.

Serves 4

FISH SOUP PROVENÇAL
(soupe à l'aïgo saou)

France

Preparation time: 20 minutes   **Cooking time:** 20 minutes

Ingredients

2	*pounds white fish (cod, halibut, flounder), cut in chunks*		*Freshly ground pepper*
5	*potatoes, peeled and sliced*	8	*cups boiling water*

2	*pounds white fish (cod, halibut, flounder), cut in chunks*
5	*potatoes, peeled and sliced*
1	*onion, sliced*
2	*tomatoes, peeled, seeded and chopped*
2	*cloves garlic, crushed*
	Herb bouquet (parsley, fennel, celery, orange peel, bay leaf)
½	*cup olive oil*
1	*tablespoon salt*

	Freshly ground pepper
8	*cups boiling water*
Rouille:	
1	*slice white bread*
1	*hot red chili pepper or 1 jalapeño pepper*
1	*clove garlic*
½	*cup olive oil*
	Salt
8 to 12	*thinly sliced pieces of French bread, toasted*
	Chopped fresh parsley

1. In an enameled cast-iron casserole, combine the fish, potatoes, onions, tomatoes, garlic, herb bouquet, oil, salt and pepper. Pour in the boiling water and cook uncovered over moderately high heat for 20 minutes.

2. While the fish is cooking, prepare the *rouille*: Briefly soak the bread in water and squeeze dry. In a mortar, pound the bread, hot pepper and garlic into a smooth paste. Add the oil by drops, beating as for mayonnaise. Add 2 tablespoons of the fish broth and season with salt and pepper. Reserve.

3. Transfer the fish and potatoes to a warmed platter. Sprinkle with parsley and keep warm. Line a soup tureen with the toasted bread and strain in the broth. Serve the fish and potatoes separately, with the *rouille* on the side.

Serves 4 to 6

NEAPOLITAN FISHERMAN'S STEW *(pesca alla pescatora)*

Fish pieces marinate—
2 to 3 hours

Cooking time: 35 to 45 minutes

Italy

Ingredients

—

½	sweet red pepper, diced
2	onions, minced
1 to 2	cloves garlic, minced
1	teaspoon marjoram
	Salt
	Freshly ground pepper
¼	cup olive oil
3	cups red wine
2	tablespoons lemon juice

3	pounds assorted fish, cut into serving pieces
2	dozen clams
2	dozen shrimp, cleaned, shelled and deveined
3	tablespoons butter
2	tablespoons flour
	Chopped fresh parsley

1. Combine the first nine ingredients. Gently coat the fish, then cover and let stand at room temperature for 2 to 3 hours.

2. Transfer the fish and the marinade to a cast-iron casserole. Bring to a boil, then lower heat and simmer fish for 10 minutes. When nearly tender, add the shrimp. Simmer until the fish flakes easily and the shrimp are pink.

3. Remove the fish and shrimp, then reduce the liquid by ⅓.

4. Steam the clams until the shells open, about 10 minutes. Drain and discard any that do not open. Keep warm.

5. Melt the butter, then sprinkle in the flour and cook for 1 minute, stirring constantly. Blend in the reduced liquid and continue stirring until sauce is smooth. Correct seasoning.

6. Arrange the fish, and shellfish in a heated serving dish, cover with the sauce and garnish with the parsley.

Serves 8

SOLE AND MUSSEL STEW
(matelote de sole à la campagnarde)

France   **Preparation time:** 20 minutes   **Cooking time:** 20 minutes

Ingredients

7	tablespoons butter	2	dozen mussels, scrubbed
2	pounds sole fillets		
1	onion, chopped	¼	cup white wine
¼	pound mushrooms	3	tablespoons flour
	Freshly ground pepper	½	cup light cream
1½	cups dry cider or dry white wine		Salt
2	tablespoons brandy	8	slices French bread, fried in butter

1. Heat 4 tablespoons of the butter in a large skillet and lightly brown the fish. Remove and reserve.

2. Sauté the onion and mushrooms in the skillet for 5 minutes. Return the fillets to the pan. Season with pepper, then pour in the cider and brandy. Cover and simmer until the fish flakes easily, about 10 minutes. Remove and arrange in a heated serving dish. Keep warm.

3. Steam the mussels in the wine over high heat until the shells open, about 5 minutes. Discard any mussels that have not opened. Drain mussels and reserve liquid. Remove the shells, saving 6 whole mussels for final decoration. Arrange the shelled mussels with the sole.

4. Reduce the liquid over high heat to ½ cup.

5. Make a roux (page 476) with the remaining butter and the flour. Slowly add the cream. Stir the roux into the liquid and adjust seasoning. Pour the sauce over the fish, then garnish with the fried bread and the reserved whole mussels.

Serves 4

Fish and Shellfish

STEAMED SEA BASS *(tsing lu yu)*

Preparation time: 10 minutes   **Cooking time:** 25 minutes

China   Ingredients

A 1½-pound sea bass, cleaned and scaled	2 scallions, shredded
5 one-inch slices fresh ginger root	¼ cup peanut oil or flavorless vegetable oil
3 scallions, minced	2 slices fresh ginger root, peeled and slivered
Salt	3 tablespoons soy sauce

1. Rinse the fish in cold water, then wrap in a thin layer of cheesecloth.

2. Pour enough cold water into an enameled cast-iron casserole to completely cover the fish when it is steamed. Add the ginger, minced scallions and salt, then bring rapidly to a boil.

3. Add the wrapped fish to the casserole and return to a boil.

4. As soon as the water reaches a full boil, cover casserole and remove from heat. Allow fish to steam (off heat) until the flesh flakes when tested with a fork, about 25 minutes. (Do not uncover casserole during this time.) While the fish steams, heat the oil in a small heavy saucepan. Keep hot.

5. Remove the steamed bass from the casserole and drain, then gently unwrap and transfer to a heated platter.

6. Salt fish lightly, then top with the shredded scallions. Keep hot.

7. Bring the hot oil almost to the smoking point, then add the slivered ginger. Remove from heat immediately and pour over the fish.

8. Sprinkle fish with the soy sauce and serve immediately.

Serves 4

BAKED SEA BREAM PROVENÇALE
(daurade à la Provençale)

Preparation time: 20 minutes   **Cooking time:** 40 minutes   *France*

Ingredients

A   *5-pound sea bream or sea bass*

5 to 6   *sprigs fennel or 1 tablespoon fennel seed*

5   *tablespoons olive oil*

6   *tomatoes, peeled and quartered*

3   *yellow onions, thinly sliced*

2   *tablespoons fresh parsley, chopped*

1   *tablespoon fresh thyme, chopped, or 1 teaspoon dried thyme*
  Salt
  Freshly ground pepper

1   *lemon, thinly sliced*

3   *tablespoons vinaigrette dressing (page 482)*
  Lemon wedges and parsley sprigs for garnish

1. Set oven at 400°.

2. Wash and dry fish.

3. Insert fennel into fish cavity.

4. Pour the oil into a baking dish. Add the fish and coat with oil on both sides. Surround fish with the tomatoes, onion, parsley and thyme. Season with salt and pepper. Place lemon slices on top of fish.

5. Bake fish for 30 minutes, then add the vinaigrette dressing. Baste fish and vegetables thoroughly.

6. Continue baking until fish flakes easily when tested with a fork, about 10 minutes.

7. To serve, transfer fish to a heated platter. Arrange tomatoes and onions on the side and sprinkle the pan juices over the fish. Garnish with lemon wedges and sprigs of parsley.

Serves 4

GRILLED FISH WITH WHITE WINE SAUCE *(brêmes à la mode du Loing)*

France

Preparation time: 15 minutes
Fish marinates—2 hours

Cooking time: 15 minutes

Ingredients

A   3-pound bream, pike,
scrod or whitefish,
cleaned and split

3   tablespoons olive oil
Salt
Freshly ground pepper

2   tablespoons mixed
herbs (chervil, dill,
thyme, basil)

2   tablespoons butter

Sauce:

3   shallots, minced

½   cup dry white wine

1   teaspoon mustard

10   tablespoons butter

2   hard-boiled egg yolks,
sieved
Juice of 1 lemon

2   tablespoons parsley

1. Put the fish on a plate, skin side down. Sprinkle with the oil,
   salt and pepper. Rub the mixed herbs into the flesh and
   marinate for 2 hours.

2. Set broiler at 425°.

3. Pat the fish dry and place on a broiling pan. Dot with the 2
   tablespoons butter. Broil the fish until it flakes easily, about
   12 minutes. Baste frequently.

4. While the fish broils, make the sauce: a) In a small saucepan,
   combine the shallots and wine; b) reduce over moderately
   high heat until almost all the liquid has evaporated; c) remove
   from heat and beat in the mustard; d) place the pan over hot
   water; e) beating constantly, add the butter, a bit at a time,
   then the egg yolks, salt and pepper. Keep warm.

5. Transfer the fish to a heated serving dish. Beat the lemon
   juice and parsley into the sauce and pour over the fish.

Serves 4

BURBOT IN WHITE WINE
(lotte à la Bordelaise)

Preparation time: 15 minutes   **Cooking time:** 40 minutes   *France*

Ingredients

1½ pounds burbot, cod or
    haddock, cut in
    ¾-inch slices
    Flour for dusting fish
6 tablespoons olive oil
1 pound tomatoes,
    peeled, seeded and
    chopped

2 shallots, sliced
    Salt
    Freshly ground pepper
    Herb bouquet (bay leaf,
    parsley, thyme,
    peppercorns)
½ cup dry white wine

1. Rinse the fish under cold running water. Pat dry and dust lightly with flour.

2. Heat the oil in a skillet. Add the fish and brown on both sides over moderately high heat. Remove fish with a slotted spoon and reserve.

3. Add the tomatoes and shallots to the skillet. Sauté for 5 minutes.

4. Season with salt and pepper and add the herb bouquet. Pour in the white wine and cook rapidly for 10 minutes.

5. Return the slices of fish to the skillet, reduce heat and cover. Simmer gently until fish flakes when tested with a fork, about 20 minutes.

Serves 4

COLD MARINATED CARP
(carpe Alsacienne)

France

Preparation time: 15 minutes
Fish marinates—12 hours

Cooking time: 20 minutes
Prepared dish chills—24 hours

Ingredients

A   2-pound carp,
    whitefish, pike, cod or
    hake, boned and cut
    into serving pieces

Marinade:

½   cup dry white wine
    Salt
    Freshly ground pepper
2   onions, chopped
1   clove garlic, minced

Herb bouquet (dill,
chervil, peppercorns,
thyme) ___

3   shallots, chopped
3   tablespoons olive oil
1   tablespoon flour
1   cup water
1   tablespoon fresh
    parsley, chopped

1. Place fish in a glass bowl with the marinade of white wine, salt, pepper, chopped onion, garlic and herb bouquet. Cover and marinate in the refrigerator for 12 hours.

2. Remove fish from bowl and reserve. Strain marinade and reserve.

3. In a saucepan, cook the shallots with the oil until translucent, about 5 minutes.

4. Stir in the flour and cook for 1 minute. Slowly pour in the water and strained marinade. Bring to a boil.

5. Add the fish, then cover and simmer gently until the fish pieces flake easily when tested with a fork, about 15 minutes.

6. Remove fish and arrange on a serving platter.

7. Reduce the sauce by half over high heat. Strain, add the chopped parsley and pour over the fish. Cover and keep in the refrigerator until the following day.

Serves 4

CARP WITH RED WINE SAUCE
(carpe au vin rouge à la Berrichonne)

Preparation time: 15 minutes   **Cooking time:** 45 minutes   *France*

Ingredients

A   2-pound carp,
    whitefish, perch, pike,
    cod or hake, cleaned
    and boned
2   cups red wine
12   small white onions
1   clove garlic, minced
½   teaspoon salt
    Freshly ground pepper

    Herb bouquet (bay leaf,
    chervil, dill, basil,
    peppercorns)
4   tablespoons butter, at
    room temperature
¼   cup flour
    Chopped fresh parsley
    for garnish

1. Cut the boned fish into 2-inch-thick serving pieces. Reserve.

2. Pour the wine into an enameled cast-iron casserole. Add the onions, garlic, salt, pepper and herb bouquet. Boil for 10 minutes.

3. Add the fish to the casserole. Lower heat, cover and simmer gently, until fish flakes easily with a fork, about 15 to 20 minutes.

4. Prepare a *beurre manié* by blending together the butter and flour. Reserve.

5. Using a slotted spoon, remove the fish and onions. Arrange on a heated platter and keep warm.

6. Strain the casserole liquid through a fine sieve into a small saucepan. Reduce over moderate heat for 10 minutes. Remove from heat and beat in the *beurre manié*. Return to a boil for 1 minute, stirring constantly.

7. Pour the sauce over the fish, sprinkle with chopped parsley and serve.

Serves 4

CARP STUFFED WITH FOIE GRAS
(carpe farcie au foie gras)

France   **Preparation time:** 15 minutes   **Cooking time:** 30 minutes

Ingredients

A   *2-pound carp, pike,*
perch or whitefish

Carp's roe, chopped
2   *ounces foie gras*

Stuffing:

1½   *cups bread crumbs*
½   *cup milk*
2   *tablespoons butter*

Salt
Freshly ground pepper
2½   *cups cream*

1. Clean and bone the fish. Reserve.

2. Set oven at 350°.

3. Briefly soak the bread crumbs in the milk. Squeeze out the excess milk and reserve bread crumbs.

4. Heat the butter in a skillet and sauté the chopped roe for 5 minutes. Remove from heat. Add the bread crumbs, *foie gras*, salt and pepper. Mix thoroughly.

5. Fill the carp with the stuffing, then sew up. Place in a buttered baking dish. Salt the fish and cover with the cream.

6. Basting frequently, bake fish until it flakes easily when tested with a fork, about 30 minutes.

Serves 4

SUMMER FISH SALAD (serenate)

Preparation time: 15 minutes   **Cooking time:** 15 minutes
Court bouillon simmers—20 minutes

West Indies

Ingredients

Court Bouillon:

5	*cups water*
½	*cup dry white wine*
	Herb bouquet (bay leaf, thyme, parsley, peppercorns)
2	*carrots, chopped*
2	*stalks celery, chopped*
	Salt
1	*pound fresh codfish, boned*
	—

Vinaigrette Sauce:

1	*cup olive oil*
1	*clove garlic, pressed*
½	*cup lemon or lime juice*
	Salt
	Freshly ground pepper
	—
¼	*cup fresh parsley, chopped*
2	*onions, minced*
3	*tomatoes, peeled and diced*
	Watercress for garnish

1. Using the ingredients listed above, prepare a court bouillon **(page 473)** in a soup kettle. Simmer for 20 minutes.

2. Add the fish, cover and simmer until fish flakes easily when tested with a fork, about 15 minutes. Remove from heat and allow fish to cool in broth.

3. Drain fish, then flake in a large bowl. Reserve.

4. Using the ingredients listed above, prepare a vinaigrette sauce **(page 482)**.

5. Add the onions, tomatoes and chopped parsley to the fish. Mix, then toss with the vinaigrette. Correct seasoning.

6. Cover bowl and refrigerate for 1 hour. Garnish with watercress when served.

Serves 2

COD BAKED IN SOUR CREAM
(fisk med kremsaus)

Norway

Preparation time: 15 minutes   **Baking time:** 20 minutes

Ingredients

4	tablespoons butter
3	shallots, minced
¾	pound mushrooms, sliced
1	tablespoon fresh dill
1	tablespoon fresh parsley, chopped
	Salt
	Freshly ground pepper

2	pounds fresh cod or any white-fleshed fish, cut in serving pieces
	Flour seasoned with salt, pepper and paprika
1½	ounces Parmesan cheese, grated
2	teaspoons paprika
½	pint sour cream
	Dry bread crumbs

1. Set oven at 375°.

2. Heat 3 tablespoons of the butter in a frying pan. Add the shallots and sauté over moderate heat until translucent.

3. Add the mushrooms to the frying pan. Stirring gently over moderate heat, sauté mushrooms until barely golden. Remove frying pan from heat and stir in the dill and parsley. Season to taste with salt and pepper. Reserve.

4. Rinse the fish pieces under cold water, then pat dry and dust with the seasoned flour.

5. Arrange half the mushrooms in a buttered dish. Cover with the fish, then top with the remaining mushrooms.

6. Sprinkle on the grated cheese and paprika, spoon in the sour cream and top with a thin layer of bread crumbs.

7. Dot dish with the remaining butter and bake until the fish flakes easily when tested with a fork, about 20 minutes. Serve from the baking dish.

Serves 4

CREAMED SALT COD
(brandade Nîmoise)

Preparation time: 15 minutes   **Cooking time:** 30 minutes   *France*
Cod soaks—10 hours

Ingredients

1½ pounds salt cod fillets

1¾ cups olive oil, warmed

1 clove garlic, pressed

1 cup light cream, warmed

Salt

Freshly ground white pepper

4 to 6 slices French bread, cut in triangles and fried in olive oil

1. Soak the cod fillets in cold water for 10 hours, changing the water 3 or 4 times.

2. Rinse the fillets under cold water and place in a large saucepan.

3. Cover with cold water. Bring to a boil, then lower heat and poach fish gently for 8 minutes. (Do not let water boil while fish poaches.)

4. Drain the fillets and separate into flakes.

5. Pour ⅓ cup of the warmed olive oil into a saucepan. Place over low heat. Using a wooden spoon, mash the cod flakes and the garlic into the oil.

6. Make a thick paste of the *brandade* by continuing to mash the mixture, adding the remaining oil and the cream a tablespoon at a time. Mash until all the liquid has been thoroughly absorbed. Do not allow *brandade* to boil.

7. Add salt and pepper to taste, garnish with the fried bread triangles and serve immediately.

Serves 4 to 6

BAKED SALT COD IN TOMATO SAUCE *(bacalhau)*

Portugal

Preparation time: 15 minutes
Salt cod soaks—10 hours

Cooking time: 35 minutes

Ingredients

1½	pounds salt cod fillets
4	tablespoons olive oil
1	pound tomatoes, peeled, seeded and chopped
2	shallots, minced
1	clove garlic, minced

4	onions, thinly sliced
	Freshly ground pepper
3	pimientos, cut into strips
¼	cup dry bread crumbs
2	tablespoons butter

1. Soak cod fillets for 10 hours in cold water to desalt. Change the water 3 or 4 imes.

2. Heat the oil in a frying pan. Add the tomatoes, shallots, garlic and onions. Cover and simmer over very low heat until the mixture is creamy. (Stir occasionally during cooking to prevent sticking.) Season with pepper, then remove from heat. Reserve.

3. Rinse the cod fillets under cold water. Place in a saucepan and cover with cold water. Bring to a boil, then lower heat and simmer for 8 minutes. Remove fillets and drain.

4. Set oven at 400°.

5. Pour the tomato and onion mixture into a buttered baking dish, add the fish and garnish with the pimiento.

6. Sprinkle on the bread crumbs, dot with the butter and brown in oven for 10 to 15 minutes.

Serves 4

EEL IN WHITE WINE SAUCE
(anguille à la mode du Clos de Sens)

Preparation time: 50 minutes   **Cooking time:** 40 minutes   *France*

Ingredients

Court Bouillon:

3	cups dry white wine
3	cups water
2	cloves garlic, minced
2	shallots, chopped
1	carrot, sliced
1	onion, sliced
	Herb bouquet (rosemary, thyme, chervil, bay leaf)
	Salt
10	peppercorns

1½	pounds eel, skinned and cut into serving pieces
	Flour for dusting eel
7	tablespoons butter
½	cup cognac, warmed
8	crayfish or jumbo shrimp, deveined
2	tablespoons cream
1	egg yolk, beaten

1. Prepare the court bouillon **(page 473)**. Simmer for 30 minutes.

2. Lightly dust the eel with flour, then sauté in 3 tablespoons butter. Add the warmed cognac and flambé.

3. Add the eel to the court bouillon, cover and simmer over low heat for 25 minutes. Add the shellfish and cook until pink. Remove the eel and shellfish to a heated serving dish.

4. Reduce the court bouillon to 2 cups and strain. Over low heat, beat in the remaining butter, a little at a time, then stir in the cream.

5. Beat ¼ cup of the sauce into the egg. Stirring constantly, pour the mixture back into the sauce. Heat through, then pour over the eel and shellfish and serve.

Serves 4

FROGS' LEGS WITH GARLIC HERB BUTTER *(grenouilles à la Luçonnaise)*

France

Preparation time: 15 minutes   **Cooking time:** 10 minutes

Ingredients

6   pairs frogs' legs
4   cups water
¼   cup white wine vinegar
    Milk for coating frogs' legs
    Flour for coating frogs' legs
2   tablespoons butter

Garlic Herb Butter:

¼   cup butter
2   cloves garlic, pressed

1   tablespoon fresh basil, finely chopped
1   tablespoon fresh oregano
1   tablespoon fresh tarragon
1   tablespoon fresh thyme, chopped

Chopped fresh parsley for garnish
Lemon slices for garnish

1. Place frogs' legs in a shallow, non-metallic pan. Pour in the water and white vinegar. Soak frogs' legs for 10 minutes, then remove and pat dry.

2. Dip frogs' legs in milk, then in flour.

3. Heat the butter in a skillet. Add the frogs' legs and sauté on both sides until tender, about 4 minutes per side. Transfer to a heated platter and keep warm.

4. While the frogs' legs are cooking, melt the butter in a small heavy saucepan; blend in the garlic and herbs. Stir over low heat for 3 minutes.

5. Pour garlic herb butter over frogs' legs, sprinkle with fresh chopped parsley and garnish with lemon slices.

Serves 2

OSLO FISH PUDDING *(fiskepudding)*

Preparation time: 45 minutes   **Baking time:** 1 hour

Ingredients

Norway

1	*pound haddock or cod fillets, chopped*
6	*tablespoons butter*
3	*eggs, separated*
2	*tablespoons flour*
1/2	*cup milk*
	Peel of 1 lemon, grated
1	*tablespoon fresh dill*
	Salt
	Freshly ground pepper
	Pinch nutmeg
1/2	*pint heavy cream, whipped*

Dill Sauce:

2	*tablespoons butter*
2	*tablespoons flour*
1	*cup fish stock, heated*
1	*cup heavy cream*
6	*ounces shrimp, chopped*
	Salt
	Freshly ground pepper
2	*tablespoons fresh dill*

Fresh dill for garnish

1. Grind the fish to a fine paste. Gradually incorporate the butter. One by one, add the egg yolks. Beat until fluffy. Sprinkle in the flour, then beat in the milk. Stir in the lemon peel, dill, nutmeg, salt and pepper.

2. Set oven at 325°. Beat the egg whites until stiff. Fold the egg whites into the fish mixture, then fold in the cream. Pour into a buttered 2-quart mold. Cover with buttered paper and place in a shallow pan of hot water. Bake until set, about 1 hour. Run a knife around the edge, then quickly invert over a platter.

3. About 10 minutes before serving, prepare the sauce: Melt the butter, sprinkle in the flour and stir over low heat for 1 minute. Beat in the fish stock, then gradually add the cream. Simmer for 3 minutes, then add the shrimp. Season, then stir in the dill. Pour the sauce over the pudding and garnish with fresh dill.

Serves 6

BRITISH BRUNCH *(kedgeree)*

Great Britain

Preparation time: 15 minutes   **Cooking time:** 10 minutes

Ingredients

10 ounces smoked haddock fillet, cooked	Salt
6 tablespoons butter	Freshly ground pepper
1 large onion, minced	Cayenne pepper
3 cups cooked rice, heated	Parsley sprigs for garnish
2 hard-boiled eggs	

1. In a large bowl, flake the fish with a fork. Reserve.

2. Melt half the butter in a large frying pan. Add the onion and sauté over moderately low heat until limp, about 5 minutes. Keep hot.

3. Add the flaked fish and mix thoroughly, then add the hot rice and toss well. Keep hot.

4. Coarsely chop the hard-boiled egg whites, then add to the fish and rice. Keep hot.

5. Sieve the hard-boiled egg yolks into the kedgeree, then season highly with salt, pepper and cayenne. Mix well.

6. Dot the kedgeree with the remaining butter, then transfer to a heated platter, garnish with parsley sprigs and serve piping hot.

Serves 4

VARIATION: *Kedgeree may be prepared with any leftover cooked fish.*

CREAMED SMOKED HADDOCK
(finnan haddie)

Preparation time: 10 minutes

Great Britain

Ingredients

½ *pound smoked haddock fillet*	*Pinch cayenne pepper*
⅔ *cup heavy cream*	*Lemon wedges for garnish*
Juice of ½ lemon	*Chopped parsley for garnish*
Salt	
Freshly ground pepper	

1. Remove any skin and bones from the haddock and flake the fish. Put half the fish in a food mill or blender with half the cream and purée to a creamy texture.

2. Pour the purée into a bowl and blend in the remaining fish and cream. Add the lemon juice and season to taste. Place in a serving dish and garnish with lemon wedges and parsley. Serve with hot buttered toast or crackers.

Serves 2

FRIED HERRING WITH MUSTARD SAUCE

Scotland

Preparation time: 10 minutes   **Cooking time:** 8 to 10 minutes

Ingredients

Mustard Sauce:

1	tablespoon butter
1	tablespoon flour
1	cup milk
2	teaspoons mustard

—

4	fresh herring, cleaned and filleted
1	egg, beaten
1	cup coarse oatmeal
4	tablespoons butter

1. To prepare the mustard sauce, melt the butter in a small saucepan. Blend in the flour and gradually add the milk. Stir until thickened, then blend in the mustard. Keep warm.

2. Dip the herring into the egg and coat with the oatmeal.

3. Melt the butter in a skillet and fry the herring until tender, about 8 to 10 minutes. Serve with the mustard sauce.

Serves 2

BAKED STUFFED MACKEREL
(maquereaux à la Flamande)

Preparation time: 15 minutes   **Cooking time:** 20 to 30 minutes

France

Ingredients

4 medium-sized mackerel or 8 porgy	¼ cup scallions, finely chopped
4 tablespoons butter, at room temperature	Salt
3 shallots, minced	Freshly ground pepper
¼ cup fresh parsley, finely chopped	Juice of 1 lemon

1. Set oven at 350°.

2. Wash fish and pat dry.

3. Cream the butter in a bowl. Blend in the shallots, parsley, scallions, salt and pepper. Stuff the fish with this mixture.

4. Wrap each fish in well-buttered aluminum foil, securing the ends to prevent juices from leaking. Place on a cookie sheet.

5. Bake for 20 to 30 minutes, depending on size of fish.

6. Before serving, remove foil and sprinkle fish with lemon juice.

Serves 4

MACKEREL IN CAPER SAUCE
(maquereaux de Roscoff)

France

Preparation time: 10 minutes
Fish marinates—1 hour

Cooking time: 35 minutes

Ingredients

Marinade:

3   tablespoons olive oil
1   onion, sliced
    Salt
    Freshly ground pepper

4   mackerel (with heads and tails reserved), filleted

Court Bouillon:

2   quarts water
1   cup cider vinegar
1   carrot, chopped
1   onion, chopped
    Fish heads and tails
1   tablespoon coarse salt
10 peppercorns, crushed
    Herb bouquet (bay leaf, parsley, thyme)

Caper Sauce:

3   tablespoons butter
3   tablespoons flour
3   tablespoons capers
1   tablespoon scallions
    Juice of ½ lemon

1. Combine marinade ingredients. Coat the mackerel fillets well and let stand 1 hour.

2. Prepare the court bouillon **(page 473)**. Simmer for 30 minutes. Poach the fillets in the court bouillon for 15 minutes. Remove and arrange in an ovenproof baking dish. Strain the court bouillon, bring to a boil and reduce to 2 cups.

3. Preheat oven to 425°.

4. Prepare the caper sauce: Melt the butter, blend in the flour and cook for 1 minute. Still stirring, pour in the court bouillon. Simmer until thickened, then add the capers, scallions and lemon juice. Cover the fish with the sauce. Bake until the fish flakes easily, about 7 minutes. Serve immediately.

Serves 4

FILLETS OF PERCH IN CHABLIS
(perches au Chablis)

Preparation time: 10 minutes   **Cooking time:** 20 to 25 minutes

France

Ingredients

2	*pounds perch or porgy fillets*
4	*shallots, finely minced*
5	*tablespoons butter*
	Salt

	Freshly ground pepper
1	*cup Chablis, hot*
½	*cup fresh bread crumbs*
¾	*cup Gruyère or other Swiss cheese, grated*

1. Set oven at 400°.

2. Place the fillets in a buttered shallow baking dish. Add the shallots and dot with the butter. Season with salt and pepper.

3. Cover fish with the hot wine and bake until fish is almost done, about 15 minutes.

4. Remove dish from oven and sprinkle with the bread crumbs and grated cheese.

5. Brown under the broiler for 5 to 10 minutes and serve immediately.

Serves 4

COLD POACHED PIKE WITH BLUE CHEESE SAUCE

(brochet de dombes au bleu de Bresse)

France

Preparation time: 20 minutes   **Cooking time:** 20 minutes
Court bouillon simmers—30 minutes

Ingredients

Court Bouillon:

2	*quarts water*
2	*cups dry white wine*
	Herb bouquet (parsley, bay leaf, thyme, peppercorns)
2	*carrots, chopped*
2	*onions, chopped*
	Salt
	Freshly ground pepper
A	*3-pound pike, cleaned*

Blue Cheese Sauce:

1	*tablespoon blue cheese (preferably bleu de Bresse)*
1	*teaspoon Dijon mustard*
5	*tomatoes, peeled, seeded and chopped*
¼	*cup fresh parsley, chopped*
	Parsley sprigs for garnish

1. Using the ingredients listed above, prepare a court bouillon (page 473). Simmer for 30 minutes.

2. Add the fish to the court bouillon and poach gently until the flesh flakes easily when tested with a fork, about 20 minutes. Remove fish and allow it to cool.

3. Prepare the sauce: Combine the blue cheese and mustard in a bowl. Mix until smooth, then add the tomatoes and chopped parsley. Blend well.

4. To serve: place the pike on a serving platter and garnish with parsley sprigs. Serve the sauce separately.

Serves 4

sage

cloves

saffron

celery seed

chili powder

fennel

ginger

peppercorns

rosemary

turmeric

caraway seed

curry powder

coriander

sesame seed

cayenne pepper

anise

paprika

basil

cinnamon

juniper berries

PIKE POACHED IN CREAM AND ROSÉ WINE

(matelote de brochet au vin rosé)

France

Preparation time: 15 minutes   **Cooking time:** 25 minutes

Ingredients

- 3 *pounds pike, cut into serving pieces*
- 6 *tablespoons butter*
- 2 *tablespoons eau de vie de mirabelle or kirsch, warmed*
- 3 *cups rosé wine*
- 2 *shallots, minced*
- *Salt*

- *Freshly ground pepper*
- *Herb bouquet (parsley, chervil, thyme, peppercorns)*
- 3 *tablespoons flour*
- 1 *cup heavy cream*
- 8 *slices French bread, fried in butter*

1. Heat 3 tablespoons of the butter in an enameled casserole. Add the pieces of fish and brown lightly. Pour in the warmed *eau de vie* (or kirsch) and flambé.

2. Add the wine, shallots, salt, pepper and herb bouquet. Simmer for 5 minutes. Remove fish and keep warm. Strain the liquid.

3. In a small saucepan prepare a roux (**page 478**) with the remaining butter and the flour. Stirring constantly, slowly add the liquid to the roux and cook over low heat until the sauce is well blended.

4. Return the fish to the casserole. Cover with the sauce and cook over low heat for 15 minutes. Stir in the cream and heat slightly. Do not boil. Transfer to a deep dish, surround with the fried bread and serve.

Serves 4

POACHED PIKE WITH MUSTARD HOLLANDAISE *(brochet de la Loire)*

France

Preparation time: 20 minutes   **Cooking time:** 20 to 30 minutes

Ingredients

Court Bouillon:

2	quarts water
2	cups dry white wine
½	cup vinegar
1	carrot, sliced
2	onions, sliced
	Herb bouquet (chervil, dill, fennel, bay leaf, basil)
3 to 4	cloves
3	tablespoons coarse salt
10	peppercorns

A	4-pound pike

Mustard Hollandaise:

3	egg yolks
1	teaspoon tarragon mustard
1	tablespoon vinegar
	Salt
	Freshly ground pepper
12	tablespoons butter, at room temperature
	Chopped fresh parsley for garnish

1. Using the ingredients listed above, prepare a court bouillon (page 473) in a fish poacher. Simmer 30 minutes.

2. Add the fish to the court bouillon. Cover and poach gently until the fish flakes easily when tested with a fork, about 20 minutes.

3. While the fish is cooking, prepare the sauce: Beat the egg yolks well with the mustard, then proceed as usual for hollandaise (page 475).

4. Gently transfer the fish from poaching liquid to a heated platter. Garnish with chopped parsley. Serve the mustard hollandaise in a sauceboat.

Serves 4

POACHED FISH WITH MUSHROOMS AND ONIONS
(brochet de la Marne)

France

Preparation time: 25 minutes **Cooking time:** 20 minutes

Ingredients

4 carrots, finely sliced	2 cups champagne or dry white Burgundy
1 onion, chopped	
2 tablespoons parsley	12 tiny white onions
1 tablespoon tarragon	8 tiny mushrooms
3 shallots, chopped	2 tablespoons flour
Salt	¾ cup milk
Freshly ground pepper	Salt
12 tablespoons butter	White pepper
A 3-pound pike, cleaned, boned and split	2 egg yolks
	Parsley sprigs and lemon wedges for garnish

1. In an enameled casserole sauté the carrots, onion, parsley, tarragon, shallots, salt and pepper in 2 tablespoons butter. Place the pike on the vegetables and add the wine. Cover and poach until fish flakes when tested, about 20 minutes. Transfer to a hot platter. Reduce liquid to ½ cup.

2. Heat 2 more tablespoons of butter in a skillet and sauté the onions until tender. Add the mushrooms and sauté briefly.

3. Prepare a béchamel sauce (page 471): Melt 2 tablespoons of the remaining butter, sprinkle in the flour, then stir in the milk, salt and pepper. Beat in the reduced liquid.

4. Beat the egg yolks in a bowl. Gradually stir in ½ cup of the sauce, then slowly beat the egg yolk mixture back into the remaining sauce. Beat in the remaining butter. Add the mushrooms and onions. Do not boil. Cover the fish with the sauce and garnish with parsley and lemon wedges.

Serves 4

STUFFED PIKE WITH HOLLANDAISE SAUCE
(brochet de la Dordogne)

France

Preparation time: 20 minutes   **Cooking time:** 35 to 40 minutes

Ingredients

A	3-pound pike, split		2	shallots, minced
	Salt		2½	cups dry white wine
	Freshly ground pepper			Herb bouquet

Stuffing:

1	cup fresh bread crumbs, moistened
2	eggs, beaten
3	ounces sorrel or spinach, finely chopped
7 to 8	sprigs parsley or chervil, chopped
2 to 3	sprigs tarragon, chopped

2   shallots, minced
2½   cups dry white wine

Herb bouquet
(rosemary, thyme,
peppercorns, bay leaf)

Hollandaise Sauce:

3	egg yolks
8	tablespoons butter
1	tablespoon water
	Juice of ½ lemon
	White pepper

1. Set oven at 350°. Season the pike with salt and pepper.

2. Combine all the ingredients for the stuffing. Mix well, then season with salt and pepper. Stuff the pike and sew up the belly. Place in a buttered baking dish. Pour in 2 cups of the wine, add the herb bouquet and bake until fish flakes easily, about 35 minutes.

3. While the fish is cooking, prepare the hollandaise sauce (page 475). Keep warm in a double boiler.

4. When the pike is done, discard the herb bouquet and transfer fish to a heated serving dish. Keep warm.

5. Add the remaining wine to the baking dish. Place over high heat and reduce liquid by half. Pour the wine sauce over the fish and serve immediately, accompanied by the hollandaise.

Serves 4

PAN-FRIED FISH WITH WHITE WINE AND MUSHROOMS
(brochet au vin blanc)

France

Preparation time: 10 minutes   **Cooking time:** 35 minutes

Ingredients

A   2-pound pike, cleaned
3   tablespoons milk
    Flour for dusting pike
    Salt
    Freshly ground pepper
6   tablespoons butter

2   cups dry white wine
¾   pound mushrooms, quartered
2   tablespoons fresh parsley, chopped

1. Set oven at 400°.

2. Dip pike in the milk and then dust with flour. Season with salt and pepper.

3. Heat the butter in a large frying pan. Add fish and brown on both sides over moderately high heat. Remove pike and place in a lightly buttered baking dish.

4. Pour the wine into the frying pan and scrape up the browned pieces remaining in the pan. Boil for 5 minutes to reduce the liquid a bit.

5. Place the mushrooms around the fish. Season with salt and pepper, then sprinkle with the parsley and pour in the wine mixture.

6. Bake until the fish flakes easily when tested with a fork, about 20 minutes.

Serves 2

FRIED FISH IN SAVORY SAUCE
(escabeche de pescado frito)

Peru

Preparation time: 15 minutes
Fish fillets stand—½ hour

Cooking time: 15 minutes

Ingredients

2   *pounds fillet of pompano, bass or red snapper*
    Salt
5   *tablespoons olive oil*
1   *clove garlic, minced*
2   *large onions, sliced*
1   *egg, lightly beaten*
    Dry bread crumbs or cornmeal

Vinegar Sauce:
1   *bay leaf*
8   *peppercorns*
¼   *teaspoon allspice*
½   *cup cold water*
___
½   *cup red wine vinegar*
1   *green pepper, cut into rings*
    Chopped coriander

1. Rub fillets with salt and let stand for ½ hour.

2. In a large skillet, heat the olive oil and sauté the garlic and half the sliced onions until translucent. Remove with a slotted spoon and reserve.

3. Pat fish dry. Dip in the egg, then in the bread crumbs. Fry fish over moderately high heat until evenly browned and the flesh flakes easily when tested with a fork.

4. While the fish is cooking, prepare vinegar sauce: In a small saucepan, combine the spices and water. Bring rapidly to a boil, then lower heat and simmer for 5 minutes. Add the vinegar, sautéed onions and garlic. Simmer for 5 more minutes.

5. Transfer fish to a hot platter and cover with hot vinegar sauce. Top the fish with remaining uncooked onion slices and the green pepper rings. Garnish with coriander.

Serves 4

RED SNAPPER COZUMEL
(huauhchinango Cozumel)

Preparation time: 20 minutes   **Cooking time:** 25 minutes   *Mexico*

Ingredients

A *5-pound red snapper, cleaned, head and tail left on*

Hot Sauce:

¼ *cup olive oil*

1 *medium onion, chopped*

1 *tablespoon ground coriander*

¼ *teaspoon cayenne pepper*

1 *sweet pepper (green or red), seeded and chopped*

2 *tomatoes, peeled, seeded and quartered*

1 *cup lime juice*
   Salt
   Freshly ground pepper

1. Preheat oven to 375°.

2. Rinse fish well under cold water. Pat dry and reserve.

3. In a saucepan, heat the oil and sauté the onion over moderate heat until translucent. Stir in the coriander and cayenne pepper and blend well. Add the chopped sweet pepper and cook for 5 minutes.

4. Add the tomatoes and lime juice. Season to taste with salt and pepper. Remove from heat.

5. Arrange the fish in a buttered shallow ovenproof pan. Cover with the sauce. Bake, uncovered, until the fish flakes easily when tested with a fork, about 25 minutes.

Serves 4

BAKED RIVER FISH
(omble chevalier du lac du Bourget)

France

Preparation time: 15 minutes

Cooking time: 25 minutes

Ingredients

4   char* or 4 small river trout, cleaned

1   egg, beaten
    Flour for dusting fish

4   tablespoons butter

¾   pound mushrooms, sliced

2   tablespoons cream

2   cups dry white wine
    Salt
    Freshly ground pepper
    Juice of 1 lemon

2   tablespoons fresh parsley, chopped

1. Set oven at 325°.

2. Rinse the fish under cold running water and pat dry.

3. Dip in the beaten egg and then in flour.

4. Melt the butter in a long baking dish and add the fish. Turn them once to allow undersides to get coated with butter. Arrange the mushroom slices around the fish.

5. Mix the cream with the wine and pour around the fish. Sprinkle with salt and pepper.

6. Bake until the fish flakes easily when tested with a fork, about 25 minutes.

7. Serve in the baking dish, sprinkled with the lemon juice and garnished with the chopped parsley.

Serves 4

*NOTE: Char is a delicate fresh-water fish resembling trout, native to Switzerland and Savoy.

COLD SALMON IN ASPIC

Preparation time: 4 hours   **Cooking time:** 20 minutes

Ingredients

Court Bouillon:

3	*quarts water*
1	*quart dry white wine*
2	*carrots, chopped*
2	*stalks celery, chopped*
2	*onions, sliced*
4	*sprigs parsley*
1	*bay leaf*
3	*cloves*
1	*tablespoon salt*
1	*teaspoon thyme*

A	*4- to 6-pound salmon (whole or center cut)*

Aspic:

2	*ounces unflavored gelatin*
6	*cups fish stock*
2	*egg whites, beaten until frothy*
2	*eggs shells, crushed*
½	*cup mayonnaise*
	Cucumber and lemon slices for garnish

Canada

1. Prepare the court bouillon **(page 473)**. Simmer for 1 hour. Wrap the fish in cheesecloth and poach gently in the court bouillon until the fish flakes easily. Refrigerate the fish. Strain the liquid into a saucepan and reduce to 6 cups.

2. Sprinkle the gelatin into ½ cup cold water, then pour in the reduced stock and stir until dissolved. Return the liquid to a saucepan and add the egg whites and egg shells. Bring to a boil, stirring constantly, and cook until foamy. Let cool, then strain through a sieve lined with a damp cloth. Combine 1 cup of the aspic with the mayonnaise and refrigerate until thickened. Reserve remaining aspic at room temperature.

3. Coat the salmon with the thickened aspic-mayonnaise mixture, then chill until set. Chill reserved aspic to the point of setting. Apply a thin layer of clear aspic over the fish, then chill until set. Reserve remaining aspic at room temperature.

4. Repeat layering aspic until the coating is of the desired thickness. Refrigerate until needed and chill the remaining aspic until set. Before serving, finely chop the aspic and arrange around the fish. Garnish with the cucumber and lemon.

Serves 6 to 8

GRILLED SALMON STEAKS WITH MUSHROOMS

(côtelettes de saumon de la Loire)

France

Preparation time: 10 minutes   **Cooking time:** 10 to 16 minutes

Ingredients

4	salmon steaks		1	clove garlic, minced
1	egg		¾	pound mushrooms, quartered
4	tablespoons olive oil		3	tablespoons cream
	Salt			Juice of ½ lemon
	Freshly ground pepper			Parsley for garnish
	Fresh bread crumbs for coating fish			Lemon wedges for garnish
6	tablespoons butter			

1. Rinse the salmon steaks under cold water. Pat dry. In a bowl, beat the egg with 1 tablespoon of the olive oil, salt and pepper.

2. Dip the salmon steaks in the egg mixture and then in the bread crumbs.

3. In a skillet, heat the remaining olive oil and 3 tablespoons of the butter. Over fairly high heat, brown the salmon steaks on both sides. This should take 5 to 8 minutes per side.

4. While the steaks are cooking, heat the remaining butter with the garlic in another skillet. Add the mushrooms and sauté over moderate heat.

5. Add the cream to the mushrooms and heat slightly.

6. Arrange the fish on a heated platter and sprinkle with the lemon juice. Surround with the mushrooms and a garnish of parsley and lemon wedges.

Serves 4

SHAD STUFFED WITH SORREL
(alose farcie à l'oseille)

Preparation time: 15 minutes   **Baking time:** 35 to 45 minutes   *France*

Ingredients

Stuffing:

2	tablespoons butter
2	shallots, minced
½	cup sorrel or spinach, chopped
	Shad's roe, chopped
1	cup fresh bread crumbs
2	tablespoons white wine
2	tablespoons fresh parsley, chopped
2	tablespoons fresh chervil, chopped

	Salt
	Freshly ground pepper
	Freshly grated nutmeg
2	eggs, lightly beaten
A	2½- to 3-pound shad (with roe), boned
4	leeks (white part only)
1	pound sorrel or spinach
2	cups white wine
3	tablespoons butter

1. Make the stuffing: a) Melt the butter in a frying pan and cook the shallots over low heat until translucent; b) add the sorrel and cook briefly to wilt; c) add the chopped roe and sauté briefly; d) remove pan from heat and add the bread crumbs, white wine, parsley and chervil; e) season to taste with salt, pepper and nutmeg; f) bind with the beaten eggs.

2. Preheat oven to 325°. Pat fish dry and lightly salt the inside surfaces. Stuff the fish. Sew up and reserve.

3. Blanch the leeks in a pot of rapidly boiling water. Rinse, then drain. Arrange the leeks and sorrel in a ovenproof dish. Place the shad on the vegetables and cover with the wine. Dot with the butter and bake until fish flakes easily when tested with a fork, about 35 to 45 minutes. Baste frequently.

Serves 4

SWORDFISH PALERMO
(pesce spada alla griglia)

Italy

Preparation time: 5 minutes   **Cooking time:** 7 minutes

Ingredients

4   *swordfish steaks*
    Salt
    Freshly ground pepper
    Pinch paprika
4   *tablespoons butter,*
    softened

Fresh parsley for
garnish
Lemon wedges for
garnish

1. Preheat the broiler.

2. Pat the swordfish pieces dry. Season to taste with salt, pepper and paprika. Dot with half the butter.

3. Place the fish on a buttered broiler pan and broil for 3 minutes on the top side. Turn the steaks, dot with the remaining butter and broil until light brown, about 4 minutes. Arrange the fish on a heated serving platter, pour over any pan juices and garnish with the parsley and lemon wedges.

Serves 4

ALPINE BROOK TROUT
(truites de torrent à la Jurassienne)

Preparation time: 5 minutes   **Cooking time:** 12 to 15 minutes

France

Ingredients

4	trout, cleaned	1	tablespoon butter, at room temperature
	Salt		
	Freshly ground pepper	2	tablespoon fresh parsley, chopped
	Juice of 2 lemons		
	Flour for dusting fish		Parsley sprigs for garnish
1	egg, well beaten		
¼	cup olive oil		Lemon wedges for garnish
2	tablespoons chicken stock, heated		

1. Rinse the trout under cold running water and pat dry. Season with salt, pepper and the juice of 1 lemon. Let stand for 15 minutes.

2. Dust fish with flour and dip in the beaten egg.

3. Heat the oil until sizzling in a frying pan. Add the trout, lower heat and fry until lightly brown, about 5 to 7 minutes on each side. (Fish should flake when tested with a fork.)

4. Arrange fish on a hot platter. Sprinkle on the chicken stock and the juice of the second lemon, then dot with butter and sprinkle on the parsley. Garnish with parsley sprigs and lemon wedges.

Serves 4

STUFFED TROUT *(truites farcies)*

Preparation time: 20 minutes   **Cooking time:** 15 minutes

France **Ingredients**

2 to 3 slices stale bread, cut
     into cubes
     Milk for soaking bread
   3 ounces foie gras
   1 shallot, minced
   1 egg, well beaten
     Salt
     Freshly ground pepper

   1 clove garlic, pressed
   1 teaspoon fresh parsley,
     chopped
   2 tablespoons butter, at
     room temperature
   4 trout, cleaned and
     gutted
   3 tablespoons olive oil

1. Briefly soak the stale bread cubes in a little milk. Squeeze out and transfer to a mixing bowl.

2. Add the *foie gras* and minced shallot. Blend well, then bind with the beaten egg. Season with salt and pepper.

3. Cream the garlic and parsley into the butter. Form into small balls and refrigerate until needed.

4. Stuff each trout with the *foie gras* mixture. Sew closed or secure with toothpicks or skewers.

5. Heat the olive oil in a skillet. Pan-fry the trout over moderately high heat until flesh flakes easily when tested with a fork, about 15 minutes (7½ minutes on each side). Spoon the oil over the fish while they cook.

6. Serve trout piping hot, topping each trout with a piece of the parsley-garlic-butter mixture.

Serves 4

SEA TROUT IN WHITE WINE, DAUPHINÉ *(truites saumonnées du Vercors)*

France

Preparation time: 15 minutes   **Cooking time:** 15 minutes

Ingredients

4	sea trout, cleaned
1	cup milk
	Flour for dusting fish
6	tablespoons butter
⅛	pound mushrooms, diced
	Peel of 1 truffle (optional)

1	cup dry white wine
1	shallot, minced
	Salt
	Freshly ground pepper
1	cup cream
	Juice of ½ lemon

1. Set oven at 425°.

2. Rinse the trout under cold running water and pat dry. Dip in the milk and then dust with flour.

3. Melt 4 tablespoons of the butter in a frying pan. Cook the trout over moderately high heat until golden, about 5 minutes on each side.

4. In another frying pan, sauté the mushrooms (and truffle peel) in the remaining butter.

5. When the fish are done, transfer them to a baking dish.

6. Mix the wine into the pan juices, add the shallots, and salt and pepper to taste. Reduce over high heat for 1 or 2 minutes.

7. Add the mushrooms, truffle peel, cream and lemon juice. Pour the mixture over the trout and bake for 5 minutes.

Serves 4

STUFFED FISH EN PAPILLOTE
(tanches farcies tourangelles)

France

Preparation time: 20 minutes

Cooking time: 20 minutes

Ingredients

2 tench or trout, cleaned

Stuffing:

1 cup fresh bread crumbs

2 tablespoons milk

½ pound mushrooms, chopped

4 shallots, finely minced

¼ cup fresh parsley, chopped

Salt

Freshly ground pepper

1 egg, beaten

6 tablespoons butter

1 cup white wine

Lemon wedges for garnish

1. Rinse the fish under cold water. Pat dry and reserve.

2. Set oven at 400°.

3. Make the stuffing: a) Combine the bread crumbs and milk in a mixing bowl; b) add the mushrooms, shallots and parsley; c) season with salt and pepper; d) bind with the beaten egg.

4. Heat 3 tablespoons of the butter in a frying pan and briefly sauté the stuffing. Remove pan from heat.

5. Stuff the fish, then rub the skins with the remaining butter. Wrap each fish *en papillote* (in greaseproof paper or parchment).

6. Place the fish in a baking dish. Pour in the wine and bake until fish are cooked through, about 20 minutes.

7. Remove the paper from the cooked fish, then transfer fish to a warmed platter. Spoon the cooking juices over the fish, garnish with lemon wedges and serve immediately.

Serves 2

PAN-FRIED FISH IN THE POITOU STYLE *(tanches à la Poitevine)*

France

Preparation time: 5 minutes   **Cooking time:** 12 to 15 minutes

Ingredients

2	tench or trout, cleaned
2	tablespoons olive oil
6	tablespoons butter
2	shallots, minced
	Salt
	Freshly ground pepper

2	tablespoons white wine vinegar
1	clove garlic, pressed
3	tablespoons fresh parsley, chopped

1. Rinse the fish under cold water. Pat dry.

2. In a skillet heat the oil and 2 tablespoons of the butter. Add the fish and sauté over moderately high heat until nicely browned, about 5 to 7 minutes on each side. Remove to a serving platter. Keep warm.

3. Add the rest of the butter to the skillet. Stir in the shallots and sauté over moderate heat until lightly browned. Season with salt and pepper.

4. Add the vinegar, garlic and parsley to the skillet and bring to a boil.

5. Pour over the fish and serve.

Serves 2

FISH FRY NIÇOISE *(poutina)*

France

Preparation time: 10 minutes   **Cooking time:** 15 minutes

Ingredients

¾ *pound tiny fish (smelts or whitebait)*

½ *cup white wine vinegar*

Flour for coating fish

5 *tablespoons olive oil*

3 *medium-sized onions, chopped*

Salt

Freshly ground pepper

Lemon wedges for garnish

1. Spread the fish out on a dish and sprinkle with the vinegar.

2. Dry the fish and roll in flour.

3. Heat the olive oil in a large frying pan and add the chopped onions. Brown the onions and then add the fish. Cook over moderately high heat until fish are golden, about 15 minutes.

4. Season with salt and pepper. Garnish with lemon wedges and serve piping hot.

Serves 2

FISH CURRY WITH RICE
(machi pulao)

Preparation time: 30 minutes   **Cooking time:** 45 minutes   *India*
Rice soaks—1 hour

Ingredients

1 *pound raw rice*	½ *teaspoon fenugreek*
1½ *pounds filleted white-fleshed fish, cut into serving pieces*	½ *teaspoon chili powder*

Curry Mixture:

1 *tablespoon coriander*	3 *tablespoons peanut oil*
2 *teaspoons cumin*	4 *whole dried chili peppers*
½ *teaspoon ground ginger*	2 *cups water*
1 *teaspoon turmeric*	*Salt*
	2 *large onions, sliced*
	2 *tablespoons lemon juice*

1. Soak rice in a bowl of cold water for 1 hour.

2. In a small bowl, combine the curry ingredients. Mix thoroughly, then blend in enough water to make a thick paste. Heat half the oil in a casserole and briskly stir the paste and the chili peppers over moderate heat until spices darken, about 3 minutes.

3. Blend in the water, then add the fish and season with salt. Bring to a boil, then simmer until fish flakes easily when tested with a fork, about 20 minutes. Carefully remove the fish and keep warm.

4. Heat the remaining oil and sauté the onion for about 5 minutes. Add to the fish liquid and bring to a boil. Stir in the drained rice and the lemon juice. Lower heat, cover and simmer until rice is fluffy, about 15 minutes.

5. When rice is tender, return fish pieces to the casserole. Heat through and serve.

Serves 4

TUNA FISH CROQUETTES
(tuna kuroke)

Japan   **Preparation time:** 10 minutes   **Cooking time:** 8 minutes

Ingredients

2   *6½-ounce cans tuna*   *Salt*
1   *pound potatoes, boiled*   *Freshly ground pepper*
    and mashed   *Bread crumbs for*
4   *scallions chopped*   *coating croquettes*
2   *eggs, beaten*   ½   *cup vegetable oil*

1. Drain the tuna fish. Transfer to a bowl and flake.

2. Add the mashed potatoes and scallions. Mix well. Bind with the beaten eggs, then season with salt and pepper.

3. Shape mixture into 8 croquettes. Roll in bread crumbs.

4. Heat the oil in a skillet and fry the croquettes until golden brown. Serve immediately.

Serves 4

PASTA WITH RED CLAM SAUCE
(spaghettini alla vongole)

Preparation time: 15 minutes
Fresh clams steam—10 minutes

Cooking time: 20 minutes

Italy

Ingredients

2	*dozen clams or 2 eight-ounce cans minced clams*
4	*shallots, minced*
1	*onion, minced*
3	*cloves garlic, minced*
¼	*cup oil*
8	*tomatoes, chopped*
2	*tablespoons tomato paste*

½	*cup white wine*
1	*cup clam juice*
½	*teaspoon dried oregano*
½	*teaspoon dried basil*
	Salt
	Freshly ground pepper
1	*tablespoon olive oil*
1	*pound thin spaghetti*
2	*tablespoons butter*
¼	*cup fresh parsley*

1. Prepare the clams: Scrub the shells with a stiff brush. Rinse until no sand remains. Discard any open clams. Steam remaining clams in a little water until shells open, about 10 minutes. Drain, discarding any unopened clams. Shell, trim and mince the remaining clams. Reserve. (If canned minced clams used, drain and reserve clams and juice.)

2. Sauté the shallots, onion and garlic in the oil for 5 minutes. Add the tomatoes, tomato paste, white wine, oregano and basil. Mix well. Season with salt and pepper. Bring to a boil, then lower heat and simmer for 20 minutes.

3. Add the olive oil to a large kettle of rapidly boiling salted water, then cook the spaghetti over moderate heat until barely tender (*al dente*), about 10 minutes. Drain and return to the kettle. Toss with the butter then transfer to a platter.

4. Add the clams to the sauce. Heat through, then stir in the parsley. Pour sauce over the spaghetti and serve.

Serves 4 to 6

SHELLFISH BRILLAT-SAVARIN
(écrevisses à la Brillat-Savarin)

France

Preparation time: 25 minutes   **Cooking time:** 40 minutes

Ingredients

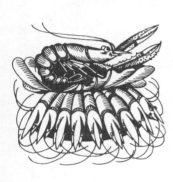

6	*tablespoons butter*		*Herb bouquet*
1	*carrot, thinly sliced*		*(rosemary, thyme, bay leaf, peppercorns)*
1	*onion, sliced*	2	*cups dry white wine*
3	*shallots, minced*		*Salt*
3	*dozen crayfish or jumbo shrimp, cleaned, shelled and deveined*		*Freshly ground pepper*
			Cayenne pepper
3	*tablespoons cognac, warmed*	½	*cup cream*
		2	*tablespoons butter, at room temperature*
3	*tomatoes, chopped*	1	*tablespoon flour*

1. In a large skillet, melt the butter and braise the carrot, onion and shallots for 10 minutes Add the shellfish and sauté until pink, about 10 minutes.

2. Pour in the warmed cognac and flambé.

3. Add the tomatoes, herb bouquet and white wine. Bring to a boil. Cover, lower heat and simmer for 10 minutes. Stir occasionally and season to taste. Remove the shellfish and arrange on a serving dish. Keep warm.

4. Prepare a *beurre manié* by blending the butter and flour.

5. Strain the cooking liquid and reduce by half over high heat. Lower heat and thicken sauce by beating in the *beurre manié* and the cream. Pour over shellfish and serve immediately.

Serves 6

SHELLFISH IN WHITE WINE
SAUCE *(écrevisses de Guyenne)*

Preparation time: 25 minutes   **Cooking time:** 40 minutes   *France*

Ingredients

2 dozen crayfish or jumbo shrimp, cleaned, shelled and deveined

2 carrots, finely sliced

2 onions, minced

1 clove garlic, minced

2 shallots, minced

2 stalks celery, finely sliced

8 tablespoons butter
   Salt

   Freshly ground pepper

3 tablespoons cognac, warmed

1½ cups dry white wine
    Herb bouquet (parsley, bay leaf, peppercorns)

1 tablespoon fresh tarragon, chopped

2 egg yolks

1 tablespoon heavy cream

1. Clean, shell and devein the crayfish (or shrimp). Reserve.

2. Sauté the carrots, onions, garlic, shallots and celery in a pan with ¼ of the butter. Season with salt and pepper.

3. Heat the remaining butter in a deep skillet. Stir in the shell-fish and cook until they turn color, about 10 minutes. Pour the warmed cognac over the shellfish and flambé.

4. Add the wine, sautéed vegetables and herb bouquet. Bring to a boil. Cover and simmer for 5 minutes, stirring occasionally. Remove the herb bouquet and sprinkle shellfish with the chopped tarragon. Transfer shellfish to a warmed shallow dish. Strain the broth and reduce slightly.

5. In a bowl, beat the egg yolks well with the cream. Slowly add ½ cup of the hot broth. Slowly stir the mixture back into the broth. Heat gently until slightly thickened. Do not boil. Pour the sauce over the shellfish and serve.

Serves 4

CRAYFISH TAILS IN CREAM
SAUCE *(gratin de queues d'écrevisses)*

France

Preparation time: 30 minutes   **Cooking time:** 25 minutes

Ingredients

Court Bouillon:

3	cups water
1½	cups dry white wine
1	onion, minced
	Herb bouquet (bay leaf, peppercorns, thyme, dill)
2	dozen crayfish tails or 2½ pounds shrimp, cleaned, shelled and deveined

Béchamel Sauce:

4	tablespoons butter
¼	cup flour
1½	cup hot milk
¼	cup court bouillon
3	egg yolks, well beaten
2	cups cream
	Salt
	Freshly ground pepper
1	cup Swiss cheese, grated

1. Using the ingredients listed above, prepare a court bouillon (page 473). Simmer for 20 minutes.

2. Poach crayfish (or shrimp) in the court bouillon for 5 minutes. Remove shellfish with a slotted spoon and keep warm.

3. Using the ingredients listed above, prepare a béchamel sauce (page 471).

4. Set oven at 400°.

5. Remove béchamel from heat and gradually incorporate the egg yolks and cream. Season with salt and pepper. (If sauce is too thick, thin it with a little of the bouillon.)

6. Transfer shellfish to a buttered baking dish, cover with the sauce, then sprinkle evenly with the cheese.

7. Bake until golden, about 25 minutes. Serve in baking dish.

Serves 4 to 6

BRITTANY BROILED LOBSTER
(homard grillé du Finistère)

Preparation time: 15 minutes   **Cooking time:** 20 to 25 minutes

France

Ingredients

A   2-pound live lobster
     Salt
     Cayenne pepper
½   cup butter, melted
2   tablespoons Calvados, warmed

1   cup crème fraîche or heavy cream
1   tablespoon fresh chervil, chopped, or ½ teaspoon dried chervil

1. Rinse the lobster. Cut its spinal cord by inserting a knife at the juncture where the tail and body meet. Turn lobster on its back and split the undershell lengthwise. Remove and discard the dark vein, the sac behind the eyes and spongy tissue. Separate the tails from the chest. Cut off the claws and crack them.

2. Set broiler at 350°.

3. Place the lobster, flesh side up, in a pan. Sprinkle with salt and cayenne pepper.

4. Brush lobster with half the melted butter and broil for 12 to 15 minutes. Baste at 3-minute intervals to keep the flesh tender.

5. Transfer lobster to an overproof serving dish. Baste with the remaining melted butter and pan juices.

6. Set oven at 425°.

7. Sprinkle lobster with the warmed Calvados and flambé.

8. Pour the *crème fraîche* (**page 473**) or heavy cream over lobster and sprinkle with the chervil. Put the dish in the oven for a few minutes to brown. Serve at once.

Serves 2

NORMANDY-STYLE LOBSTER
(homard à la Normande)

France   **Preparation time:** 25 minutes   **Cooking time:** 35 minutes

Ingredients

A	2-pound lobster, cleaned (page 476)
	Salt
	Freshly ground pepper
¼	cup olive oil
3	tomatoes, peeled, seeded and chopped
2	tablespoons Calvados, warmed

1	cup dry imported cider or dry white wine
½	teaspoon saffron
1	shallot, minced
½	clove garlic, pressed
2	tablespoons butter
1	egg yolk
	Chopped fresh parsley for garnish

1. Season the lobster pieces with salt and pepper. Heat the oil in a large skillet and sauté the lobster over high heat for several minutes, turning the shells constantly until bright red. Add the tomatoes and bring to a boil. Lower heat, add the warmed Calvados and flambé. Add the cider (or wine) and saffron. Cover pan and simmer for 20 minutes.

2. Sauté the shallot and garlic in butter until translucent. Add the lobster coral and tomalley. Cover and simmer for 3 minutes. Keep saucepan over very low heat.

3. Remove the lobster from the skillet and keep hot. Reduce the lobster liquid slightly over high heat, then add it to the coral and tomalley. Beat the egg yolk well in a bowl. Slowly beat in a few tablespoons of the sauce, then gently stir the mixture into the remainder of the sauce. Heat very gently. Do not boil.

4. Arrange the lobster on a heated serving platter and pour the sauce over it. Garnish with parsley.

Serves 2

MUSSELS ANGOUMOIS IN CREAM SAUCE *(mouclade)*

Preparation time: 1 hour

Cooking time: 20 minutes

France

Ingredients

3	quarts mussels, scrubbed
1	cup white wine or water
	Herb bouquet (bay leaf, parsley, thyme)
1	clove garlic
3	tablespoons butter

3	shallots, minced
	Freshly ground pepper
2	tablespoons flour
1	egg yolk
½	cup cream
	Juice of ½ lemon

1. In a large pot, combine the mussels with the white wine, herb bouquet and garlic. Cover and steam until shells open, about 10 minutes. Drain, reserving the liquor.

2. Discard the herb bouquet, garlic and any unopened mussels. Remove half the shell from each opened mussel. Arrange on a heated serving platter and keep warm.

3. In a saucepan, heat the butter and sauté the shallots. Season with pepper. Stirring constantly, blend in the flour. Slowly pour in the mussel liquor. Cook for 10 minutes, then remove from heat.

4. Beat the egg yolk and cream in a bowl. Slowly pour a little of the hot sauce into egg mixture, stirring constantly to prevent curdling. Add the lemon juice and heat through. Do not boil.

5. Pour sauce over mussels and serve at once.

Serves 4

FLAMBÉ SCALLOPS, BORDEAUX
(coquilles Saint-Jacques à la Bordelaise)

France

Preparation time: 15 minutes   **Cooking time:** 25 minutes

Ingredients

1   pound whole bay
    scallops or sliced sea
    scallops
5   tablespoons butter
1   onion, sliced
1   shallot, minced
3   tablespoons cognac,
    warmed

1   tomato, peeled, seeded
     and chopped
1½   cloves garlic, minced
     Salt
     Freshly ground pepper
½   cup white wine
     (preferably Bordeaux)

1. Rinse the scallops under cold running water. Pat dry.

2. Heat the butter in a skillet. Add the onion and shallot and cook over moderate heat until translucent.

3. Add the scallops, raise heat and brown lightly. Pour on the cognac and flambé.

4. Add the tomato and garlic. Season with salt and pepper. Pour in the white wine and simmer for 5 to 6 minutes. Stir gently.

5. Using a slotted spoon, transfer the cooked scallops to 4 warmed scallop shells or individual shallow baking dishes. Keep warm.

6. Reduce the sauce over moderately high heat. Strain through a fine sieve and pour over the scallops. Serve at once.

Serves 4

SAVORY SAUTÉED SCALLOPS
(coquilles Saint-Jacques de Cornouaille)

Preparation time: 10 minutes   **Cooking time:** 17 minutes   *France*

Ingredients

1½   pounds whole bay
      scallops or sliced sea
      scallops

8   tablespoons butter

2   shallots, minced

1   tablespoon fresh
      chervil, chopped, or 1
      teaspoon dried chervil

1   clove garlic, pressed

*Pinch freshly grated
nutmeg*

Dash cayenne pepper

Salt

1⅓ cups fresh bread
      crumbs

6   tablespoons dry bread
      crumbs

1. Rinse the scallops under cold running water. Pat dry.

2. Melt 5 tablespoons of the butter in a saucepan. Add the shallots and chervil and sauté gently for 2 minutes.

3. Add the scallops, garlic, nutmeg, cayenne and salt. Cook for 6 minutes, stirring occasionally.

4. Add the fresh bread crumbs and continue cooking for 6 more minutes. Remove from heat.

5. Spoon the scallop mixture into 6 scallop shells or individual baking dishes. Sprinkle with the dry bread crumbs and dot with the remaining butter.

6. Place under the broiler until nicely browned, about 3 minutes. Serve piping hot.

Serves 6

SHRIMP BAKED IN PORT, EGGS AND CREAM

(camarões com vinho do Porto)

Portugal

Preparation time: 15 minutes   **Baking time:** 35 minutes

Ingredients

4 *tablespoons butter*	4 *egg yolks*
8 *scallions, chopped*	1 *cup heavy cream*
1 *pound small shrimp, cleaned, shelled and deveined*	½ *cup fresh parsley, coarsely chopped*
¼ *cup dry port*	*Salt*
	Freshly ground pepper

1. Preheat oven to 325°.

2. Melt the butter in a large frying pan. Add the scallions and sauté over moderate heat until limp.

3. Add the shrimp and cook gently until pink, about 5 minutes.

4. Add the port and simmer for 5 minutes.

5. Transfer the shrimp mixture to an ovenproof dish. Reserve.

6. In a bowl, beat together the egg yolks and cream. Add the parsley and season with salt and pepper.

7. Pour the custard mixture into the ovenproof dish. Mix thoroughly. Bake until set, about 35 minutes.

Serves 4

BEAN CURD AND SHRIMP
(tofu to ebi no kuzuni)

Preparation time: 10 minutes   **Cooking time:** 7 minutes   *Japan*

Ingredients

2 teaspoons cornstarch	3 cups chicken stock
2 tablespoons peanut oil or vegetable oil	4 scallions, cut into 1-inch pieces
1 thin slice fresh ginger root, peeled and minced	¼ cup sake or dry sherry
1 pound shrimp, cleaned, shelled and deveined	4 three-inch squares fresh bean curd (tofu), diced

1. In a cup, dissolve the cornstarch in a little water. Reserve.

2. Heat the oil in a frying pan. Add the ginger and shrimp. Stir-fry over high heat until shrimp turns pink, about 3 minutes.

3. Add the stock, scallions and *sake* (or sherry). Bring to a boil, then reduce heat to low and briskly stir in cornstarch mixture.

4. Continue stirring until liquid clears, then add the diced bean curd. Stir gently until heated through. Serve immediately.

Serves 2 to 4

SHRIMP AND OKRA GUMBO

(crevettes Pelée)

Martinique

Preparation time: 30 minutes   **Cooking time:** 20 minutes

Ingredients

½   *cup vegetable oil*
1   *onion, chopped*
1   *pound fresh okra,
    trimmed and sliced*
1   *pound tomatoes, peeled
    and chopped*
1   *large banana, peeled
    and sliced*

1   *pound shrimp,
    cleaned, shelled,
    deveined and coarsely
    chopped*
2   *tablespoons lemon juice
    Salt
    Cayenne pepper*
½   *cup boiling water
    Boiled rice*

1. Heat the oil in a large saucepan. Add the onion and sauté over low heat until translucent, about 5 minutes.

2. Stirring constantly, add the okra and cook over low heat for 2 minutes.

3. Add the tomatoes, then the banana slices and mix thoroughly. Simmer over moderately low heat for 5 minutes.

4. Add the chopped shrimp and lemon juice, then season to taste with salt and cayenne pepper.

5. Pour in the boiling water, cover and simmer until shrimp are pink and firm, about 10 minutes.

6. Adjust seasonings, transfer to a bed of boiled rice and serve immediately.

Serves 4

STIR-FRIED SHRIMP *(chao sha)*

Preparation time: 25 minutes

Cooking time: 7 minutes

Ingredients

China

4½   tablespoons peanut oil

1½   teaspoons salt

2   green peppers, seeded and chopped

1   pound canned bamboo shoots, diced

3   cloves garlic, minced

1   thick slice fresh ginger root, minced

1   pound shrimp, shelled, deveined and diced

2   tablespoons Chinese rice wine or dry sherry

½   teaspoon sugar

1   tablespoon cornstarch

2   tablespoons chicken stock or water

1. Place a wok (or skillet) over high heat for ½ minute. Add 1 tablespoon of the oil and ½ teaspoon of the salt. Wait ½ minute, then add the peppers and stir-fry for 1 minute. Remove with a slotted spoon and reserve.

2. Add another ½ tablespoon oil and ½ teaspoon of salt to the wok. Wait ½ minute, then add the bamboo shoots and stir-fry for 1 minute. Remove and reserve.

3. Add the remaining oil and salt to the wok. Wait 10 seconds, then add the garlic and ginger. Stir-fry for 1 minute, then raise heat and add the shrimp. Stir-fry over high heat until pink, about 1½ minutes. Remove wok from heat. Add the rice wine (or sherry) and sugar. Stir briefly to blend, then allow mixture to rest for 1 or 2 minutes.

4. In a cup dissolve the cornstarch in the stock (or water.) Add reserved peppers and bamboo shoots to the wok, then briskly stir in the cornstarch mixture.

5. Return wok to high heat and toss ingredients until the shrimp are thoroughly glazed, about 1 minute. Serve immediately.

Serves 3 to 4

SHRIMP CROQUETTES
(Garnalen Croquetten)

The Netherlands

Preparation time: 40 minutes   **Cooking time:** 8 minutes

Ingredients

6 tablespoons butter	Freshly grated nutmeg
⅓ cup flour	2 eggs, beaten
1 cup milk, heated	Dry bread crumbs for coating croquettes
½ pint heavy cream, heated	Vegetable oil for deep-frying
2 cups cooked shrimp, minced	1 tablespoon fresh parsley, chopped
Salt	Flour for dredging
Freshly ground pepper	

1. Melt the butter in a saucepan. Sprinkle in the flour, stirring constantly over low heat for 2 minutes. Gradually blend in the milk and the cream. Stir over low heat until sauce thickens, about 10 minutes. Remove pan from heat.

2. Add the shrimp and mix thoroughly, then season to taste with salt, pepper and nutmeg. Spread the shrimp mixture out on a large platter. Let stand until completely cool, about 30 minutes.

3. Shape the cooled shrimp mixture into sausagelike rolls about 2 inches long. On a lightly floured board roll each croquette to lightly coat. Dip in the beaten egg, then roll in the dry bread crumbs until well coated. Cover and let stand for 30 minutes.

4. Pour enough vegetable oil into a large saucepan to reach a depth of 4 inches. Heat oil almost to the smoking point (385°–390°). Arrange the croquettes in a frying basket. Plunge basket into the hot oil and fry croquettes until crisp and golden, about 8 minutes.

5. Transfer the croquettes to absorbent paper or to a wire rack and drain. Serve piping hot.

Serves 4

POULTRY AND GAME

ROAST CHICKEN IN MADEIRA
SAUCE *(poularde de Bresse)*

France

Preparation time: 20 minutes   **Cooking time:** 1¼ hours
Truffles and pork fat marinate—4 hours

Ingredients

¼	cup cognac	6	tablespoons butter, at room temperature
¼	cup Madeira		
2	ounces truffles, cut into fine strips	A	4-pound chicken
			Salt
½	pound fresh pork fat or bacon, diced		Freshly ground pepper
		1	cup chicken stock

1. In a non-metallic bowl, combine the cognac and Madeira. Add the truffle strips and the diced pork fat (or bacon). Marinate for 4 hours, then drain. Reserve marinade.

2. Preheat oven to 350°.

3. Insert the truffle strips along the chicken breast between the flesh and the skin. Put 3 tablespoons of the butter and half the marinated pork fat inside the chicken. Truss the chicken and coat the skin thoroughly with the remaining butter. Sprinkle with salt and pepper.

4. Put the rest of the pork fat and the marinade in an ovenproof casserole. Add the chicken and roast until tender, about 1¼ hours, basting frequently. Transfer chicken to a board and carve.

5. Place the casserole over high heat and reduce the stock to ¾ cup. Pour the sauce and serve immediately.

Serves 4

ROAST CHICKEN WITH HONEY AND ORANGE SAUCE

Preparation time: 20 minutes   **Cooking time:** 1½ hours   *Israel*

Ingredients

2 tablespoons chicken fat	2 scallions, chopped
¼ cup honey	¼ green pepper, chopped
1 teaspoon salt	½ teaspoon ginger
1 teaspoon paprika	½ teaspoon prepared horseradish
A 5-pound roasting chicken	Salt
1 cup orange juice, heated	Orange slices for garnish
2 cups orange juice	1 tablespoon cornstarch
2 tablespoons grated orange rind	

1. Preheat oven to 350°.

2. In a saucepan, melt the chicken fat. Remove from heat and blend in the honey, salt and paprika.

3. Place the chicken in a roasting pan. Coat inside and out with the honey mixture, then pour the juice over the bird. Place the pan in the oven and roast chicken until tender, about 1½ hours. (Baste frequently during roasting.)

4. About 20 minutes before chicken is done, combine the orange juice, rind, scallions, green pepper, ginger, horse-radish and salt. Bring slowly to a boil and simmer for 15 minutes. Keep hot.

5. Transfer the roasted chicken to a platter and garnish with orange slices. Pour the pan juices into the sauce.

6. Dissolve the cornstarch in a little cold water, then briskly stir into sauce. Stir over low heat until thickened. Pour into a warmed sauceboat and serve.

Serves 6

CHICKEN WITH CHESTNUT STUFFING *(poulet à la Limousine)*

France

Preparation time: 45 minutes   **Cooking time:** 1¼ hours

Ingredients

Stuffing:

24	*chestnuts*
1	*cup chicken stock*
1	*stalk celery, chopped*
3	*tablespoons butter*
2	*onions, chopped*
¼	*pound sausage meat*

¼	*cup fresh parsley, chopped*
	Salt
	Freshly ground pepper
A	*3-pound chicken*
1	*tablespoon butter*

1. Score the chestnuts and cook in rapidly boiling water for 3 minutes. Drain, peel and skin.

2. In a saucepan, combine the chestnuts with the chicken stock, celery and 1 tablespoon of the butter. Cook over low heat for 20 minutes. Drain and chop the chestnuts.

3. Set oven at 425°.

4. In a bowl, mix the chestnuts with the onions, sausage meat and parsley. Salt and pepper to taste, then brown lightly in the remaining 2 tablespoons of the butter.

5. Stuff the chicken with this mixture and truss. Place in a roasting pan and coat with 1 tablespoon butter.

6. Roast the chicken for 15 minutes, then reduce heat to 350° and continue roasting until done, about 1 hour. Baste chicken frequently as it roasts.

Serves 4

CHICKEN IN SOUR CREAM
SAUCE *(hons i sur grädde)*

Preparation time: 30 minutes   **Roasting time:** 1¼ hours   *Sweden*

Ingredients

A 4-pound roasting
   chicken, cleaned
   Salt
1 teaspoon dried thyme
3 tablespoons butter
2 tablespoons vegetable
   oil
3 onions, chopped

1 bay leaf
6 juniper berries or 1
   ounce gin
1 teaspoon ginger
   Freshly ground pepper
3 strips lean bacon
1 pint sour cream
   Parsley for garnish

1. Preheat oven to 350°. Dry the chicken well. Season with salt
   and the thyme. Truss bird and coat with 1 tablespoon butter.

2. Heat the remaining butter and the oil in an enameled cast-
   iron casserole. Brown the chicken and then reserve.

3. Add the onions, bay leaf, juniper berries (or gin), ginger and
   pepper to the casserole. Sauté briskly for 5 minutes.

4. Cover the breast and legs with the bacon strips and return the
   chicken to the casserole. Cover and bake for 30 minutes.

5. Add the sour cream. Continue cooking until bird is tender,
   about 45 minutes. Take casserole from oven and remove
   chicken. Place casserole over moderate heat and stir to blend
   sauce. Taste and correct seasoning, if necessary. Keep warm.

6. Carve the chicken. Strain the sauce and pour over chicken.
   Garnish with parsley.

Serves 4

CHICKEN IN CHAMPAGNE SAUCE *(poulet à la Champenoise)*

France

Preparation time: 30 minutes

Cooking time: 1 hour

Ingredients

Stuffing:

½   *pound sausage meat*
1½   *tablespoons butter*
1   *small onion, chopped*
1   *shallot, chopped*
½   *clove garlic, minced*
½   *cup dry white wine*
1   *chicken liver, chopped*
¼   *cup fresh parsley*
    Salt
    Freshly ground pepper
    Pinch nutmeg

—

A   *3-pound chicken*
1   *thin strip pork fat*
¼   *pound bacon, diced*
1   *carrot, sliced*
1   *turnip, sliced*
½   *calf's foot*
1   *stalk celery, sliced*
    Salt
    Freshly ground pepper
2   *cups champagne or dry white wine*

1. Brown the sausage meat in a skillet; remove and reserve. Add the butter and sauté the onion, shallot and garlic. Pour in the wine and reduce liquid by half. Add the liver, parsley, sausage, and seasonings. Mix well.

2. Stuff the chicken. Truss and tie the strip of pork fat over the breast. Preheat oven to 325°.

3. In a large casserole brown the bacon with the carrot and turnip. Add the chicken and brown evenly.

4. Blanch the calf's foot for 5 minutes, then rinse. Add the calf's foot, celery, salt and pepper to the casserole. Pour in the champagne and bring rapidly to a boil. Remove casserole from heat, cover and place in oven. Bake until chicken is tender, about 45 minutes. To serve, transfer the chicken to a warm platter. Strain sauce, skim and pour into a warm gravy boat.

Serves 4

BRAISED CHICKEN WITH RED WINE AND ARMAGNAC
(coq au vin à la Quercynoise)

France

Preparation time: 30 minutes   **Cooking time:** 1½ hours

Ingredients

1	tablespoon olive oil
¼	pound bacon, diced
A	3-pound chicken
3	tablespoons Armagnac brandy, warmed
1	onion, chopped
1	tablespoon flour
2	tablespoons tomato paste

3 to 3½	cups red Bordeaux wine
4	shallots, chopped
	Herb bouquet (bay leaf, parsley, thyme)
	Salt
	Freshly ground pepper
2	tablespoons butter
½	pound mushrooms

1. In an earthenware casserole, sauté the bacon in the oil, drain and reserve.

2. Sauté the chicken until nicely browned, about 10 minutes. Pour in the brandy and flambé. Remove and reserve.

3. Sauté the onion until translucent, about 5 minutes. Stir in the flour and cook for 1 minute, then blend in the tomato paste, wine, shallots and herb bouquet. Season with salt and pepper. Bring rapidly to a boil, then lower heat and add the chicken and bacon. Cover and simmer gently for 45 minutes. Turn the chicken, re-cover and simmer for another 35 minutes.

4. Heat the butter in a frying pan. Sauté the mushrooms until golden, then add to the casserole. Continue cooking until chicken is tender, about 10 minutes.

5. Remove chicken and carve. Remove herb bouquet and reduce the sauce to the desired consistency. Return chicken with juices to the casserole. Heat through.

Serves 4

CHICKEN LYONNAISE WITH MUSHROOMS *(poulet célestine)*

France

Preparation time: 15 minutes   **Cooking time:** 40 minutes

Ingredients

5 tablespoons butter	½ cup white wine
A 3-pound chicken, cut into serving pieces	3 tablespoons rich chicken stock
1 pound mushrooms, sliced	1 clove garlic, minced
2 large tomatoes, peeled, seeded and chopped	Salt
	Freshly ground pepper
3 tablespoons cognac, warmed	Dash cayenne pepper
	Chopped fresh parsley for garnish

1. Heat 3 tablespoons of the butter in a large frying pan and brown the chicken over fairly high heat.

2. Add the remaining butter, sliced mushrooms and chopped tomatoes to the pan. Sprinkle on the cognac and flambé, then sauté for 5 minutes.

3. Add the wine, chicken stock and minced garlic. Season lightly with salt, pepper and cayenne pepper.

4. Cover the pan and cook over low heat until chicken is tender, about 20 minutes.

5. Using a slotted spoon, transfer the chicken and mushrooms to a heated serving dish and keep warm.

6. Reduce sauce to desired consistency over high heat. Taste and adjust seasoning, if necessary. Pour over the chicken and garnish with parsley.

Serves 4

POACHED CHICKEN IN "HALF-MOURNING"

(poularde à la Lyonnaise, dîte "demi-deuil")

France

Preparation time: 1½ hours

Cooking time: 1 hour

Ingredients

- 2   *black truffles, sliced*
- A   *4-pound chicken (with giblets)*
- *Juice of 1 lemon*

Stock:

- 3   *quarts water*
- 3   *carrots, chopped*
- 3   *turnips, chopped*
- 1   *celery heart, chopped*
- 4   *leeks, chopped*
- 1   *onion stuck with 3 to 4 cloves*

Herb bouquet (thyme, bay leaf, parsley, peppercorns)
- ¼   *pound bacon, sliced*
- 2   *veal bones*
- *Chicken's giblets*
- *Salt*
- *Freshly ground pepper*
- *Freshly grated nutmeg*

Assorted cooked spring vegetables for garnish

1. Insert the truffle slices between the skin and the flesh of the chicken—use 3 slices in each side of the breast and 2 in each of the thighs. Secure with string. Truss the bird and sprinkle with lemon juice. Cover with foil and refrigerate overnight.

2. In a soup kettle combine all the above-listed stock ingredients. Cover and simmer for 1 hour. Add the chicken. Return to a boil and skim, then reduce heat, cover and poach chicken gently until tender, about 1 hour. Strain the liquid in which the chicken has poached and reserve for future use.

3. Transfer the chicken to a warmed platter and garnish with separately cooked assorted spring vegetables, such as baby carrots, small white onions, tiny green peas, mushrooms and asparagus.

Serves 4 to 6

POACHED STUFFED CHICKEN
(poule à la mode de Gray)

France

Preparation time: 30 minutes   **Cooking time:** 1½ to 2 hours
Court bouillon simmers—30 minutes

Ingredients

A 4-pound stewing
chicken (with livers
and giblets)

Court Bouillon:

2½ quarts water

Chicken's giblets

2 leeks

2 carrots

2 turnips

1 stalk celery

Herb bouquet (parsley,
rosemary, bay leaf,
sage)

Salt
Freshly ground pepper

Stuffing:

Chicken's liver,
chopped

2 tablespoons butter

1 egg, beaten

5 ounces foie gras

Salt
Freshly ground pepper
Pinch of freshly grated
nutmeg

1. Using the ingredients listed above, prepare the court bouillon (page 473) and simmer for 30 minutes.

2. Lightly sauté the chopped chicken liver in the butter. Remove from heat.

3. Combine the sautéed mixture with the egg, *foie gras*, salt, pepper and nutmeg.

4. Stuff the chicken with this mixture, truss and secure the vent.

5. Add the chicken to the court bouillon and return to a boil. Lower heat, cover and simmer gently until the chicken is tender, about 1½ to 2 hours. Serve with rice.

Serves 4

A rich broth is left after the chicken is cooked. Rice served with the chicken may be cooked in it, or it can provide the basis for many other soups and sauces.

CHICKEN-IN-THE-POT
(poule-au-pot Henri IV)

Preparation time: 40 minutes
Stock simmers—2 hours

Cooking time: 1⅓ hours

France

Ingredients

Stock:

A	2-pound piece beef shin
1	beef marrow bone
	Chicken's giblets
1	pound carrots, sliced
1	pound turnips, sliced
4	leeks, sliced
1	celery stalk, quartered
1	large onion
	Herb bouquet (rosemary, parsley, thyme, bay leaf)
4½	quarts water

Stuffing:

	Chicken's liver
2	tablespoons butter

1	cup dry bread crumbs
2	tablespoons milk
6 to 8	ounces ham, diced
2	cloves garlic, minced
1	shallot, chopped
¼	cup fresh parsley
	Salt
	Freshly ground pepper
¼	teaspoon nutmeg
1	egg, beaten
A	4-pound stewing chicken
6	cabbage leaves
4 to 6	boiling potatoes, peeled

1. Combine all the ingredients listed for stock, bring to a boil and skim, then cover and simmer for 2 hours.

2. Lightly sauté the liver in the butter. Chop, then mix with the stuffing ingredients. Stuff the bird, reserving 6 spoonfuls of stuffing. Add the chicken to the stock and simmer for 1 hour.

3. Blanch the cabbage leaves in boiling water. Place a spoonful of the stuffing on each leaf. Roll into sausage shapes and tie. Add the cabbage and the potatoes to the soup kettle. Simmer until the potatoes are tender, about 20 minutes. Transfer the chicken to a platter and surround with the vegetables. Serve the broth separately.

Serves 4 to 6

SESAME SEED CHICKEN *(jee ma jee)*

Preparation time: 20 minutes   **Cooking time:** 20 minutes
Chicken steeps—20 to 30 minutes

China

Ingredients

A *3-pound chicken*
   Salt

8 *scallions*

6 *whole Szechwan peppercorns (optional)*

3 *one-inch lengths fresh ginger root, peeled*

2 *tablespoons sesame-seed oil*

1 *tablespoon soy sauce*

1 *tablespoon sesame seeds, toasted*

1. Wash the chicken under cold running water. Pat dry.

2. Rub the cavity with salt, then insert 2 scallions (the peppercorns) and the ginger.

3. Place the chicken, breast up, in a heavy pot. Add cold water to half cover the chicken. Season with 1 teaspoon salt.

4. Bring rapidly to a boil, then reduce heat, cover and simmer until chicken is tender, about 20 minutes.

5. Remove pot from heat and allow chicken to steep in water for 20 to 30 minutes.

6. Transfer chicken to a cutting board. Remove skin. Cut meat into thin slices, then shred. Cool to room temperature.

7. While the chicken is cooling, mince the remaining scallions.

8. Transfer the shredded chicken to a bowl. Toss with the sesame oil, the soy sauce and the minced scallions.

9. To serve, arrange on a platter and garnish with the toasted sesame seeds.

Serves 2 to 4

BRAISED CHICKEN WITH PEANUTS *(maffé)*

Preparation time: 20 minutes   **Cooking time:** 45 minutes   *Senegal*

Ingredients

½ cup peanut oil	4 ounces tomato paste
A 3-pound chicken, cut in serving pieces	Salt
	Freshly ground pepper
2 onions, chopped	Cayenne pepper
2 cups chicken broth, heated	Chopped hard-boiled eggs for garnish
½ cup chunky peanut butter	Chopped roasted peanuts for garnish

1. Heat the oil in a large enameled cast-iron casserole. Add the chicken pieces and sauté over moderately high heat until nicely browned on all sides, about 10 minutes.

2. Add the chopped onion and stir over moderate heat until onion is golden, about 5 minutes. Keep hot.

3. In a bowl, combine the chicken broth, peanut butter and tomato paste. Blend until smooth, then pour over the chicken.

4. Season casserole with salt, pepper and cayenne, then cover and simmer over low heat until chicken is tender, about 30 minutes.

5. To serve, arrange on a bed of rice and garnish with chopped hard-boiled eggs and chopped roasted peanuts.

Serves 4

CHICKEN BRAISED IN RED WINE
(poulet à la Nivernais)

France

Preparation time: 25 minutes   **Cooking time:** 45 minutes

Ingredients

7	tablespoons butter
1	large onion, chopped
A	3-pound chicken, cut into serving pieces
4	carrots, sliced
½	pound salsify or eggplant, peeled and sliced

2	tablespoons flour
1	cup water
1½	cups red wine
	Salt
	Freshly ground pepper
	Herb bouquet (parsley, bay leaf, thyme)

1. Heat half of the butter in a skillet and brown the chopped onion and chicken pieces over moderately high heat.

2. Transfer the chicken and chopped onion to an enameled cast-iron casserole. Reserve.

3. Sauté the vegetables for 8 to 10 minutes in the skillet used to brown the chicken. Transfer to the casserole.

4. Melt the remaining butter in the skillet. Stirring constantly, blend in the flour and cook for 1 minutes. Still stirring, gradually add the water and bring the sauce to a boil.

5. Remove sauce from heat and add the wine, salt, pepper and herb bouquet. Blend well, then pour into casserole. Cover casserole and simmer over very low heat until chicken is tender, about 45 minutes.

Serves 4

CHICKEN WITH RED WINE AUVERGNAISE
(coq au vin de Chanturgues)

France

Preparation time: 25 minutes
Chicken marinates—12 hours

Cooking time: 1 hour

Ingredients
Marinade:

½	teaspoon thyme
1	bay leaf
3 or 4	sprigs parsley
12	peppercorns
4½	cups red wine
—	
A	5-pound chicken, cut into serving pieces
7	tablespoons butter
¼	pound bacon, diced

10	small white onions
½	pound mushrooms, sliced
3	tablespoons Armagnac brandy, warmed
3	tablespoons flour
1	clove garlic, pressed
	Salt
	Freshly ground pepper

1. Combine the marinade ingredients and marinate chicken for 12 hours. Remove chicken and reserve marinade.

2. Heat 5 tablespoons of the butter in an enameled cast-iron casserole. Sauté the diced bacon, onions and mushrooms briefly over moderate heat. Add the chicken and brown. Pour in the brandy and flambé.

3. Add 1 tablespoon of the flour, stir constantly for 5 minutes, then strain in the marinade. Secure the strained herbs into a bouquet and add with the garlic to the casserole. Cover and simmer until the chicken is tender, about 45 minutes

4. Before serving, transfer chicken, onions and mushrooms to a warm platter. Over high heat, reduce sauce in casserole.

5. Prepare a *beurre manié* (page 471) with the remaining butter and flour and beat into the reduced sauce, simmer for 5 minutes, then pour over chicken.

Serves 6

CHICKEN WITH TOMATOES AND GREEN PEPPERS

(poulet Basquaise)

France

Preparation time: 25 minutes   **Cooking time:** 30 minutes

Ingredients

A *3-pound chicken, cut into serving pieces*
    Flour for dusting chicken
3 *tablespoons olive oil*
1 *clove garlic*
4 *ounces mushrooms, sliced*
4 *tomatoes, peeled, seeded and chopped*

2 *green peppers, seeded and sliced*
4 *ounces ham, diced*
½ *cup dry white wine*
    Salt
    Freshly ground pepper
    Chopped fresh parsley for garnish

1. Lightly dust the chicken pieces with flour.

2. Put the oil in an enameled cast-iron casserole rubbed with the garlic. Add the chicken pieces and brown evenly over moderately high heat.

3. Add the mushrooms and sauté briefly. Stir in the tomatoes, peppers and ham.

4. Pour in the wine and season with salt and pepper. Cover and simmer until chicken is tender, about 30 minutes.

5. Transfer the pieces of chicken to a warmed serving platter. Reduce the sauce over high heat if necessary, then pour over the chicken. Garnish with chopped parsley. Serve with rice.

Serves 4

CHICKEN CASSEROLE WITH SAFFRON RICE *(arroz con pollo)*

Preparation time: 15 minutes   **Cooking time:** 1¼ hours   *Mexico*

Ingredients

2	3-pound chickens, cut into serving pieces
½	cup olive oil
3	cloves garlic, minced
1	large onion, minced·
1	green pepper, seeded and chopped
1⅓	cup rice
1	teaspoon oregano
½	pound ham, diced
1	tablespoon salt

	Freshly ground pepper
1 to 2	teaspoons saffron
8	tomatoes, peeled and quartered
2	cups water
2	cups green peas
½	cup stuffed green olives
⅓	cup capers
	Fresh parsley, chopped
	Pimiento for garnish

1. Set oven at 350°. Rinse the chicken pieces and pat dry. Heat the oil in a large casserole and brown a few chicken pieces at a time. Reserve.

2. Sauté the garlic, onion and green pepper until soft, about 5 minutes. Add the rice and stir to coat. Cook over moderate heat until golden, about 3 minutes.

3. Return the chicken pieces to the casserole. Stir in the oregano, ham, salt, pepper, saffron, tomatoes and water. Bring to a boil on top of the stove. Cover and place in the oven for 30 minutes.

4. Reduce the heat to 250°. Add the peas, olives and capers. Continue baking, uncovered, until chicken is tender, about 20 minutes. Garnish with the parsley and pimiento.

Serves 8

ANJOU-STYLE CHICKEN
FRICASSEE *(fricassée de poulet à l'Angevine)*

France

Preparation time: 15 minutes   **Cooking time:** 45 minutes

Ingredients

5	*tablespoons butter*
A	*3-pound chicken, cut into serving pieces*
10	*small white onions*
½	*pound mushrooms, cut in half*

1 *cup white wine*
Salt
Freshly ground pepper
½ *cup heavy cream*

1. Melt the butter in a large skillet and brown the chicken pieces evenly over moderately high heat.

2. Reduce heat and add the onions. Continue cooking for 5 minutes, then stir in the mushrooms.

3. Pour in the wine and season with salt and pepper.

4. Cover pan and simmer over low heat for 30 minutes.

5. Just before serving, stir in the cream and heat through. Do not boil.

Serves 4

EGER CHICKEN PAPRIKA
(csirke paprikás)

Preparation time: 30 minutes

Cooking time: 35 minutes

Hungary

Ingredients

2   *chickens, cut into
    serving pieces*
    *Flour for dredging
    chicken*
    Salt
    Freshly ground pepper
6   *tablespoons butter*
2   *tablespoons vegetable
    oil*
2   *onions, chopped*

1   *clove garlic, pressed*
2   *tablespoons paprika*
1   *cup chicken stock*
1   *tablespoon heavy cream*
½   *pint sour cream*
    *Chopped fresh parsley
    for garnish*
    Paprika for garnish

1. Dry the chicken pieces well, then dredge in flour seasoned with salt and pepper.

2. Heat the butter and oil in a large skillet or enameled cast-iron casserole. Add the chicken pieces and sauté until golden. Remove chicken and reserve.

3. Add the onions and garlic and sauté lightly, then stir in the paprika and half the stock. Blend thoroughly. Return the chicken to the skillet, cover and simmer for 20 minutes.

4. Add the remaining stock and the cream. Continue simmering, uncovered, until chicken is tender, about 10 minutes.

5. Remove chicken from skillet and keep warm. Stir in the sour cream and simmer gently for 5 minutes. Taste sauce and correct seasoning.

6. To serve, arrange chicken on a heated platter, cover with the sauce, garnish with parsley and a sprinkling of paprika.

Serves 6

CHICKEN CREOLE *(poulet Magloire)*

Preparation time: 30 minutes   **Cooking time:** 45 minutes

Haiti

Ingredients

A   3- to 4-pound chicken, cut in serving pieces

3   tablespoons vegetable oil

2   medium onions, chopped

2   green peppers, seeded and chopped

2   stalks celery, chopped

2   cloves garlic, minced

2   tablespoons fresh parsley, chopped

2   whole cloves

¼   teaspoon dried basil

3   whole dried red chili peppers (optional)

¼   teaspoon chili powder

¼   teaspoon cayenne

¼   teaspoon dried thyme

2   bay leaves, crushed

1   tablespoon salt
    Freshly ground pepper

3   cups water

1   large can Italian plum tomatoes

1   cup raw long-grain rice

1. Wash the chicken pieces and pat dry.

2. Heat the oil in a large enameled cast-iron casserole. Add the chicken and sauté until nicely browned, about 15 minutes. Remove chicken pieces and reserve.

3. Add the onions, green peppers, celery and garlic to the casserole and sauté over moderate heat until onions are translucent, about 5 minutes. Add the remaining seasonings, water and plum tomatoes (with juice). Mix well.

4. Return the reserved chicken to the casserole. Bring to a boil, then lower heat, cover and simmer gently for 15 minutes.

5. Stir in the rice, then re-cover the casserole and simmer until rice is tender, about 15 minutes. Uncover the casserole, raise heat to moderate and boil briefly until liquid is slightly reduced. Serve immediately from the casserole.

Serves 4 to 6

CHICKEN WITH HOT SAUCE
(doro-weutt)

Preparation time: 20 minutes   **Cooking time:** 45 minutes   *Ethiopia*

Ingredients

A 3-pound chicken, cut into serving pieces

3 cups boiling water
   Juice of 1 lemon

1 teaspoon salt

4 tablespoons butter

6 onions, chopped

2 tablespoons chili powder

2 tablespoons tomato paste

4 tablespoons red wine

½ teaspoon ground ginger
   Freshly ground pepper

4 hard-cooked eggs, shelled

1. Place the chicken in a large pot and cover with the boiling water. Add the lemon juice and salt and simmer for 10 minutes. Remove the chicken and reserve the broth.

2. Melt the butter in a large casserole and sauté the onions for 10 minutes. Add 1 cup of hot chicken broth, the chili powder and tomato paste to the onions. Simmer for 5 minutes, then add the red wine, ginger, pepper and another cup of the broth.

3. Place the chicken in the sauce and simmer until tender, about 40 minutes.

4. Prick the hard-cooked eggs with a fork and add to the sauce about 3 minutes before serving.

Serves 4

CHICKEN CURRY (*murga korma*)

Preparation time: 30 minutes   **Cooking time:** 20 minutes

Ingredients

India

Curry Powder:

4	tablespoons cumin
1	tablespoon coriander
1	teaspoon turmeric
1	teaspoon chili powder
½	teaspoon ginger
½	teaspoon fenugreek
½	teaspoon garam masala (optional)

———

4	large onions, minced
4	dried chili peppers

¼	cup peanut oil
¼	cup water
4	chicken breasts, diced
	Salt
4	cardamom pods (seeds only), ground
4	ounces coconut, toasted
1	ounce walnuts, chopped
¾	pint yoghurt
3	tablespoons lemon juice
	Walnut halves

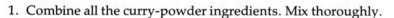

1. Combine all the curry-powder ingredients. Mix thoroughly.

2. Sauté the onions and the chilies in the oil for 10 minutes. Blend the curry mixture into the onions. Stir over moderate heat until the spices darken, about 3 minutes. Add 2 tablespoons of the water to prevent scorching.

3. Season with salt, then add the chicken and the cardamom. Stir briskly for 4 minutes, then blend in the remaining water. Add ¾ of the coconut and the walnuts. Mix thoroughly. Reduce heat to low and blend in half the yoghurt. Stirring frequently, simmer chicken until tender, about 5 minutes. (If the heat is too high, the yoghurt will curdle.)

4. Blend in the remaining yoghurt and the lemon juice. Heat through. Discard the chilies. Transfer to a heated platter and garnish with the remaining coconut and halved walnuts. Serve hot, accompanied by chutney and rice.

Serves 4 to 6

YOGHURT MARINATED
CHICKEN *(tandoori murgi)*

Preparation time: 20 minutes
Chicken marinates—24 hours

Cooking time: 1¼ hours

India

Ingredients

A   3-pound roasting
chicken

Marinade:

1   cup plain yoghurt

3   cloves garlic, crushed

1   teaspoon ginger

1   medium onion, finely
chopped

¼   cup lemon or lime juice

1   tablespoon ground
coriander

1   teaspoon turmeric

1   teaspoon cumin

1   teaspoon garam masala
(optional)

Salt

Freshly ground pepper

¼   cup vegetable oil

1   onion, thinly sliced

1   lemon or lime,
quartered

1. Quarter and skin the chicken. Reserve.

2. In a large bowl, combine the yoghurt, garlic, ginger, onion, lemon (or lime) juice, coriander, turmeric, cumin, *garam masala*, salt, pepper and oil.

3. Cut several deep slits (nearly to the bone) in each piece of chicken, then thoroughly rub with marinade. Place chicken in marinade and refrigerate for at least 24 hours, turning occasionally.

4. Preheat oven to 375°.

5. Transfer chicken pieces to a greased rack in a baking pan. Baste chicken pieces with the marinade and roast until tender, about 1¼ hours. (Baste occasionally during roasting.)

6. To serve, arrange chicken pieces on a heated platter and garnish with onion rings and lemon or lime wedges.

Serves 2 to 4

CHICKEN KIEV *(kotlety po-kyivskomu)*

Preparation time: 20 minutes   **Cooking time:** 20 minutes

Ingredients

½	*pound unsalted butter, at room temperature*
3	*tablespoons parsley*
2	*cloves garlic, pressed*
½	*teaspoon tarragon*
6	*chicken breasts*
	Salt and pepper
	Flour for dredging
1	*egg, lightly beaten*
1	*cup dry bread crumbs*

Mushroom-Cream Sauce:

¾	*cup butter*
1½	*pounds fresh mushrooms, chopped*
6	*tablespoons flour*
3	*cups chicken broth*
	Salt and pepper
	Pinch cayenne pepper
¾	*cup sherry*
1	*cup light cream*
	Butter or fat for frying

1. Blend the butter, parsley, garlic and tarragon. Shape into 6 small rolls (about 2 inches long and ½ inch thick). Place a roll of butter on each flattened breast of chicken. Sprinkle with salt and pepper. Roll up each chicken breast around the butter, folding in the ends. Skewer with toothpicks. Dredge in flour, dip in egg and thoroughly coat with bread crumbs. Refrigerate while preparing the sauce.

2. Sauté the mushrooms in butter. Blend in the flour. Mix well. Add the broth and seasonings. Stir constantly for 5 minutes, then add the sherry and simmer for another 5 minutes. Remove from heat, blend in the cream and keep warm.

3. In a large skillet, melt enough butter or fat to cover the chicken. Heat to 375° (or until a 1-inch cube of bread browns in 1 minute). Fry each roll until golden. Drain and place on a heated platter. Serve sauce separately or poured over the chicken breasts.

Serves 6

CHICKEN WITH BAMBOO SHOOTS AND MUSHROOMS
(jam bao chee ting)

Preparation time: 30 minutes   **Cooking time:** 8 minutes   *China*

Ingredients

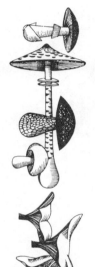

6	dried Chinese mushrooms	½	cup canned bamboo shoots, sliced
2	chicken breasts	2	cloves garlic, minced
1	tablespoon cornstarch	2	tablespoons Chinese rice wine or dry sherry
2	tablespoons hoisin sauce (optional)	1 to 3	tablespoons soy sauce
1	tablespoon water		Salt
3	tablespoons peanut oil		

1. Soak the mushrooms in a bowl of lukewarm water for 30 minutes. Drain. Discard stems. Dry caps, dice and reserve.

2. Slice chicken into julienne strips, then dice. In a bowl, toss diced chicken with 1 tablespoon cornstarch. Reserve.

3. In a cup, combine the hoisin sauce and the water. Reserve.

4. Place a wok (or 10-inch skillet) over high heat for ½ minute. Lower heat and swirl in 1 tablespoon of the oil. Wait ½ minute, then add the bamboo shoots and the mushrooms. Stir-fry for 2 minutes. Remove vegetables with a slotted spoon.

5. Add the remaining oil to the wok. Wait ½ minute, then add the garlic and chicken. Stir-fry briskly until the chicken changes color, about 1½ minutes.

6. Over low heat, stir in the rice wine (or sherry), then the hoisin sauce mixture and the soy sauce. Season to taste with salt. Add the mushrooms and bamboo shoots to the wok. Mix briefly and serve immediately.

Serves 4

PINEAPPLE CHICKEN *(po lo jee)*

Preparation time: 30 minutes   **Cooking time:** 6 minutes

China

Ingredients

2   chicken breasts, boned and diced

2   tablespoons cornstarch

1   medium (14- to 16-ounce) can pineapple tidbits in juice

2   tablespoons peanut oil or flavorless vegetable oil

2   slices fresh ginger root, peeled and minced

½   green pepper, seeded and diced

1   medium onion, minced

2   tablespoons Chinese rice wine or dry sherry

Salt

1. In a bowl, toss the diced chicken with 1 tablespoon cornstarch. Reserve.

2. Drain pineapple tidbits and reserve. Pour juice into a measuring cup. For each cup add 1 heaping teaspoon cornstarch. Blend well and reserve.

3. Place a wok (or skillet) over high heat for ½ minute. Add the oil and swirl pan for ½ minute. Add the ginger and green pepper. Stir-fry for 1 minute, then add the chicken pieces and the onion. Stir-fry until chicken changes color, about 1½ to 2 minutes. Remove wok from heat.

4. Add the wine and salt. Mix, then add the pineapple tidbits.

5. Stir cornstarch-pineapple juice to remix, then add to wok.

6. Return wok to high heat. Stir lightly until ingredients are thoroughly coated, then boil until sauce clears. Serve immediately.

Serves 3 to 4

CHICKEN WITH ASPARAGUS
(lu sun chao jee pien)

Preparation time: 10 minutes   **Cooking time:** 10 minutes   *China*

Ingredients

2 to 3 *tablespoons vegetable oil*

1 *thick slice ginger, diced*

1 *clove garlic, minced*

½ *pound asparagus, cut into 1-inch pieces*

3 *chicken breasts, slivered*

4 *tablespoons chicken broth*

1 *tablespoon Chinese rice wine or dry sherry*

2 *tablespoons water*

2 *teaspoons cornstarch*

1. Heat 1 tablespoon of the oil in a wok or skillet. Stir-fry the ginger and garlic for ½ minute. Then add the asparagus. Stir-fry for 1 minute and remove with a slotted spoon.

2. Add 1 or 2 tablespoons of the remaining oil to the wok. Stir-fry the chicken for 1 minute, then add the broth, wine and water. Simmer briefly, then sprinkle in the cornstarch. Mix well and heat through.

3. Return the asparagus to the wok and toss lightly to coat with the sauce. Serve immediately.

Serves 2 to 3

CHICKEN WINGS WITH GINGER
(chiang jee yeh)

China

Preparation time: 5 minutes

Cooking time: 25 minutes

Ingredients

- 1 tablespoon peanut oil or flavorless vegetable oil
- 1 thick slice fresh ginger root, peeled and rinsed
- 8 chicken wings
- 1 clove garlic, crushed
- 1 tablespoon soy sauce
- ¼ teaspoon salt
- 2 teaspoons sugar
- 1 tablespoon Chinese rice wine or pale dry sherry
- ½ cup water
- Bok choy (Chinese cabbage) for garnish

1. Place a wok (or 12-inch skillet) over high heat for ½ minute.

2. Swirl in the oil. Heat for ½ minute, then add the ginger and stir-fry. Add the chicken wings and garlic and stir-fry for 2 minutes.

3. Add the soy sauce. Mix briefly. Then add the salt, sugar and rice wine (or sherry).

4. Pour in the water and bring to a boil, then lower heat and simmer gently for 20 minutes.

5. Serve on a bed of cabbage.

Serves 2

UKRAINIAN CHICKEN PIE *(kurnik)*

Preparation time: 2¼ hours

Baking time: 45 minutes

Ingredients

2	*onions, halved*
1	*stalk celery, halved*
1	*clove garlic, pressed*
2	*teaspoons salt*
5	*cups water*
—	
A	*4-pound chicken*

Sour Cream Pastry:

3½	*cups flour*
1	*teaspoon baking powder*
½	*teaspoon salt*
¼	*pound butter, chilled*
2	*eggs, lightly beaten*

½	*pint sour cream*
1	*egg yolk, beaten*
—	
¼	*pint sour cream*
2	*tablespoons parsley*
¼	*teaspoon nutmeg*
1	*tablespoon lemon juice*
	Salt
3	*cups cooked rice*
1	*pound mushrooms, sautéed in butter*
5	*hard-cooked eggs, chopped*
¼	*cup fresh dill, chopped*

USSR

1. In a kettle combine the first 5 ingredients and boil for 15 minutes. Add the chicken, cover and simmer until chicken is tender, about 1½ hours. When the chicken is done, remove the meat and chop. Reserve the stock.

2. Prepare the pastry as for flaky pastry (**page 474**).

3. Blend 1½ cups of the stock and the sour cream and bring to a simmer, stirring constantly. Remove from heat and blend in the parsley, nutmeg, lemon juice, chicken and salt.

4. On a lightly floured surface, roll out the pastry to ⅛-inch thickness and line a deep pie dish. Beginning and ending with a layer of rice, alternate a layer of the chicken mixture with a layer of the mushrooms and a layer of the chopped eggs and dill. Press down filling, then cover with the remaining pastry, crimping the edges to seal. Cut a 1-inch hole in the center, then brush lid with egg. Bake 15 minutes in a 400° oven, then reduce heat to 350° and bake until the kurnik bubbles at the edges, about 30 minutes. Serve hot.

Serves 8

SOUTHERN FRIED CHICKEN

Preparation time: 10 minutes   **Cooking time:** 25 minutes

USA   **Ingredients**

A   *3-pound frying chicken, cut into 12 pieces*
    Salt
    Freshly ground pepper

3 to 4   *cups peanut oil or bacon drippings*
1   *cup flour*

1. Rinse the chicken pieces, pat dry and season with salt and pepper. Over very high heat, pour enough oil into a casserole to cover the chicken pieces.

2. Place the flour, salt and pepper in a bag. Beginning with the legs and thighs, add a few chicken pieces at a time and shake vigorously to coat thoroughly. Remove and press the flour into the skin of each piece.

3. Fry the legs and thighs for about 10 minutes. Add the remaining pieces one by one, keeping the temperature of the oil constant. Continue frying until each piece is crisp and golden brown, about 15 minutes.

4. As each piece is cooked, remove with a slotted spoon and drain on absorbent paper. Keep warm in a slow oven or cool to room temperature before serving.

Serves 2 to 4

MEXICAN-STYLE TURKEY
(mole de guajolote)

Preparation time: 15 minutes **Cooking time:** 2 hours *Mexico*

Ingredients

½	*cup flour*
	Salt
A	*12-pound turkey (giblets reserved), cut into serving pieces*
½	*cup lard or oil*

Mole Sauce:

2	*tablespoons oil*
3	*medium onions, chopped*
2	*cloves garlic, chopped*
½	*cup seedless raisins*
2	*ounces unsweetened chocolate, cut in pieces*
1	*teaspoon cinnamon*

¼	*teaspoon each of anise seed, cumin and cloves*
3	*tablespoons chili powder*
2	*tablespoons white sesame seeds, toasted*
3 to 4	*dry tortillas, broken in pieces*
3	*tomatoes, chopped*
	Freshly grated pepper
6	*cups turkey broth*
	Lime slices and toasted sesame seeds for garnish

1. Season the flour with the salt. Dredge the turkey pieces in the flour. Heat lard in large skillet. Brown the turkey, then transfer the turkey to a large casserole. Cover with water and season with salt. Bring to a boil, cover and simmer until turkey is tender, about 45 minutes.

2. Remove turkey pieces from casserole. Remove meat and reserve. Return turkey bones to casserole. Add the giblets and bring to a boil, then lower heat and simmer for ½ hour.

3. Heat the oil in a skillet. Sauté the onions, then add the remaining *mole* ingredients. Mix well. Using 2 cups of turkey broth, purée the onion mixture until the sauce is smooth. Add the sauce and turkey to the casserole and simmer for 30 minutes. Garnish with lime slices and sesame seeds.

Serves 10

ROAST STUFFED DUCK
(canard à la solognote)

France

Preparation time: 20 minutes   **Cooking time:** 1½ hours

Ingredients

Stuffing:

Duck's liver, chopped	Salt
⅔ cup fresh bread crumbs, moistened with milk	Freshly ground pepper
	6 tablespoons brandy
1 onion, chopped	A 4½-pound duck (with liver)
½ clove garlic, minced	2 tomatoes, halved
½ clove dried thyme	1 cup chicken stock
½ teaspoon dried savory	Salt
1 teaspoon dried rosemary	Freshly ground pepper

1. Combine the duck's liver, bread crumbs, onion, garlic and herbs. Season with salt and pepper, then sprinkle on the brandy, cover and refrigerate 1 hour.

2. Preheat oven to 350°.

3. Stuff the duck, then truss and secure the vent. Place the duck in a roasting pan. Surround with the tomatoes. Roast until the juices running from the thigh, when pricked, are pale yellow, about 1½ hours.

4. Transfer duck to a heated serving platter and keep warm.

5. Spoon out all but 1 tablespoon of the fat in the roasting pan. Pour in the chicken stock and boil rapidly for a few minutes, deglazing the pan. Add the tomatoes. Strain and season with salt and pepper, then pour into a heated sauceboat.

6. Carve duck at the table, spooning the sauce over individual portions of the stuffing as they are served.

Serves 4

BRAISED DUCK WITH TURNIPS
(canard aux navets à la mode Poitevine)

Preparation time: 35 minutes   **Cooking time:** 1½ to 2 hours

France

Ingredients

Stuffing:

Duck's liver and giblets, diced	1 teaspoon basil
2 chicken livers, diced	1 teaspoon rosemary
3 ounces bacon, diced	7 tablespoons butter
1 cup fresh bread crumbs	A 4½-pound duck
2 tablespoons milk	3 tablespoons tomato purée
2 eggs, beaten	6 tablespoons Madeira
1 shallot, finely chopped	10 small white onions
Salt and pepper	20 small turnips, sliced
1 tablespoon fresh parsley, chopped	2 tablespoons cream
½ teaspoon sage	1 tablespoon cognac

1. Combine the stuffing ingredients listed above. Lightly brown the mixture in a frying pan in 2 tablespoons of the butter.

2. Rinse the duck well and rub with salt. Stuff the bird, then truss and secure the vent. Preheat oven to 325°.

3. Brown the duck in 3 tablespoons of butter. Mix the tomato purée with the Madeira and stir into casserole. Season with salt and pepper. Cover and braise the duck for 1 hour.

4. Brown the onions and turnips in a frying pan with the rest of the butter. Add the cream and cognac. Reserve.

5. After the duck has cooked about 1 hour, degrease the casserole and add the turnips and onions. Continue to braise until the vegetables are tender and the juices from the duck's thigh run pale yellow. Transfer the duck to a hot platter and surround with the vegetables.

Serves 4

BRAISED DUCK AND PERSIAN
RICE *(morghabi polo)*

Iran

Preparation time: 30 minutes
Duck marinates—2 hours

Cooking time: 50 minutes

Ingredients

A   *5- to 6-pound duck,*
    cut into serving pieces
½   *pint yoghurt*
2   *tablespoons butter*
2   *onions, chopped*
4   *cups water*
    Salt
    Freshly ground pepper

½   *duck's giblets, chopped*
1½ *ounces pistachio nuts,*
    chopped
1½ *ounces seedless raisins*
2   *cups long-grained*
    raw rice
    Salt
    Freshly ground pepper
½   *teaspoon cinnamon*
4   *cups chicken stock, hot*

Persian Rice:
3   *tablespoons butter*

1. Coat the duck pieces with the yoghurt. Cover and let stand
    for 2 hours. Remove duck pieces and reserve yoghurt.

2. Melt the butter in an enameled cast-iron casserole. Sauté the
    onions for 5 minutes. Add the duck pieces and sauté until
    browned, about 10 minutes. Pour in the water and scrape up
    any particles in the casserole. Season with salt and pepper.
    Bring to a boil, then lower heat, cover and simmer until duck
    is tender, about 40 minutes.

3. Prepare the Persian rice: Melt the butter and sauté the duck's
    giblets until lightly browned. Add the nuts, raisins, rice, salt,
    pepper and cinnamon and stir-fry for 2 minutes. Pour in the
    chicken stock, then lower heat, cover and simmer gently until
    rice is nearly tender, about 25 minutes. Drain and reserve.

4. Preheat oven to 400°. Drain the duck pieces and then alter-
    nate layers of the Persian rice and the duck in the casserole
    used to cook the duck. Cover and bake until heated through,
    about 10 minutes.

Serves 6

DUCKLING BRAISED IN RED WINE *(caneton Rouennais)*

Preparation time: 20 minutes

Cooking time 1½ hours

Ingredients

France

½	*pound bacon, diced*
4	*tablespoons butter*
15	*small white onions*
4	*shallots, chopped*
A	*4½-pound duckling, cut into serving pieces*
3	*tablespoons Calvados or applejack, warmed*
¼	*cup flour*
3½	*cups red wine*

½	*cup bouillon*
	Salt
	Freshly ground pepper
	Herb bouquet (parsley, sage, rosemary, bay leaf, peppercorns)
½	*pound mushrooms, sliced*
1	*duck liver, ground*
3	*tablespoons flour*
2	*tablespoons butter*

1. In an enameled cast-iron casserole, sauté the bacon until brown. Remove the bacon and reserve. Add the butter, onions and shallots to the casserole and sauté until onions are golden, but not brown. Remove and reserve.

2. Brown the pieces of duck in the casserole. Pour in the brandy and flambé. Mix in the flour and stir, then add the wine and bouillon and continue stirring until the sauce is smooth. Return the reserved bacon, onions and shallots to the casserole. Add salt, pepper and the herb bouquet. Cover and simmer for 1 hour over low heat.

3. Add the mushrooms and cook for an additional 30 minutes. Before serving, remove herb bouquet and transfer duck pieces, onions and mushrooms to a heated serving dish.

4. Add the liver and the *beurre manié* (page 471) to the sauce. Correct seasoning, then pour the sauce over the duck.

Serves 4

WILD DUCK IN MUSTARD SAUCE *(canard sauvage sauce infernale)*

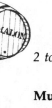

France

Preparation time: 20 minutes   **Cooking time:** 20 to 30 minutes

Ingredients

A *2-pound wild duck*	1 *cup rosé wine*
Salt	*Juice of ½ lemon*
Freshly ground pepper	*Grated lemon peel*
2 to 3 *strips pork fatback*	1 *teaspoon prepared Dijon mustard*
Butter for basting	*Salt*

Mustard Sauce:

Duck's liver
2   *tablespoons butter*
2   *shallots, finely chopped*

Freshly ground pepper
2   *tablespoons fresh parsley, chopped*

1. Set the oven at 450°.

2. Season the inside of the duck with salt and pepper. Lard the breast by covering it with strips of pork fatback (or bacon) and securing with string.

3. Place the duck, breast side up, on a trivet in a roasting pan. Baste frequently with butter. Roast 20 to 30 minutes for pink to well-done meat.

4. While the duck is roasting, prepare the mustard sauce: a) Sauté the duck liver in 1 tablespoon of the butter for 5 minutes; b) remove liver, mash to a paste and set aside; c) using the same pan, sauté the shallots with an additional tablespoon of butter until translucent; d) pour in the wine and bring to a boil; e) lower heat and add the duck liver, lemon juice, grated lemon peel, mustard, salt, pepper and parsley.

5. Remove the duck from the pan, carve and arrange on a heated serving dish. Add the pan juices to the mustard sauce and serve in a separate sauceboat.

Serves 2

SAUTÉED DUCK LIVER WITH BRANDY SAUCE

(foie de canard à la Bigourdane)

France

Preparation time: 5 minutes   **Cooking time:** 10 minutes

Ingredients

½	pound duck livers, cut in ½-inch slices
2	tablespoons flour
	Salt
	Freshly ground pepper
3	tablespoons goose fat or olive oil

12	thin slices French bread, fried in olive oil
½	pound small green seedless grapes
3	tablespoons Armagnac brandy

1. Dust livers with flour and season with salt and pepper.

2. Heat the goose fat (or olive oil) in a frying pan, add liver slices and sauté for 3 minutes on one side and 2 minutes on the other. They should be pink on the inside.

3. Arrange livers and bread slices in a circle on a hot serving dish. Keep warm.

4. Sauté the grapes in the pan juices for 3 minutes. Remove with a slotted spoon and arrange in the center of the serving platter. Keep warm.

5. Dilute pan juices with the brandy, bring to a boil and pour over the livers. Serve immediately.

Serves 2

GOOSE WITH CHESTNUT STUFFING *(oie farcie a la mode de Segré)*

France

Preparation time: 1 hour   **Roasting time:** 2¼ hours

Ingredients

Chestnut Stuffing:

1 *pound chestnuts*	3 *tablespoons white wine*
1 *cup Madeira*	3 *tablespoons cream*
1 *cup chicken broth*	½ *tablespoon sage*
4 *tablespoons butter*	*Salt*
2 *goose or chicken livers*	*Freshly ground pepper*
1 *onion, minced*	*Pinch allspice*
6 *shallots, minced*	1 *egg, beaten*
1 *clove garlic, minced*	
½ *cup parsley, chopped*	An *8-pound goose*
2½ *cups bread crumbs*	*Salt*

1. Score the chestnuts, then blanch in a pot of boiling water for 3 minutes. Drain and peel. Combine the chestnuts, Madeira and stock and simmer until tender, about 20 minutes.

2. Sauté the livers, onion, shallot and garlic in butter for 3 minutes. Chop the livers, then add to the chestnuts. Add the remaining stuffing ingredients. Mix thoroughly.

3. Preheat oven to 450°. Stuff and truss the goose. Place the goose on a rack in a roasting pan. Salt lightly and prick the breast with a fork. Roast for 20 minutes, then baste with the pan juices. Reduce oven temperature to 325° and continue roasting until the juices from the thigh run pale yellow when pricked, about 2 hours.

4. When the goose is done, transfer to a heated serving platter. Skim the fat from the pan, then deglaze with the chestnut liquid. Reduce gravy to desired consistency. Carve the goose at the table, topping each portion with the hot gravy.

Serves 6

PARTRIDGES BRAISED IN RED WINE *(perdreaux à la Languedocienne)*

Preparation time: 35 minutes   **Cooking time:** 1 to 1½ hours

France

Ingredients

Stuffing:

	Partridges' livers, chopped
4	*ounces ham, diced*
2	*tablespoons fresh parsley, chopped*
1	*egg, beaten*
	Salt
	Freshly ground pepper
2	*partridges*

	Salt
	Freshly ground pepper
4	*tablespoons olive oil*
1	*tablespoon flour*
1	*cup red wine*
1	*cup chicken stock*
1	*tablespoon tomato purée*
	Herb bouquet (thyme, bay leaf, parsley)
½	*teaspoon grated orange peel*
6	*cloves garlic, blanched*

1. Combine the partridge livers, ¾ of the ham and the parsley. Bind with the egg, then season with salt and pepper.

2. Stuff the partridges. Truss and season with salt and pepper.

3. In an earthenware casserole, heat the olive oil. Add the partridges and brown evenly over moderately high heat, about 10 minutes. Remove birds and keep warm.

4. Add the remaining ham to the casserole. Sprinkle with the flour, then stir in the red wine, chicken stock and tomato purée.

5. Add the herb bouquet and orange peel. Bring rapidly to a boil, then lower heat, cover and simmer for 10 minutes.

6. Return the partridges to the casserole and add the blanched garlic cloves. Cover and simmer until birds are tender, about 1 to 1½ hours, depending on the age of the birds.

Serves 2

PARTRIDGES WITH GRAPES
(perdreaux aux raisins)

France

Preparation time: 15 minutes   **Cooking time:** 30 minutes

Ingredients

4 *partridges, cleaned*	*Salt*
6 *tablespoons butter*	*Freshly ground pepper*
4 *thin slices pork fat or blanched larding bacon*	¼ *cup brandy, warmed*
7 *dozen Muscat or other green seedless grapes*	4 *slices of French bread, fried in butter*

1. Rub the partridges with a little butter, bard with the pork fat (or bacon) slices and truss.

2. Heat the remaining butter in a casserole large enough to hold the partridges side by side. Add the birds and brown on all sides over moderately high heat. (This will take about 15 minutes.)

3. Add the grapes, salt and pepper, cover and continue cooking over moderate heat until birds are tender, about 15 minutes.

4. Remove the partridges, untruss and take off the barding strips.

5. Return birds to the casserole, sprinkle on the brandy and flambé.

6. Arrange the partridges on a heated serving platter. Garnish each bird with the grapes and the fried bread slices and cover with the remaining pan juices.

Serves 4

Partridges should be young and small to be cooked in this manner. Quail or small Rock Cornish hens could very well be substituted.

PARTRIDGES WITH LENTILS
(estouffade de perdrix aux lentilles)

Preparation time: 30 minutes
Lentils soak—overnight

Cooking time: 1½ hours

France

Ingredients

2	*cups dry lentils*	6	*shallots, chopped*
8	*partridges*	2	*herb bouquets (parsley, rosemary, thyme, peppercorns)*
	Salt		
	Freshly ground pepper	1	*cup dry white wine*
8	*slices bacon, blanched*	1	*cup chicken stock*
4	*tablespoons butter*	3	*onions, chopped*
2	*carrots, quartered*		

1. Soak lentils overnight in a bowl of cold water.

2. Season the cavities of the partridges with salt and pepper. Wrap a slice of blanched bacon around each breast and secure with string. Truss the legs and wings.

3. Heat the butter in a large casserole. Add the partridges and brown evenly over fairly high heat. Add the carrots, shallots and 1 herb bouquet. Pour in the wine and stock. Cover and simmer over low heat until birds are tender, about 1½ hours.

4. While the partridges are cooking, prepare the lentils: a) Drain the soaked lentils; b) place them in a large saucepan; c) cover with cold water; d) add the remaining herb bouquet and the onions; e) bring to a boil, then lower heat, cover and simmer until tender, about 30 to 40 minutes; f) drain and keep hot.

5. Transfer the cooked partridges to a heated serving platter and surround them with the lentils. Strain the casserole juices and sprinkle it over the birds.

Serves 8

YOUNG HARE IN WHITE WINE
(meurette de lapereau Bourbonnaise)

France

Preparation time: 30 minutes   **Cooking time:** 50 minutes

Ingredients

2   young hare (less than
    one year old), saddles
    and legs only
1   tablespoon butter
12 tiny white onions
1   tablespoon flour
1   cup dry white wine
½   cup water
    Salt

Freshly ground pepper
Herb bouquet (bay leaf,
    oregano, thyme)
2   egg yolks
½   cup heavy cream
    Juice of ½ lemon
2   tablespoons fresh
    parsley, chopped

1. Cut the meat into serving pieces.

2. Heat the butter in a skillet. Add the meat and brown evenly over moderately high heat. Remove meat from skillet and reserve.

3. Add the onions to the skillet and brown lightly. Stirring continuously, sprinkle in the flour and cook for 30 seconds. Blend in the wine and water.

4. Return the meat to the skillet and season to taste with salt and pepper. Add the herb bouquet, cover and simmer until the meat is tender, about 50 minutes.

5. Discard the herb bouquet. Transfer the meat to a heated serving platter. Keep warm.

6. In a small bowl, beat the egg yolks well. Add the cream, lemon juice and parsley.

7. Blend a little of the liquid from the skillet into the cream and egg mixture, then gently stir the mixture into the remaining liquid in the skillet. Stirring constantly, heat through. Do not allow the sauce to boil. Cover the meat with the sauce and serve immediately.

Serves 4 to 6

HARE IN RED WINE SAUCE
(lièvre à la Niçoise)

Preparation time: 20 minutes   **Cooking time:** 1 hour   *France*

Ingredients

½   cup olive oil
A   5-pound hare, cut into serving pieces
3   tablespoons cognac, warmed
3½ cups dry red wine
Salt
Freshly ground pepper

Herb bouquet (bay leaf, parsley, oregano, thyme)
10 small white onions
½   pound small pork sausages
4   ounces pitted black olives
Chopped fresh parsley for garnish

1. Heat the oil in an enameled cast-iron casserole. Add the pieces of hare and brown evenly over moderately high heat.

2. Sprinkle on the warmed cognac and flambé.

3. Add the red wine, salt, pepper and herb bouquet. Cover and simmer over low heat for 30 minutes.

4. While the hare is cooking, blanch the onions in boiling water for 5 minutes and brown the sausages in a skillet.

5. Add the onions, sausages and olives to the casserole. Correct seasoning, if necessary, then continue to simmer hare for another 30 minutes.

6. Transfer the hare, sausages, olives and onions to a heated platter. Keep warm.

7. Reduce the sauce by about ½ over high heat. Pour sauce over the hare and garnish with chopped parsley.

Serves 4

FRICASSEE OF RABBIT ÎLE DE FRANCE *(gibelotte de lapin)*

France

Preparation time: 20 minutes   **Cooking time:** 1 hour

Ingredients

2	tablespoons butter	1	clove garlic, finely chopped
¼	pound lean bacon, diced		Herb bouquet (bay leaf, parsley, oregano, thyme)
A	3-pound rabbit, cut into serving pieces		Salt
2	tablespoons brandy, warmed	12	small white onions
¼	cup flour	½	pound white mushrooms, halved
1	cup beef bouillon		
1	cup white wine		

1. Heat the butter in an enameled cast-iron casserole. Add the bacon and brown. Using a slotted spoon, remove bacon and reserve.

2. Add the rabbit pieces to the casserole. Brown slightly over high heat, then sprinkle on the warmed brandy and flambé.

3. Stirring constantly, gradually add the flour and cook for 1 minute over low heat.

4. Blend in the bouillon and wine, then add the garlic, herb bouquet and salt. Cover and simmer over low heat for 30 minutes.

5. While the rabbit is cooking, blanch the onions in boiling water for 5 minutes. Drain and reserve.

6. Add the reserved bacon and onions and the mushrooms to the casserole. Re–cover and cook until the rabbit is tender, about 30 minutes.

Serves 4

MEATS

ROAST BEEF AND YORKSHIRE PUDDING

Great Britain

Preparation time: 15 minutes
Batter stands—15 minutes

Cooking time: 15 to 18 minutes per pound for rare meat

Ingredients

A 3-pound roast beef, sirloin, top round or standing rib
Salt
Freshly ground pepper

Yorkshire Pudding:

1 cup flour
   Salt
1 egg
1¼ cups milk
1¼ cups beef stock

1. Preheat the oven to 500°. Season the meat with salt and pepper and place in a small roasting pan. Sear the roast for 15 minutes, then reduce the temperature to 350° and continue roasting until the meat reaches the desired degree of doneness. Remove from the oven and allow to rest for 15 minutes before carving.

2. About ½ hour before the roast is done, prepare the Yorkshire pudding: Sift the flour and salt into a bowl. Make a well in the center and break the egg into it. Add a little milk and beat until the batter is smooth. Stir in the remaining milk. Let the batter stand for 15 minutes.

3. Pour 4 tablespoons of drippings from the roast into a muffin tin or a shallow baking dish. Heat the fat to sizzling. Pour in the batter and bake until crisp and brown, about 15 minutes for individual puddings or about 30 minutes for a large one. Cut the pudding into squares and arrange on the serving platter with the carved meat.

4. For the gravy, slowly pour off the fat from the roasting pan, saving the sediment and meat juices. Season with salt and pepper and stir over low heat until dark brown. Add the beef stock, bring to the boil and reduce slightly. Pour into a gravy boat and skim off any remaining fat.

Serves 4

POT ROAST WITH DUMPLINGS
(Sauerbraten mit Kartoffelklösse)

Preparation time: 45 minutes
Meat marinates—4 days

Cooking time: 3½ hours
Dumplings cook—10 minutes

Germany

Ingredients
Marinade:

2	onions, chopped
4	carrots, chopped
2	stalks celery, chopped
2	cloves
10	peppercorns
4	bay leaves
4	sprigs parsley
2½	cups red wine vinegar
A	4-pound beef round

Salt and pepper
Flour

4	tablespoons butter
2	cups beef stock

Dumplings:

6	potatoes
	Salt
2	eggs, well beaten
1	cup flour
	Nutmeg
24	croutons

1. Combine the marinade ingredients. Rub the roast with salt and pepper. Place the meat in the marinade and refrigerate for 4 days, turning occasionally. Remove meat, pat dry and dredge in flour. Strain the marinade.

2. Melt the butter in a large casserole and brown the meat evenly. Sauté the vegetables for 10 minutes, then add the stock and ½ of the marinade. Cover and simmer for 3 hours, turning the meat once. About 30 minutes before serving, stir 3 tablespoons flour and water together and mix into the sauce. Continue to simmer.

3. Boil the potatoes until soft, then peel and rice. Mix in the eggs, flour and seasonings. Press a crouton into the center of a spoonful of dumpling mixture. Repeat to make 24 balls. Boil the dumplings for 10 minutes.

4. Place the meat and vegetables on a serving dish with the dumplings. Reduce the gravy slightly and pour over the dish.

Serves 8

BRISKET OF BEEF WITH FRUIT

Israel

Preparation time: 10 minutes

Cooking time: 1½ hours

Ingredients

A 3-pound brisket of beef
1 large onion, chopped
   Salt
   Freshly ground pepper
½ teaspoon ginger
¼ teaspoon cinnamon
6 cloves
3 ounces dried apricots
3 ounces dried prunes
1½ ounces currants

1 pound potatoes, peeled and cubed

Sauce:
4 tablespoons beef drippings
3 tablespoons flour
   Reserved liquid from cooking fruit
1 tablespoon sugar
1 cup red wine

1. Place the beef and chopped onion in an enameled cast-iron casserole. Cover with boiling water. Return water to a boil. Skim surface until clear, then season with salt, pepper and the spices. Cover casserole and simmer for ½ hour.

2. While meat is cooking, place the fruits in a saucepan, cover with water and simmer for ½ hour. Drain and reserve liquid. Add the fruits and potatoes to casserole. Cover tightly and simmer until potatoes are nearly tender, about 20 minutes.

3. Preheat oven to 375°.

4. While the casserole is simmering, prepare the sauce: a) In a saucepan, heat the beef drippings; b) stirring constantly over moderate heat, blend in the flour and cook until lightly browned; c) add the reserved fruit liquid and continue stirring until sauce thickens, then add the sugar and wine; d) continue stirring until the sauce is smooth. Keep warm.

5. When the potatoes are nearly tender, blend in the sauce. Transfer the casserole to the oven and cook until the meat is tender, about ½ hour.

Serves 6

BEEF TENDERLOIN FILLETS WITH ARTICHOKE HEARTS

(tournedos à l'Angevine)

France

Preparation time: 15 minutes

Cooking time: 40 minutes

Ingredients

4	artichokes
	Salt
1	lemon, cut in half
4	beef marrow bones
¾	cup crème fraîche (page 473) or heavy cream
3	tablespoons butter

4	beef tenderloin fillets each wrapped with a strip of fat
	Freshly ground pepper
1	tablespoon Calvados or other brandy, warmed
4	rounds of bread, fried in butter
1	tablespoon fresh tarragon or parsley, chopped

1. Drop the artichokes into a large soup kettle of lightly salted boiling water. Return water to a boil, then lower heat to moderate and cook artichokes until tender, about 35 minutes. Drain the artichokes. Discard leaves and remove the choke. Rub the artichokes hearts with the cut lemon and keep warm.

2. Poach the marrow bones in salted water for 10 minutes. Remove the marrow from the bones and reserve.

3. In a frying pan, melt the butter and sear the fillets on both sides over high heat. Reduce heat and cook steaks for 3 to 4 minutes on each side. Remove from heat. Season with salt and pepper, then sprinkle on the brandy and flambé.

4. Arrange the bread rounds on a heated platter. Place one fillet, topped with an artichoke heart, on each round.

5. Stir the *crème fraîche* into the meat juices. Heat sauce through to thicken, then season with salt and pepper and sprinkle in the tarragon. Pour sauce over the artichoke hearts and top with strips of marrow.

Serves 4

STEAK WITH BORDELAISE SAUCE
(entrecôte à la Bordelaise)

France

Preparation time: 10 minutes   **Cooking time:** 12 minutes

Ingredients

  2 *one-pound shell steaks*

Bordelaise Sauce:

  4 *shallots, minced*
  ⅛ *teaspoon dried thyme*
  ½ *cup red Bordeaux wine*
  6 *tablespoons butter, at room temperature*
    Salt
    Freshly ground pepper

  1 *tablespoon tomato paste*
  4 *tablespoons poached beef marrow (page 476), diced (optional)*
  1 *tablespoon fresh parsley, chopped*

1. Preheat broiler.

2. Broil steaks to preferred rareness. (For medium-rare steaks, figure about 6 minutes on each side.)

3. While the steaks are cooking, prepare the sauce: a) In a saucepan, combine the shallots, thyme and wine; b) reduce the liquid over high heat until syrupy; c) place the saucepan over hot water; d) using a wire whisk, beat in the butter, a little at a time (the butter should not melt but should retain a creamy consistency); e) season with salt and pepper, then add the tomato paste, marrow and parsley.

4. To serve, arrange the steaks on a hot platter and cover with the sauce.

Serves 2 to 4

STEAK WITH BERCY SAUCE
(entrecôte Bercy)

Preparation time: 10 minutes **Cooking time:** 12 to 15 minutes

France

Ingredients

2 *one-and-a-half- to two-inch-thick shell steaks*

Bercy Sauce:

3 *shallots, minced*
½ *cup white wine*
   Salt
   Freshly ground pepper
7 *tablespoons butter, at room temperature*

2 *tablespoons fresh parsley, chopped*
   Juice of ¼ lemon

   Salt
   Freshly ground pepper
   Watercress for garnish

1. Broil steaks as desired. (For medium-rare meat, figure 6 to 8 minutes on one side and 6 minutes on the other.)

2. While the steaks are cooking, prepare the sauce: a) In an enameled saucepan, combine the shallots, white wine, salt and pepper; b) reduce to ⅓ over high heat; c) place the pan over hot water and beat in the butter a little at a time (the butter should not melt completely, but remain soft and creamy); d) add the chopped parsley and lemon juice.

3. When the steaks are done, season with salt and pepper and transfer to a heated platter. Pour the Bercy sauce over the steaks, garnish with watercress and serve.

Serves 2

A sauce with red wine instead of white wine as its base turns this dish into steak marchand de vin.

STEAK WITH VEGETABLE GARNISH

(bifteck à la landaise)

France

Preparation time: 20 minutes
Meat marinates—6 hours

Cooking time: 40 minutes

Ingredients

Marinade:

½	cup dry white wine
3	tablespoons Armagnac
1	teaspoon peppercorns
¼	teaspoon nutmeg
1	teaspoon thyme
1	bay leaf
2	pounds beef loin strip or top round
¼	cup olive oil
2	small eggplants, peeled and diced

2	zucchini, sliced
2	tomatoes, sliced
2	green peppers, seeded and coarsely chopped
2	onions, chopped
1	clove garlic, minced
	Salt
	Freshly ground pepper
2	tablespoons parsley
½	cup fresh bread crumbs
2	tablespoons butter

1. Combine the marinade ingredients. Add the meat and let stand at room temperature for 6 hours, turning it occasionally. Drain and dry the meat. Reserve the marinade.

2. Preheat the broiler. Heat the oil in a skillet. Add the vegetables, garlic, salt and pepper. Add 2 tablespoons of the marinade, cover and cçok over low heat for 30 minutes.

3. Broil steaks for 8 to 10 minutes (for rare steak), then turn steaks over and broil for approximately 8 more minutes. Baste occasionally with the marinade.

4. Ten minutes before the meat is done, transfer the vegetables to a baking dish. Sprinkle with the parsley and bread crumbs, dot with the butter and brown in the oven for 10 minutes.

5. Transfer the meat to a hot platter. Dilute the cooking juices with the marinade, scrape up any brown particles and reduce the sauce. Pour the sauce over the meat and serve the vegetables on the side.

Serves 4

SUKIYAKI

Preparation time: 30 minutes
Meat chills—to the freezing point

Cooking time: 6 minutes

Japan

Ingredients

 2 *pounds beef tenderloin or sirloin*
 ½ *cup soy sauce*
 ¼ *cup sake or dry sherry*
 ¼ *cup sugar*
 ¾ *cup chicken broth*
    Salt
    Freshly ground pepper
 4 *tablespoons vegetable oil*
 ½ *head bok choy (Chinese cabbage), cut in thin diagonal slices*
 2 *onions, thinly sliced*
 1 *cup celery, sliced*
 1 *cup bamboo shoots, sliced lengthwise*
 8 *mushrooms, sliced*
 ½ *pound fresh spinach, leaves trimmed*
12 *scallions, julienned*
 1 *cake tofu (bean curd), cubed*

1. Chill meat to freezing point. Cut crossgrain into very thin slices, then allow to warm to room temperature.

2. In a non-metallic bowl, combine the soy sauce, *sake* (or sherry), sugar, chicken broth, salt and pepper. Reserve.

3. Heat the oil in a large skillet. Add the sliced meat and brown lightly over fairly high heat. Push meat to the side of the pan. Pour in half the soy mixture, then add the cabbage, onions, celery, bamboo and mushrooms. Stirring constantly, sauté briskly for 3 minutes. Add the spinach, scallions and bean curd. Stirring gently but briskly, sauté another 3 minutes.

4. Serve immediately with hot rice and individual bowls of lightly beaten raw egg for dipping. (The hot *sukiyaki* placed in the egg has an unusual creamy texture. This can be omitted.) The remaining marinade is served as a dipping sauce.

Serves 4

If you follow the Japanese custom and cook sukiyaki *at the table, present the uncooked ingredients attractively arranged on a large platter and cook in an electric skillet or a chafing dish.*

BEEF ROLLS BRAISED IN RED WINE *(biftecks à la Boulonnaise)*

France

Preparation time: 15 minutes

Cooking time: 1½ hours

Ingredients

Stuffing:

⅓   cup fresh parsley, chopped

1   shallot, minced

¼   pound sausage meat
    Salt
    Freshly ground pepper

——

4   very thin slices flank steak or 4 quarter-inch-thick slices top round pounded to ⅛-inch thickness

2½   tablespoons butter

1   tablespoon tomato paste

½   cup red wine

½   cup beef bouillon

1. In a bowl, combine the parsley, shallot and sausage meat. Season to taste with salt and pepper. (To check seasoning, sauté a teaspoonful of the stuffing in butter until well cooked, then taste.)

2. Spread a layer of the stuffing on each slice of beef. Roll up and tie.

3. Heat the butter in a skillet. Add the beef rolls and brown evenly on all sides.

4. Dilute the tomato paste with the wine and bouillon. Pour over the beef rolls.

5. Season with pepper, then cover and simmer over low heat for 1½ hours.

Serves 4

STUFFED BEEF ROLLS *(benlöse fugle)*

Preparation time: 30 minutes   **Cooking time:** 1 hour

Ingredients

Norway

1 pound round or flank steak, thinly sliced	¼ pound ground beef
1 teaspoon salt	2 tablespoons fresh parsley, chopped
½ teaspoon freshly ground pepper	Flour for dredging beef rolls
¼ teaspoon ground ginger	4 tablespoons butter
¼ teaspoon ground cloves	2 cups beef bouillon, heated

1. Place the meat slices between pieces of waxed paper and pound as thin as possible. (Each slice should be about 3 × 4 inches when pounded.)

2. Sprinkle each slice with salt, pepper, ginger and cloves. Place some of the ground beef on each slice of seasoned steak, then sprinkle with the chopped parsley.

3. Roll up each slice, tucking in the edges as the slice is rolled and securing each end with string. Dredge the beef rolls in the flour. Reserve.

4. Melt the butter in a heavy skillet. Add the beef rolls and brown evenly over fairly high heat. Pour in the heated bouillon, adding water if necessary, to cover rolls with liquid. Lower heat, cover skillet and simmer for ½ hour. Uncover the skillet and simmer for another ½ hour.

5. Remove the rolls with a slotted spoon and keep warm. Reduce the gravy to desired consistency over high heat.

6. To serve, discard strings from the beef rolls and transfer the meat to a heated platter. Pour the gravy over the meat or serve it in a warmed sauceboat.

Serves 4

SHREDDED BEEF WITH BAMBOO SHOOTS AND GREEN PEPPERS

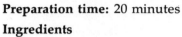

(tung sun chao new ru)

China

Preparation time: 20 minutes

Cooking time: 6 minutes

Ingredients

¾	pound flank steak, sliced thinly and then shredded	5	thick slices fresh ginger root, peeled and slivered
	Cornstarch for dredging meat	¼	teaspoon cayenne pepper
3	tablespoons peanut oil	1	tablespoon soy sauce
½	cup canned bamboo shoots, slivered	½	teaspoon sugar
1	green pepper, chopped	1	tablespoon Chinese rice wine or dry sherry
	Salt		

1. Dredge the beef in cornstarch. Reserve.

2. Place a wok (or 12-inch skillet) over high heat for ½ minute. Lower heat slightly and add 1 tablespoon of the oil. Swirl pan for ½ minute, then add the bamboo shoots, green pepper and a pinch of salt. Stir-fry for 2 minutes. Remove vegetables with a slotted spoon and reserve.

3. Add the remaining 2 tablespoons oil to the wok. Wait ½ minute, then add the ginger and stir-fry for ½ minute.

4. Add the cayenne pepper and the reserved beef. Stir-fry until the meat is nicely browned, about 1½ minutes. Remove wok from heat.

5. Stir in the soy sauce, sugar and rice wine (or sherry). Return pan to high heat. Stirring briskly, heat through. Add the vegetables and mix for ½ minute. Serve immediately.

Serves 2 to 4

BARBECUED SHORT RIBS *(kal bi kui)*

Preparation time: 15 minutes   **Cooking time:** 45 minutes
Ribs marinate—2 to 4 hours

Korea

Ingredients

3   *pounds short ribs of beef*

Marinade:

2   *tablespoons fresh ginger root, peeled and minced*

½   *cup soy sauce*
¼   *cup sugar or honey*
2   *cloves garlic, crushed*
¼   *cup ground sesame seeds*
6   *scallions, chopped*

1. Trim any excess fat or gristle from ribs.

2. Combine marinade ingredients in a non-metallic bowl.

3. Place ribs in shallow pan and pour marinade over them. Brush meat thoroughly with the marinade, then let stand 2 to 4 hours at room temperature, turning meat occasionally.

4. Preheat oven to 375°.

5. Transfer marinated ribs to a rack in a roasting pan. Reserve marinade.

6. Roast ribs for 40 minutes, turning meat often and basting with the marinade.

7. Raise oven heat to 450° and continue roasting until ribs are crisp, about 5 minutes.

Serves 4 to 6

If ribs are to be charcoal-grilled, prepare as above but baste more frequently while cooking to keep ribs from drying out.

BEEF BRAISED IN RED WINE
(daube à la Saint-André)

France

Preparation time: 20 minutes   **Cooking time:** 3 hours

Ingredients

3	pounds rump steak, cut into 1½-inch cubes
	Salt
	Freshly ground pepper
¼	teaspoon ground allspice
½	pound salt pork
½	pound lean bacon, diced

¼	cup fresh parsley, chopped
1	clove garlic, minced
2	shallots, minced
	Herb bouquet (rosemary, thyme, mace, peppercorns)
1	onion, stuck with 4 cloves
3	cups red wine

1. Season the steak with salt, pepper and allspice. Reserve.

2. Blanch the salt pork in boiling water for 10 minutes. Drain, slice and reserve.

3. In a bowl, combine the diced bacon, parsley, garlic and shallots. Mix well.

4. Place a layer of the salt pork slices in an enameled cast-iron casserole. Add a layer of rump steak, then one of the chopped mixture. Continue layering, ending with a layer of steak.

5. Add the herb bouquet and the onion stuck with cloves. Pour in the red wine.

6. Bring to a boil, then cover tightly and simmer over low heat for 3 hours.

7. Skim off the fat. Remove the onion and herb bouquet. Serve in the casserole.

Serves 6

BRAISED BEEF WITH RICE AND OLIVES *(marketzeit)*

Preparation time: 15 minutes   **Cooking time:** 1½ hours   *Tunisia*

Ingredients

2	tablespoons olive oil	2	cups canned tomatoes
1	pound stewing beef, cut into 1-inch cubes		Salt Freshly ground pepper
2	onions, chopped	½	cup pitted green olives, sliced
1	clove garlic, minced		
4	ounces raw long-grain rice		Chopped fresh parsley for garnish
1	cup beef broth		

1. Heat the olive oil in a Dutch oven or enameled casserole. Add the beef cubes and sauté evenly over moderately high heat until barely browned, about 10 minutes.

2. Stirring constantly, add the onions, garlic and rice and cook for a minute or two.

3. Reduce heat and stir in beef broth and tomatoes. Season with salt and pepper.

4. Bring to a boil, then lower heat and simmer for 1 hour.

5. Add the sliced olives and continue simmering until meat is tender, about 30 minutes.

6. Serve in the casserole, garnished with chopped parsley.

Serves 4

BRAISED BEEF AND ONIONS
(biftecks des bateliers de la Loire)

France

Preparation time: 10 minutes   **Cooking time:** 4 hours

Ingredients

2 pounds beefsteak (chuck, flank, brisket), sliced	2 cups water
3 tablespoons butter	Dash red wine vinegar
2½ pounds onions, thinly sliced	4 sour gherkins, finely sliced
Salt	Butter
Freshly ground pepper	

1. Layer the meat and onions in a buttered, enameled cast-iron casserole. (Begin and end with a layer of onions and season each layer with salt and pepper.)

2. Add the water, cover and simmer over very low heat until the meat is tender, about 4 hours.

3. Just before serving, add a dash of vinegar and the finely sliced gherkins. Dot with butter and serve from the casserole.

Serves 4 to 6

STEWED BEEF WITH OKRA *(bamia)*

Preparation time: 30 minutes   **Cooking time:** 1½ hours

Egypt

Ingredients

2	tablespoons vegetable oil
2	tablespoons butter
1½	pounds stewing beef or lamb or veal, cut into 1½-inch cubes
2	onions, chopped
2	cloves garlic, minced
½	teaspoon ground coriander

1	pound tomatoes, peeled and sliced
1	tablespoon tomato paste
2	pounds fresh okra, trimmed, or 2 ten-ounce packages frozen okra
	Salt
	Freshly ground pepper

1. Heat the oil and butter in an enameled cast-iron casserole. Add the meat cubes and sauté on all sides over moderate heat until nearly brown.

2. Add the onions, garlic and coriander and stir-fry for a minute or two.

3. Add the tomatoes and tomato paste and fresh okra. Correct seasoning. (If frozen okra is used, add in step 5 where indicated.)

4. Cover stew mixture with water and bring to a boil, then reduce heat, cover casserole and simmer for 1 hour.

5. (Add the frozen okra.) Check level of liquid and add additional water, if necessary. Cover casserole again and continue simmering until the meat and vegetables are very tender, about ½ hour.

Serves 4

SPICY SHREDDED BEEF
(pabellon criollo)

Venezuela

Preparation time: 25 minutes

Cooking time: 1½ hours

Ingredients

2   *pounds skirt or flank steak*

2   *cups beef stock or water*

⅓   *cup olive oil*

2   *onions, finely chopped*

3   *cloves garlic, pressed*

6   *tomatoes, blanched, peeled and chopped*

½   *teaspoon ground cumin*

1   *teaspoon salt*

Freshly ground pepper

Cooked black beans and cooked rice for garnish

1. Combine the steak and beef stock (or water) in an enameled cast-iron casserole. Bring rapidly to a boil, then reduce heat, cover and simmer meat until extremely tender, about 1½ hours.

2. Remove kettle from heat and allow meat to cool in its broth.

3. Heat the olive oil in a large frying pan. Add the onions and garlic and sauté over moderately high heat until onions are translucent, about 5 minutes. Keep hot.

4. Add the tomatoes to the skillet, then season with the cumin, salt and pepper. Blend sauce thoroughly, then simmer for 5 minutes. Keep hot.

5. Transfer the cooled meat to a carving board. Slice thinly, then shred.

6. Add the meat to the sauce and heat through.

7. To serve, spoon the *pabellon criollo* onto the center of a heated platter. Surround with mounds of black beans and rice.

Serves 6

Try **tajadas de plátano** *(diagonal slices of plantain [tropical green banana] fried in vegetable oil) for an unusual and tasty garnish.*

YANKEE MEATLOAF

Preparation time: 15 minutes   **Baking time:** 1 hour

Ingredients   *USA*

1 pound ground beef	Dash tabasco sauce
1 cup milk	1 tablespoon oregano
1 cup seasoned bread	1 teaspoon tarragon
crumbs	1½ teaspoons parsley
1 egg	1 teaspoon thyme
1 onion, parboiled and	½ teaspoon sage
chopped	Freshly grated pepper
1 green pepper, chopped	1 tomato, sliced
Dash Worcestershire	1 tablespoon butter
sauce	

1. Preheat oven to 325°.

2. Combine the first 14 ingredients and mix thoroughly. Shape into a loaf and place in a baking pan. Arrange tomato slices on top and dot with the butter.

3. Bake for 45 minutes. Remove from oven and let rest for 15 minutes before serving.

Serves 4

Many cooks enjoy experimenting with different combinations and quantities of herbs. Try adding mustard, rosemary, dill, mushrooms, fresh parsley or pimiento to spice up your meatloaf.

BEEFSTEAK AND KIDNEY PIE

Australia

Preparation time: 15 minutes
Pastry chills—1 hour

Cooking time: 1¾ hours

Ingredients

Flaky Pastry:

2¾ cups flour
10 tablespoons butter
½ cup iced water
1 teaspoon salt
—
1 tablespoon flour
   Salt
   Freshly ground pepper
1 pound beefsteak, cubed

2 lamb or beef kidneys, skinned, cored and sliced
3 tablespoons oil
1 onion, chopped
   Dash Worcestershire sauce
1½ cups beef stock
1 egg, beaten

1. Prepare the flaky pastry (**page 474**). Chill for 1 hour.

2. Season the flour with salt and pepper. Dredge the meats in the flour mixture. Heat the oil in an enameled casserole and lightly brown the meat and onion. Add the Worcestershire sauce and stock and simmer over low heat for 1 hour.

3. Roll out the pastry to ¼-inch thickness. Preheat the oven to 350°.

4. Transfer the meat to a deep pie dish and pour in the juice. Cover with the crust. Cut a hole in the center of the crust and brush with the beaten egg. Bake until the crust is golden about 45 minutes.

Serves 4

NOTE: *Leftover cooked steak can be substituted for the raw beefsteak. Add it to the casserole 10 minutes before the end of the cooking time in Step 2.*

TOKÁNY OF VEAL
(tokány borjubul)

Preparation time: 30 minutes   **Cooking time:** 1¼ hours   *Hungary*

Ingredients

2	*pounds veal shoulder, cubed*
	Flour for dredging veal
3	*tablespoons oil*
2	*tablespoons butter*
3	*onions, chopped*
1	*cup dry white wine*
1	*green pepper, seeded and sliced into rings*
2	*carrots, sliced*
3	*tomatoes, peeled and chopped*

½	*teaspoon marjoram*
1	*tablespoon paprika*
	Salt
	Freshly ground pepper
1	*cup veal or beef stock*
6	*ounces bacon, diced*
½	*pound mushrooms, chopped*
1	*cup sour cream*

1. Dredge the veal in flour. Heat the oil and butter in an enameled cast-iron casserole. Brown the veal evenly over moderately high heat. Remove and reserve.

2. Add the onions to the casserole and sauté until tender, about 5 minutes. Pour in the wine, scraping up any browned particles in the casserole. Add the green pepper, carrots and tomatoes to the casserole. Simmer for 10 minutes.

3. Return the veal to the casserole. Add the seasonings and stock and bring to a boil, then lower heat, cover and simmer for 45 minutes.

4. Blanch the bacon for 5 minutes. Drain, rinse under cold water and pat dry. Sauté bacon until lightly browned and add to the casserole. Replace cover and simmer for another 20 minutes.

5. Ten minutes before serving, add the mushrooms. Reduce the heat to low and stir in the sour cream. Heat to thicken but do not boil.

Serves 4

BREAST OF VEAL WITH CHESTNUT STUFFING
(poitrine de veau à l'Auvergnate)

France

Preparation time: 40 minutes   **Cooking time:** 2½ hours

Ingredients

1½ pounds chestnuts	4 to 5 tablespoons milk
1 cabbage, quartered	2 onions, chopped
A 2½-pound veal breast	3 tablespoons butter
Salt	2 tablespoons lard
Freshly ground pepper	2½ cups dry white wine
6 slices smoked bacon	2 tablespoons fresh parsley, chopped
1½ cups bread crumbs	

1. Blanch the scored chestnuts in boiling water for 3 minutes. Drain and peel. Return chestnuts to the pot, cover with cold water and simmer for 15 minutes. Drain and chop half the chestnuts.

2. Blanch the cabbage for 3 minutes. Drain and refresh.

3. Blanch the bacon for 10 minutes. Drain, then arrange on the bottom of a large casserole.

4. Moisten the crumbs with the milk. Combine with the chopped chestnuts, onions and butter. Season with salt and pepper. Slit a pocket in the veal and season inside. Stuff and secure the opening. Place the veal, cabbage, lard and whole chestnuts in the casserole. Pour in the wine and cover tightly. Simmer over low heat for 2½ hours.

5. Transfer the veal to a platter and garnish with the chestnuts and cabbage. Reduce the liquid in the casserole, skim off the fat and pour over the meat and vegetables. Sprinkle with parsley.

Serves 4 to 6

BRAISED VEAL SHANKS *(osso buco)*

Preparation time: 25 minutes

Cooking time: 2 hours

Italy

Ingredients

2 veal shanks, sawed into 2-inch sections
Flour for dredging veal
2 tablespoons olive oil
2 tablespoons butter
2 carrots, finely chopped
2 onions, finely chopped
2 stalks celery, chopped
1 clove garlic, minced
2 pieces lemon peel
1 bay leaf

½ teaspoon dried thyme
Salt
Freshly ground pepper
2 tablespoons tomato paste
2 cups dry white wine
2 cups veal or beef stock
¼ cup fresh parsley, chopped
1 tablespoon lemon rind, grated

1. Roll the veal pieces in flour.

2. Heat the oil and butter in an enameled cast-iron casserole. Add the floured veal and brown evenly over moderately high heat. Remove veal and reserve.

3. Add the carrots, onions, celery and garlic to the casserole. Stir over moderate heat until onions are tender, about 5 minutes. (Do not let vegetables brown.)

4. Arrange the reserved veal on top of the vegetables. Add the lemon peel and bay leaf. Sprinkle on the thyme, then season with salt and pepper.

5. In a bowl, combine the tomato paste, wine and stock. Add to the casserole. Bring to a boil, then reduce heat, cover and simmer very gently for 2 hours. Discard bay leaf and lemon peel. Stir in the parsley and grated lemon rind. Cook for 5 more minutes. Taste and correct seasoning, if necessary, then serve with steamed rice or a *risotto* (page 339).

Serves 4

BREADED VEAL SCALLOPS WITH ANCHOVY BUTTER

(Schnitzel mit Sardelenbutter)

Austria

Preparation time: 10 minutes   **Cooking time:** 10 minutes

Ingredients

Anchovy Butter:

2	anchovy fillets, chopped
6	tablespoons butter, at room temperature
4	veal scallops, pounded flat

	Seasoned flour
2	eggs, beaten
1	cup dry bread crumbs
3	tablespoons butter
	Chopped fresh parsley for garnish
	Lemon wedges for garnish

1. Prepare the anchovy butter: In a mortar, pound the anchovies and mix in softened butter. Form into 4 pats, transfer to waxed paper and refrigerate until needed.

2. Dry the scallops and dredge in seasoned flour. Dip in the beaten egg and then in the bread crumbs.

3. Melt the butter in a large skillet. Add the scallops and sauté over high heat until nicely browned and crisp, about 5 minutes per side.

4. Arrange the scallops on a serving platter. Top each scallop with a pat of anchovy butter, garnish with chopped fresh parsley and lemon wedges. Serve immediately.

Serves 2 to 4

Topping each scallop with a fried egg and an anchovy fillet instead of the anchovy butter turns this dish into Veal à la Holstein.

VEAL SCALLOPS IN CREAM
SAUCE *(escalopes de veau à la Berrichonne)*

Preparation time: 15 minutes   **Cooking time:** 30 minutes   *France*

Ingredients

4 veal scallops	½ pound mushrooms, chopped
Flour for dusting veal	3 ounces ham, cut in julienne strips
4 tablespoons butter	
Salt	2 tablespoons flour
Freshly ground pepper	1 cup milk
2 onions, chopped	¾ cup Gruyère or other Swiss cheese, grated
2 shallots, minced	2 tablespoons cream

1. Dust the veal scallops with flour.

2. Heat the butter in a skillet and lightly brown the scallops on both sides over moderately high heat. Transfer to an oven-proof baking dish, season to taste and set aside.

3. Set oven at 425°.

4. Add the onions and shallots to the skillet. Sauté briefly, then add the mushrooms. Cook until the onions are nearly tender.

5. Add the ham to the skillet, stir in the flour and then slowly pour in the milk.

6. Stirring constantly, bring sauce to a boil, then lower heat and cook until thickened. Salt and pepper to taste.

7. Cover scallops with half the grated cheese, pour sauce over and top with the remaining cheese.

8. Bake until nicely browned, about 15 minutes. Just before serving, sprinkle on the cream.

Serves 4

VEAL SCALLOPS WITH PIPÉRADE SAUCE

(escalopes de veau à la mode de Biscaye)

France

Preparation time: 15 minutes   **Cooking time:** 30 minutes

Ingredients

Pipérade:

2 tablespoons olive oil	2 pounds tomatoes, peeled, seeded and chopped
2 green peppers, seeded and thinly sliced	
1 small hot red pepper, chopped	4 veal scallops
	Flour for dusting veal
1 onion, chopped	1 egg, beaten
2 cloves garlic, minced	¼ cup dry bread crumbs
¼ teaspoon sugar	3 tablespoons butter
Salt	4 slices ham
Freshly ground pepper	¾ cup Gruyère or other Swiss cheese, grated

1. Prepare the *pipérade*: a) Heat the olive oil in a skillet; b) add the green peppers, hot pepper, onion, garlic and sugar; c) season with salt and pepper and sauté until onion is translucent; d) add the tomatoes, then cover and simmer gently for 15 minutes; e) uncover and continue to cook until liquid has evaporated. Remove from heat and reserve.

2. Set oven at 425°.

3. Dust the scallops with a little flour. Dip them in the beaten egg and then in the bread crumbs.

4. Melt the butter in a skillet and sauté the scallops over moderate heat until golden brown on both sides, about 5 minutes.

5. Arrange the scallops in a buttered ovenproof baking dish. Place a slice of ham on each scallop and cover thoroughly with the *pipérade*. Sprinkle with the grated cheese and bake until nicely browned, about 10 minutes.

Serves 4

VEAL WITH MUSHROOMS LYONNAISE

(sauté de veau aux champignons)

France

Preparation time: 15 minutes   **Cooking time:** 1 hour

Ingredients

1½ *pounds veal rump or shoulder, cut into 1½-inch cubes*	*Salt*
Flour for dusting veal	*Freshly ground pepper*
3 *tablespoons olive oil*	¾ *pound mushrooms, sliced*
6 *tablespoons butter*	1½ *cups chicken broth*
4 *shallots, finely chopped*	½ *cup heavy cream*
2 *onions, chopped*	*Juice of 1 lemon*
¼ *pound thickly sliced bacon, diced*	6 *slices French bread, fried in butter*

1. Pat the veal cubes dry and dust with flour.

2. Heat the olive oil and 3 tablespoons butter in a large skillet. Add the pieces of veal and brown evenly on all sides over high heat.

3. Lower heat to moderate and add the shallots, onions and bacon. Cook for 10 minutes, then add salt and pepper.

4. While the onions and bacon are cooking, heat the remaining butter in another skillet and sauté the mushrooms. Add the sautéed mushrooms and the chicken broth to the veal. Simmer gently until the veal is tender, about 40 minutes.

5. Add the cream and lemon juice to the skillet. Bring sauce to a boil and thicken by cooking over moderate heat for about 3 minutes.

6. Serve in a deep heated platter garnished with the slices of fried bread.

Serves 4

VEAL AND HAM ROLLS
(rollatini di vitello)

Italy **Preparation time:** 45 minutes   **Cooking time:** 25 minutes

Ingredients

8	veal scallops, pounded very thin	2	tablespoons vegetable oil
	Salt	5	shallots, minced
	Freshly ground pepper	½	cup white wine
8	thin slices cooked ham	¼	cup Marsala
	Flour for dusting veal rolls	2	tomatoes, peeled, seeded and chopped
2	tablespoons butter	2	teaspoons dried basil

1. Season the veal scallops with salt and pepper.

2. Place a slice of ham on each scallop. Roll up scallops and secure with thread. Dust lightly with flour.

3. Heat the butter and oil in a skillet. Add the rolled scallops and sauté evenly over moderately high heat until nicely browned, about 10 minutes. Remove veal rolls and reserve.

4. Add the shallots to the skillet and sauté over moderate heat until tender, about 5 minutes.

5. Stir in the white wine and the Marsala. Bring rapidly to a boil, scraping up any brown particles in skillet.

6. Reduce heat to low and return the reserved veal rolls to the skillet. Stir in the tomatoes and basil. Season generously with salt and pepper.

7. Cover skillet and simmer gently until *rollatini* are tender, about 25 minutes.

8. Remove veal rolls from skillet and discard trussing thread, then arrange on a heated platter and cover with the sauce.

Serves 4

STUFFED VEAL ROLLS *(Blindle Vinken)*

Preparation time: 45 minutes   **Cooking time:** 45 minutes

The Netherlands

Ingredients

Stuffing:

2	tablespoons butter
1	onion, chopped
¼	pound veal, ground
2	tablespoons parsley
2	eggs, hard-boiled
	Salt
	Freshly ground pepper
	Freshly grated nutmeg

—

6	thin slices veal
	Seasoned flour for dredging veal
4	tablespoons butter
½	cup beef stock
2	slices lemon
	Chopped fresh herbs for garnish

1. Prepare the stuffing: a) Heat the butter in a frying pan; add the onion and sauté over moderately low heat until translucent, about 5 minutes; remove from heat; b) in a bowl, combine the sautéed onions, ground veal and parsley; c) put eggs through a sieve, then add to mixture and blend thoroughly. Season to taste with salt, pepper and a little nutmeg. Reserve.

2. Pound the veal slices to about ⅛-inch thickness. Trim and season lightly with salt and pepper. Place some of the stuffing on each veal slice. Roll up the slices, then secure the rolls with string. Dredge rolls lightly in seasoned flour.

3. Heat the butter in a large frying pan. Add the veal rolls and sauté evenly over moderately high heat until nicely browned on all sides, about 10 minutes. Add the stock and the lemon slices to the skillet. Bring to a boil, then lower heat, cover and simmer until veal is tender, about 45 minutes.

4. Remove the veal rolls from the frying pan, untie them and arrange on a heated serving platter. Keep hot. Reduce the pan juices slightly, then discard the lemon slices and pour sauce over the veal rolls. Garnish with chopped fresh herbs.

Serves 6

ROAST LEG OF LAMB WITH GARLIC SAUCE *(Gasconnade)*

France

Preparation time: 15 minutes **Cooking time:** 12 to 15 minutes per pound (140° F.) for pink lamb

Ingredients

A   5-pound leg of lamb
½   pound garlic cloves, peeled
6   anchovy fillets, halved

Salt
Freshly ground pepper
1   cup beef bouillon

1. Preheat oven to 425° or prepare a spit rotisserie.

2. Sliver 1 large clove garlic.

3. Make slits in the leg of lamb and insert the slivered garlic and the anchovy fillets. Lightly salt and pepper the meat.

4. Roast the lamb in the oven or on a spit. (For pink lamb, cook 12 to 15 minutes per pound, or until the internal temperature of the lamb reaches 140° on a meat thermometer.)

5. While the meat is cooking, prepare the remaining garlic cloves: Drop the garlic cloves into a pot of rapidly boiling water and cook until tender, about 8 minutes. Rinse under cold water, then drain and mash. Reserve.

6. When the lamb is done, remove the roasting pan from the oven and transfer lamb to a heated platter.

7. Stir the mashed garlic cloves into the roasting pan juices, add the bouillon and reduce sauce slightly over high heat.

8. Carve the lamb at the table and serve the sauce on the side.

Serves 4 to 6

ROAST LEG OF LAMB WITH PÉRIGORD SAUCE

(gigot de mouton à la Périgourdine)

France

Preparation time: 15 minutes   **Cooking time:** 12 to 15 minutes per pound (140° F.) for pink lamb

Ingredients

A 5-pound leg of lamb	Freshly ground pepper
2 truffles, slivered	3 tablespoons Armagnac or other brandy, warmed
¼ pound bacon, sliced	
2 tablespoons goose fat (page 475) or olive oil	½ cup beef bouillon
Salt	

1. Preheat oven to 450°.

2. Make small slits in the lamb and insert the truffle slivers. Lard the lamb with the bacon, then brush on the goose fat (or olive oil). Place lamb on a rack in a roasting pan. Season with salt and pepper. Roast, uncovered, for 15 minutes.

3. Reduce heat to 350°, baste lamb and then continue roasting until done. (For pink lamb, figure 12 to 15 minutes per pound, or until the internal temperature of the lamb reaches 140° on a meat thermometer.)

4. About 15 minutes before the end of cooking time, sprinkle on the brandy and flambé.

5. Transfer the roasted lamb to a heated serving platter. Keep warm.

6. Place the roasting pan on top of the stove. Add the bouillon and scrape up any browned particles in the roasting pan. Reduce slightly over high heat. Pour into a heated sauceboat and serve with the lamb.

Serves 4 to 6

ROAST LEG OF LAMB WITH POTATOES *(gigot aux pommes de terre)*

France

Preparation time: 20 minutes   **Cooking time:** 12 to 15 minutes per pound (140° F.) for pink lamb

Ingredients

A	5- to 6-pound leg of lamb
3	cloves garlic, slivered
¼	pound bacon, sliced
4	tablespoons butter

3	pounds potatoes, peeled and thinly sliced
	Salt
	Freshly ground pepper
	Freshly grated nutmeg
¼	cup beef bouillon

1. Preheat oven to 425°.

2. Make slits in the lamb and insert ⅓ of the slivered garlic. Mince the remaining garlic and sliver 1 slice bacon.

3. Coat a casserole with 1 tablespoon of the butter. Layer the potato slices in the casserole, seasoning each layer with the bacon, garlic, salt, pepper and nutmeg.

4. Place the leg of lamb on top of the potatoes. Lard with the remaining bacon slices and dot with the remaining butter. Place casserole in the oven and sear lamb for 15 minutes. Reduce oven temperature to 350° and baste lamb. Continue roasting until the meat is done. Baste frequently. (To determine total roasting time for pink lamb, figure 12 to 15 minutes per pound, or until the internal temperature of the meat reaches 140° on a meat thermometer.)

5. About 15 minutes before the end of the cooking time, pour the beef bouillon over the meat and potatoes.

6. When the lamb is done, remove from the casserole and carve. Cover the potatoes with the sliced lamb, pour on the carving juices and present dish in the casserole.

Serves 6 to 8

BRAISED LEG OF LAMB WITH ONIONS *(gigot braisé aux oignons)*

Preparation time: 30 minutes   **Cooking time:** 2 hours   *France*

Ingredients

A 5-pound leg of lamb	36 tiny white onions, unpeeled
4 tablespoons butter	1 teaspoon sugar
¼ cup olive oil	Salt
2 tablespoons tomato paste	Freshly ground pepper
2½ cups beef bouillon	2 teaspoons potato or corn starch, dissolved in 2 tablespoons cold water
¼ cup cold water	
Herb bouquet (bay leaf, thyme, garlic)	

1. Rub the leg of lamb with 1 tablespoon of the butter. Heat the olive oil in an enameled cast-iron casserole and brown the lamb on all sides over high heat. Pour in the cold water and scrape up any brown particles sticking to the casserole.

2. Mix the tomato paste with 2 cups of the bouillon. Add the tomato paste mixture and the herb bouquet. Bring to a boil, then lower heat, cover and simmer for 2 hours.

3. Drop the unpeeled onions into a large pot of rapidly boiling water. Cook for 3 minutes, then rinse under cold water. Drain and peel. About 30 minutes before the meat is done, heat the remaining butter in a large skillet and sauté the onions until golden, about 5 minutes. Sprinkle the onions with the sugar, pour in the remaining bouillon and cook until nearly all the liquid has evaporated, about 30 minutes.

4. Season the cooked lamb with salt and pepper. Transfer to a heated serving platter and surround with the onions. Thicken the pan juices by stirring in the potato (or corn) starch mixture. Heat through and pour over the dish.

Serves 4 to 6

LEG OF LAMB WITH WHITE BEANS (gigot de mouton aux haricots)

France

Preparation time: 20 minutes   **Cooking time: Lamb**—12 to
Beans soak—overnight   15 minutes per pound for pink lamb
                                            Beans—2 hours

Ingredients

2 pounds dry white beans or white peas	3 cloves garlic, slivered
Herb bouquet (thyme, rosemary, parsley)	A 6-pound leg of lamb
Salt	4 tablespoons butter
Freshly ground pepper	2 tomatoes, peeled, seeded and quartered
4 onions, chopped	2 shallots, minced

1. Soak the beans in cold water overnight. Drain beans and transfer them to a saucepan. Add cold water to cover, the herb bouquet, salt, pepper and half the onions. Bring to a boil and simmer the beans until tender, at least 2 hours. When done, drain and discard the herb bouquet.

2. Preheat oven to 450°.

3. While the beans are cooking, insert garlic slivers in the meat. Rub with 2 tablespoons butter and season to taste. Sear in a 450° oven for 15 minutes. Reduce heat to 350° and roast for about 1¼ hours, or until internal temperature reaches 140° on meat thermometer. Baste frequently. The outside of the meat should be golden brown and the inside quite rare.

4. Prepare the garnish while the lamb and beans are cooking: Heat 2 tablespoons butter in a saucepan. Add the tomatoes, remaining onions and shallots. Cook slowly for 10 minutes, then add the beans. Simmer for about 5 minutes.

5. Transfer bean and tomato mixture to an ovenproof platter. Remove lamb and place it on top of the beans. Baste with pan juices and return to oven. Continue roasting until done.

Serves 8 to 10

STUFFED SHOULDER OF LAMB

(Gevulde Lamsborst)

The Netherlands

Preparation time: 30 minutes

Roasting time: 15 minutes per pound for pink meat

Ingredients

A 4-pound shoulder of lamb, boned

1 garlic clove, crushed
   Salt

Stuffing:

2 tablespoons butter

1 onion, chopped

2 tablespoons flour

2 teaspoons curry powder

1 cup milk

1 apple, peeled, cored and diced

¼ cup fresh parsley, chopped

¾ cup cooked rice
   Salt
   Freshly ground pepper

─

¼ cup butter, melted

1 cup beef stock

2 tablespoons flour

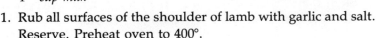

1. Rub all surfaces of the shoulder of lamb with garlic and salt. Reserve. Preheat oven to 400°.

2. To make the stuffing: Melt the butter in a saucepan and sauté the onion over moderate heat until translucent, about 5 minutes. Remove pan from heat and sprinkle on the flour and curry powder. Return pan to low heat and stir for 1 minute. Gradually add the milk and stir until smooth. Add in the apple, parsley, rice and salt and pepper.

3. Fill the pocket of the lamb shoulder with the stuffing. Secure the opening with skewers, then sew up. Place in a roasting pan and baste with the melted butter, then roast to desired tenderness. (For pink meat allow 15 minutes per pound.) When lamb is done, remove from oven and cool slightly, then carve and serve. To prepare a gravy, deglaze the roasting pan with the beef stock and the flour. Serve in a sauceboat.

Serves 4 to 6

P. J. MORIARTY'S IRISH STEW

Ireland

Preparation time: 30 minutes

Cooking time: 2½ hours

Ingredients

3 *pounds potatoes, peeled and thinly sliced*
   Salt
   Freshly ground pepper
1 *pound onions, thinly sliced*

3 *pounds stewing lamb, cut into cubes*
1 *quart water or beef stock*
   Chopped fresh parsley for garnish

1. Line the bottom of an enameled cast-iron casserole with a layer of sliced potatoes. Season with salt and pepper. Add a layer of onions and seasonings, then a layer of lamb. Continue layering, seasoning each layer with salt and pepper. End with a layer of potatoes.

2. Pour in the water (or stock) and bring rapidly to a boil.

3. Skim the surface of the stew, then lower heat, cover and simmer until meat is tender, about 2½ hours.

4. Sprinkle stew with fresh chopped parsley and serve from the casserole.

Serves 6

LAMB PILAF WITH APRICOTS
(chelow-khoresh)

Preparation time: 30 minutes   **Cooking time:** 2 hours   *Iran*

Ingredients

4	tablespoons butter	¼	teaspoon ground allspice
2	pounds lean stewing lamb, cut into 1-inch cubes	¼	teaspoon freshly grated nutmeg
2	onions, finely chopped	1	ounce seedless raisins
	Salt	1	cup dried apricots
	Freshly ground pepper	1	pound raw long-grain rice
¼	teaspoon ground cinnamon	4	cups water

1. Heat the butter in an enameled cast-iron casserole. Add the meat and sauté evenly over moderate heat for 10 minutes.

2. Reduce heat, add the onion and stir-fry until the onion is golden and the meat nicely browned.

3. Add the seasonings, raisins and apricots. Sauté for a minute or two, then cover with cold water. Bring to a boil, then lower heat, cover and simmer until the meat is very tender, about 1½ hours.

4. Fifteen minutes before the meat is done, prepare the rice: a) Pour 4 cups of water into a saucepan and salt lightly; b) bring rapidly to a boil, then sprinkle in the rice; c) boil rapidly for 2 minutes, then lower heat, cover tightly and simmer for 10 minutes; d) drain.

5. Layer the rice and the cooked meat (with sauce) in another casserole, beginning and ending with a layer of rice.

6. Cover and steam over moderate heat until the rice is tender, about 20 minutes.

Serves 6

BAKED LAMB WITH CRACKED WHEAT *(kibbeh bil sanieh)*

Lebanon

Preparation time: 30 minutes
Bulgur soaks—15 minutes

Baking time: 1 hour

Ingredients

1	pound bulgur (cracked wheat)
2	pounds lean lamb, ground twice
½	onion, grated
2	teaspoons salt
	Freshly ground pepper

½	pound lean lamb, ground twice
1	ounce pine nuts
	Salt
	Freshly ground pepper
½	teaspoon cinnamon
	Pinch grated nutmeg
	Pinch ground allspice
¼	pound butter

Filling:

2   tablespoons oil
1   onion, chopped

1. Soak the bulgur in water for 15 minutes. Drain, pressing out excess water, until dry. Combine the bulgur, lamb, onion, salt and pepper. Knead vigorously (or whirl in a blender) until mixture is smooth.

2. Set oven at 375°.

3. Prepare the filling: Sauté the onion in the oil until soft, then mix in the remaining ingredients and sauté over high heat until the meat is lightly browned. Remove from heat.

4. Melt the butter in a saucepan. Reserve.

5. Spread half the reserved bulgur-lamb mixture in the bottom of a buttered 9 x 12-inch baking pan. Press down firmly. Cover with the filling and then top with remaining bulgur-lamb mixture. Smooth the top, pressing it down firmly. Cut diagonal lines across the surface to make diamond shapes. Pour the melted butter over the *kibbeh*. Bake until crisp and brown, about 1 hour. Serve hot or cold.

Serves 8

CAUCASIAN SKEWERED LAMB
(shashlik)

Preparation time: 20 minutes   **Cooking time:** 10 to 15 minutes

Lamb marinates—24 hours

USSR

Ingredients

Marinade:

1	cup olive oil
1	cup red wine
¼	cup lemon juice
2	tablespoons fresh dill, chopped
1	clove garlic, minced
1	bay leaf

Freshly ground pepper

2	pounds lamb, trimmed and cut into 1-inch cubes
16	small onions
4	green peppers, seeded and quartered

1. In a large non-metallic bowl, combine the marinade ingredients listed above.

2. Add the lamb chunks and stir to coat well. Cover and marinate in refrigerator for 24 hours (turn lamb frequently while it marinates).

3. Preheat broiler or charcoal grill.

4. Parboil the onions for 6 minutes. Drain and reserve.

5. Drain marinated lamb and reserve marinade.

6. Thread 4 skewers with the marinated lamb, onions and pepper quarters, alternating ingredients.

7. Baste *shashlik* with the reserved marinade, then broil. (For pink lamb, broil 10 minutes; for well-done, 15 minutes.) Once or twice during broiling turn skewers and baste again.

8. Serve immediately with rice pilaf or kasha.

Serves 4

CANBERRA LAMB FONDUE

Preparation time: 20 minutes

Cooking time: at table

Australia

Ingredients

Mint Sauce:

12	sprigs fresh mint, chopped
5	tablespoons wine vinegar
½	onion, finely minced
1	cup corn or peanut oil
2	teaspoons salt
	Freshly ground pepper

Garlic Sauce:

6	large cloves garlic, mashed
2	egg yolks
1	cup fine olive oil
	Juice of ½ lemon
	Salt
	Freshly ground pepper
4	cups corn or peanut oil
1½	pounds leg of lamb, cubed

1. Combine the above-listed ingredients for the mint sauce. Mix well and reserve.

2. Prepare the garlic sauce: Beat the garlic and yolks together, add the oil drop by drop, beating constantly, as for a mayonnaise (page 476). When thickened, add the lemon juice, salt and pepper. Reserve.

3. Heat oil to 400° (or until a bread cube browns in 1 minute) in a fondue pot or chafing dish. To serve, place the fondue pot on the table, keeping the temperature constant. Spear a cube of lamb and cook to desired doneness—rare: 10 to 20 seconds; medium: 40 seconds; well done: 1 to 1½ minutes. Dip in either the mint or garlic sauce.

Serves 4

MEATBALLS WITH EGG-LEMON SAUCE *(keftaides avgolemono)*

Preparation time: 30 minutes   **Cooking time:** 20 minutes   *Greece*

Ingredients

2	slices white bread
1½	pounds lamb, ground twice
1	onion, chopped
1	clove garlic, pressed
	Salt
	Freshly ground pepper

Egg-Lemon Sauce:

3 egg yolks
   Juice of 1 lemon
¾ cup water
   Salt
   Freshly ground pepper

1. Soak the bread in water, squeeze dry and crumble.

2. In a blender or mixing bowl, combine the crumbled bread, lamb, onion, garlic, salt and pepper. Blend at high speed (or knead vigorously) until very smooth.

3. Form mixture into small teaspoon-size balls.

4. Drop the meatballs into a pot of lightly salted boiling water and poach over moderate heat until well cooked, about 20 minutes.

5. While the meatballs are poaching, prepare the sauce: a) In the top of a double boiler, beat the egg yolks until light; b) add the lemon juice, water, salt and pepper and blend well; c) place over simmering water and heat gently until the sauce thickens slightly. (Do not allow the water under the sauce to boil.) Keep warm.

6. Drain the cooked meatballs thoroughly, then add them to the egg-lemon sauce and heat through. Serve immediately.

Serves 4

STUFFED VINE LEAVES *(sarap dolma)*

Preparation time: 30 minutes   **Cooking time:** 1½ to 2 hours
Preserved vine leaves soak—20 minutes

Turkey

Ingredients

20	*large fresh vine leaves or 1 one-pound jar preserved vine leaves*

Salt
Freshly ground pepper
½ *teaspoon cinnamon*

Filling:

½ *cup uncooked long-grain rice*
1 *pound ground lamb*
2 *onions, finely chopped*
1 *clove garlic, pressed*
1½ *ounces seedless raisins*

Olive oil
1 *egg yolk*
1 *tablespoon flour*
2 *cups beef broth*

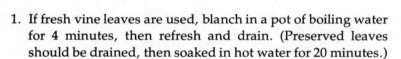

1. If fresh vine leaves are used, blanch in a pot of boiling water for 4 minutes, then refresh and drain. (Preserved leaves should be drained, then soaked in hot water for 20 minutes.)

2. Simmer the rice in a saucepan of boiling water for 5 minutes, then drain well and transfer to a mixing bowl. Add the other filling ingredients to the rice. Mix thoroughly.

3. Spread out the vine leaves, vein side up. Place a spoonful of filling in each leaf center, toward the stem end. Fold the leaf over the filling, tucking in the tip. Fold each side toward the middle, then roll up into a compact sausage-shape. Arrange in closely packed rows in a casserole coated with olive oil.

4. In a bowl, blend together the egg yolk, flour and a little of the beef broth. Mix until smooth, then blend in the remaining broth. Pour the broth mixture over the vine leaves, then weight with a heavy plate.

5. Cover casserole and cook until tender, about 1½ to 2 hours. Using a slotted spoon, transfer cooked stuffed vine leaves to a heated platter and top with an egg-lemon sauce (page 247).

Serves 4

CHRISTMAS BAKED HAM
(kokt griljerad skinka)

Preparation time: 15 minutes   **Cooking time:** 3¾ hours

Ingredients

Sweden

A   10- to 12-pound
     smoked ham, precooked
4   bay leaves
6   whole cloves
6   peppercorns
4   cups Madeira

Coating:

1   egg white
1   tablespoon dry mustard
4   tablespoons brown sugar

1   cup dry bread crumbs

Sauce:

4   tablespoons butter
¼   cup flour
2   cups stock from ham
2   cups beef bouillon

     Cooked prunes and
     apple rings for garnish

1. Place ham in a kettle and cover with boiling water. Add the spices and simmer until nearly tender, about 2½ hours. Drain, then pour in wine and simmer for 30 minutes more.

2. Preheat oven to 350°. Combine the egg white, mustard and sugar. Mix thoroughly. Reserve.

3. Remove kettle from heat and allow ham to cool slightly in liquid. Remove cooled ham from kettle, reserving the wine. Strain the reserved wine and reserve 2 cups of the stock. Skin ham but leave a collar of skin around the shank bone.

4. Place the ham in a baking pan. Coat the surface of the meat with the egg-white mixture, then pat on the bread crumbs. Bake for 45 minutes.

5. For the sauce, melt the butter in a saucepan and blend in the flour; cook for 1 to 2 minutes. Gradually stir in the reserved wine stock and bouillon until desired consistency is reached.

6. To serve, transfer the ham to a heated platter. Garnish with cooked prunes and apple rings. Serve the sauce in a heated gravy boat.

Serves 12 to 14

HAM AND ENDIVE ROLLS AU GRATIN *(Lof, Ham en Kaasaus)*

Belgium

Preparation time: 15 minutes

Baking time: 30 minutes

Ingredients

8   firm heads Belgian
     endive

8   thin slices baked ham

Cheese Sauce:

2   tablespoons butter

2   tablespoons flour

¾   cup milk

4   ounces Gruyère cheese,
     grated

    Salt

    Freshly ground pepper

1. Drop the heads of endive into a saucepan of boiling water and cook for 2 minutes. Drain, then refresh under cold water and pat dry.

2. Roll up each head of endive in a slice of the ham. Place rolls in a buttered baking dish. Reserve.

3. Set oven at 350°.

4. Melt the butter in a saucepan, add the flour and milk, as for a béchamel sauce (page 471). Stirring constantly over low heat, gradually add ½ the grated cheese and cook until the cheese melts. Season to taste with salt and pepper. Keep warm.

5. Pour off any liquid that has accumulated in the baking dish, then cover the ham and Belgian endive rolls with the sauce.

6. Top with the remaining grated cheese and bake for 30 minutes. Serve immediately.

Serves 4

ROAST PORK WITH APPLES
(Varkensschrif)

The
Netherlands

Preparation time: 15 minutes   **Cooking time:** 2 hours

Ingredients

8	tablespoons butter			Freshly ground pepper
A	4-pound pork loin, boned		1	teaspoon marjoram
8	apples, peeled and sliced		1	teaspoon oregano
	Salt		1	clove garlic, minced
				Juice of 2 oranges

1. Preheat oven to 350°.

2. Melt the butter in a shallow roasting pan and brown the meat. Place in the oven and roast for ½ hour, then add the apples and seasonings. Continue roasting until a meat thermometer registers 185°, about 1½ hours. Let the roast stand for 15 minutes, then carve and arrange on a serving platter with the apples.

3. Deglaze the pan with the orange juice and reduce the liquid slightly. Spoon over the meat and serve.

Serves 6

ROAST PORK WITH PLUM
COMPOTE *(filet de porc rôti aux quetsches)*

France

Preparation time: 20 minutes

Cooking time: 2¼ hours

Ingredients

¼ cup olive oil

3 pounds pork loin (bone in)

3 tablespoons butter

Salt

Freshly ground pepper

2 teaspoons rosemary

1 teaspoon ground sage

2 carrots, sliced

1 onion, sliced

3 cloves garlic, peeled

1 cabbage, cut into eighths

1 pound potatoes, peeled

¼ cup chicken stock

Plum Compote:

1 pound purple plums, halved and pitted

3 tablespoons sugar

1 tablespoon water

Peel of 1 lemon

1. Set oven at 325°. Heat the oil and brown the pork.

2. Melt the butter in a casserole and add the pork. Season with salt, pepper, and herbs. Add the carrots, onions, and garlic. Cover casserole and cook for 1 hour.

3. Blanch the cabbage in rapidly boiling salted water for 2 minutes. Remove and rinse under cold water. Drain.

4. After the pork has cooked for 1 hour, add the potatoes and the cabbage. Baste with cooking juices. (Add ¼ cup chicken stock if there are not enough cooking juices for basting.) Season with salt and pepper. Re-cover and cook for another hour, basting a few times.

5. For the compote, put the plums in a saucepan with the sugar, water and lemon peel. Simmer until plums are soft, about 20 minutes; discard lemon peel.

6. Present the pork on a platter surrounded by the vegetables and sprinkled with 2 to 3 tablespoons of cooking juices. Serve the hot plum compote separately in a bowl.

Serves 4

ANDEAN-STYLE SWEET ROAST
PORK *(lomo de cerdo)*

Preparation time: 15 minutes   **Cooking time:** 1½ hours   *Peru*
Pork marinates—24 hours

Ingredients

A	3-pound pork loin	¼	cup butter, melted
1	tablespoon salt	1	cup milk

Marinade:

		½	teaspoon ground cinnamon
1	cup dry white wine	½	teaspoon nutmeg
4	whole cloves	¾	cup seedless raisins
⅓	cup brown sugar	½	cup fresh bread crumbs

1. Rub the pork loin with the salt. Let stand 20 minutes.

2. In a large non-metallic pan, combine marinade ingredients listed above. Add the pork loin, spooning marinade over meat to coat thoroughly. Cover and refrigerate 24 hours.

3. Preheat oven to 325°.

4. Remove meat, pat dry and reserve.

5. Gradually add the melted butter, milk, cinnamon, nutmeg and raisins to the marinade. Mix thoroughly.

6. Sprinkle the pork with the bread crumbs, then place in a roasting pan. Cover with the marinade mixture and cook until tender, about 1½ hours (or until internal temperature is 185°). Baste meat frequently. Serve at once, spooning the gravy over the pork.

Serves 6

PORK STEWED IN CUMIN
(porco com cominho)

Portugal

Preparation time: 25 minutes
Pork marinates—24 hours

Cooking time: 45 minutes

Ingredients

Marinade:

½   *cup white wine*
    Juice of 1 lemon
1½ *teaspoons ground
    cumin*
3   *cloves garlic, crushed*
1   *bay leaf*
1   *teaspoon salt*
    Freshly ground pepper

2   *pounds lean boneless
    pork, cubed*
2   *tablespoons vegetable
    oil*
1   *bunch cilantro
    (Chinese parsley),
    chopped*
    *Lemon wedges for
    garnish*
    Olives for garnish

1. In a shallow non-metallic bowl, combine the marinade ingredients.

2. Add the pork cubes and stir to coat thoroughly. Cover and refrigerate for 24 hours, turning meat occasionally.

3. Remove marinated pork from bowl with a slotted spoon. Pat dry. Reserve marinade.

4. Heat the oil in a heavy casserole, add the meat and sauté over moderately high heat until golden brown. Add the marinade. Reduce heat to low, cover and cook until the meat is tender, about 45 minutes. Lower heat, stir in cilantro. Mix well and transfer to heated serving platter.

5. Garnish with lemon wedges and olives. Serve with fried potatoes.

Serves 6

SAVOY-STYLE FRICASSEE OF
PORK *(fricassée de porc à la Savoyarde)*

Preparation time: 20 minutes   **Cooking time:** 2 hours   *France*
Pork marinates—12 hours or overnight

Ingredients
Marinade:

2	cups dry white wine		1	tablespoon flour
3	tablespoons olive oil		1	tablespoon marinade (see above)
	Salt		1	cup red wine
6	peppercorns		1	cup water
2	onions, chopped			Salt
	Herb bouquet (sage, rosemary, basil, chervil)			Freshly ground pepper
			2	tablespoons butter
2	pounds pork loin, cut into serving pieces		1	tablespoon flour
3	tablespoons butter		1	cup cream
3	tablespoons vegetable oil		8	slices French bread, fried in butter

1. Combine the above-listed marinade ingredients in a non-metallic bowl. Add the pieces of pork, cover and refrigerate for 12 hours or overnight. Remove the pieces of meat from the marinade and pat dry. Reserve 1 tablespoon of the marinade.

2. In a large skillet, heat the butter and oil. Add the meat and sauté over moderate heat until nicely browned. Lower heat and sprinkle in the flour. Stir in the reserved marinade, then add the red wine and water. Season with salt and pepper. Bring to a boil, then lower heat, cover and simmer until the meat is tender, about 2 hours.

3. Prepare a *beurre manié* by combining the flour and butter. About 15 minutes before serving, thicken the sauce with the *beurre manié* and the cream. Serve garnished with fried bread.

Serves 4

PORK CHOPS BAKED WITH CABBAGE *(côtes de porc à l'Auvergnate)*

France

Preparation time: 40 minutes

Baking time: 40 minutes

Ingredients

1   *cabbage, quartered*
5   *tablespoons cream*
    Salt
    Freshly ground pepper
4   *tablespoons butter*
4   *loin pork chops*

½   *cup dry white wine*
4   *leaves fresh sage, chopped, or ¼ teaspoon dried sage*
½   *cup Cantal or Cheddar cheese, grated*

1. Blanch the cabbage quarters for 5 minutes in a large kettle of boiling salted water. Refresh under cold running water, then drain and chop coarsely.

2. In a saucepan, combine the cabbage and cream. Season to taste with salt and pepper. Cover and cook over low heat for 15 minutes. Remove from heat.

3. Heat half the butter in a large skillet and sauté the pork chops until nicely browned, about 10 minutes on each side. Season with salt and pepper. Remove chops from the skillet and reserve.

4. Preheat oven to 325°.

5. Add the wine and sage to the skillet. Boil for a few minutes, then remove from heat and add the cabbage. Mix well.

6. Spread half the cabbage in a baking dish, add the chops and then cover with the remaining cabbage. Top with the grated cheese.

7. Dot with the remaining butter and bake, uncovered, for 40 minutes.

Serves 4

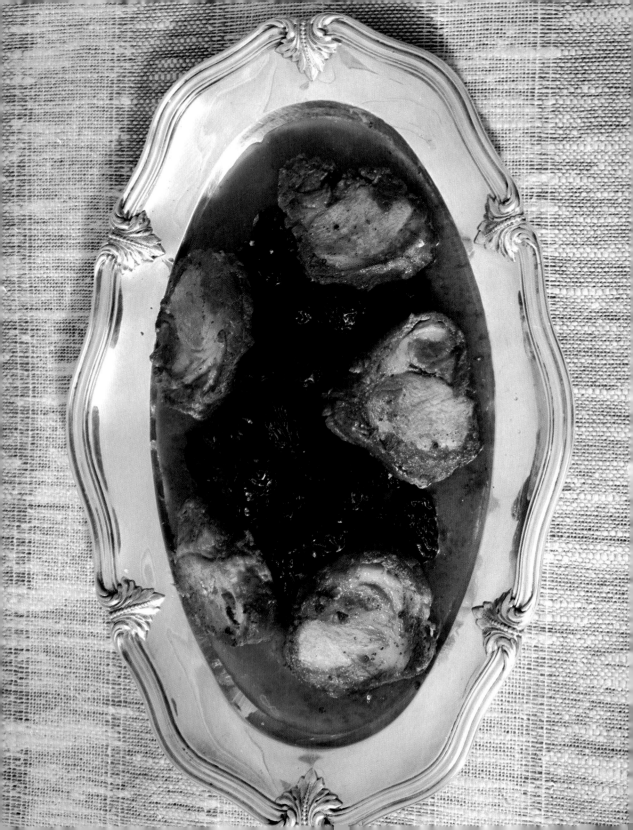

PORK CHOPS WITH
SAUERKRAUT *(varzá cu porc)*

Preparation time: 1 hour   **Cooking time:** 45 minutes   *Rumania*

Ingredients

3 *pounds sauerkraut*
4 *tablespoons vegetable oil*
½ *pound bacon, diced*
4 *onions, chopped*
2 *cloves garlic, pressed*
3 *carrots, sliced*
¼ *cup tomato paste*
   Herb bouquet (juniper

berries, peppercorns, parsley, bay leaf)
2 *cups beer*
2 *cups beef or chicken stock*
6 *pork chops*
   Chopped fresh dill for garnish
½ *pint sour cream*

1. Briefly rinse the sauerkraut under cold running water. Squeeze out and reserve.

2. Heat half the oil in a casserole. Add the bacon and sauté until fat is rendered, about 10 minutes. Add the onions, garlic and carrots and sauté until golden, about 10 minutes.

3. Add the reserved sauerkraut and stir until coated with the fat. Blend in the tomato paste, then add the herb bouquet. Salt lightly. Pour in the beer and stock. Bring rapidly to a boil, then lower heat, cover and simmer for 20 minutes.

4. While the sauerkraut simmers, prepare the pork chops: Heat the remaining oil in a skillet. Pat the chops dry, then sauté over moderately high heat until nicely browned on both sides. (This will take about 8 minutes per side.)

5. Transfer the browned pork chops to the casserole, burying them in the sauerkraut. Cover and simmer until pork is tender, about 45 minutes.

6. Discard herb bouquet. Garnish with chopped fresh dill and serve piping hot, accompanied by a dish of sour cream.

Serves 6

PORK FILLETS WITH PRUNES
(filets de porc aux pruneaux)

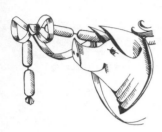

France

Preparation time: 15 minutes
Prunes soak—overnight

Cooking time: 35 minutes

Ingredients

½ pound dried pitted prunes	¼ cup flour, seasoned with salt and pepper
1 cup dry white wine	3 tablespoons butter
4 one-half-inch-thick slices pork fillet, boned	1 teaspoon red currant jelly
	1 cup cream

1. Combine the prunes and wine in an enameled cast-iron casserole. Soak prunes overnight.

2. Place the casserole over low heat and gently poach the prunes for 20 minutes. Remove from heat.

3. While the prunes are cooking, dust the pork fillets with the seasoned flour. Heat the butter in a skillet and sauté the pork fillets over high heat for 10 minutes on each side. Lower heat, cover and cook for 10 minutes.

4. Using a slotted spoon, transfer the poached prunes to a heated serving dish. Surround with the fillets. Keep warm.

5. Pour the poaching liquid from the prunes into the juices in the meat skillet. Over high heat, reduce liquid to about ½ cup.

6. Lower heat to moderate. Stirring constantly, add the red currant jelly and the cream. Heat until sauce thickens slightly, then pour over the prunes and meat and serve immediately.

Serves 4

ROAST PORK STRIPS *(tsa sow ru)*

Preparation time: 20 minutes
Pork marinates—3 hours

Roasting time: 50 minutes

China

Ingredients

1½ *pounds pork tenderloin
     or butt*

Marinade:

¼   *cup water*

¼   *teaspoon red food
     coloring*

2   *tablespoons sugar*

¼   *cup soy sauce*

2   *tablespoons hoisin
     sauce (optional)*

2   *tablespoons Chinese
     rice wine or dry sherry*

3   *cloves garlic, minced*

½   *teaspoon salt*

1. Cut the pork into strips 5 inches long, 2 inches wide and 2 inches thick. Reserve.

2. In a shallow non-metallic pan, combine the marinade ingredients. Mix thoroughly. Add the pork strips to the marinade, coat well, then let stand at room temperature for 3 hours. (Baste strips with marinade from time to time.)

3. Preheat oven to 475°.

4. Baste the pork one more time with the marinade, then transfer to a rack in a roasting pan. Discard marinade.

5. Place roasting pan on the top shelf of oven. Roast pork strips for 30 minutes, then turn meat over, baste with the pan juices and continue roasting until pork is tender, about 20 minutes. Transfer the roasted pork strips to a cutting board and slice at an angle into ¼-inch-thick pieces. Serve hot or cold.

Serves 4

Roast pork strips will keep for up to a week in the refrigerator. It can be reheated for a main course or used to supplement a variety of dishes, such as fried rice or wonton soup.

SWEET AND SOUR PORK *(koo lu ru)*

China

Preparation time: 20 minutes

Cooking time: 20 minutes

Ingredients

Batter:

1	cup flour
½	teaspoon salt
1	egg, beaten
1	cup cold water

Marinade:

2	tablespoons soy sauce
2	tablespoons dry sherry
2	teaspoons sugar
1	pound lean pork, cut in 1-inch cubes
3	cups peanut oil

Sweet and Sour Sauce:

2	tablespoons peanut oil
2	cloves garlic, minced
3	green peppers, diced
½	cup sweet pickled vegetables, chopped
¾	cup water
¼	cup sugar
1	tablespoon molasses
½	cup malt vinegar
2	tablespoons catsup
1	tablespoon cornstarch, dissolved in water

1. Combine the batter ingredients and beat until smooth. Let stand for 2 hours. Combine the marinade ingredients. Add the pork and let stand for 30 minutes.

2. Drain the pork and reserve the marinade. Heat the oil in a wok until nearly smoking. Dip the pork in the batter and fry until brown, about 12 minutes. Drain.

3. Prepare the sauce: Add the garlic to the hot oil and stir-fry for ½ minute. Add the peppers and pickled vegetables and stir-fry for 2 minutes. Blend in the water, reserved marinade, sugar, molasses, vinegar and catsup and stir for 3 minutes. Blend in the cornstarch and simmer until sauce clears, about 2 minutes. Pour the sauce over the pork and serve.

Serves 3 to 4

BOK CHOY WITH PORK OR BEEF
(bai tsai ru)

Preparation time: 20 minutes

Cooking time: 8 minutes

China

Ingredients

1 *pound bok choy (Chinese cabbage) or celery cabbage*	1 *teaspoon salt*
	1 *teaspoon fresh ginger root, minced*
1 *pound pork or flank steak, cubed*	1 *tablespoon Chinese rice wine or dry sherry*
Cornstarch	2 *tablespoons soy sauce*
1 *egg white, beaten*	¼ *teaspoon sugar*
4 *tablespoons peanut oil*	

1. Trim the leaves and stalks of the *bok choy*. Wash thoroughly and pat dry. Cut into 1- to 1½-inch chunks. Reserve.

2. Dredge the pork (or beef) cubes in cornstarch and dip in the egg white. (If using pork, omit egg white coating.)

3. Place a 12-inch wok (or skillet) over high heat for ½ minute. Swirl in 2 tablespoons of the oil. Wait ½ minute, then reduce heat to moderate and add the stalks of *bok choy*. Stir-fry for 1 minute, then add the rest of the cabbage. Stir-fry until barely tender, about 1½ minutes. Remove wok from heat. Season with ½ teaspoon salt, then transfer to a heated serving platter. Keep warm.

4. Return wok to high heat. Wait ½ minute, then swirl in the remaining oil. Heat oil, then add the ginger and stir-fry for 1 minute. Add the meat and ½ teaspoon salt. Stir-fry meat until tender (pork — 3 to 4 minutes; beef — 2 to 3 minutes). Remove from heat.

5. One by one, add the rice wine (or sherry), soy sauce and sugar. Return wok to high heat and toss briefly. Pour over the bed of cabbage and serve immediately.

Serves 2 to 4

BEAN CURD AND PORK *(dou fu ru)*

China

Preparation time: 15 minutes
Dried shrimp soaks—10 minutes

Cooking time: 7 minutes

Ingredients

1	tablespoon dried shrimp
½	pound boneless lean pork, finely chopped
	Cornstarch
3	tablespoons peanut oil
3	thick slices ginger root, peeled and minced
1	green chili pepper, finely chopped
3	tablespoons soy sauce

1	tablespoon Chinese rice wine or dry sherry
½	teaspoon sugar
4	large scallions, minced
3	three-inch-square bean curd cakes
¼	cup chicken stock
1	tablespoon sesame-seed oil

1. Soak the dried shrimp in cold water for 10 minutes. Drain.

2. Dredge the pork in cornstarch. Place a wok (or 10-inch skillet) over high heat for ½ minute. Heat 1 tablespoon of the oil for ½ minute, then add the ginger, pork and chili pepper. Stir-fry for 1½ minutes.

3. Stir in 2 tablespoons of the soy sauce, then add wine and sugar. Stir briskly for 1 minute, then mix in the white parts of the scallions. Remove all ingredients from wok with a slotted spoon and reserve.

4. Add the remaining 2 tablespoons peanut oil to the wok. Swirl over high heat for ½ minute, then add the bean curd cakes. Lower heat to moderate and stir-fry for 2 minutes, mashing down the cakes as they cook to separate them.

5. Stir in shrimp and remaining tablespoon soy sauce. Mix briefly. Return all ingredients to the wok and blend together. Add the chicken stock and the sesame oil. Stir briefly, then add the green portion of the scallions. Toss lightly, transfer to a heated platter and serve immediately.

Serves 2 to 4

STEAMED GROUND PORK
(tsing tzu ru)

Preparation time: 10 minutes   **Cooking time:** 1½ hours   *China*
Chinese mushrooms soak—30 minutes

Ingredients

4 *dried Chinese mushrooms*	¼ *cup soy sauce*
4 *ounces canned water chestnuts, drained and chopped*	1½ *tablespoons Chinese rice wine or dry sherry* Salt
1 *pound lean ground pork*	

1. Soak the Chinese mushrooms in a bowl of warm water for ½ hour. Remove with a slotted spoon, drain and pat dry. Discard stems. Chop caps finely.

2. In a bowl, combine the chopped mushroom caps with the water chestnuts and ground pork. Mix thoroughly, then gradually blend in the soy sauce, Chinese rice wine (or sherry) and salt.

3. Transfer mixture to an ovenproof serving bowl. Place bowl in a large pot of boiling water. Cover pot and steam for 1½ hours.

4. Serve the pork cake in the bowl as an accompaniment to other Chinese dishes.

Serves 2 to 4

VARIATION: *Fifteen minutes before the end of cooking time, break an egg over the pork cake. Re-cover and continue steaming until done.*

PORK SAUSAGE POACHED IN WHITE WINE
(saucisson de Morteau au vin blanc)

France

Preparation time: 15 minutes   **Cooking time:** 45 minutes

Ingredients

- 1   tablespoon butter
- 1   one-pound Morteau sausage or any large fresh pork sausage such as cotechino or kielbasa
- 1   cup dry white wine
- 1   cup chicken stock
- 1   onion, chopped
- 2   cloves garlic, minced
  Herb bouquet (marjoram, mace, thyme, basil, peppercorns)
- 1   tablespoon tomato paste
- 1   pound boiling potatoes, peeled and halved
  Salt
  Freshly ground pepper
- 1   tablespoon fresh parsley, chopped

1. In an enameled cast-iron casserole, melt the butter and lightly brown the sausage. Cover with the wine and chicken stock. Add the onion, garlic, herb bouquet, tomato paste, potatoes, salt and pepper.

2. Bring to a boil. Cover and simmer gently for 40 minutes.

3. Transfer the sausage to a warmed platter and arrange the potatoes around it.

4. Reduce the cooking liquid by half over moderately high heat. Correct seasoning and pour the strained liquid over the sausage. Sprinkle with the parsley.

Serves 2 to 4

Traditionally the people of Franche-Compté serve this dish with French bread and a selection of French mustards.

BRAISED PORK SAUSAGE WITH RED CABBAGE AND APPLES

(kiełbasa w czerwonej kapuście)

Poland

Preparation time: 20 minutes   **Cooking time:** 30 minutes

Ingredients

2	tablespoons vegetable oil	2	pounds kielbasa (Polish sausage)
1	tablespoon butter		Bay leaf
2	onions, chopped	¼	cup red wine vinegar
1	small red cabbage, shredded	½	cup beef stock or water
2	apples, peeled, cored and chopped		Salt
			Freshly ground pepper

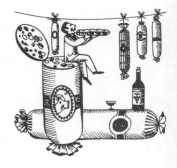

1. Heat the oil and butter in a heavy pot or casserole. Add the chopped onions and sauté until tender, about 5 minutes.

2. Add the cabbage and apples. Mix well, then bury the sausage and bay leaf in the mixture.

3. Pour in the wine vinegar and stock (or water). Season with salt and pepper.

4. Cover pot and simmer over moderate heat for 30 minutes.

5. Discard bay leaf. Remove sausage from pot and cut into serving pieces.

6. Transfer the cabbage mixture to a heated serving platter and arrange the sausage on top. Serve piping hot.

Serves 4

PHILADELPHIA SCRAPPLE

Preparation time: 30 minutes   **Cooking time:** 3½ hours

USA   **Ingredients**

1 *pound pork*	*Freshly ground pepper*
3 *pigs' knuckles*	1¼ *cups buckwheat*
½ *teaspoon thyme*	1¼ *cups cornmeal*
½ *teaspoon marjoram*	*Flour for coating scrapple*
1 *teaspoon sage*	*Oil or butter for frying*
2 *teaspoons salt*	

1. Cover the meats with water and simmer until the meat separates easily from the bones, about 2½ hours.

2. Remove the meat from the bones and chop. Discard the bones. Strain the broth and return 1 quart of broth to the kettle. Add the chopped meats and the seasonings. Bring to a boil.

3. Combine the buckwheat and cornmeal with 1 quart cooled broth. Pour into the kettle and stir the mixture until thickened into a mush, about 1 hour.

4. Remove the scrapple from the heat and allow to cool. To serve, slice and coat lightly with flour. Fry in oil or butter until golden brown.

Serves 6 to 8

BAKED LIVER IN WINE SAUCE
(sikotaki yahni)

Preparation time: 25 minutes   **Baking time:** 40 minutes   *Greece*

Ingredients

3	tablespoons olive oil
3	onions, chopped
1	pound beef liver, trimmed and cut in 1-inch squares
	Flour for dredging liver
2	tablespoons tomato paste

1½	cups beef stock
¾	cup red wine
	Salt
	Freshly ground pepper
	Oregano
12	green olives, pitted

1. Set oven at 375°.

2. Heat the olive oil in an enameled cast-iron casserole. Add the onions and sauté over moderately high heat until golden, about 5 minutes. Remove with a slotted spoon and reserve.

3. Dredge the liver in flour.

4. Add the liver to the casserole and brown evenly, stirring over high heat for 2 minutes.

5. Add the tomato paste, stock, wine and the reserved onions. Season to taste with salt, pepper and oregano. Bring rapidly to a boil, then remove casserole from heat.

6. Cover and bake for 30 minutes, then add the olives. Re-cover again and bake for 10 more minutes.

7. Serve with rice pilaf, if desired.

Serves 4

TONGUE WITH ALMOND SAUCE
(lengua con salsa alemendras)

Argentina

Preparation time: 15 minutes   **Cooking time:** 3 hours

Ingredients

A   5- to 6-pound fresh
     beef tongue
1   onion studded with 2
     cloves
4   sprigs parsley
1   tablespoon salt
1   teaspoon oregano
4   peppercorns
2   bay leaves

1   clove garlic, minced
2   cups beef broth
2   ounces toasted
     almonds, slivered
2   teaspoons fresh
     parsley, chopped
     Dry bread crumbs for
     thickening sauce
     (optional)
     ———
     Capers for garnish

Almond Sauce:
1   tablespoon olive oil

1. Rinse tongue and place in a large soup kettle. Cover with cold water, then add the onion, parsley and seasonings.

2. Bring rapidly to a boil. Skim the surface, then lower heat, cover and simmer for 1½ hours. Skim foam off surface of broth and turn tongue over. Re-cover and continue simmering until tender, about 1½ hours.

3. Remove kettle from heat and allow tongue to cool slightly in its broth, then skin and trim gristle. Keep hot.

4. Prepare the almond sauce: a) Heat the olive oil in a large skillet; b) add the garlic and sauté briefly, then add the broth, almonds and parsley; c) bring to a boil, then lower heat and simmer gently for 10 minutes. (If necessary, thicken with sifted dry bread crumbs.)

5. To serve, slice tongue and arrange on a heated platter. Cover with the sauce and garnish with capers. Serve immediately.

Serves 6 to 8

TRIPE AND ONIONS
(gras-double à la Lyonnaise)

Preparation time: 40 minutes   **Cooking time:** 30 minutes

France

Precooked tripe simmers—1 to 4 hours

Ingredients

2 pounds fresh honeycomb tripe	Salt
1 onion stuck with 4 cloves	Freshly ground pepper
Herb bouquet (bay leaf, marjoram, peppercorns)	3 tablespoons butter
	½ cup olive oil
	3 onions, sliced
2 carrots, quartered	¼ cup vinegar
	Chopped fresh parsley

1. Wash tripe and blanch in boiling water for 2 minutes. Refresh under cold water and repeat process. Drain.

2. Put tripe in saucepan. Cover generously with cold water. Add the onion stuck with cloves, herb bouquet, carrots, salt and pepper. Cover and simmer until tender.

3. Drain the tripe and pat dry. Cut into strips. Reserve.

4. Heat the butter in a skillet, add the onions and cook over low heat for 20 minutes. Do not brown.

5. In another skillet heat the oil and sauté the tripe until golden, about 10 minutes.

6. Add the sautéed onions to the tripe. Pour in the vinegar and heat through. Transfer to a heated platter and garnish with fresh chopped parsley.

Serves 6

Most fresh tripe sold in the U. S., Britain and France has been cleaned, blanched and precooked. Additional cooking needed to make tripe fork-tender may vary from 1 to 4 hours. If the tripe has not been precooked, it will have to simmer 10 to 12 hours.

TRIPE IN WHITE WINE
(tripes à la Saintongeaise)

France

Preparation time: 30 minutes

Baking time: 4 hours

Ingredients

2	*pounds honeycomb tripe*
2	*leeks, thinly sliced*
4	*carrots, thinly sliced*
10	*small white onions*
1	*stalk celery, thinly sliced*
2	*cloves garlic, crushed*
	Herb bouquet (bay leaf, parsley, thyme,

	marjoram, peppercorns)
¼	*teaspoon freshly grated nutmeg*
	Salt
	Freshly ground pepper
4	*cups dry white wine*
4	*cups water*
1	*calf's foot or knuckle, quartered (optional)*

1. Set oven at 250°.

2. Prepare the tripe: Wash tripe under cold running water, then transfer to a large pot of rapidly boiling water and blanch for 2 minutes. Refresh tripe under cold water, then repeat blanching process. Drain tripe, dry thoroughly and cut into small serving pieces.

3. Line a buttered earthenware casserole with the leeks, carrots, onions and celery. Add the tripe pieces (calf's foot or knuckle), garlic, herb bouquet and nutmeg. Season with salt and pepper.

4. Pour in the wine and water and bring rapidly to a boil, then remove casserole from heat.

5. Cover casserole tightly and bake for at least 4 hours. (Since the flavor of the casserole improves with prolonged cooking, it may be cooked for much longer, if desired.)

Serves 4 to 6

LISBON-STYLE CALVES' LIVER
(iscas)

Preparation time: 10 minutes   **Cooking time:** 10 minutes   *Portugal*
Liver marinates—24 hours

Ingredients

Marinade:

1	cup dry white wine
1	bay leaf
2	cloves garlic, pressed
	Salt

Freshly ground pepper

1	pound calves' liver, thinly sliced
½	pound bacon, diced

1. Combine the marinade ingredients in a shallow, non-metallic pan.

2. Add liver slices and stir to coat thoroughly. Cover and refrigerate for 24 hours, turning occasionally.

3. Remove liver slices, pat dry and reserve. Strain marinade and reserve.

4. In a skillet, fry bacon until crisp. Add the liver and sauté over moderate heat until tender, about 3 minutes per side.

5. Transfer meat to a heated platter and keep warm.

6. Pour the reserved marinade into the skillet and reduce by half over high heat.

7. Spoon reduced marinade over the liver and serve at once.

Serves 4

VEAL SWEETBREADS WITH SORREL *(ris de veau à l'oseille)*

France

Preparation time: 35 minutes
Sweetbreads soak—4 hours

Cooking time: 45 minutes

Ingredients

2 pounds sweetbreads	Freshly ground pepper
3 tablespoons goose fat (page 475) or olive oil	Herb bouquet (chervil, thyme, bay leaf, peppercorns)
8 small white onions	½ cup dry white wine
2 carrots, sliced	½ cup bouillon
2 tomatoes, peeled, seeded and chopped	2 pounds sorrel or spinach
Salt	

1. Soak the sweetbreads in cold water until they turn white, about 4 hours. (Change the water every hour.) Drain sweetbreads, then blanch in a pot of simmering water for 10 minutes. Plunge them into ice water and soak for 5 minutes to firm. Remove and pat dry, then trim skin and membranes.

2. Heat 2 tablespoons of the goose fat (or oil) in a large skillet and brown the sweetbreads, onions and carrots. Add the tomatoes, salt, pepper, herb bouquet, wine and bouillon. Cover and simmer gently for 40 minutes.

3. Rinse the sorrel (or spinach) and trim the stalks. Blanch for 2 minutes in boiling salted water, then refresh. Drain well and chop. In another skillet, heat the remaining fat. Add the sorrel, cover and cook gently for 20 minutes. Season to taste.

4. When the sweetbreads are done, discard herb bouquet and reserve juices. Arrange the sweetbreads and vegetables on a heated platter. Keep warm. Over high heat, reduce juice in skillet by half. Strain and pour over the meat and vegetables.

Serves 4

VEAL KIDNEYS IN MADEIRA
SAUCE *(rognons de veau au Madère)*

Preparation time: 10 minutes   **Cooking time:** 15 minutes   *France*

Ingredients

2 whole veal kidneys	2 tablespoons Calvados, warmed
4 tablespoons butter	½ cup Madeira
½ pound mushrooms, sliced	½ cup cream
¼ pound ham, diced	2 tablespoons fresh parsley, chopped
Salt	
Freshly ground pepper	

1. Remove most of the fat and the very fine membrane from the kidneys. Slice and pat dry. Reserve.

2. Melt half the butter in a skillet and sauté the mushrooms over high heat for 5 minutes. Add the ham and season with salt and pepper. Remove skillet from heat.

3. In another skillet, heat the remaining butter. Stirring constantly, sauté the kidneys over moderately high heat for about 6 minutes. Pour in the warmed Calvados and flambé. Remove skillet from heat.

4. Add the Madeira to the skillet with the mushrooms. Place over high heat. Stirring constantly, bring to a boil. Lower heat and stir in the cream. Heat slightly, then remove skillet from stove.

5. Add the kidneys to the mushrooms, sprinkle with the parsley and serve immediately. (The kidneys should not stand or they will get hard.)

Serves 2

This dish is often served with artichoke hearts braised in butter. Steamed rice would be another good accompaniment.

VEAL KIDNEYS WITH NOODLES
(rognons de veau aux nouilles)

France

Preparation time: 20 minutes   **Cooking time:** 25 minutes

Ingredients

2 *whole veal kidneys*	1 *clove garlic, minced*
12 *ounces flat egg noodles*	3 *shallots, minced*
Salt	*Freshly ground pepper*
3 *tablespoons butter*	3 *tablespoons cognac,*
3 *tablespoons olive oil*	*warmed*

1. Preheat oven to 350°.

2. Prepare the kidneys: a) Remove most of the fat as well as the very fine membrane; b) cut each kidney into four sections, following its natural divisions so that it will cook quickly and evenly; c) rinse very briefly under cold running water, pat dry and reserve.

3. Drop the noodles into salted boiling water and cook for 10 minutes.

4. While the noodles are cooking, sauté the kidneys in butter for about 10 minutes. Spoon butter over the kidneys as they cook. Drain the noodles and rinse with cold water.

5. In a separate pan, heat the olive oil and sauté the minced garlic and the shallots. Add the noodles, coating them thoroughly with the sauce. Season with salt and pepper and turn into a warm buttered baking dish.

6. Remove kidneys from heat, reserving pan juices. Slice the kidneys and season with salt and pepper. Place kidneys around noodles in the baking dish. Spoon half the pan juices onto the casserole. Bake for 15 minutes. Just before serving, add the warmed cognac to the remaining pan juices. Flambé and sprinkle over the top of the casserole.

Serves 4

LAMB KIDNEYS IN CHAMPAGNE SAUCE *(rognons d'agneau au champagne)*

Preparation time: 15 minutes   **Cooking time:** 30 minutes

France

Ingredients

10	lamb kidneys, peeled and trimmed of fat	3	tablespoons fresh parsley, chopped
8	tablespoons butter	3	shallots, minced
½	pound mushrooms, sliced	1	tablespoon flour
	Salt	¾	cup champagne (or dry white wine)
	Freshly ground pepper	2	tablespoons beef stock
	Pinch grated nutmeg		Juice of ½ lemon

1. Prepare the kidneys by removing most of the fat and the fine membrane. Rinse under cold water. Pat dry and reserve.

2. Heat 3 tablespoons of the butter in a skillet, add the mushrooms and sauté for 5 minutes. Remove from heat and sprinkle lightly with salt and pepper. Reserve.

3. In another skillet, heat 4 tablespoons of the remaining butter. Add kidneys and cook over high heat for 5 minutes. Transfer the kidneys to a warm plate and season with salt, pepper, nutmeg and half the parsley. Keep warm.

4. In the same skillet, cook the shallots over low heat until translucent. Stir in the flour and then add the wine and the stock. Blend well. Stir in the mushrooms. Cook sauce for 10 minutes, stirring to prevent boiling. Swirl in the rest of the butter and the lemon juice. Remove from heat.

5. Cut the kidneys crosswise into slices ⅛ inch thick. Add the kidneys and the juices to the sauce. Return skillet to low heat for a few minutes to allow kidneys to warm through. Garnish the dish with the remaining parsley.

Serves 4

CALVES' BRAINS IN BURGUNDY SAUCE *(cervelles en meurette)*

France

Preparation time: 45 minutes
Brains soak—4 hours

Cooking time: 30 minutes

Ingredients

1	*pound calves' brains*
1	*onion, sliced*
2	*carrots, sliced*
	Herb bouquet (bay leaf, parsley, thyme)
1	*clove garlic, pressed*
	Salt and pepper

2	*teaspoons sugar*
3	*cups red wine*
3	*tablespoons butter*
2	*tablespoons flour*
1	*egg yolk*
8	*slices French bread, fried in butter*
	Chopped fresh parsley

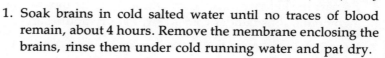

1. Soak brains in cold salted water until no traces of blood remain, about 4 hours. Remove the membrane enclosing the brains, rinse them under cold running water and pat dry.

2. In a large saucepan combine the onion, carrots, herb bouquet, garlic, salt, pepper and sugar. Place the brains on top and pour in the wine. Bring to a boil, then lower heat, cover and simmer gently for 20 to 25 minutes.

3. Remove saucepan from heat and allow brains to cool for 20 minutes. Transfer brains to a dish and keep warm.

4. Strain the sauce through a sieve into a saucepan. Over high heat, reduce sauce to about 1½ cups. Keep over low heat.

5. Prepare a *beurre manié* by blending together the butter and flour. Beat the yolk well in a bowl. Beat in ¼ cup of the sauce, a tablespoon at a time. Slowly pour mixture into the remaining sauce, then beat in the *beurre manié*. Do not boil.

6. Slice the brains and arrange them in the center of a warm serving dish. Surround with the fried bread, cover with the sauce and garnish with chopped parsley.

Serves 4

Composite Dishes and Casseroles

JANSSON'S TEMPTATION

(Janssons frestelse)

Sweden

Preparation time: 15 minutes

Baking time: 1 hour

Ingredients

8	medium potatoes, peeled and thinly sliced	16	anchovy fillets, chopped
	Freshly ground pepper	¼	cup dry bread crumbs
2	onions, minced	1½	cups heavy cream
		2	tablespoons butter

1. Set oven at 375°.

2. Place a layer of potatoes in a buttered ovenproof dish. Season lightly with pepper, then cover with a thin layer of onions and anchovies. Continue layering with the remaining potatoes, onions and anchovies, lightly seasoning the potato layers with pepper.

3. Sprinkle the top with the bread crumbs, then pour in the cream and dot with the butter.

4. Bake until the potatoes are tender when tested with a knife, about 1 hour. Serve from the baking dish.

Serves 4

HERRING, POTATO AND ONION CASSEROLE *(sillgratäng)*

Preparation time: 15 minutes   **Cooking time:** 50 minutes   *Sweden*
Herring fillets soak—overnight

Ingredients

6 salt herring fillets	Freshly ground pepper
5 potatoes, peeled and sliced thinly	2 tablespoons butter
4 onions, sliced thinly	2 tablespoons dry bread crumbs

1. Soak the salt herring fillets overnight in cold water.

2. Drain the herring fillets and pat dry, then cut into bite-size pieces.

3. Set oven at 400°.

4. In a well-buttered rectangular baking dish, arrange the potatoes, herring and onions in alternating rows. Season lightly with pepper.

5. Sprinkle the top with bread crumbs and dot with the butter.

6. Bake for 30 minutes, then turn oven heat down to 300° and continue baking until potatoes are tender, about 20 minutes. Serve immediately from the baking dish.

Serves 4

COBBLER'S PIE *(Schuster Pastete)*

Germany

Preparation time: 20 minutes
Herring fillets soak—4 hours

Baking time: 1 hour

Ingredients

1   *pound herring fillets*
1   *pint sour cream*
¼   *cup milk*
3   *pounds cooked potatoes, thinly sliced*
1   *pound cooked ham, cut in julienne strips*

2   *onions, minced*
    Dry bread crumbs for topping pie
1   *tablespoon butter*

1. Soak the herring fillets for 4 hours in a bowl of cold water.

2. Drain herring fillets and pat dry, then mince. Reserve.

3. Set oven at 350°.

4. In a bowl, blend together the sour cream and milk. Reserve.

5. Line the bottom of a well-buttered soufflé dish with a thin layer of sliced potatoes. Cover with a layer of minced herring and onions, then top with a layer of julienned ham. Continue layering with the remaining potatoes, herring, onions and ham. (End with a layer of potatoes.)

6. Cover the mixture with the sour cream and milk mixture, then top with dry bread crumbs and dot with the butter.

7. Bake cobbler's pie for 1 hour. Serve piping hot from the soufflé dish.

Serves 4 to 6

PAELLA VALENCIANA

Preparation time: 40 minutes   **Baking time:** 40 minutes

Ingredients

Spain

5	tablespoons olive oil
A	3-pound frying chicken, cut into serving pieces
⅓	cup water
1	large onion, chopped
1	clove garlic, minced
4	tablespoons butter
2	cups raw rice
¼	teaspoon saffron
3½	cups chicken stock
3	medium tomatoes, quartered
	Salt

	Freshly ground pepper
½	teaspoon cayenne pepper
A	2-pound lobster, cleaned (page 476)
1	pound hot or sweet sausage, cooked and sliced
1	cup peas, shelled
½	pound shrimp, cleaned and shelled
18	cherrystone clams, cleaned
	Fresh parsley for garnish

1. Heat the olive oil in a casserole dish and brown the chicken. Add the water, cover and simmer for 30 minutes. Remove the chicken and reserve.

2. In the same pan, sauté the onion and garlic until soft, about 5 minutes. Add the butter, rice and saffron. Stir for 5 minutes to coat the rice thoroughly, then pour in the stock. Add the tomatoes and seasonings, cover and simmer for 15 minutes.

3. In a large baking dish, assemble the paella. Start with a layer of ½ the rice mixture and cover with layers of the chicken, lobster and sausage. Cover with the remaining rice. Bake, covered, for 20 minutes, then add the peas and shrimp to the top layer of rice. Add the clams and more stock if the rice seems too dry. Cover the dish again and bake until the clams open, about 12 minutes. Discard any clams that do not open. Garnish with the parsley and serve.

Serves 8

LIBERIAN CHICKEN CASSEROLE
(jollof)

West Africa

Preparation time: 30 minutes   **Cooking time:** 30 minutes

Ingredients

¼ cup vegetable oil	Freshly ground pepper
A 3-pound chicken, cut into serving pieces	1 cup long-grained rice
½ pound ham, chopped	6 tomatoes, peeled
2 onions, chopped	6 ounces tomato paste
½ teaspoon ground allspice	3 cups chicken broth
Salt	½ pound green beans, snapped

1. Heat the oil in an enameled cast-iron casserole. Add the chicken pieces and brown evenly over moderate heat.

2. Add the ham, onions and allspice to the casserole. Season with salt and pepper. Cook over moderate heat until the onions are tender, about 5 minutes.

3. Add the rice and mix well to coat grains. Stir in the tomatoes, tomato paste and chicken broth. Top with the green beans.

4. Cover casserole and simmer for 20 minutes.

5. Check amount of liquid in casserole. Add additional stock or water, if necessary, then cover casserole again and continue simmering until rice is done, about 10 minutes.

Serves 4

CHICKEN TETRAZZINI
(spaghettini Tetrazzini)

Preparation time: 30 minutes

Ingredients

Sauce:

8 tablespoons butter

3 tablespoons flour

3 cups milk

1 teaspoon salt

 Freshly ground pepper

¼ cup Parmesan cheese, grated

1 egg yolk

—

1½ cups cooked chicken, cubed

Baking time: 20 minutes

¼ pound mushrooms, sliced

4 tablespoons butter

 Salt

 Freshly ground pepper

¼ cup white wine

1 pound spaghettini

1 cup Parmesan cheese, grated

2 tablespoons bread crumbs

Italy

1. Prepare the sauce: Melt the butter in a saucepan and add the flour. Stirring constantly, add the milk a little at a time. Stir over low heat for 10 minutes. Add the salt and pepper. Remove from the heat and stir in the cheese and egg yolk. Reserve.

2. Sauté the chicken and mushrooms in the butter for about 3 minutes. Add salt, pepper and the wine and cook over medium heat for about 5 minutes. Reserve.

3. Preheat the oven to 350°.

4. Cook the spaghettini in boiling salted water until *al dente*, about 6 to 8 minutes. Drain and return to pot. Add the sauce, the chicken-mushroom mixture and the Parmesan cheese. Mix well. Pour into a large buttered casserole and sprinkle with the bread crumbs. Bake for 20 minutes and serve.

Serves 4 to 6

BEEF TAJINE
(tajine de boeuf et haricots verts)

Morocco

Preparation time: 20 minutes　　　　**Cooking time:** 2 hours

Ingredients

2　pounds beef round, cubed	1　cinnamon stick
Salt	½　cup parsley, chopped
Freshly ground pepper	4　tomatoes, peeled and chopped
3　tablespoons olive oil	3　tablespoons tomato paste
2　onions, chopped	¾　cup water
1　teaspoon cumin	1　pound green beans, sliced lengthwise
½　teaspoon ground ginger	1　tablespoon sesame seeds, toasted
½　teaspoon turmeric	
Pinch cayenne pepper	

1. Pat the meat dry and season with salt and pepper. Heat the oil in a large casserole and brown the meat. Remove and reserve.

2. In the same pan, add the onions and sauté until lightly browned, about 10 minutes. Add the spices, parsley, tomatoes, tomato paste and water. Return the beef to the casserole, cover and simmer for 1½ to 2 hours, stirring occasionally. Add more water if necessary.

3. In a separate saucepan, cook the green beans in boiling salted water until nearly tender. Reserve.

4. Preheat the oven to 400°.

5. Place the green beans in the casserole, cover and bake for 15 minutes. Remove from the oven, sprinkle with the sesame seeds and serve with hot white rice.

Serves 4

DUTCH HOT POT *(Leyden Hutspot)*

Preparation time: 30 minutes   **Cooking time:** 1½ hours

Ingredients

The Netherlands

A 3-pound beef brisket or flank	3 knockwurst
1 soup bone	4 tablespoons beef suet or chicken fat, rendered
5 onions, chopped	Salt
6 carrots, chopped	Freshly ground pepper
6 potatoes, cubed	Cayenne pepper

1. Place the brisket (or flank) and the soup bone in a kettle. Cover generously with cold water and bring to a boil over moderately high heat. Skim the surface of the water, then lower heat and simmer meat for 1 hour.

2. Add the vegetables and knockwurst to the kettle. Return to a boil, then lower heat and simmer until brisket is tender, about ½ hour. Remove kettle from heat and discard the soup bone. Remove the brisket and knockwurst. Reserve.

3. Using a fine colander or sieve, drain the vegetables, then purée in a food mill or blender. Transfer vegetable purée to a mixing bowl. Blend in the suet (or fat), then season to taste with salt, pepper and cayenne. Reserve.

4. Remove the casing from the knockwurst. Slice the peeled knockwurst into ½-inch-thick rounds. Fold into the vegetable purée. Transfer mixture to a heated serving platter.

5. Slice the brisket. Arrange the slices on top of the vegetable purée and knockwurst. Serve immediately.

Serves 6

The strained cooking broth from this dish may be kept hot and used as an accompaniment to the dish, or it may be reserved for future use.

GOULASH WITH SAUERKRAUT
(Szeged goulasch)

Austria

Preparation time: 30 minutes

Cooking time: 1½ hours

Ingredients

1½	pounds beef chuck, cubed
	Seasoned flour for dredging meat
3	tablespoons vegetable oil
2	large onions, chopped
1	clove garlic, chopped
4	tomatoes, peeled, seeded and chopped
2	tablespoons tomato paste

	Herb bouquet (parsley, bay leaf, thyme)
1	cup white wine
1	cup water
	Salt
	Freshly ground pepper
¾	pound sauerkraut
3	potatoes, peeled
2	teaspoons paprika
½	cup sour cream

1. Dry the meat and dredge in seasoned flour.

2. Heat the oil in a large skillet. Add the meat and brown evenly over moderately high heat. Using a slotted spoon, transfer meat to an enameled cast-iron casserole. Reserve.

3. Add the onions to the skillet and sauté until lightly browned, about 10 minutes. Transfer onions to the casserole. Add the garlic, tomatoes, tomato paste, herb bouquet, white wine and water. Season with salt and pepper. Bring to a boil, then lower heat. Cover and simmer for 45 minutes.

4. While the casserole simmers, rinse the sauerkraut in cold water and squeeze dry. Add the sauerkraut, potatoes and paprika to the casserole. Re-cover and continue simmering until the potatoes are tender, about 45 minutes.

5. Correct seasoning. Stir in the sour cream and heat through. (Do not boil.)

Serves 6

CABBAGE ROLLS IN TOMATO SAUCE *(golubtsi)*

Preparation time: 30 minutes

Cooking time: 35 minutes

USSR

Ingredients

   12   *large cabbage leaves*

Stuffing:

   1   *large onion, chopped*
   6   *tablespoons butter*
   1   *pound ground round*
   ½   *pound ground pork*
   1   *cup cooked rice*
   2   *tablespoons fresh parsley, minced*
   1   *egg, lightly beaten*

      Salt
      Freshly ground pepper

Sour Cream Sauce:

   2   *tablespoons flour*
   1   *cup tomato juice*
   ½   *cup water*
   ½   *pint sour cream*
      Salt
      Freshly ground pepper
   ¼   *cup fresh dill, chopped*

1. Blanch the trimmed cabbage leaves in a pot of boiling water for 5 minutes. Refresh and drain well.

2. Sauté the onion in 2 tablespoons of the butter. Combine the onion, meats, rice and parsley. Mix thoroughly, then bind with the egg and season with salt and pepper.

3. Flatten the cabbage leaves. Place a portion of the meat mixture on the end of each leaf. Roll up the leaves, tucking the edges around the mixture. Secure with string.

4. Sauté the *golubtsi* in the remaining butter until lightly browned, about 5 minutes. Reduce heat to low, cover pan and cook gently for 30 minutes. Remove from pan and discard string. Arrange on a heated platter and keep warm.

5. Stirring constantly over moderate heat, add the flour and cook for 2 minutes. Blend in the tomato juice and water. Bring to a boil, blend in the sour cream, dill and salt and pepper. Pour sauce over the *golubtsi* and serve.

Serves 6

GROUND BEEF WITH RICE AND BEANS *(carne con arroz y frijoles)*

Cuba

Preparation time: 20 minutes   **Cooking time:** 35 minutes

Ingredients

4 slices bacon	1 cup long-grained rice
1 large onion, chopped	1 pound ground beef
2 cloves garlic, minced	3 tomatoes, peeled and quartered
3 stalks celery, chopped	A 16-ounce can kidney beans, partially drained
1 green pepper, seeded and chopped	Freshly ground pepper
2½ cups water	Dash cumin
Salt	

1. In a large skillet, fry the bacon until crisp. Remove, drain and reserve. Sauté the onion, garlic, celery and green pepper in the bacon drippings until soft, about 10 minutes.

2. Bring the water and ½ teaspoon salt to a boil in a saucepan. Add the rice, cover and simmer for 25 minutes.

3. Add the beef to the onion mixture, stirring constantly, until the meat is browned. Add the tomatoes and kidney beans. Mix and season with salt, pepper and cumin. Cover and simmer over low heat for 20 minutes. Serve the bean mixture spooned over the rice and crumble the bacon on top.

Serves 4

BLACK BEAN AND MEAT STEW
(feijoada à Brasileira)

Preparation time: 30 minutes   **Cooking time:** 5 hours   *Brazil*
Dried beef and black beans soak—overnight

Ingredients

1 *pound carne seca (sun-dried salted beef)*	1½ *pounds chuck beef*
3 *cups dry black beans*	2 *tablespoons oil*
A *3-pound smoked tongue*	3 *cups onions, chopped*
1 *pound pork sausage*	2 *cloves garlic, minced*
1 *pound linguica defumada (Portuguese sausage)*	¼ *cup parsley, chopped*
A *½-pound piece bacon*	1 *tomato, chopped*
	2 *chili peppers, chopped*
	Salt and pepper

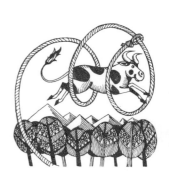

1. Soak the dried beef and black beans overnight in separate bowls of cold water.

2. Place the tongue in a soup kettle and cover with water. Simmer until tongue is tender, about 2½ hours. Remove from heat and cool tongue in its broth. Skin and trim the tongue.

3. Place the beans in a large kettle and cover with cold water. Cover and simmer for 30 minutes.

4. Drain the dried beef, then cut into 1-inch cubes. Add all the meats to beans. Cover and simmer until the meats and beans are tender, about 2 hours.

5. Heat the oil in a skillet. Sauté the onions, garlic, parsley, tomato and peppers until tender, about 5 minutes. Add 1 cup of the cooked beans to the vegetables and mash. Simmer for 5 minutes. Stir the vegetable mixture into the large pot of beans. Adjust seasonings and heat through.

6. Remove meats, slice and arrange on a heated platter. Serve the vegetable mixture separately.

Serves 8 to 10

SOUTH AMERICAN MIXED-MEATS STEW *(puchero)*

Uruguay

Preparation time: 30 minutes

Cooking time: 2 hours

Ingredients

2	*pounds stewing beef, cubed*
1	*small smoked ham butt*
2 to 3	*sweet sausages*
	Salt
2	*onions, quartered*
3	*carrots, sliced*
½	*small cabbage, cut in wedges*
4	*potatoes, peeled and quartered*
1	*stalk celery, chopped*

	Small hot chili peppers, to taste
1½	*cups fresh corn kernels*
1	*green pepper, quartered*
2	*turnips, quartered*
3	*cloves garlic, minced*
3	*sprigs fresh parsley, chopped*
	Herb bouquet (bay leaf, oregano, cumin)
	Freshly ground pepper
1	*cup cooked chick-peas*

1. Place the beef, ham and sausages in a soup kettle. Cover with cold water, salt generously and bring to a boil. Reduce heat, skim the surface and simmer until tender, about 1½ hours.

2. Add the remaining ingredients. Bring rapidly to a boil, then lower heat, cover and simmer until vegetables are tender, about 30 minutes. Skim the fat from the broth and correct seasoning. Discard the herb bouquet.

3. Transfer the ham butt and sausages to a carving board. Slice into bite-sized pieces. Return to the casserole and heat through. To serve, arrange the meats and vegetables on a heated serving platter. Serve the broth in a tureen.

Serves 8

CORSICAN MEAT AND MACARONI CASSEROLE *(stuffato)*

Preparation time: 20 minutes   **Cooking time:** 3 hours   *France*

Ingredients

½ *cup olive oil*	1 *tomato, chopped*
6 *slices bacon*	4 *cups red wine*
½ *pound beef (sirloin tip, eye round or bottom round), cut in serving pieces*	1 *cup water*
	Salt
	Freshly ground pepper
½ *pound veal shoulder, cut in serving pieces*	*Herb bouquet (rosemary, bay leaf, parsley)*
½ *pound pork shoulder, cut in serving pieces*	8 *ounces macaroni*
1 *onion, sliced*	1½ *cup Gruyère or other Swiss cheese, grated*
1 *clove garlic, minced*	

1. Heat the olive oil in a skillet. Sauté the bacon strips and the meats over moderately high heat until nicely browned, about 10 minutes. Remove with slotted spoon and drain.

2. Transfer the meats to an enameled cast-iron casserole. Add the onion, garlic and tomato. Pour in the wine and water. Salt and pepper to taste, then add the herb bouquet. Bring to a boil, then lower heat, cover and simmer gently until meats are tender, about 2½ hours.

3. Set oven at 350°.

4. Drop the macaroni into a pot of boiling, salted water. Cook until *al dente*, about 10 minutes, then drain and reserve.

5. When the meats are tender, remove with a slotted spoon and reserve. Reduce casserole liquid to 2 cups over high heat. Arrange a layer of meat in a large ovenproof dish. Cover with a layer of macaroni and then a layer of cheese. Pour in the reduced casserole liquid and bake for 20 minutes.

Serves 6

COTTAGE PIE

Great Britain

Preparation time: 35 minutes   **Baking time:** 15 minutes

Ingredients

6	tablespoons butter
2	onions, chopped
2	cloves garlic, minced
1	pound beef, ground
4	carrots, sliced
1½	tablespoons tomato paste
2	tablespoons fresh parsley, chopped
1	tablespoon dried thyme

1	bay leaf
1½	cups beef stock
	Salt
	Freshly ground pepper
6	medium potatoes, peeled
1	sprig mint
¼	cup Swiss or Cheddar cheese, grated

1. Heat 2 tablespoons of the butter in a skillet. Sauté the onions, garlic and beef over moderate heat 10 minutes. Add the carrots, tomato paste, herbs and stock. Mix thoroughly, then season heavily with salt and pepper. Bring mixture to a boil, then lower heat and simmer until most of the stock has evaporated and the carrots are tender, about 20 minutes. Discard bay leaf. Keep warm.

2. While the meat mixture simmers, drop the potatoes and mint into a pot of rapidly boiling salted water and cook until tender, about 20 minutes. Drain and discard the mint. Return the potatoes to the pot and toss briefly over low heat to remove excess moisture. Transfer potatoes to a bowl and mash well. Beat in the remaining butter and season to taste with salt and pepper.

3. Set oven at 375° or preheat broiler.

4. Spoon the meat mixture into an oven-proof dish. Cover with the mashed potatoes, smoothing the surface. Sprinkle with the grated cheese, then bake for 15 minutes or place briefly under broiler.

Serves 4

MEAT TIMBALES *(bobotee)*

Preparation time: 20 minutes   **Baking time:** 45 minutes

Union of South Africa

Ingredients

2 *tablespoons butter*	*Juice of 1 lemon*
1 *onion, chopped*	1 *ounce almonds, chopped*
1 *clove garlic, minced*	8 *dried apricots, soaked and chopped*
1 *slice white bread*	
1 *cup milk*	1½ *ounces raisins*
2 *eggs, beaten*	¼ *cup chutney*
1 *pound ground beef or lamb*	*Salt*
1 *tablespoon curry powder*	*Freshly ground pepper*

1. Preheat oven to 350°.

2. Melt the butter and sauté the onion and garlic for 10 minutes.

3. Soak the bread in the milk, then squeeze dry. Beat the eggs into the milk.

4. Combine the meat, bread and onions with the remaining ingredients. Stir in half the egg-milk mixture.

5. Place the mixture in a greased baking dish or 6 individual casseroles. Top with the remaining egg mixture and bake until the custard sets, about 45 minutes. Serve with plain rice.

Serves 6

BEEF, LAMB AND PORK HOT POT

(karjalanpaisti)

Finland

Preparation time: 20 minutes

Cooking time: 5 hours

Ingredients

1   *pound beef chuck, cut into 1½-inch cubes*

1   *pound boneless stewing lamb or mutton, cut into 1½-inch cubes*

1   *pound boneless pork shoulder, cut into 1½-inch cubes*

5   *onions, thinly sliced*
     Allspice
     Salt

4   *cups hot water or beef stock*

1. Set oven at 275°.

2. Layer the meats and sliced onion in an enameled cast-iron casserole, alternating the ingredients. Season each layer with allspice and salt.

3. Pour in the water or stock, cover and bake until the meats are tender, about 5 hours.

Serves 8

GASCON LAMB AND CHICKEN BOILED DINNER *(pot-au-feu du Lot)*

Preparation time: 20 minutes   **Cooking time:** 3 hours   *France*

Ingredients

A	4-pound piece lamb shoulder			Salt
1	veal knuckle			Freshly ground pepper
	Herb bouquet (juniper berries, bay leaf, parsley, thyme)	A	3-pound stewing chicken, trussed
1	celery stalk with leaves	8	carrots, quartered
1	onion stuck with 3 cloves	3	small white turnips, scraped
2	cloves garlic	4	leeks
		1	cup dry white wine

1. Put the lamb and veal knuckle in a large soup kettle. Cover with cold water.

2. Bring to a boil. Skimming the surface occasionally, continue to boil until the broth is clear.

3. Add the herb bouquet, celery, onion, garlic, salt and pepper. Lower heat, cover and simmer for 1½ hours.

4. Add the chicken, carrots, turnips, leeks and wine. Continue cooking until chicken is tender, about 1½ hours. Taste and correct seasoning, if necessary.

5. To serve, arrange the meats, chicken and vegetables on a hot platter and strain the broth into a warmed soup tureen.

Serves 6 to 8

LAMB AND CHICKEN STEW
WITH SEMOLINA *(couscous)*

Morocco

Preparation time: 1½ hours
Couscous stands—15 minutes

Cooking time: 3 hours

Ingredients

½	cup olive oil
3	pounds lamb, cubed
A	3-pound chicken, cut into serving pieces
3	onions, chopped
3	leeks, cleaned and split
3	green peppers, seeded and cut in strips
4	carrots, cut in 2-inch lengths
4	turnips, cut in 2-inch lengths
2	cloves garlic, pressed
1	tablespoon coriander
	Salt
	Freshly ground pepper

Couscous:

1	pound couscous (wheat-grain semolina)
1	teaspoon saffron
1	cup hot water

2½	tablespoons butter, at room temperature
¼	cup olive oil
¼	pound raisins
3	zucchini, sliced
3	tomatoes, peeled and quartered
1	teaspoon paprika
1	twenty-ounce can chick-peas

Hot Sauce:

2	cups meat-vegetable broth
⅛	teaspoon turmeric
1	teaspoon fresh ginger root, grated
½ to ¾	teaspoon harissa (red pimiento concentrate) or cayenne pepper

1. Heat the olive oil in the bottom section of a *couscoussière* or in a large soup kettle. Add the lamb, chicken, onions, leeks, peppers, carrots and turnips. Sauté evenly over moderately high heat until lightly browned, about 10 minutes. Cover the meats and vegetables with cold water. Add the garlic, coriander and season to taste with salt and pepper. Bring rapidly to a boil, then lower heat and simmer for about 3 hours.

2. Prepare the *couscous:* a) Spread out the *couscous* on a large platter; sprinkle on the saffron and hot water, then dot with 1 tablespoon of the butter; b) rub the moistened grains between your palms until the water has been completely absorbed, then cover platter tightly with aluminum foil and let stand 15 minutes; c) stir the *couscous* thoroughly, then transfer it to the upper section of the *couscoussière* (or a cheesecloth-lined sieve that fits snugly above the simmering stew in the kettle); d) place the meats and vegetables on top and steam until the grains are puffy, about 30 to 45 minutes. Spread the partially cooked *couscous* on a platter and sprinkle with a little cold water, the olive oil and 1 tablespoon of butter.

3. Add the raisins, zucchini, tomatoes and paprika to the simmering stew. Mix thoroughly. Continue simmering.

4. Place the top sections of the *couscoussière* over the simmering stew. A handful at a time, add the *couscous* to the *couscoussière*, making sure each addition has warmed thoroughly before adding the next. Steam until grains are well swollen and separate easily, about 30 minutes.

5. While the *couscous* steams, drain the chick-peas, then transfer to a sieve and steam over lightly salted boiling water until tender, about 20 minutes. Drain and keep hot.

6. When the *couscous* is done, transfer to a platter and work in the remaining ½ teaspoon butter. Keep hot. (Allow meats and vegetables to continue simmering until tender.) When the meats and vegetables are done, remove and keep warm. Strain the cooking liquid into a saucepan and keep hot.

7. Prepare the hot sauce: Transfer 2 cups of the strained broth to another saucepan. Bring to a boil, then stir in the turmeric, ginger, harissa (or cayenne pepper) and nutmeg. Keep hot.

8. To serve, pile the *couscous* in the center of a large wooden or earthenware serving platter. Make a well in the center and fill with the meats and vegetables. Surround with the chick-peas. Serve the hot sauce and meat-vegetable broth in separate sauceboats.

Serves 10 to 12

Morocco

AEGEAN PASTA WITH LAMB *(pastitsio)*

Greece

Preparation time: 2 hours

Baking time: 45 minutes

Ingredients

5	tablespoons butter
2	onions, chopped
5	garlic cloves, minced
1	pound lamb, ground
2½	cups Italian plum tomatoes, chopped
	Pinch oregano
	Salt and pepper
¼	teaspoon each nutmeg, allspice and cinnamon
3	eggs, lightly beaten
¾	cup grated Parmesan

1	large eggplant, peeled and thinly sliced
	Olive oil
3	cups macaroni, cooked

Custard Sauce:

2	tablespoons butter
2	tablespoons flour
3	cups milk, heated
	Salt and pepper
4	eggs, lightly beaten
1	cup ricotta cheese

1. Sauté the lamb, onions and garlic in 3 tablespoons of butter for 10 minutes. Blend in the tomatoes and seasonings. Cook uncovered until the liquid is nearly evaporated, about 45 minutes. Remove from heat and allow to cool slightly, then stir in the eggs and ½ cup of the Parmesan cheese.

2. Preheat broiler. Arrange the eggplant on a baking sheet, sprinkle lightly with olive oil and broil until both sides are golden. Turn oven to 325°.

3. Add the macaroni to the meat mixture. Pour into a greased baking dish. Sprinkle with half the remaining Parmesan cheese, then layer in the eggplant slices.

4. Melt the butter for the custard sauce. Sprinkle in the flour and stir over low heat for 2 minutes. Add the milk, salt and pepper, stir over low heat until mixture thickens, about 5 minutes. Blend a little of the heated mixture into the eggs, then stir the eggs into the saucepan. Blend in the ricotta. Pour the custard over the eggplant. Dot with remaining butter and cheese. Bake until custard sets, about 45 minutes.

Serves 6 to 8

MOUSSAKA

Preparation time: 30 minutes   **Baking time:** 1¼ hours

Ingredients

Bulgaria

4	*medium eggplants, peeled and sliced*		*Freshly ground pepper*
1	*onion, chopped*		*Pinch oregano*
2	*tablespoons butter*		*Olive oil*
2	*pounds ground lamb*	4	*tomatoes, sliced*
2	*teaspoons salt*	1	*cup yoghurt*
1	*teaspoon paprika*	4	*egg yolks*
		½	*cup flour*

1. Salt both sides of the eggplant slices and let stand 1 hour.

2. Sauté the onions in the butter for 10 minutes. Add the lamb, salt, paprika, pepper and oregano. Brown the mixture and reserve.

3. Preheat the oven to 250°.

4. Sprinkle the eggplant slices with olive oil and broil under the flame until lightly browned on one side, then turn and broil on other side. Reset oven to 350°.

5. In a greased baking dish, arrange alternate layers of the meat mixture with the eggplant slices. Top with the tomato slices. Bake for 1 hour.

6. Combine the yoghurt, egg yolks and flour, mixing well. Pour over the casserole and bake until custard is golden, about 15 minutes.

Serves 6

ALSATIAN MEAT AND POTATO CASSEROLE (beckenhofe)

France

Preparation time: 20 minutes   **Cooking time:** 3 hours

Ingredients

2½	*pounds potatoes, peeled and thinly sliced*
¾	*pound lean pork (boned shoulder butt), thinly sliced*
¾	*pound lamb (boned shoulder), thinly sliced*
1	*pound onions, thinly sliced*

Salt
Freshly ground pepper
Freshly grated nutmeg
Herb bouquet (bay leaf, parsley, thyme)
2   *tablespoons butter*
2½   *cups dry white wine*

1. Set oven at 325°.

2. Place a layer of potatoes in a buttered casserole, add a layer of pork and lamb and then a layer of onions. Season with salt, pepper and a dash of nutmeg. Continue alternating layers, seasoning each layer with salt, pepper and nutmeg and finishing with a layer of potatoes.

3. Bury the herb bouquet in the middle of the casserole, then dot casserole with the butter and pour in the white wine.

4. Cover tightly and bake until meat is tender, about 3 hours. Serve from the casserole.

Serves 6

ANDALUSIAN STEW *(olla podrida)*

Preparation time: 30 minutes
Chick-peas soak—overnight

Cooking time: 2¾ hours

Spain

Ingredients

¼ cup olive oil	4 carrots, chopped
¼ pound salt pork, diced	4 onions, quartered
¼ pound ham hock, cubed	½ pound green beans
¾ pound pork loin, cubed	1 small cabbage, quartered
¾ pound chicken, chopped	3 medium potatoes, quartered
Salt	3 cloves garlic, pressed
Freshly ground pepper	Pinch saffron
3 quarts cold water	½ teaspoon cumin
2 cups cooked chick-peas	Pinch coriander
6 turnips	

1. In a large casserole, heat the olive oil. Add the salt pork and sauté over fairly high heat for 5 minutes. Remove with a slotted spoon and reserve.

2. Add the pieces of ham, pork and chicken to the casserole. Brown over high heat, then season with salt and pepper.

3. Return the reserved salt pork to the casserole. Pour in the cold water and bring rapidly to a boil. Skim the surface. Add the chick-peas and return to a boil, then lower heat, cover and simmer gently for 1½ hours. Add the vegetables, re-cover and continue simmering for 1 more hour.

4. Season the stew with the garlic, saffron, cumin and coriander, then remove vegetables and meats with a slotted spoon and arrange on a heated serving platter. Bring broth to a boil and reduce slightly over high heat. Pour broth over meat and vegetables. Serve immediately.

Serves 4 to 6

CASSOULET

Preparation time: 20 minutes
Beans soak—overnight

Cooking time: 3 hours

France

Ingredients

1½	pounds white beans
4½	cups beef bouillon
¼	pound pork rind or bacon, blanched
2	carrots, quartered
3	whole cloves garlic
1	onion
3	tablespoons flour
½	cup tomato purée
10	tablespoons pork or goose fat (page 475)
½	pound pork, cubed

1	pound lamb, cubed
¼	pound lean salt pork
2	onions, chopped
3	cloves garlic, minced
	Herb bouquet (thyme, bay leaf, rosemary)
	Salt and pepper
¾	pound garlic sausage
½	pound pork sausages
1	cup fresh bread crumbs
¼	cup fresh parsley

1. Soak the beans overnight in cold water. Drain and place in a soup kettle. Add the bouillon, pork rind, carrots, garlic and onion. Cover and simmer for 1 hour. Remove the pork rind and the beans. Reserve. Strain the bean liquid, sprinkle with the flour and mix in the tomato purée.

2. Heat 6 tablespoons of the fat in a casserole. Brown the cubes of fresh pork, lamb and salt pork. Pour the bean liquid over the meats, then add the onions and seasonings. Cover and simmer for 1¾ hours, then add the garlic sausage. Simmer for another 20 minutes.

3. Set oven at 350°. Heat the remaining fat and brown the pork sausages. Slice the pork rind into thin strips and layer in a large earthenware casserole. Cover with half the beans.

4. Discard the herb bouquet. Transfer the pork, lamb and salt pork to the beans. Cover meat with the remaining beans, then add the sausages. Pour the liquid from the casserole into the *cassoulet*, then sprinkle with bread crumbs and parsley and bake for 1 hour, basting occasionally.

Serves 8

PORK AND SEAFOOD
MAGELLAN *(porco com amêijoas)*

Preparation time: 30 minutes
Pork marinates—overnight

Cooking time: 1 hour

Portugal

Ingredients

Marinade:

¾   cup dry white wine
1   tablespoon paprika
1   bay leaf
2   cloves
3   cloves garlic, pressed

2   pounds lean boneless
    pork, cubed
2   tablespoons lard

2   onions, sliced
2   cloves garlic, minced
4   tomatoes, chopped
2   pounds clams or
    mussels, scrubbed

Chopped fresh parsley
Chopped fresh
coriander
Lemon wedges

1. Combine the marinade ingredients and coat the pork cubes
    thoroughly. Cover bowl and refrigerate overnight, turning
    occasionally. Remove pork from marinade and pat dry. Re-
    serve the marinade.

2. Heat 1 tablespoon of the lard in a large frying pan and brown
    the pork. Add the marinade to the skillet, cover and simmer
    for 30 minutes. Remove cover before end of cooking time to
    reduce liquid by half. Reserve.

3. Melt the remaining lard and sauté the onions and garlic for 5
    minutes. Add the tomatoes, the reserved pork and its liquid.
    Simmer for 10 minutes.

4. Add the clams, cover and simmer over moderate heat until
    the clams open, about 5 minutes. Discard bay leaf and any
    clams that do not open. Arrange the pork and clams (in their
    shells) on a heated serving platter. Top with the sauce from
    the casserole, then garnish with parsley, coriander and
    lemon wedges.

Serves 6

PORK AND SAUERKRAUT
(choucroute à l'Alsacienne)

France

Preparation time: 15 minutes

Cooking time: 4 hours

Ingredients

2	onions, sliced	2	cups dry white wine
3	tablespoons goose fat (page 475) or olive oil	2	cups beef bouillon
1	pound sauerkraut, rinsed and drained	A	1-pound piece of lean bacon or salt pork
2	apples, peeled and sliced	4	smoked pork loin chops
20	juniper berries	3	tablespoons kirsch
6 to 8	peppercorns	8	potatoes, in jackets
		4	frankfurters

1. In a large enameled cast-iron casserole, sauté the onions in the goose fat (or oil). Add the sauerkraut and apples. Tie the juniper berries and peppercorns in muslin and add to the pot. Pour in enough wine and bouillon to cover the sauerkraut. Cover and cook over low heat for 2½ hours.

2. While the sauerkraut is stewing, blanch the bacon (or salt pork) in 3 quarts of simmering water for 15 minutes. Drain.

3. Add the bacon and the pork chops to the sauerkraut. Cover and simmer for 1 hour, then stir in the kirsch, re-cover and continue simmering for an additional 30 minutes.

4. Boil the potatoes in salted water until tender and then peel. Keep warm.

5. In a separate saucepan, simmer the frankfurters in water for 15 minutes.

6. Place the sauerkraut in a serving dish. Cut the bacon into slices and arrange on top with the chops. Surround the sauerkraut with the potatoes and frankfurters.

Serves 4

PORK AND VEAL PIE *(tourte Lorraine)*

Preparation time: 25 minutes
Meats marinate—24 hours

Baking time: 50 minutes
Pastry chills—1 hour

France

Ingredients

½   *pound pork fillet*
½   *pound veal*

Marinade:

½   *cup dry white wine*
2   *shallots, minced*
2   *teaspoons salt*
   Freshly ground pepper
⅛   *teaspoon allspice*

Flaky Pastry:

2¾   *cups flour*
10   *tablespoons butter*
½   *cup iced water*
1   *teaspoon salt*

3   *eggs*
½   *cup cream*

1. Cut the pork fillet and the veal into julienne strips.

2. In a glass bowl, combine the marinade ingredients listed above. Add the julienned pork and veal. Cover and marinate in the refrigerator for 24 hours.

3. Prepare flaky pastry (**page 474**) with the ingredients listed above. Chill for 1 hour.

4. Set oven at 425°. Roll out ⅔ of the pastry into a rectangle ¼ inch thick. Place on a buttered baking sheet.

5. Drain the marinated meats and pat dry. Arrange on the pastry, leaving a ¾-inch margin around the edge of the pastry. Roll out the rest of the pastry to form the top crust. (This should be thinner than the bottom portion.) Place pastry top over the meat, moisten the edges and seal. Cut a ½-inch opening in the top crust.

6. Beat 1 egg well in a small bowl, then brush on the top crust for a glaze. Bake pie for 40 minutes. Remove from oven. Beat together the remaining eggs and the cream. Pour the mixture into the pie opening. Return pie to oven for 10 more minutes. Serve immediately.

Serves 6

EASTER PIE *(pâte de Pâques de Berry)*

France

Preparation time: 30 minutes
Pastry chills—2 hours

Baking time: 1 hour

Ingredients

Flaky Pastry:

2¾	cups flour
10	tablespoons butter
½	cup ice water
1	teaspoon salt

Filling:

4	hard-cooked eggs, peeled and halved

1	pound sausage meat
3	tablespoons fresh parsley, chopped
1	tablespoon salt
1	tablespoon pepper
⅛	teaspoon ground allspice
1	beaten egg for glazing

1. Using the ingredients listed above, prepare the flaky pastry (page 474). Chill for 2 hours.

2. In a bowl, combine the sausage meat, parsley, salt, pepper and allspice.

3. Set oven at 325°. Roll out ⅔ of the pastry into a rectangle about ½ inch thick. Cut off the corners to form a 6-sided piece of pastry. Place on a buttered baking sheet.

4. Spread half the sausage mixture in the middle of the pastry, leaving a fairly wide border. Place the hard-cooked eggs on top, cut side down, then add the rest of the filling.

5. Cover filling with a 6-sided pastry lid made from remaining dough. Moisten, pinch and seal the edges. Make 2 or 3 slits in the lid. Brush pie with the beaten egg and bake for 1 hour. Serve at room temperature.

Serves 4 to 6

HAM AND PORK CUSTARD
(rigodon de Basse-Bourgogne)

Preparation time: 10 minutes   **Baking time:** 30 minutes   *France*

Ingredients

½ *pound ham, sliced*	*Salt*
½ *pound cooked pork, sliced*	6 *eggs*
3 *cups milk*	⅓ *cup flour*
	1 *tablespoon butter*

1. Set oven at 325°.

2. Arrange the meats in a buttered 2-quart ovenproof dish. Reserve.

3. Pour the milk into a saucepan, salt lightly, bring to a boil, then lower heat.

4. In a mixing bowl, beat together the eggs and the flour. Beating constantly, add the hot milk.

5. Pour custard mixture over the meat, then dot with the butter.

6. Bake until set, about 30 minutes. Serve warm or cold as a breakfast or light luncheon dish.

Serves 4 to 6

This savory custard somewhat resembles a **quiche.** *In Burgundy it has many variations. Without meat and made with sweetened milk, the* **rigodon** *is often topped with fruit purée to serve as dessert.*

FRIED NOODLES WITH PORK

(tzu ru chao mien)

China

Preparation time: 20 minutes
Cooked noodles chill—24 hours

Cooking time: 10 minutes

Ingredients

8 ounces Chinese or other egg noodles	½ pound boneless pork or chicken, julienned
7 tablespoons peanut oil	2 tablespoons soy sauce
10 dried Chinese mushrooms	1 tablespoon Chinese rice wine or dry sherry
1 pound fresh mung bean sprouts or 1 large can bean sprouts	¼ teaspoon salt
	1 clove garlic, minced
1 slice ginger, minced	3 scallions, minced

1. Cook the noodles in a large pot of rapidly boiling unsalted water until tender, about 5 to 8 minutes. Drain and spread out on a platter to cool. Toss with 1 tablespoon of the oil, then cover and refrigerate for at least 24 hours.

2. Soak the mushrooms in warm water for ½ hour. Pat dry. Discard stems and slice caps into julienne strips. Reserve. Rinse bean sprouts. Discard husks, drain and pat dry.

4. Place a wok (or skillet) over high heat for 1 minute. Add 2 tablespoons of the oil and heat for ½ minute. Add the ginger and stir-fry for 1 minute. Add the pork (or chicken) and stir-fry for 3 minutes. Remove from heat. Mix in 1 tablespoon of the soy sauce, the Chinese rice wine and salt. Remove ingredients from wok and reserve.

5. Return wok to high heat. Add 2 more tablespoons of the oil to the wok. Wait ½ minute, then add the garlic, bean sprouts, scallions and mushrooms. Stir-fry for 2 minutes. Season with salt. Remove ingredients from pan and reserve.

6. Heat the remaining oil in the wok and stir-fry the noodles for 1 minute. Return all the reserved ingredients. Mix well and season with the remaining soy sauce. Serve immediately.

Serves 4

LASAGNE AL FORNO

Preparation time: 2¼ hours   **Baking time:** 45 minutes

Ingredients

Italy

1	*pound ground beef*
1	*large onion, chopped*
1	*clove garlic, minced*
A	*1-pound can Italian plum tomatoes*
2	*eight-ounce cans tomato sauce*
2	*teaspoons oregano*
1	*teaspoon basil*
2	*tablespoons fresh parsley, chopped*

2	*teaspoons salt*
1	*tablespoon sugar*
½	*pound cooked sweet or hot Italian sausage, sliced*
½	*pound lasagne noodles*
3	*cups ricotta cheese*
1	*cup freshly grated Parmesan cheese*
2	*cups mozzarella cheese, shredded*

1. Sauté the beef, onion and garlic in a large saucepan until the meat is brown and the onion is tender, about 5 minutes. Drain off any fat. Add the plum tomatoes, tomato sauce, 1 teaspoon of the oregano, basil, parsley, 1 teaspoon salt and the sugar. Stir well and heat to boiling. Add the sausage and simmer, uncovered, for about 1½ hours.

2. While the sauce is cooking, prepare the lasagne noodles, according to package directions. This should take about 25 minutes. Drain and separate the noodles.

3. Preheat the oven to 350°. Mix together the ricotta, ½ cup of the Parmesan cheese, 1 teaspoon salt and the remaining teaspoon of oregano.

4. In an ungreased 13 × 9 × 2½-inch baking dish, assemble the lasagne. Start with a layer of ¼ of the sauce, then ⅓ of the noodles, ⅓ of the ricotta mixture and ⅓ of the mozzarella. Repeat twice. End with the remaining sauce and sprinkle with the remaining Parmesan cheese. Bake for 45 minutes. Remove from oven and let stand for 10 minutes before cutting and serving.

Serves 8 to 10

CHINESE FRIED RICE *(chow fan)*

China

Preparation time: 10 minutes   **Cooking time:** 15 minutes

Ingredients

5 tablespoons peanut oil or vegetable oil	½ pound raw shrimp, shelled and deveined
2 eggs, lightly beaten	½ pound ham, minced
8 scallions, minced	½ cup peas
1 thick slice fresh ginger root, minced	3 cups cooked rice
	2 tablespoons soy sauce

1. Place a wok (or 10-inch skillet) over high heat for 1 minute. Add 2 tablespoons of the oil and swirl pan for ½ minute. Lower heat and pour in the beaten eggs with a few scallions. Cook until eggs set, then transfer to a bowl and break up into small pieces. Reserve.

2. Swirl 1 more tablespoon oil into the wok. Heat through, then add the ginger and stir-fry over moderate heat for 1 minute.

3. Add the shrimp and stir-fry over high heat until firm and pink, about 2 minutes. Add the ham and stir-fry for 1 minute. Add the peas and stir-fry for 1 more minute. Remove all ingredients from wok and reserve.

4. Heat the remaining 2 tablespoons oil in the wok for ½ minute. Add the cooked rice and stir-fry for 2 to 3 minutes. Stir in the soy sauce. Return all the ingredients to the wok, mix briefly over high heat, then transfer to a platter and serve immediately.

Serves 4 to 6

Meatless Dishes and Vegetables

BAKED EGGS WITH BÉCHAMEL SAUCE *(oeufs Brayens)*

France

Preparation time: 10 minutes

Baking time: 20 minutes

Ingredients

4	eggs
¼	cup cream
	Salt
	Freshly ground pepper

Béchamel Sauce:

2	tablespoons butter
2	tablespoons flour
1	cup milk

2	tablespoons cream
	Salt
	Freshly ground pepper
4	slices white bread, toasted and buttered
	Chopped fresh parsley for garnish

1. Set oven at 350°.

2. Beat the eggs well, as for an omelet, and add the cream, salt and pepper.

3. Butter 4 individual ovenproof ramekins and pour ¼ of the egg mixture into each one. Place ramekins on a shallow baking pan filled with hot water and bake until set, about 20 minutes.

4. While the eggs are baking, prepare the béchamel sauce (page 471), using the above-listed ingredients. Keep warm.

5. When eggs are done, turn out the ramekins onto slices of buttered toast. Cover with béchamel sauce and sprinkle with chopped parsley.

Serves 2

BAKED EGGS EINDHOVEN
(Gebakken Eieren met Vien en Kaas)

The
Netherlands

Preparation time: 10 minutes   **Baking time:** 15 minutes

Ingredients

4	*tablespoons butter*
1	*onion, grated*
	Salt
½	*cup Cheddar cheese,*
	grated

6	*eggs*
½	*cup heavy cream*
	Cayenne pepper

1. Preheat oven to 350°.

2. In a small frying pan, heat the butter. Add the grated onion and sauté over moderate heat until onion is translucent, about 5 minutes. Remove from heat.

3. Pour the sautéed onions into a shallow baking dish. Salt lightly, then sprinkle with ½ the grated cheese.

4. One by one, gently break the eggs onto the bed of cheese. (Do not break the yolks.) Cover with the heavy cream, then top with the remaining grated cheese.

5. Sprinkle dish with cayenne, then bake for 15 minutes. Serve piping hot from the baking dish.

Serves 4 to 6

CORSICAN CHEESE OMELET
(omelette au broccio)

France

Preparation time: 5 minutes   **Cooking time:** 6 minutes

Ingredients

6   *eggs*
3   *tablespoons cold water*
⅛   *teaspoon crushed mint*
    Salt
    Freshly ground pepper

3   *tablespoons butter*
1   *cup Broccio or other fresh goat cheese*
    Parsley sprigs for garnish

1. In a bowl, combine eggs and water. Beat eggs until light and fluffy, then add the mint and season with salt and pepper.

2. Place a large omelet pan over moderate heat. Heat until a drop of water sprinkled in pan disappears immediately, then swirl in the butter.

3. When the foam of the butter begins to subside, quickly pour in the eggs. Using the flat side of a fork, briskly swirl the eggs in the pan until they begin to set. (Shake pan back and forth while stirring to prevent omelet from sticking.)

4. Crumble in the cheese, fold omelet over and remove from heat. Garnish with parsley sprigs and serve.

Serves 2

BASQUE EGGS WITH PIPÉRADE SAUCE *(oeufs à la pipérade)*

Preparation time: 15 minutes   **Cooking time:** 30 minutes

France

Ingredients

Pipérade:

- 2   tablespoons olive oil
- 2   green peppers, seeded and thinly sliced
- 1   small hot red pepper, chopped
- 1   onion, chopped
- 2   cloves garlic, minced
-      Salt
-      Freshly ground pepper

- 2   pounds tomatoes, peeled, seeded and chopped
- ¼   teaspoon sugar
- 8   slices of ham, cut in strips
- 2   tablespoons olive oil
- 8   eggs, lightly beaten
-      Fresh parsley for garnish

1. Prepare the *pipérade:* a) Heat the olive oil in a skillet; b) add the green peppers, hot pepper, onion and garlic; c) season with salt and pepper and sauté until onion is translucent; d) add the tomatoes and sugar, cover and simmer gently for 15 minutes; e) uncover and continue to cook until liquid has evaporated; f) correct seasoning. Keep warm.

2. In another skillet, brown the ham in the olive oil. Remove ham and keep warm.

3. Stirring constantly over high heat, pour eggs into the skillet in which the ham was cooked. Continue stirring until lightly scrambled. With a spatula, transfer the eggs to a hot platter and spoon the *pipérade* over them. Surround with the reserved ham and garnish with fresh parsley. Serve immediately.

Serves 4

EGGS POACHED IN WINE SAUCE
(oeufs à la Bourguignonne ou en meurette)

France

Preparation time: 30 minutes   **Cooking time:** 10 minutes

Ingredients

Meurette Sauce:

1	onion, sliced
2	shallots, sliced
2	cloves garlic, minced
2	leeks (white part only), sliced
2	carrots, sliced
2½	cups red Burgundy wine
1	herb bouquet (rosemary, basil, dill)

	Salt
	Freshly ground pepper
1	teaspoon sugar
3	tablespoons cognac
1	tablespoon flour
3	tablespoons butter
8	eggs
8	slices French bread, fried in butter

1. Prepare the *meurette* sauce: a) In a saucepan combine the vegetables, wine, herb bouquet, salt, pepper and sugar; b) bring to a boil, then lower heat and simmer gently for 15 minutes; c) using a fine sieve, strain the sauce into a skillet; d) add the cognac and flambé. Keep sauce over moderate heat.

2. Prepare a *beurre manié* (**page 471**) by kneading the flour and butter together. Reserve.

3. Poach the eggs in the simmering sauce. Transfer the poached eggs to a warm platter and keep hot.

4. Thicken the *meurette* with the *beurre manié*. Correct seasoning. Place the eggs on the fried bread and cover with the sauce. Serve immediately.

Serves 4

VARIATION: *In lower Burgundy the* **meurette** *is made with dry white wine, and sautéed mushrooms are added to the sauce.*

FRIED EGGS WITH HAM AND EGGPLANT *(oeufs frits à la Gasconne)*

Preparation time: 25 minutes
Eggplant stands—1 hour

Cooking time: 10 minutes

France

Ingredients

1	eggplant, peeled and sliced
	Salt
6	tablespoons olive oil
8	slices ham

8	eggs
1½	cups tomato sauce flavored with garlic
	Chopped fresh parsley for garnish

1. Sprinkle the eggplant slices with salt and allow to stand for 1 hour. Pat dry.

2. Heat half the oil in a skillet and sauté the eggplant slices until tender, about 5 minutes on each side. Arrange on a heated platter. Keep warm.

3. In another skillet, heat the remaining oil. Brown the ham and fry the eggs.

4. In a small saucepan, heat the tomato sauce. Keep warm.

5. Arrange the ham and eggs on top of the eggplant, cover with the tomato sauce and sprinkle with chopped fresh parsley.

Serves 4

CHEESE FONDUE *(fondue Neuchâtel)*

Switzerland

Preparation time: 10 minutes

Cooking time: 15 minutes

Ingredients

2   *cups dry white wine*
1   *clove garlic, split*
½   *pound Gruyère cheese, grated*
½   *pound Emmenthaler cheese, grated*
1   *tablespoon cornstarch*

3   *tablespoons kirsch*
    Salt
    Freshly ground pepper
    Freshly grated nutmeg
1   *loaf French bread, cubed*

1. Pour the wine into a fondue pot or chafing dish rubbed with garlic. Heat almost to the boiling point.

2. Little by little, slowly add the grated cheese to the hot wine. (Make sure each addition is thoroughly melted and blended in before adding the next.) Keep hot.

3. In a small cup, combine the cornstarch and the kirsch. Reserve.

4. Stirring constantly, bring the cheese and wine mixture to a boil, then reduce heat and blend in the cornstarch and kirsch mixture. Continue stirring over moderately low heat until mixture thickens, about 3 minutes, then season to taste with salt, freshly ground pepper and nutmeg.

5. To serve, place the fondue pot over low heat at the table, regulating the heat so that the fondue barely simmers. Spear small pieces of the French bread with long-handled forks and swirl in the fondue until nicely coated.

Serves 4

WELSH RAREBIT

Preparation time: 10 minutes

Ingredients

Wales

3 cups Cheddar cheese, grated	Dash cayenne pepper
4 tablespoons butter, at room temperature	1 tablespoon milk or beer
1 to 2 teaspoons mustard	4 slices bread, toasted and buttered

1. Preheat the broiler.

2. Combine the cheese, butter, mustard and pepper. Add the milk (or beer) and stir until smooth.

3. Spread the mixture onto the hot toast and place under the broiler until the cheese has melted. Serve immediately.

Serves 2 to 3

CHEESE RAMEKIN LORRAINE

(ramequin Messin)

France

Preparation time: 15 minutes   **Baking time:** 30 to 35 minutes

Ingredients

2 *cups milk*	4 *eggs, separated*
⅓ *cup flour*	¼ *cup cottage cheese,*
1⅓ *cups Gruyère or other*	*sieved*
Swiss cheese, grated	3 *tablespoons heavy*
Salt	*cream*
Freshly ground pepper	

1. Set oven at 325°.

2. In a saucepan, bring the milk to the boiling point. Remove pan from heat. Beating well, add the flour. Cook over moderate heat for 5 minutes.

3. Remove mixture from heat, blend in the grated cheese and season with salt and pepper.

4. Beat the egg yolks and mix into the custard.

5. Beat the egg whites until stiff and fold into the mixture.

6. Whip the sieved cottage cheese with the cream.

7. Transfer the custard to a buttered 2-quart ovenproof soufflé dish and cover with the cottage cheese mixture.

8. Bake custard until set, about 30 to 35 minutes. Serve immediately as a luncheon or supper dish.

Serves 6

QUICHE LORRAINE

Preparation time: 20 minutes
Pastry chills—1 hour

Baking time: 30 minutes

France

Ingredients

Flaky Pastry:

1¾	cups flour
8	tablespoons butter
4 to 6	tablespoons iced water
½	teaspoon salt

Filling:

6   slices lean bacon

2   tablespoons butter, cut in small pieces

3   eggs

1½   cups light cream

¼   teaspoon nutmeg
Salt
Freshly ground pepper

1. Using the above-listed ingredients, prepare the flaky pastry **(page 474)** and chill for 1 hour.

2. Set oven at 350°.

3. Roll out pastry to ⅛-inch thickness and line a buttered 9-inch pie pan. Pre-bake shell until golden, about 10 minutes. Remove from oven.

4. Cut bacon into fourths and brown the pieces in a skillet. Remove and drain.

5. Place the bacon and 1 tablespoon butter in the partially cooked pastry shell. Reserve.

6. Beat the eggs and cream together. Season with nutmeg, salt and pepper. Pour mixture over the bacon and dot with the rest of the butter.

7. Bake quiche until a knife inserted in the middle of the filling comes out clean, about 30 minutes. Cool slightly before cutting. The quiche may be served hot or cold.

Serves 4

THREE-CHEESE QUICHE
(goyère de Valenciennes)

France

Preparation time: 15 minutes
Pastry chills—1 hour

Baking time: 30 minutes

Ingredients

Flaky Pastry:

1¾	cups flour
8	tablespoons butter
½	teaspoon salt
4 to 6	tablespoons iced water

Filling:

¼	pound creamed small-curd cottage cheese

2	tablespoons milk
1	teaspoon salt
½	cup Gruyère or other Swiss cheese, grated
½	heaped cup diced Maroilles or Pont l'Evêque cheese
2	eggs, beaten
	Freshly ground pepper

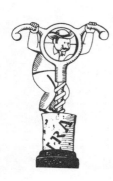

1. Using the above-listed ingredients, prepare the flaky pastry (page 474) and chill for 1 hour.

2. Preheat oven to 400°.

3. Roll out the pastry to ¼-inch thickness and line a 9-inch pie pan. Pre-bake shell for 10 minutes. Remove from oven and reserve.

4. Reduce oven temperature to 325°.

5. In a bowl, combine the cottage cheese, milk and salt. Blend in the other cheeses and the eggs. Season well with pepper.

6. Pour the cheese mixture into the partially cooked pastry shell and bake until the filling is golden and the pastry lightly browned, about 20 minutes. Serve immediately.

Serves 4 to 6

VARIATION: *Make bite-size quiches and serve as an appetizer.*

CHEESE AND ONION TART
(quiche aux oignons)

Preparation time: 30 minutes   **Cooking time:** 1 hour   *France*
Pastry chills—1 hour

Ingredients

Flaky Pastry:

1¾	cups flour
8	tablespoons butter
4 to 6	tablespoons iced water
½	teaspoon salt

2	tablespoons cream
½	cup milk
1	teaspoon flour
4	tablespoons Gruyère or other Swiss cheese, grated
	Salt
	Freshly ground pepper

Filling:

2	tablespoons butter
4	large onions, sliced
2	eggs

1. Using the above-listed ingredients, prepare the flaky pastry (page 474). Chill for 1 hour.

2. Heat the butter in a skillet. Add the onions, cover and cook over low heat for 30 minutes. Stir the onions occasionally. Do not brown. Remove pan from heat.

3. In a bowl, beat the eggs, cream and milk. Blend in the flour and cheese. Season with salt and pepper. Reserve.

4. Set oven at 400°.

5. Roll out pastry and line a 9-inch buttered pie pan. Pre-bake pastry for 10 minutes.

6. Beat the egg mixture into the onions. Pour mixture into the pastry shell and bake until the filling has set and the pastry is lightly browned, about 30 minutes. Serve hot or cold.

Serves 4 to 6

ALSATIAN ONION TART (zewelwaï)

France

Preparation time: 25 minutes
Pastry chills—1 hour

Baking time: 1 hour

Ingredients

Flaky Pastry:

1¾	cups flour
8	tablespoons butter
4 to 6	tablespoons iced water
½	teaspoon salt

Salt
Freshly ground pepper
Freshly grated nutmeg

5	*slices lean bacon, cut into small strips*
2	*eggs*
½	*cup heavy cream*
5	*tablespoons butter*

Filling:

1½	*pounds onions, sliced*
½	*cup water*

1. Using the above-listed ingredients, prepare the flaky pastry (page 474) and chill for 1 hour.

2. Simmer the onions in ½ cup water until all the liquid has evaporated, about 15 minutes. Season with salt, pepper and nutmeg. Reserve.

3. While the onions are cooking, briefly sauté bacon to eliminate some of the fat. Remove the bacon and reserve.

4. Set oven at 325°.

5. In a bowl, beat the eggs and add the cream. Reserve.

6. Roll out the pastry and line a 9-inch pie pan. Pre-bake for 10 minutes.

7. Melt the butter in a saucepan and stir in the onions. Remove pan from heat and pour in the egg and cream mixture. Correct seasoning. Pour mixture into the pastry shell. Dot with the bacon and bake for 1 hour. Serve immediately.

Serves 6

ONION FLAN *(pissaladière Dauphinoise)*

Preparation time: 45 minutes
Pastry chills—1 hour

Baking time: 30 minutes

France

Ingredients

Flaky Pastry:

1¾   *cups flour*
  8   *tablespoons butter*
4 to 6 *tablespoons iced water*
  ½   *teaspoon salt*

Filling:

  5   *tablespoons olive oil*

1½   *pounds onions, thinly sliced*
  1   *clove garlic, minced*
      Salt
      Freshly ground pepper
 12   *anchovy fillets*
 15   *black olives, sliced*

1. Prepare the flaky pastry (page 474) using the above-listed ingredients. Chill for 1 hour.

2. Heat 4 tablespoons of the oil in a skillet. Add the onions and garlic and season with salt and pepper. Cover pan and braise over low heat for 30 minutes. Do not allow onions to brown.

3. Preheat the oven to 400°.

4. While onions are cooking, roll out dough into a circle ⅛-inch thick. Line a buttered 9-inch pie pan with the pastry and pre-bake for 10 minutes. Remove pan from oven and lower oven heat to 325°.

5. Place the onions in the pastry shell. Lay the anchovy fillets in a lattice arrangement over the onions. Top with the olive slices and sprinkle with remaining oil.

6. Return pan to oven and bake flan for 30 minutes.

Serves 4 to 6

LEEK PIE *(flamîche aux poireaux)*

France

Preparation time: 40 minutes
Pastry chills—1 hour

Baking time: 45 minutes

Ingredients

Flaky Pastry:

2	*cups flour*
10	*tablespoons butter*
½	*cup iced water*
1	*teaspoon salt*

5	*tablespoons butter*
1	*tablespoon flour*
½	*cup light cream*
	Salt
	Freshly ground pepper
1	*egg, beaten*

Filling:

12	*leeks (white parts only), split*

1. Using the above-listed ingredients, prepare the flaky pastry (page 474) and chill for 1 hour.

2. Wash the leeks thoroughly, then blanch for 2 minutes in boiling water. Drain and refresh in cold water. Pat dry.

3. Heat 3 tablespoons of the butter in a skillet. Add the blanched leeks, cover pan and braise leeks over low heat until barely tender, about 30 minutes.

4. While the leeks are cooking, prepare a béchamel sauce (page 471) with the remaining butter, flour and cream. Season to taste with salt and pepper. Remove from heat. Add the braised leeks to the sauce. Mix well. Reserve.

5. Set oven at 400°.

6. Roll out half the chilled pastry to ⅜-inch thickness and line a buttered 9-inch pie or flan dish. Pour in the reserved leek mixture. Roll out the remaining pastry. Cover the leeks with the lid and seal the edges of the pie. Brush the crust with the beaten egg and bake for 45 minutes. Serve at once.

Serves 6

PASTA ST. AMBROSE
(spaghettini Sant'Ambrose)

Preparation time: 20 minutes   **Cooking time:** 20 minutes

Italy

Ingredients

Sauce:

8 tablespoons unsalted butter	1 cup heavy cream
1 onion, finely chopped	1 tablespoon tomato paste
1 large stalk celery, finely chopped	___
1 clove garlic, minced	1 pound thin Italian spaghetti (spaghettini)
½ cup dry white wine or ¼ cup dry vermouth	4 ounces Parmesan cheese, grated

1. In a saucepan, melt 2 tablespoons of the butter. Add the chopped onion and celery and sauté over low heat until translucent, about 5 minutes. Add the remaining butter and the garlic. Stir over low heat until the butter has melted. Add the wine (or vermouth) and cook over high heat until nearly all the liquid has evaporated. Reduce heat to low. Add the cream and tomato paste and stir for 1 minute. Stir in the Parmesan cheese. Continue stirring over low heat until sauce is smooth. Keep warm.

2. In a large pot of rapidly boiling salted water, cook spaghetti until barely tender (*al dente*), about 8 to 10 minutes. Drain in a colander.

3. Return spaghetti to pot. Cover with the sauce and toss lightly. Transfer to a heated serving bowl and serve immediately, accompanied by a dish of freshly grated Parmesan cheese.

Serves 4

ALSATIAN DUMPLINGS *(knepfl)*

France

Preparation time: 20 minutes
Dough stands—2 hours

Cooking time: 10 minutes
per batch

Ingredients

3½ cups flour	3 tablespoons butter, melted
3 eggs, beaten	¾ cup Gruyère or other Swiss cheese, grated
1 cup milk	
1 teaspoon salt	

1. Prepare the dough with the flour, eggs, milk and salt and allow it to stand for 2 hours.

2. Using a teaspoon dipped in boiling water, form the dough into little balls.

3. Into a large kettle of boiling water, drop as many dumplings as can be accommodated without crowding. Cook over moderate heat for 10 minutes. Remove dumplings with a slotted spoon and drain. Add another batch to the boiling water.

4. Transfer cooked dumplings to a buttered baking dish and keep warm. Continue as above until all dumplings are cooked.

5. Just before serving, preheat broiler. Pour the melted butter over the dumplings, sprinkle with the grated cheese and heat under the broiler until the cheese turns golden. Serve hot as a side dish with a meat stew or casserole.

Serves 8 to 10

POTATO AND SAUERKRAUT
SALAD *(salade Alsacienne)*

Preparation time: 20 minutes   **Cooking time:** 20 minutes   *France*

Ingredients

1 *pound medium potatoes*	½ *teaspoon salt*
Salt	*Freshly ground pepper*
Freshly ground pepper	3 *tablespoons mayonnaise*
Vinaigrette Sauce:	¾ *pound garlic sausage*
3 *tablespoons wine vinegar*	6 *slices bacon*
10 *tablespoons olive oil*	1 *pound sauerkraut, rinsed and drained*

1. Cook the potatoes in salted boiling water until just tender, about 15 to 20 minutes. (It is important not to overcook potatoes for a salad.) Drain, peel and cut into thin slices.

2. Prepare the vinaigrette sauce by combining the above-listed ingredients.

3. Marinate the warm potato slices in a mixture of 3 tablespoons of the vinaigrette sauce and 1 tablespoon mayonnaise.

4. Poach the sausage in boiling water for 10 minutes. Drain, slice and toss with 3 tablespoons of vinaigrette.

5. Sauté the bacon until crisp, drain on absorbent paper and crumble.

6. Drop the sauerkraut into boiling water. Bring back to a boil, then remove from the heat. Leave sauerkraut in hot water for 2 minutes, drain, refresh and squeeze dry. Transfer to a platter and toss with the remaining vinaigrette and mayonnaise. To serve, sprinkle the bacon over the sauerkraut and arrange the sausage and potatoes around it.

Serves 2 to 4

POTATO AND ONION CASSEROLE *(galette Lyonnaise)*

France   **Preparation time:** 15 minutes   **Baking time:** 20 minutes
Potatoes boil—20 minutes

Ingredients

2 *pounds medium potatoes*	*Salt*
3 *medium onions, chopped*	*Freshly ground pepper*
8 *tablespoons butter*	*Freshly grated nutmeg*

1. Boil the potatoes in their jackets until barely tender, about 20 minutes.

2. While the potatoes are cooking, prepare the onions.

3. Heat half the butter in a frying pan. Add the onions and sauté gently until translucent, about 5 minutes. Do not brown. Remove from heat and reserve.

4. Set oven at 375°.

5. Peel the potatoes, then transfer to a mixing bowl and mash.

6. Mix the sautéed onions into the mashed potatoes. Season to taste with salt, pepper and nutmeg. Blend in 2 tablespoons of the remaining butter.

7. Scrape mixture into a buttered 2-quart baking dish, dot with the remaining butter and bake in the oven until top is nicely browned, about 20 minutes. Serve in the baking dish.

Serves 4 to 6

GAND-STYLE POTATO CASSEROLE *(potée de Gand)*

Preparation time: 30 minutes   **Baking time:** 20 minutes   *Belgium*

Ingredients

6	large potatoes, peeled and quartered
2	leeks, chopped
12	stalks celery, coarsely chopped
3	tablespoons butter, melted

2	egg yolks, beaten
6	ounces Swiss cheese, grated
	Salt
	Freshly ground pepper

1. Set oven at 350°.

2. Drop potatoes into a large pot of boiling salted water and cook for 10 minutes.

3. Add the leeks and celery to the pot and simmer until the vegetables are tender, about 15 minutes.

4. Drain the vegetables. Purée through a food mill or blender.

5. Transfer the vegetable mixture to a large bowl and beat in the butter, the egg yolks and half the grated cheese. Season to taste with salt and pepper.

6. Pour the vegetable mixture into a buttered baking dish. Bake for 20 minutes.

7. Sprinkle the casserole with the remaining grated cheese and put under the broiler until the cheese is golden, about 2 minutes. Serve immediately.

Serves 4

SAVOY POTATOES *(gratin Savoyard)*

France

Preparation time: 20 minutes **Baking time:** 1½ hours

Ingredients

2 pounds potatoes, peeled and thinly sliced	1¼ cups Beaufort or Swiss cheese, grated
Salt	2 cups beef bouillon
Freshly ground pepper	4 tablespoons butter

1. Set oven at 325°.

2. Butter an ovenproof casserole.

3. Dry the potato slices. Place one thin layer of potatoes in the casserole. Season with salt and pepper, then cover with a layer of grated cheese. Continue layering and seasoning, ending with a layer of grated cheese.

4. Pour the bouillon over the cheese and dot with the butter.

5. Bake until all the liquid has evaporated, about 1½ hours.

Serves 4 to 6

DAUPHINÉ POTATOES
(gratin Dauphinois)

Preparation time: 15 minutes   **Baking time:** 1½ hours   *France*

Ingredients

2 *pounds potatoes, peeled and thinly sliced*
1 *clove garlic, crushed*
3 *tablespoons butter*
   Salt
   Freshly ground pepper

½ *teaspoon freshly grated nutmeg*
2 *eggs, beaten*
2 *cups milk*
1 *tablespoon cream*

1. Set oven at 325°.

2. Pat the potato slices dry.

3. Rub a baking dish with the crushed garlic, then coat with 1 tablespoon of the butter.

4. Layer the potato slices in the dish, seasoning each layer with salt, pepper and nutmeg.

5. In a bowl, beat together the eggs, milk and cream.

6. Pour the mixture over the potatoes, dot with the remaining butter and bake for 1½ hours.

Serves 4 to 6

BAKED STUFFED POTATOES
(pommes de terre à la Roussillonnaise)

France

Preparation time: 30 minutes

Cooking time: 1 hour

Ingredients

8	baking potatoes
8	anchovy fillets
2	eggs, hard-boiled
4	shallots, chopped
2	tablespoons fresh parsley, chopped
2	tablespoons fresh chives, chopped
1	tablespoon butter

Béchamel Sauce:

3	tablespoons butter
2	tablespoons flour
1	cup milk
3	tablespoons cream
	Salt
	Freshly ground pepper
½	teaspoon freshly grated nutmeg

1. Preheat oven to 350°.

2. Spear potatoes with a fork and bake until tender, about 40 minutes.

3. In a bowl, mash together the anchovies, eggs, shallots, parsley and chives. Reserve.

4. Fifteen minutes before the potatoes are done, prepare the béchamel sauce (page 471). Blend in the reserved anchovy-herb mixture. Keep warm over hot water.

5. When the potatoes are done, cut them in half and scoop out the pulp. Reserve jackets. Mash the pulp and the sauce together. Fill the jackets with the mixture and dot with the butter.

6. Arrange the stuffed potatoes in a buttered baking dish and bake for 15 minutes.

Serves 8

HASH-BROWN POTATOES ANGOUMOIS
(farcidure de pommes de terre)

France

Preparation time: 15 minutes   **Cooking time:** 35 minutes

Ingredients

1½ *pounds potatoes, peeled and grated*	*Salt*
	Freshly ground pepper
6 *slices bacon, diced*	4 *tablespoons lard or*
1 *clove garlic, minced*	*vegetable oil*

1. In a bowl, combine the potatoes, bacon and garlic. Mix well, then season with salt and pepper.

2. Heat the lard (or oil) in a frying pan. Add the potato mixture and cook over moderate heat until underside is golden.

3. Turn potatoes and continue cooking until the second side is crisp and golden, about 15 minutes.

Serves 4

YAM FRITTERS (ntomo krakro)

Ghana

Preparation time: 30 minutes
Yams boil—20 minutes

Cooking time: 15 minutes
per batch

Ingredients

1	pound yams or sweet potatoes
	Salt
2	eggs, lightly beaten
¼	cup light cream
1	onion, grated
	Flour

Ground cloves
Freshly grated nutmeg
Freshly ground pepper
Flour for dredging fritters
Vegetable oil or lard for frying

1. Drop the yams (or sweet potatoes) into a pot of rapidly boiling salted water and boil until tender, about 20 minutes.

2. Drain yams, then peel and trim any discolored areas.

3. Mash the yams in a large mixing bowl until smooth.

4. Incorporate the eggs, beat in the cream and then add the grated onion and the flour. Mix thoroughly, then season to taste with ground cloves, grated nutmeg, salt and pepper.

5. Shape the mixture into flat cakes, then dredge lightly in flour.

6. Pour enough oil (or lard) into a large heavy skillet to reach a depth of ¼ inch. Heat until oil is almost at smoking point.

7. Add a few fritters to the hot oil and fry until crisp and brown, about 8 minutes per side. Remove fritters with a slotted spoon, drain and keep hot.

8. Repeat until all fritters are fried, then transfer to a heated platter and serve immediately.

Serves 6

BARLEY AND MUSHROOM CASSEROLE

Preparation time: 30 minutes   **Baking time:** 45 minutes   *Scotland*

Ingredients

6	tablespoons butter
2	cloves garlic, minced
2	onions, minced
1	pound mushrooms, thinly sliced
1	cup pearl barley

½	tablespoon dried basil
1⅓	cups chicken broth
	Salt
	Freshly ground pepper
¼	cup fresh parsley, chopped

1. Set oven at 325°.

2. Melt the butter in a small enameled cast-iron casserole. Add the garlic and onion and sauté over moderately low heat until onion is translucent, about 5 minutes.

3. Add the mushrooms and sauté over moderate heat until mushrooms are golden, about 5 minutes.

4. Add the barley and the basil to the mushroom mixture and toss lightly, then pour in the chicken broth and season to taste with salt and pepper.

5. Slowly bring casserole to a boil, then remove from heat. Cover casserole and bake until barley is tender, about 45 minutes.

6. Before serving, add the chopped parsley and toss gently. Serve piping hot.

Serves 4

LENTILS WITH TOMATOES
(addis ma'a banadoora)

Syria

Preparation time: 30 minutes
Lentils soak—3 hours

Cooking time: 1 hour

Ingredients

1	cup brown lentils	½	cup beef bouillon
¼	cup vegetable oil	4	tomatoes, peeled and chopped
1	large onion, minced		Salt
2	cloves garlic, minced		Freshly ground pepper
1	teaspoon ground cumin		

1. Soak the lentils in a bowl of cold water for 3 hours.

2. Discard any lentils that have floated to the surface, then drain the remaining lentils thoroughly.

3. Transfer lentils to a pot of rapidly boiling salted water and cook over moderate heat for ½ hour. Drain and reserve.

4. Heat the oil in a large saucepan. Add the onions and garlic and sauté until translucent, about 5 minutes.

5. Stirring constantly, add the cumin and cook over high heat for 2 minutes.

6. Add the bouillon and the reserved lentils. Mix thoroughly, then simmer, uncovered, over moderately low heat until lentils are nearly tender, about 15 minutes.

7. Stir in the tomatoes and season to taste with salt and pepper. Continue simmering until tomatoes are tender, about 15 minutes.

8. Transfer to a heated serving dish and serve immediately.

Serves 4

BRAISED RICE, MILAN STYLE

(risotto alla Milanese)

Preparation time: 10 minutes   **Cooking time:** 25 minutes   *Italy*

Ingredients

2 cups beef or chicken stock, heated	1 cup raw short-grain rice
Pinch saffron	3 tablespoons Parmesan cheese, freshly grated
2 tablespoons oil	Salt
3 tablespoons butter	Freshly ground pepper
½ onion, chopped	Freshly grated Parmesan cheese
2 tablespoons beef marrow, diced	

1. In a cup, combine ¼ cup of the hot stock and the saffron. Reserve.

2. Heat the oil and 2 tablespoons of the butter in a large skillet. Add the onion and sauté over moderate heat until onion is translucent, about 5 minutes. Add the marrow and the rice. Stir briefly until rice is thoroughly coated, then sauté for 1 minute over moderate heat.

3. Add ½ cup of the remaining stock to the rice. Stir gently over moderate heat until the stock is absorbed, then add another ½ cup stock and stir until that is absorbed. Add half the remaining stock to the rice and stir as above, then add the remaining stock. Continue stirring gently until the rice is tender and creamy and all the stock has been absorbed. (This entire process will take 20 to 25 minutes.)

4. Stir the saffron and stock mixture into the rice, then blend in the remaining butter and the Parmesan cheese. Season with salt and pepper and serve, accompanied by a bowl of freshly grated Parmesan cheese.

Serves 4

GINGERED STRING BEANS
(chiang pien tou)

China

Preparation time: 10 minutes   **Cooking time:** 10 minutes

Ingredients

1 pound fresh string beans, snapped	1 tablespoon soy sauce
2 tablespoons peanut oil or flavorless vegetable oil	¼ cup chicken stock
3 thick slices fresh ginger root, minced	3 scallions, chopped Chopped walnuts for garnish

1. Plunge the green beans into a pot of lightly salted boiling water and blanch over moderately high heat for 3 minutes. Drain and refresh under cold water, then pat dry and reserve.

2. Place a wok or large skillet over high heat for ½ minute, then swirl in the oil. Wait ½ minute, then add the minced ginger and stir-fry over moderately high heat for 1 minute.

3. Add the green beans and stir-fry until barely tender, about 2 minutes.

4. Add the soy sauce and chicken stock. Bring rapidly to a boil, then cover and simmer over moderate heat until beans are tender, about 4 minutes.

5. Stir in the scallions and toss briefly over high heat, then transfer to a heated serving platter, garnish with chopped walnuts and serve immediately.

Serves 4

GASCONY GREEN BEANS
(haricots verts à la Landaise)

Preparation time: 15 minutes   **Cooking time:** 30 minutes   *France*

Ingredients

1½	*pounds green beans*	3	*thin slices ham, diced*
3	*leeks (white parts only), split*	1½	*tablespoons flour*
1	*clove garlic minced*	1	*egg yolk*
	Salt	1	*teaspoon wine vinegar*
2	*tablespoons goose fat (page 475) or olive oil*		*Chopped fresh parsley for garnish*
2	*onions, chopped*		

1. Parboil the beans, leeks and garlic in a pot of boiling salted water for 10 minutes. Drain vegetables, reserving 1 cup of the broth. Reserve vegetables.

2. In a frying pan, heat the goose fat (or olive oil) and sauté the onions and the ham over moderate heat for 10 minutes. Stirring constantly, sprinkle in the flour and pour in the reserved vegetable broth. Continue stirring over moderate heat until the sauce is smooth. Add the reserved vegetables to the sauce and simmer gently for 10 minutes. Keep hot.

3. Beat the egg yolk and vinegar in a bowl. Gradually beat a little of the hot sauce into egg mixture, then pour in the frying pan with the beans.

4. Heat until sauce thickens. (Do not boil.) Garnish with chopped parsley and serve.

Serves 4

SAVORY GRATED BEETS
(natyortya svekla)

USSR

Preparation time: 10 minutes   **Cooking time:** 30 minutes

Ingredients

3	*tablespoons butter*
1	*onion, minced*
1	*pound raw beets, grated*
1	*teaspoon lemon rind, grated*
2	*tablespoons lemon juice*
1	*tablespoon flour*

½	*cup beef broth, heated*
	Salt
	Freshly ground pepper
2	*tablespoons chives, chopped*
2	*tablespoons fresh parsley, chopped*

1. Heat the butter in a frying pan. Add the minced onion and sauté over moderately low heat until translucent, about 5 minutes.

2. Add the grated beets, lemon rind and lemon juice. Mix gently until beets are evenly coated, then cover pan and simmer beets over low heat until barely tender, about 20 minutes.

3. Sprinkle the flour into the hot broth and mix vigorously until well blended, then pour over the beets. Stir beet mixture over moderate heat until well blended, then simmer, uncovered, until beets are tender, about 10 minutes.

4. Reduce heat to low. Season beets to taste with salt and pepper, then add the chopped chives and parsley. Toss gently. Serve hot or cold.

Serves 4

BROCCOLI, BERLIN STYLE
(brocoli Allemande)

Preparation time: 10 minutes   **Cooking time:** 15 minutes

France

Ingredients

1½ *pounds broccoli*	2 *egg yolks, beaten*
Salt	1 *tablespoon lemon juice*
3 *tablespoons butter*	*Pinch nutmeg*
2 *tablespoons flour*	*Pinch freshly ground*
1 *cup milk*	*pepper*
¼ *cup chicken broth*	

1. Place the broccoli in a small amount of boiling salted water. Cover tightly and cook until just crisp-tender, about 8 to 10 minutes.

2. Prepare the sauce: Melt the butter and blend in the flour. Gradually add the milk and chicken broth and stir until thickened, about 10 minutes. Add the yolks and cook for another minute, then stir in the lemon juice, nutmeg and pepper.

3. Arrange the broccoli on a heated serving dish and cover with the sauce.

Serves 4

BRUSSELS SPROUTS WITH CELERY

Great Britain

Preparation time: 20 minutes

Baking time: 10 minutes

Ingredients

3	tablespoons butter
2	stalks celery, chopped
1	onion, chopped
1½	pounds small Brussels sprouts, trimmed
2	tablespoons flour

1	cup milk, heated
	Salt
	Freshly ground pepper
	Freshly grated nutmeg
¼	cup dry bread crumbs

1. Set oven at 350°.

2. In a skillet heat 2 tablespoons of the butter. Add the celery and onion and sauté over low heat until tender, about 10 minutes.

3. While the onions and celery are cooking, steam the Brussels sprouts for 7 minutes over boiling water. Drain and reserve.

4. Sprinkle the flour into the onion and celery mixture. Stir over low heat until well blended, then gradually add the milk and cook gently until sauce thickens.

5. Season to taste with salt, pepper and nutmeg, then add the reserved Brussels sprouts.

6. Pour mixture into a buttered baking dish. Top with the bread crumbs, dot with the remaining butter and bake for 10 minutes. Serve hot.

Serves 6

PURÉED BRUSSELS SPROUTS
(Spruiten purée)

The Netherlands

Preparation time: 10 minutes   **Cooking time:** 15 minutes

Ingredients

Salt
1   pound Brussels
    sprouts, trimmed and
    scored
1   cup water

Pinch nutmeg
1   teaspoon lemon juice
1   cup heavy cream

1. Bring salted water to a boil in a saucepan. Add the Brussels sprouts. Return to a boil, lower the heat, cover and simmer until tender, about 10 minutes. Drain and refresh under cold water.

2. Using a food mill or blender, purée the Brussels sprouts, then return to the saucepan. Add salt to taste and the nutmeg, then stir in the cream. Blend well.

3. Stir over low heat for 5 minutes. Serve piping hot.

Serves 4

Spruiten purée *makes an ideal accompaniment to duck or pork.*

BEDFORD COLESLAW

Preparation time: 20 minutes   **Marination time:** 2 hours

USA

Ingredients

1 *small head cabbage*	2 *tablespoons vinaigrette dressing (page 482)*
2 *carrots, peeled*	
½ *green pepper, chopped*	½ *cup mayonnaise*
1 *small onion, chopped*	*Salt*
1 *clove garlic, pressed (optional)*	*Freshly ground pepper*

1. In a non-metallic bowl, shred the cabbage and the carrots. Add the pepper and onion and toss well.

2. Stir in the garlic, vinaigrette and mayonnaise. Season to taste with salt and pepper. Cover and refrigerate for at least two hours (or overnight) before serving.

Serves 4

STUFFED CABBAGE *(chou farci)*

Preparation time: 30 minutes

Cooking time: 3 hours

France

Ingredients

A   *2-pound green cabbage*

Stuffing:

1   *pound sorrel, chopped*
½   *cup fresh parsley, chopped*
½   *pound lettuce, chopped*
½   *pound spinach, chopped*
½   *pound bacon, diced*
½   *pound pork, ground*

2   *onions, chopped*
2   *shallots, minced*
4   *eggs*
¼   *cup flour*
1⅓   *cups bread crumbs*
3   *tablespoons cream*
    Salt and pepper
—
6   *cups chicken broth*

1. Blanch the cabbage in boiling water for 10 minutes. Drain.

2. Combine the greens with the bacon, pork, onions and shallots. Add the eggs, flour, bread crumbs and cream. Blend until smooth and season with salt and pepper.

3. Remove a few outer leaves of the cabbage and carefully open out the remaining leaves. Cut out the central stalk, leaving the base of the core intact. Fill the cabbage with the stuffing and gently reshape the cabbage to its original form. Cover the top of the cabbage with the detached outer leaves.

4. Wrap the cabbage tightly in cheesecloth. Place in a pan just large enough to hold the cabbage. Cover with the chicken broth and simmer, covered, for 3 hours. Serve the cabbage immediately, accompanied by a sauceboat of the hot cooking liquid.

Serves 4

BAVARIAN RED CABBAGE

(Rotkohl mit Speck)

Germany   **Preparation time:** 15 minutes   **Cooking time:** 20 minutes

Ingredients

- 5   slices bacon
- 3   onions, chopped
- 1   tablespoon flour
- ¼   cup red wine vinegar
- ½   cup red wine
-     Salt
-     Freshly ground pepper

- 2   pounds red cabbage, shredded
- ¼   teaspoon caraway seed (optional)
- 1   apple, peeled, cored and diced

1. In a heavy enameled casserole, sauté the bacon over moderate heat to render the fat. Do not allow the fat to brown. Remove the bacon and reserve for other uses.

2. Add the onions to the casserole and sauté until translucent. Sprinkle in the flour while stirring. Cook for about 30 seconds, then slowly pour in the vinegar and the wine. Stir briskly to avoid lumps.

3. Add the red cabbage, caraway seed and apple. Season with salt and pepper. Mix all the ingredients together and cover.

4. Cook for about 20 minutes, or until the cabbage is tender but not soggy.

Serves 4 to 6

HONEYED CARROTS AND SWEET POTATOES *(tzimmes)*

Preparation time: 15 minutes   **Cooking time:** 1¼ hours   *Israel*

Ingredients

- 1 *pound carrots, thickly sliced*
- 3 *large sweet potatoes, peeled and quartered*
- 1 *cup water, boiling*

- ½ *pound prunes, pitted*
- ⅓ *cup honey*
- *Salt*

1. Place the carrots and sweet potatoes in a saucepan. Pour in the water, then add the prunes.

2. Cover the pan tightly and steam the mixture over low heat for 15 minutes.

3. Add the honey and season to taste with salt. Simmer over very low heat until the vegetables are tender, about 1 hour.

Serves 6

BALKAN BRAISED CARROTS

(sargarera)

Yugoslavia

Preparation time: 10 minutes

Cooking time: 15 minutes

Ingredients

4	tablespoons butter			*Salt*

4   *tablespoons butter*
1   *teaspoon sugar*
8   *carrots, thinly sliced*
3   *scallions, cut into
    1-inch pieces*
    Cayenne pepper

Salt
Freshly ground pepper
1   *cup plain yoghurt*
2   *tablespoons fresh dill,
    chopped*

1. Melt the butter in a saucepan. Add the sugar, carrot slices and scallions. Cover and braise gently until carrots are tender, about 15 minutes.

2. Season to taste with the cayenne pepper, salt and pepper.

3. Add the yoghurt and dill. Stirring constantly, heat through. (Do not allow to boil.) Serve immediately.

Serves 4

CAULIFLOWER WITH BREAD-CRUMB GARNISH

(choufleur à la Polonaise)

France

Preparation time: 10 minutes   **Cooking time:** 25 minutes

Ingredients

1   head cauliflower, trimmed

Salt

8   tablespoons butter

1   cup dry bread crumbs

Juice of ½ lemon

Freshly ground pepper

4   eggs, hard-boiled

½   cup fresh parsley, chopped

1. Drop the cauliflower into a heavy pot of boiling salted water. Quickly return to a boil, then lower heat, cover tightly and steam until tender, about 25 minutes.

2. While the cauliflower is cooking, prepare the bread-crumb garnish: a) Melt the butter in a skillet; b) add the bread crumbs and stir until the mixture is golden; c) sprinkle in the lemon juice and add salt and pepper to taste. Keep warm.

3. Remove the cauliflower and drain well. Reserve.

4. Mince the hard-boiled eggs and mix with the chopped parsley. Season to taste with salt and pepper.

5. To serve, arrange the cauliflower on a heated platter. Sprinkle on the reserved bread crumbs and surround with the egg and parsley mixture.

Serves 2 to 4

CAULIFLOWER SOUFFLÉ
(soufflé au choufleur)

France

Preparation time: 20 minutes   **Baking time:** 35 to 40 minutes

Ingredients

1 *small cauliflower, broken into flowerets*	1½ *cups milk, boiling*
½ *teaspoon salt*	1 *teaspoon rosemary*
Freshly ground pepper	5 *eggs, separated*
Freshly grated nutmeg	1½ *cups Swiss cheese, grated*
Cayenne pepper	2 *tablespoons dry bread crumbs.*
3 *tablespoons butter*	
3 *tablespoons flour*	

1. Preheat oven to 400°.

2. Cook the cauliflower in boiling salted water until tender, about 10 minutes. Purée and season with salt, pepper, nutmeg, cayenne pepper and rosemary.

3. Melt the butter in a saucepan, stir in the flour and cook for 2 minutes. Add the milk and stir until thickened. Remove the pan from the heat and blend in 4 of the egg yolks, one at a time. Add the cauliflower purée and all but 2 tablespoons of the grated cheese.

4. Beat the 5 egg whites with a pinch of salt until stiff. Fold carefully into the cheese mixture. Pour into a buttered soufflé dish and sprinkle with the remaining grated cheese and the bread crumbs. Bake for 35 to 40 minutes.

Serves 4

CORN PUDDING

Preparation time: 15 minutes   **Cooking time:** 45 minutes

Ingredients

USA

4 *tablespoons butter*	*Salt*
1 *small onion, minced*	*Freshly ground pepper*
1 *cup fresh corn*	4 *eggs, separated*
1 *cup light cream*	

1. Set oven at 325°.

2. In a skillet, melt the butter and sauté the onion over low heat for 3 minutes. Do not allow the butter to brown. Scrape into a bowl.

3. Add the corn, cream, salt and pepper. Lightly beat the egg yolks and stir into the corn. Mix well.

4. In a separate bowl, beat the egg whites until frothy. Add a pinch of salt and continue beating until stiff. Fold the egg whites into the corn mixture.

5. Pour into a buttered baking dish. Bake for 40 minutes. Increase heat to 400° and bake for an additional 5 minutes.

Serves 4

FRIED SWEET CORN *(frikadel djagung)*

Indonesia

Preparation time: 5 minutes

Cooking time: 2 minutes

Ingredients

1   *cup cooked sweet corn or an 8-ounce can corn niblets*
1   *small onion, chopped*
1   *stalk celery, chopped*
2   *tablespoons Chinese parsley, chopped*

½   *teaspoon salt*
1   *egg, lightly beaten*
1 to 2   *tablespoons flour*
3   *tablespoons peanut oil*

1. Combine the first seven ingredients in a large bowl. Mix thoroughly.

2. Heat the oil in a 12-inch wok or a large skillet. Add the vegetable mixture and stir-fry until golden, about 5 minutes.

Serves 4

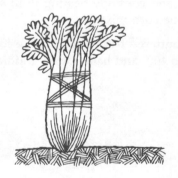

BRAISED CUCUMBERS WITH DILL AND SOUR CREAM

(svezii i solenyi oguretz so smetanoi)

USSR

Preparation time: 10 minutes   **Cooking time:** 15 minutes

Ingredients

6 small cucumbers, peeled	¼ cup sour cream
Salt	2 tablespoons fresh dill, chopped
6 tablespoons butter	Freshly ground pepper
1 onion, minced	Pinch nutmeg

1. Halve the cucumbers lengthwise and scrape out the seeds. Cut into 2-inch strips. Sprinkle the cucumbers with salt and let stand for 20 minutes. Drain and pat dry.

2. Melt 4 tablespoons of butter in a saucepan. Add the cucumbers, cover and cook over low heat until tender, about 10 minutes.

3. Melt the remaining butter and sauté the onion for 5 minutes. Remove from the heat and stir in the sour cream and dill. Season with salt, pepper and nutmeg. Stir in the cucumbers, heat through and serve.

Serves 4

STUFFED EGGPLANT AMMAN
(batinjan Amman)

Jordan

Preparation time: 30 minutes

Ingredients

3	medium eggplants
	Salt
½	cup olive oil
2	onions, chopped
1	pound mushrooms, thinly sliced
2	cloves garlic, pressed
A	28-ounce can Italian-style tomatoes, drained and chopped
1	cup fresh bread crumbs
	Freshly ground pepper

Cooking time: 30 minutes

2	tablespoons fresh parsley, chopped
1	teaspoon dried mint leaves, crushed
½	teaspoon oregano
¼	teaspoon marjoram
	Pinch cayenne pepper
¼	teaspoon ground allspice
½	cup Parmesan cheese, freshly grated

1. Preheat oven to 350°.

2. Boil the eggplants in a large kettle of water for 15 minutes. Drain and cut in half lengthwise. Scoop out most of the pulp, leaving ½-inch thickness of pulp in the skins. Sprinkle hollowed-out shells with salt and drain for ½ hour. Rinse, pat dry and reserve. Chop the scooped-out pulp.

3. Heat the olive oil in a large skillet. Add the chopped eggplant pulp, onions, mushrooms and garlic. Sauté over moderately high heat until lightly browned.

4. Add the tomatoes, bread crumbs, 1½ teaspoons salt, herbs and spices. Mix well, then remove from heat and spoon the sautéed mixture into the reserved shells.

5. Arrange the stuffed eggplant in a greased baking pan, sprinkle with the grated Parmesan and bake until cheese has melted or nearly browned.

Serves 6

SAUTÉED MUSHROOMS
(cèpes à la Bordelaise)

Preparation time: 20 minutes   **Cooking time:** 25 minutes   *France*
Chinese mushrooms soak—30 minutes

Ingredients

8 to 12   *cèpes (boletus
mushrooms) or
Chinese mushrooms or
1 pound firm white
mushrooms*
½   *cup olive oil*
2   *cloves garlic, minced*
6   *shallots, chopped*

4   *slices ham, diced*
1   *tablespoon fresh
parsley, chopped*
1   *bay leaf*
Salt
Freshly ground pepper
Juice of ½ lemon

1. Clean the mushrooms and remove stalks. Chop stalks. Reserve caps and stalks. (If Chinese mushrooms are used; soak them in lukewarm water for 30 minutes, remove with a slotted spoon and discard stalks. Pat caps dry.)

2. In a frying pan, heat half the oil with the garlic. Stir in the shallots and sauté until translucent, about 3 minutes. Add the ham, parsley, bay leaf and the chopped mushroom stalks. Lower heat and simmer for 15 minutes.

3. Heat the remaining oil in a frying pan and sauté the mushroom caps over high heat. Season with salt and pepper. Keep warm.

4. Arrange the mushroom caps on a heated platter and surround with the ham garnish. Sprinkle with the lemon juice and serve immediately.

Serves 4

CREAMED WILD MUSHROOMS
(chanterelles à la crème)

France

Preparation time: 25 minutes

Cooking time: 20 minutes

Ingredients

1	pound chanterelles or 1 pound trim white mushrooms
	Vinegar for rinsing
3	tablespoons butter
2	tablespoons oil
	Salt
	Freshly ground pepper

⅓	cup heavy cream
	Pinch freshly grated nutmeg
8	slices French bread, fried in butter
	Chopped fresh parsley for garnish

1. Carefully clean the mushrooms, rinsing them several times in water with a dash of vinegar until no dirt remains. Pat dry. (If the *chanterelles* are large, cut them lengthwise into strips.)

2. Heat the butter and oil in a skillet. Add the mushrooms and stir over moderately high heat until moisture starts coming out of the mushrooms, about 10 minutes.

3. Season with salt and pepper. Cook, uncovered, over moderate heat for 10 minutes to reduce liquid.

4. Reduce heat to low and stir in the cream and a pinch of nutmeg. Continue stirring over low heat until the cream begins to thicken, then remove skillet from heat.

5. Arrange the fried bread on a heated platter. Pour the creamed mushrooms on top and garnish with chopped fresh parsley. Serve immediately

Serves 4

OKRA OLYMPIA *(bamyes yahni)*

Preparation time: 10 minutes   **Cooking time:** 35 minutes

Greece

Ingredients

1½	pounds okra, trimmed and sliced		Salt
			Freshly ground pepper
1	cup olive oil	¼	teaspoon oregano
3	onions, minced	¼	teaspoon sugar
5	tomatoes, peeled and chopped	½	cup water
½	lemon, sliced		

1. Blanch the okra briefly in a pot of boiling salted water. Drain.

2. Heat the olive oil and sauté the onions until translucent, about 10 minutes. Add the okra slices and cook for 5 minutes.

3. Add the remaining ingredients, cover and simmer over low heat for 20 minutes. Correct seasoning and serve hot.

Serves 6

ONIONS STUFFED WITH RICE AND MEAT *(fylld lök)*

Sweden

Preparation time: 50 minutes

Cooking time: 1 hour

Ingredients

10	medium onions, peeled	1	tablespoon brown
	Salt		sugar
½	pound beef, ground	2	cups beef broth
1	cup cooked rice	1½	tablespoons flour
1	egg	½	cup cream
⅓	cup cream	2	tablespoons each fresh
	Freshly ground pepper		dill and parsley,
3	tablespoons butter		chopped

1. Parboil the onions in salted water for 5 minutes. Remove with a slotted spoon and drain. Carefully scoop out the center with a spoon, keeping the shape. Reserve centers.

2. Combine the meat, rice, egg and cream. Season well with salt and pepper. Fill the onion centers wih the mixture. Cover with reserved onion leaves and secure with string.

3. Set oven at 350°.

4. Melt the butter in a casserole, then brown the filled onions a few at a time. Sprinkle with the brown sugar. Pour in the broth, half covering the onions. Cover the casserole, place in the oven and simmer for 1 hour, basting occasionally. Discard the string and arrange the onions on a serving platter. Keep warm.

5. Heat the bouillon in a saucepan. Mix the flour and cream together, then whisk into the bouillon. Stir until thickened. Correct seasoning. Pour the sauce over the onions. Sprinkle with dill and parsley.

Serves 4 to 6

BASSE-TERRE CREAMED PEAS
(petits pois à la crème)

Preparation time: 5 minutes   **Cooking time:** 15 minutes

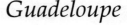

Guadeloupe

Ingredients

2	thick slices bacon, diced
2	pounds young green peas, shelled
1¼	cups beef broth
	Herb bouquet (parsley, peppercorns, small onion, bay leaf)
½	cup heavy cream

	Salt
	Freshly ground pepper
1	tablespoon butter, softened
1	teaspoon flour
1	tablespoon rum
	Pinch brown sugar

1. In a small saucepan, sauté the bacon cubes until crisp. Drain and reserve.

2. Put the peas in a medium saucepan and add the broth and the herb bouquet. Simmer over medium heat for 10 to 12 minutes, until peas are tender. Remove the herb bouquet. Add the heavy cream and season with salt and pepper.

3. Make a *roux* by combining the butter and flour and add it into the peas. Stir sauce until smooth and thick. Add the rum and sugar and serve piping hot.

Serves 4 to 6

STIR-FRIED SPINACH *(po tsai)*

Preparation time: 10 minutes   **Cooking time:** 2 minutes

China   **Ingredients**

2 pounds spinach,
   trimmed
2 tablespoons peanut or
   flavorless vegetable oil

1 clove garlic, mashed
A 1-inch piece fresh
   ginger root, peeled and
   minced

1. Wash the spinach thoroughly and dry lightly. The leaves should be slightly moist.

2. Place a wok (or casserole) over high heat for 1 minute. Add the oil, garlic and ginger. Swirl oil in pan for ½ minute.

3. Reduce heat to moderate, add the spinach and cover immediately. Steam spinach for 1 minute, then toss lightly.

4. Replace cover and steam until just tender, about 1 more minute. Serve immediately.

Serves 4

Any leafy vegetable, such as bok choy, *watercress or romaine lettuce, can be cooked this same way.*

SUMMER SQUASH AND TOMATO CASSEROLE

Preparation time: 30 minutes   **Cooking time:** 40 minutes

West Indies

Ingredients

6	*small yellow squash*
2	*small onions, diced*
½	*teaspoon salt*

Béchamel Sauce:

2   *tablespoons butter*
2   *tablespoons flour*
1   *cup milk*
    Salt
    Freshly ground pepper

2   *garlic cloves, minced*
4   *tablespoons butter*
2   *tomatoes, peeled and sliced*
    Chopped parsley for garnish

1. Cut the squash into ½-inch slices, sprinkle with salt and allow to stand for 15 minutes, then drain and pat dry.

2. Place the squash, onion and salt in a saucepan with cold water to cover. Bring to a boil, cover and lower heat. Simmer 10 minutes, drain well and transfer to a buttered baking dish.

3. Set oven at 325°.

4. Prepare the béchamel sauce using the above-listed ingredients (page 471). Pour the béchamel sauce over the vegetables, sprinkle with the garlic and dot with the butter. Cover with over-lapping slices of tomato and bake for 40 minutes. Garnish with parsley and serve.

Serves 4 to 6

ROMAN-STYLE STUFFED TOMATOES *(pomodori ripieni alla Romana)*

Italy

Preparation time: 20 minutes

Baking time: 20 minutes

Ingredients

6	*large firm tomatoes*
¾	*cup cooked rice*
8	*tablespoons butter, melted*
½	*cup mozzarella cheese, shredded*
2	*tablespoons Romano cheese, grated*

1	*teaspoon dried oregano*
1	*tablespoon parsley, finely chopped*
	Salt
	Freshly ground pepper
2	*tablespoons bread crumbs*

1. Cut off the top of each tomato and scoop out the center. Be careful not to make the walls too thin.

2. Preheat oven to 325°.

3. In a mixing bowl, toss the rice with 6 tablespoons of the butter. Add the cheeses, oregano, parsley, salt and pepper and mix well.

4. Stuff each tomato with one-sixth of the rice mixture and then place in buttered baking dish. Sprinkle the top of each tomato with 1 teaspoon bread crumbs and 1 teaspoon of the remaining melted butter. Bake for 20 minutes.

Serves 6

BAKED TURNIPS IN CREAM

(navets gratinés sauce Normande)

Preparation time: 30 minutes

Baking time: 15 minutes

France

Ingredients

2 *pounds small white turnips, peeled and quartered*

Sauce Normande:

4 *tablespoons butter*

1 *medium onion, finely sliced*

2 *tablespoons flour*

1 *cup dry cider or dry white wine*

   Salt
   Freshly ground pepper

1¼ *cups crème fraîche or heavy cream*
   Pinch freshly grated nutmeg

1 *lemon quarter*

1. Blanch the turnips in 2 quarts boiling salted water for 10 minutes. Drain and arrange in a buttered baking dish.

2. Set oven at 400°.

3. Prepare the *sauce Normande*: a) Melt the butter in a saucepan and lightly sauté the onion until translucent, b) stir in the flour and continue cooking for a few minutes; c) add the cider, stirring constantly until the sauce thickens; d) season with salt and pepper, then add the *crème fraîche* (**page 473**) or heavy cream, nutmeg and a squeeze of lemon juice.

4. Pour the sauce over the turnips and bake for 15 minutes.

Serves 4 to 6

YELLOW TURNIP SOUFFLÉ

(kålrabi soufflé)

Norway

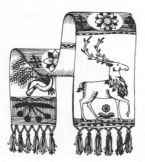

Preparation time: 15 minutes   **Baking time:** 50 minutes

Ingredients

1   *pound yellow turnips,*
    scraped and coarsely
    grated
1   *cup fresh bread-crumbs*
1   *cup milk*
3   *eggs, separated*

3   *tablespoons butter,*
    melted
    Salt
    Freshly ground pepper

1. Preheat oven to 350°.

2. Add the grated turnips to a pot of boiling water and cook over moderately high heat until barely tender, about 3 minutes.

3. While the turnips parboil, combine the bread crumbs, milk, lightly beaten egg yolks and butter in a mixing bowl. Blend thoroughly, then season to taste with salt and pepper. Reserve.

4. Drain the parboiled turnips, mash, then stir into the bread-crumb mixture. Reserve.

5. In another bowl, beat the egg whites with a wire whisk or electric beater until frothy. Add a pinch of salt, then continue beating until egg whites are stiff.

6. Gently fold the egg whites into the turnip mixture, then transfer mixture to a buttered baking dish.

7. Set the baking dish in a shallow pan of hot water and bake until the soufflé is puffed and lightly browned, about 50 minutes. (Do not open the oven door during baking.)

8. Serve piping hot from the baking dish.

Serves 6

ZUCCHINI IN TOMATO SAUCE

(courgettes Niçoises)

Preparation time: 15 minutes
Sauce simmers—15 minutes

Cooking time: 15 minutes

France

Ingredients

Tomato Sauce:

 3 tablespoons olive oil

 2 pounds ripe tomatoes,
    peeled, seeded and
    quartered

 2 onions, chopped

    Several leaves fresh
    basil or 1 teaspoon
    dried basil

 1 tablespoon fresh
    parsley, chopped
    Salt
    Freshly ground pepper
    —

 5 small zucchini, sliced

 3 sprigs fresh tarragon,
    chopped, or 1 teaspoon
    dried tarragon

1. Heat the olive oil in a pan. Add the tomatoes, onions, basil
   and parsley and mix well.

2. Cover pan and simmer over low heat until the tomatoes
   soften, about 15 minutes. Season with salt and pepper.

3. Add the zucchini, cover and cook over moderately low heat
   until the zucchini are tender, about 15 minutes.

4. Just before serving, sprinkle with the tarragon. Serve hot or
   cold.

Serves 4 to 6

ZUCCHINI IN SOUR CREAM
(tökfäzelék)

Bulgaria

Preparation time: 20 minutes
Zucchini stands—15 minutes

Cooking time: 25 minutes

Ingredients

1 *pound zucchini, coarsely grated or cut into thin strips*	1 *medium onion, chopped*
Salt	1 *clove garlic, pressed*
2 *tablespoons flour*	*Freshly ground pepper*
½ *pint sour cream*	2 *tablespoons fresh dill, chopped*
3 *tablespoons butter*	2 *tablespoons vinegar*

1. Sprinkle the zucchini with salt and let stand for 15 minutes.

2. In a small bowl, combine flour and sour cream. Reserve.

3. Melt the butter in a frying pan. Add the onion and garlic and sauté gently until translucent, about 10 minutes.

4. Drain the zucchini, then transfer to the frying pan. Season with salt and pepper. Cook until tender, about 10 minutes.

5. Spoon the reserved sour cream mixture over zucchini. Cook over low heat for 5 minutes.

6. Blend in the dill and vinegar. Heat through and serve at once.

Serves 4

ZUCCHINI STUFFED WITH LAMB AND RICE *(kolokithakia gemista)*

Preparation time: 10 minutes
Rice simmers—15 minutes

Baking time: 20 minutes

Greece

Ingredients

6 zucchini	Salt
3 tablespoons olive oil	Freshly ground pepper
2 onions, minced	1½ cups water
½ pound lamb, ground	1½ cups cooked rice
2 tablespoons fresh parsley, chopped	2 tablespoons lemon juice
1 teaspoon dried thyme	2 eggs, beaten
½ teaspoon fennel seeds	3 tablespoons butter
2 bay leaves	Dry bread crumbs for garnish
½ teaspoon dried mint	

1. Slice the zucchini in half lengthwise. Scoop out the pulp and chop.

2. Heat the oil and sauté the onion until limp, then add the lamb and sauté until browned, about 10 minutes. Add the zucchini pulp and seasonings. Pour in ½ cup water and simmer meat mixture gently, until the water has evaporated, about 15 minutes.

3. Discard the bay leaf from the meat mixture, then transfer mixture to a large bowl. Add the rice and the lemon juice and mix thoroughly, then bind with the eggs. Correct seasonings. Stuff the reserved zucchini shells with the rice and meat mixture, dot with butter, sprinkle with dry bread crumbs. Arrange on a buttered baking sheet and bake until shells are tender, about 20 minutes.

Serves 6

VEGETABLES AU GRATIN
(grönsaksgratin)

Sweden

Preparation time: 30 minutes   **Cooking time:** 10 minutes

Ingredients

Cream Sauce:

2	tablespoons butter
2	tablespoons flour
1	cup heavy cream
1	cup vegetable stock or milk
2	egg yolks
	Salt
	Freshly ground pepper

—

2	cups cauliflower, cooked
2	cups carrots, cooked
2	cups peas, cooked
1	tablespoon butter
4	tomatoes, sliced
1	ounce Emmenthaler cheese, grated

1. Preheat oven to 400°.

2. In a saucepan melt the butter. Stirring constantly over moderate heat, sprinkle in the flour and cook for 1 minute.

3. Gradually beat in the cream and vegetable stock (or milk). Stir over low heat for 10 minutes. Keep hot.

4. In a bowl, beat the egg yolks well. Gradually beat in a few tablespoons of the hot sauce, then stir mixture into the saucepan. Heat through but do not boil. Remove saucepan from heat and season to taste with salt and pepper. Reserve.

5. Layer the cauliflower, carrots and peas in a well-buttered baking dish. Pour in the sauce. Layer on the tomato slices, season well with salt and pepper, then top with the grated cheese. Bake until the cheese is melted, about 10 minutes, then brown quickly under the broiler.

Serves 6

BATTER-FRIED VEGETABLES
(tempura)

Preparation time: 20 minutes
Batter and sauce chill—15 minutes

Cooking time: 1 minute
per batch

Japan

Ingredients
Batter:

- 2   *eggs*
- 2   *cups flour*
- 2   *cups water*
-     *Salt*
- 1   *teaspoon baking powder*

Dipping Sauce:

- 1   *cup chicken stock*
- ¼   *cup sugar*
- ½   *cup soy sauce*
- 2   *tablespoons mirin (sweet rice wine) or dry sherry*
- 1   *slice fresh ginger root, peeled and minced*

- 1   *teaspoon daikon (Japanese radish), grated*
- 1   *scallion, minced*

- 3   *cups vegetable oil*
- 1   *cup sesame-seed oil*

- 4   *carrots, sliced*
- 2   *sweet potatoes, sliced*
- 2   *green peppers, sliced*
- ½   *pound small mushrooms, halved*
- 1   *small eggplant, sliced*
- 2   *onions, sliced in rings*
- 24 *green beans, snapped*
- 2   *zucchini, sliced*

1. Prepare the batter by combining eggs with water and mix well. Gradually stir in the flour, salt and baking powder. Mixture should have consistency of whipping cream. Refrigerate for 15 minutes.

2. Combine dipping-sauce ingredients and refrigerate.

3. Heat the oil in a large pot to 350°. Dip each vegetable into the batter and drop it gently into the hot fat. Fry until golden brown, about 30 seconds to 1 minute. Drain each piece briefly and serve at once. Serve with individual bowls of dipping sauce and hot rice.

Serves 6

VEGETABLE CURRY *(sabzi ka curry)*

Preparation time: 45 minutes   **Cooking time:** 25 minutes

India

Ingredients

Curry Powder:

1	tablespoon each coriander, cumin, turmeric
2	whole cardamom pods, ground
1	teaspoon each ginger, fenugreek, chili powder, garam masala (optional)
3	tablespoons peanut oil
2	large onions, minced
2	cloves garlic, minced

2	dried chili peppers
½	cup tomato sauce
¼	teaspoon sugar
4	medium potatoes
4	carrots, sliced
1	pint Brussels sprouts
2	ounces raisins
6	zucchini, sliced
4	apples, chopped
	Salt
	Lemon juice

1. In a small bowl, combine the curry-powder ingredients.

2. Heat the oil in a large pot. Add the onion, garlic and chili peppers and sauté over moderate heat for 10 minutes. Blend in the curry-powder mixture and stir until the spices darken in color, about 3 minutes. Blend in the tomato sauce and the sugar, then pour in enough water to make a thick sauce. Cover and simmer gently for 10 minutes.

3. While the sauce simmers, parboil the potatoes for 5 minutes then drain, peel and cut into small pieces. Add the potatoes, carrots, Brussels sprouts and raisins to the sauce. Mix thoroughly, then simmer for 5 minutes. Add the zucchini and the apples. Season to taste with salt and lemon juice, then continue to simmer until vegetables are tender, about 10 minutes. Serve the curry with a meat dish or as a main course with rice.

Serves 6 to 8

Baking

ARAB BREAD *(pita)*

Lebanon

Preparation time: 20 minutes   **Baking time:** 8 to 10 minutes
Dough rises—1¾ hours

Ingredients

1	package dry yeast	1	teaspoon salt
1 to 1¼	cups warm water	2	tablespoons oil
	Pinch sugar		Cornmeal
3½	cups presifted flour		

1. In a large mixing bowl, dissolve the yeast and sugar in ¼ cup of the water. Let stand for 10 minutes, then add the remaining water, the salt and the oil. Stir 1 cup of the flour at a time into the yeast mixture, forming a sticky dough. (Add a little more flour if dough is too sticky.)

2. Transfer the dough to a lightly floured board and knead vigorously until smooth, about 10 minutes. Shape the dough into a ball and coat lightly with oil. Cover and let rise until doubled in bulk, about 1½ hours.

3. Punch down the dough and form 6 or 7 balls. On a lightly floured board, roll or press out the dough with the hands into 6-inch circles that are ¼ inch thick. Dust lightly with flour, cover and let rise again for 15 minutes.

4. Preheat oven to 500°.

5. Place the bread on lightly oiled baking sheets dusted with cornmeal. Bake until puffy, about 8 to 10 minutes. Wrap the bread in foil immediately after removing from the oven to preserve moistness.

Makes 6 or 7 round loaves

IRISH SODA BREAD

Preparation time: 15 minutes   **Baking time:** 1 hour

Ireland

Ingredients

4	cups unbleached all-purpose flour	¾	cup sugar
1	teaspoon baking soda	½	cup butter, melted
1	teaspoon cream of tartar	3	ounces seedless raisins
1	teaspoon salt	1¾	cups buttermilk

1. Preheat oven to 375°.

2. Sift the dry ingredients into a large mixing bowl.

3. Add the butter, raisins and buttermilk. Mix well, making a soft, moist dough. Dust with additional flour if dough is too sticky to handle.

4. Transfer the dough to a lightly floured surface. Knead vigorously for 3 or 4 minutes until dough is firm, then shape into 2 round loaves.

5. Moisten each loaf with buttermilk and dust with flour.

6. Score the top of each loaf with an X.

7. Place the bread on a buttered and floured baking sheet and bake until nicely browned, about 1 hour. Cool on a wire rack.

Yields 2 loaves

SWEDISH SAFFRON BREAD
(saffransbröd)

Sweden

Preparation time: 20 minutes   **Baking time:** 6 to 8 minutes
Dough rises—1½ to 3½ hours

Ingredients

1	*pound butter*	½	*teaspoon salt*
¼	*cup milk*	1	*egg*
1	*envelope dry yeast*	3½ to 4	*cups flour*
½	*teaspoon ground saffron*		*Beaten egg for glaze*
½	*cup sugar*		*Raisins for decoration*

1. Melt the butter over low heat and gradually add the milk. Heat until mixture is warm, but not hot.

2. Place the yeast in a large mixing bowl. Add a little of the warm milk and blend thoroughly, then stir in the remaining milk, saffron, sugar, salt and egg. Mix well. Gradually stir in 3½ cups of the flour. Work the dough with fingers until smooth and firm.

3. Sprinkle a little of the remaining flour over the dough, then cover bowl and let stand in a warm place until the dough doubles in bulk (1 to 3 hours).

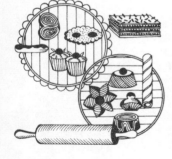

4. Transfer the dough to a lightly floured surface and knead until smooth. If dough is too moist, add some of the remaining flour. Divide into portions and shape dough into small cakes, braided loaves or buns. Arrange the breads on a buttered baking sheet, cover and let stand for ½ hour.

5. Preheat oven to 475°. Brush the breads with the egg, decorate with the raisins and bake until golden, about 6 to 8 minutes for small cakes and braided buns, about 15 minutes for larger loaves.

Serves 6

BRIOCHE

Preparation time: 30 minutes
Dough rises—2½ hours

Baking time: 20 minutes

France

Ingredients

1	envelope dry yeast	½	pound butter, softened
2	teaspoons sugar	6	eggs
¼	cup warm water	1	egg mixed with 2 tablespoons water for glazing
¾	cup milk, warmed		
4	cups presifted flour		
½	teaspoon salt		

1. In a large mixing bowl, dissolve the yeast and sugar in the warm water. Add the milk, 2 cups of the flour, and the salt, then beat well with a wooden spoon. Cover with a damp towel and let rise until doubled in bulk, about 1 hour.

2. Add the butter, eggs, and the remaining 2 cups of flour and mix well until the dough is smooth and satiny. Cover again with a damp towel and let rise until doubled in bulk, about 1½ hours.

3. With floured hands, roll 18 two-inch balls of dough. Place each one in a buttered muffin tin. Now roll 18 half-inch balls. Firmly press one small ball in the center of each large ball.

4. Preheat oven to 425°.

5. Brush each brioche with glaze and let them rise for another 15 minutes. Bake for 20 minutes, until golden brown.

Yields 18 brioches

GLAZED PRETZEL BREAD

(krendel gulevich)

USSR

Preparation time: ½ hour
Dough rises—2 hours

Baking time: 25 minutes

Ingredients

1 package dry yeast	2 eggs
¼ cup warm water	½ cup light cream
1 teaspoon sugar	1 egg lightly beaten with
2 cups flour	1 tablespoon cream
3 tablespoons sugar	2 teaspoons honey
½ teaspoon salt	2 teaspoons peach brandy
4 tablespoons butter, chilled	

1. In a cup, soak the yeast in the warm water with the sugar for about 10 minutes.

2. Sift together the flour, sugar and salt. Cut the butter into the flour until it reaches the consistency of corn meal.

3. In a large mixing bowl, lightly beat together the eggs and the cream, then stir in the yeast mixture. Gradually blend in the flour mixture. Knead the dough on a lightly floured surface until it is smooth and shiny, about 10 minutes. Shape it into a ball and coat it lightly with butter. Cover and let dough rise until doubled in bulk, about 1½ hours.

4. Preheat the oven to 425°.

5. Punch down the dough. Roll into a long 2-inch-thick rope. Twist the rope into a pretzel shape and transfer to a buttered baking sheet. Let dough rise until doubled again, about 30 minutes.

6. Brush the dough with the lightly beaten egg. Bake for 15 minutes, then cover with foil and bake for 10 more minutes. Remove from oven and transfer to a wire rack to cool. Combine the honey and brandy and glaze the krendel before serving.

Serves 6

MOLASSES GINGERBREAD

Preparation time: 15 minutes

Baking time: 1 hour

Ingredients

USA

½ *pound butter, in small pieces*

1 *cup sugar*

1 *cup molasses*

1 *cup milk, scalded*

2¼ *cups flour*

1 *teaspoon ginger*

1 *teaspoon cinnamon*

1 *teaspoon allspice*

1 *teaspoon salt*

1½ *teaspoons baking soda*

2 *eggs*

Rind of 1 navel orange, grated

Whipped cream for topping

Orange slices for garnish

1. Preheat oven to 300°.

2. In a large mixing bowl, combine the butter, sugar and molasses. Pour in the hot scalded milk and stir until the butter is melted, then let stand until cool.

3. Sift together into a bowl the flour, ginger, cinnamon, allspice, salt and baking soda. Reserve.

4. One by one, beat the eggs into the cooled milk mixture, then gradually beat in the spiced flour. Add the orange rind and mix thoroughly.

5. Scrape the batter into a 9 × 13-inch buttered baking pan and bake until a cake tester inserted in the center comes out clean, about 1 hour.

6. Cut into squares and serve piping hot, topped with whipped cream and garnished with orange slices.

Serves 6 to 8

FREE-FORM ALMOND CAKES

(galettes Charolaises)

France

Preparation time: 15 minutes
Batter chills—2 hours

Baking time: 40 minutes

Ingredients

3 ½	*cups presifted flour*
½	*pound butter, at room temperature*
2	*eggs*
1	*cup sugar*
4	*ounces almonds, ground*

2	*tablespoons water*
2	*tablespoons lemon juice*
5	*ounces mixed glacéed fruits, finely chopped*
	Black-currant preserves for topping

1. Sift the flour into a large bowl. Make a well in the middle of the flour and add the butter and eggs. Work mixture lightly with fingertips until well blended, then briskly work in the sugar, almonds, water, lemon juice and glacéed fruits.

2. Shape dough into a ball, wrap in greaseproof paper and refrigerate for 2 hours.

3. Preheat oven to 325°.

4. Transfer the chilled dough to a sheet of greaseproof paper and cut in half. Using the bottom of a plate, press each half into a flat round cake about ¾ inch thick.

5. Place the cakes on a buttered baking sheet. Streak the surfaces with a fork and bake until golden, about 40 minutes. (The cakes will be quite flat.)

6. When the cakes are done, transfer to a wire rack to cool. Serve at room temperature, topped with black-currant preserves.

Serves 6 to 8

NUTTED TEA CAKE
(gâteau aux noix de Grenoble)

Preparation time: 30 minutes   **Baking time:** 40 minutes   *France*

Ingredients

7 tablespoons unsalted butter, at room temperature	1 ounce walnuts, chopped
½ cup sugar	Juice of 1 lemon
3 eggs	Grated peel of 2 lemons
3 ounces hazelnuts, finely ground	1 cup flour
	½ teaspoon baking soda

1. Set oven at 350°.

2. Cream the butter in a bowl. Gradually add the sugar, beating well until light.

3. Using a wire whisk, gradually beat in the eggs, incorporating each one well before adding the next. Continue beating until mixture is light and fluffy.

4. Add the nuts, lemon juice, grated lemon peel, flour and soda. Mix until ingredients are thoroughly blended.

5. Pour into a buttered 1½-quart loaf pan and bake until the cake shrinks slightly from the sides of the pan and a toothpick inserted into the center of the cake comes out clean, about 40 minutes.

Serves 6

NUT CAKE *(gâteau aux noisettes)*

France

Preparation time: 10 minutes   **Baking time:** 45 minutes

Ingredients

   5   *eggs, separated*   2   *tablespoons water*
   ¾   *cup sugar*   *Pinch salt*
  10   *ounces hazelnuts,*
       walnuts or almonds,
       coarsely ground

1. Preheat oven to 350°.

2. Using a wire whisk, beat the egg yolks well in a bowl. Gradually beat in the sugar. Continue beating until the mixture is light yellow. Stir the nuts into the egg yolk mixture. Blend well, adding the water to facilitate mixing.

3. In another bowl, beat the egg whites until frothy. Add a pinch of salt, then continue beating until egg whites are stiff. Carefully fold the egg whites into the batter.

4. Pour the batter into a buttered and floured charlotte mold or 8-inch cake tin.

5. Bake until a toothpick inserted into the center of the cake comes out clean, about 45 minutes. (Do not open the oven door during baking time.)

6. When the cake is done, transfer to a cake rack and allow to cool thoroughly before removing from pan.

Serves 6 to 8

SAND CAKE *(sandkuchen)*

Preparation time: 45 minutes   **Baking time:** 50 minutes

Ingredients

Austria

½ *pound butter, at room
   temperature*

1¼ *cups sugar*

5 *eggs, separated*

½ *pound potato starch*

½ *teaspoon baking
   powder*

1 *tablespoon rum*

   *Rinds of 3 lemons,
   grated*

   Pinch salt

1. Preheat oven to 350°.

2. In a mixing bowl, cream the butter well with a wooden spoon, then beat until light and fluffy with a whisk or an electric beater. Add ¼ cup of the sugar to the butter. Beat until sugar is thoroughly incorporated, then add 1 egg yolk at a time, blending thoroughly. (This will take at least 20 minutes by hand or 10 minutes using an electric beater.)

3. A tablespoon at a time, beat the potato starch into the batter. Blend thoroughly before adding each remaining tablespoon. Beat the baking powder into the batter, then add the rum and grated lemon rind. Reserve.

4. In another mixing bowl, beat the egg whites with a pinch of salt until stiff. Gently fold the egg whites into the batter.

5. Pour the batter into a buttered loaf pan and bake until golden and a toothpick inserted into the center of the cake comes out clean, about 50 minutes.

6. Transfer cake (in pan) to a wire rack and cool for ½ hour, then remove from pan and cool to room temperature.

Serves 6 to 8

Sand cake may be prepared in advance and be stored for up to 2 weeks.

GUGELHUPF

Germany

Preparation time: 15 minutes
Dough rises—2 hours

Baking time: 1 hour

Ingredients

2   packages dry yeast
½   cup sugar
½   cup warm water
4   cups presifted flour
½   teaspoon salt
8   tablespoons butter, softened
4   eggs, lightly beaten
¾   cup milk, warmed
½   cup black raisins
½   cup white raisins

¼   cup candied citron
¼   cup candied orange peel
2   teaspoons vanilla extract
½   cup almonds, coarsely chopped
    Melted butter
    Confectioners' sugar for dusting cake

1. Dissolve the yeast and 1 teaspoon of the sugar in the warm water. Add ½ cup of the flour and mix lightly. Let the dough rise for 30 minutes in a warm draft-free corner.

2. Resift the remaining flour and the salt into the dough. With a wooden spoon, beat in the butter and eggs alternately with the milk. Beat the mixture well.

3. Add the raisins, citron, orange peel, vanilla, nuts and the remaining sugar. Beat until the batter is smooth and elastic. Cover the dough and let rise until doubled in bulk, about 1 hour.

4. Place the dough in a buttered Gugelhupf mold or tube pan. Let it rise for another 30 minutes.

5. Preheat oven to 350°. Brush the top of Gugelhupf with melted butter and bake until deep golden brown, about 1 hour. Dust with confectioners' sugar.

Serves 6 to 8

KING'S CAKE *(Königskuchen)*

Preparation time: 30 minutes

Baking time: 1¼ hours

Germany

Ingredients

¾ pound unsalted butter

1¼ cups sugar

5 eggs, separated

3 cups presifted flour

Pinch salt

¼ cup currants

¼ cup raisins

¼ cup almonds, slivered

2 tablespoons citron, chopped

Grated rind of 1 lemon

¼ teaspoon vanilla

1 ounce cognac or rum

1. Preheat oven to 350°.

2. Cream the butter, then add the sugar and beat until fluffy. Add the egg yolks, one at a time. Slowly stir in the flour, mixing well. Add the salt, currants, raisins, almonds, citron, lemon rind, vanilla and cognac.

3. Beat the egg whites with a little salt until stiff. Gently fold the egg whites into the batter, then pour into a 10-inch buttered cake pan.

4. Bake until a toothpick inserted in the cake comes out clean, about 1¼ hours. Cool the cake in the pan.

Serves 4 to 6

CHOCOLATE DREAM CAKE
(drömtårta)

Sweden

Preparation time: 30 minutes

Baking time: 10 minutes

Ingredients

⅓   cup potato starch
2   tablespoons cocoa
1   teaspoon baking powder
3   eggs
1   egg white
⅔   cup sugar

¼   pound butter, softened
1   cup confectioners' sugar
1   tablespoon cocoa
1   teaspoon vanilla extract
1   egg yolk

Mocha Butter Cream:

2   tablespoons instant coffee, dissolved in 1 teaspoon water

1. Preheat oven to 400°. Line a baking pan with greaseproof paper. Reserve.

2. Sift the potato starch, cocoa and baking powder into a bowl. Reserve.

3. In a large mixing bowl, beat the eggs and extra egg white very well. Beating constantly, gradually add the sugar. Continue beating until mixture is fluffy. A tablespoon at a time, beat the sifted ingredients into the egg and sugar mixture. Beat thoroughly after each addition.

4. Using a spatula, spread the batter into the baking pan and bake until cake springs back to the touch, about 10 minutes. Invert the cake onto a floured towel, cover with another towel and cool to room temperature.

5. Cream the butter well in a mixing bowl and blend in the sugar and cocoa. Beat mixture until fluffy. Add the coffee, vanilla, and egg yolk. Spread the mocha cream evenly on top of the cake. Holding the shorter end of the towel, roll the cake into a cylinder. Place on a platter and serve.

Serves 4

CHOCOLATE TORTE *(Schokoladentorte)*

Preparation time: 30 minutes   **Baking time:** 50 minutes

Ingredients

8	*ounces semisweet chocolate*
2	*tablespoons coffee*
1	*cup butter, softened*
1	*cup sugar*
8	*eggs, separated*
¼	*cup dry bread crumbs*
	Pinch salt

Glaze:

6	*ounces semisweet chocolate*
2	*tablespoons coffee*
1	*teaspoon butter*
	Whipped cream

Germany

1. Set oven at 375°. Combine the chocolate and coffee in a double-boiler. Melt over simmering water. Reserve.

2. In a large bowl, cream the butter. Gradually add the sugar and beat until light and fluffy. Beat the egg yolks until pale yellow, then gradually incorporate into the butter and sugar mixture. Add the bread crumbs. Blend thoroughly, then stir in the melted chocolate.

3. In another large bowl, beat the egg whites with the salt until stiff. Gently fold into the batter. Pour ¾ of the batter into a buttered cake pan. Refrigerate the rest of batter until needed.

4. Bake torte until a toothpick inserted in the center comes out clean, about 50 minutes. Cool torte slightly in the pan, then transfer to a cake rack. When it has cooled to room temperature (about 45 minutes), slice into 2 layers.

5. Remove chilled batter from refrigerator about 10 minutes before using. Spread it on the bottom layer of the torte, then cover with the other layer. Refrigerate until needed.

6. Prepare the glaze: Melt the chocolate with the coffee, then beat in the butter. Remove from heat and cool slightly. Spread the glaze over the torte. Serve, either chilled or at room temperature, with whipped cream.

Serves 6 to 8

CHEESECAKE

Preparation time: 20 minutes

Baking time: 45 minutes

Israel

Ingredients

Crust:

8	tablespoons butter, melted
2	cups graham cracker crumbs
2	tablespoons sugar

Filling:

3	eight-ounce packages cream cheese, at room temperature

4	eggs
1¼	cups sugar
2	teaspoons vanilla extract
1	tablespoon lemon juice
1	pint strawberries, hulled

1. Preheat oven to 350°.

2. Dribble the melted butter over the graham cracker crumbs and the sugar, then toss lightly. Press the crumbs firmly to all sides of a spring-form pan and refrigerate.

3. Combine the filling ingredients in a large mixing bowl. Beat until smooth, then pour into the chilled crust. Bake for 45 minutes, then turn off the heat and allow the cake to cool in the oven.

4. Place the cheesecake on a serving platter and arrange the strawberries in an attractive pattern on the top. Serve chilled.

Serves 6

PRUNE CAKE

Preparation time: 20 minutes   **Baking time:** 1 hour

Ingredients

USA

1½	cups sugar
1	teaspoon salt
1	teaspoon nutmeg
1	teaspoon cinnamon
1	teaspoon baking soda
2	cups flour
3	eggs
1	cup vegetable oil
1	cup buttermilk
1	cup prunes, chopped

6	ounces shelled filberts or walnuts, chopped
1	teaspoon vanilla

Glaze:

1	cup sugar
½	teaspoon baking soda
¼	pound butter
½	cup buttermilk
1	tablespoon corn syrup
½	teaspoon vanilla

1. Preheat oven to 300°.

2. Sift the dry ingredients into a mixing bowl. Reserve.

3. In another mixing bowl beat the eggs until pale yellow. Gradually beat in the oil and the buttermilk, then stir in the prunes, nuts and vanilla. Gradually blend the dry ingredients into the egg mixture. Continue beating until batter is thoroughly blended.

4. Pour the batter into a buttered and floured 9 × 13-inch cake pan and bake until a toothpick inserted comes out clean, about 1 hour. Transfer cake (in pan) to a wire rack. Reserve.

5. As soon as the cake is removed from the oven, prepare the glaze. Combine all the ingredients in a saucepan. Boil and stir over high heat until mixture is frothy and slightly thickened, about 2 minutes. Pour the glaze over the hot cake. Let stand for at least 3 hours. Serve at room temperature.

Serves 6

Because the glaze seeps into the cake as it stands, this prune cake tastes particularly good the day after it is prepared.

CARROT CAKE

Canada

Preparation time: 15 minutes   **Baking time:** 45 minutes

Ingredients

1½ cups sugar	1 teaspoon salt
1¼ cups vegetable oil	3 teaspoons cinnamon
4 eggs	½ teaspoon nutmeg
2 cups flour	2 teaspoons vanilla
2 teaspoons baking soda	3 cups grated carrots

1. Preheat oven to 325°.

2. Combine the sugar, oil and eggs.

3. Sift together the dry ingredients. Add to the sugar mixture, beating well. Add the vanilla and carrots.

4. Pour into a large buttered and floured pan and bake until a cake tester comes out clean, about 45 minutes.

Serves 6

DUNDEE CAKE

Preparation time: 20 minutes

Baking time: 2 hours

Scotland

Ingredients

¾	cup butter	¼	cup glacéed cherries
¾	cup granulated sugar	2½	cups mixed dried fruit
3	eggs	½	cup candied peel
2	cups flour	3	tablespoons milk
2	teaspoons baking powder	2	ounces almond flakes or chips
1	teaspoon allspice		Egg white for glaze
2	ounces almonds, chopped		

1. Preheat oven to 325°.

2. Cream the butter in a large mixing bowl. Gradually blend in the sugar and beat until fluffy. Gradually incorporate the eggs into the mixture.

3. Sift together the dry ingredients. Blend into the butter mixture, adding enough milk to make a thick batter. Stir in the fruits.

4. Pour the batter into a buttered and floured 8-inch cake tin. Cover with the almond flakes and brush with the egg white. Bake until a toothpick inserted in the cake comes out clean, about 2 hours. Cool cake in the pan before transferring to a wire rack.

Serves 6

ALMOND TORTE *(toucinho do céu)*

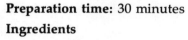

Portugal

Preparation time: 30 minutes

Baking time: 10 minutes

Ingredients

1¼	cups sugar
⅓	cup water
6	ounces almonds, finely ground
8	egg yolks
1½	teaspoons ground cinnamon

1	teaspoon almond extract
4	ounces almond flakes or chips, toasted
	Whipped cream flavored with almond extract and sugar

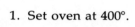

1. Set oven at 400°.

2. In a heavy saucepan, combine the sugar and water. Bring to a gentle boil until liquid clears. Stirring over moderate heat, add the ground almonds and cook for 5 minutes. Remove pan from heat and reserve.

3. In a bowl, beat the egg yolks with a wire whisk until pale yellow. Stir the almond mixture into the egg yolks a spoonful at a time, beating well. Return mixture to saucepan. Stir in cinnamon and almond extract.

4. Stirring constantly, gently cook almond mixture over low heat until it thickens slightly, about 10 minutes. Do not boil. Remove from heat.

5. Pour mixture into a buttered fluted pie pan and top with the toasted almond flakes. Bake pie until set, about 10 minutes. Serve cold accompanied by whipped cream flavored with almond extract and sugar.

Serves 6

RASPBERRY JAM TART *(Linzer Torte)*

Preparation time: 30 minutes · **Baking time:** 25 minutes
Pastry chills—30 minutes

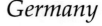

Germany

Ingredients

1	cup flour	2	egg yolks
1	teaspoon cinnamon	An	8-ounce jar raspberry
½	pound hazelnuts, ground		jam
½	cup sugar		Confectioners' sugar for dusting top of tart
½	pound unsalted butter, chilled		

1. Sift the flour and cinnamon into a large mixing bowl, then add the hazelnuts and sugar. Using a pastry blender or 2 knives, cut the butter into the dry ingredients until pastry has the consistency of fine cornmeal. Add the egg yolks and briskly work mixture with fingertips until smooth. Do not overhandle the pastry. Wrap in greaseproof paper and refrigerate for 30 minutes.

2. Preheat oven to 350°.

3. On a lightly floured surface, roll out ⅔ of the chilled pastry to ¼-inch thickness and line a 9-inch false-bottomed pie plate.

4. Spoon the raspberry jam into the prepared tart shell, then spread jam over entire bottom surface.

5. Roll out the remaining pastry on a lightly floured surface. Cut into long ½-inch-wide strips with a fluted pastry wheel or knife. Lay the strips in a lattice pattern on top of the filled tart. Pinch the strips together with the edges of tart shell, then refrigerate for 15 minutes.

6. Bake tart until pastry is lightly browned, about 25 minutes. Cool in the pan for 15 minutes, then remove tart from pan and cool to room temperature on a cake rack. Dust with confectioners' sugar.

Serves 6

MERINGUE SPONGE CAKE
(Génoise meringuée)

France

Preparation time: 30 minutes   **Baking time:** 30 minutes
Meringue syrup simmers—15 minutes

Ingredients

A one-pound Génoise or
    other sponge cake
½ cup apricot jam
2 tablespoons cognac
3 tablespoons sugar

½ cup sugar
4 egg whites
    Pinch salt
    Pinch cream of tartar
    Glacéed cherries

Meringue:

½ cup water

1. Cut the cake into 2 layers. Reserve.

2. Combine the apricot jam, cognac and sugar in a small heavy saucepan. Stir over moderate heat until sugar dissolves and mixture is runny, then remove from heat and cool slightly. Using a knife or spatula, spread the filling over one layer of the cake. Top with the remaining layer. Transfer to an oven-proof platter and reserve.

3. Set oven at 200°.

4. In another saucepan, combine the sugar and water. Stir over moderate heat until sugar dissolves and liquid clears, about 2 to 3 minutes. Then boil until syrup reaches the soft ball stage (238° on a candy thermometer), about 10 minutes.

5. While the syrup cooks, beat the egg whites in a large bowl with the salt and the cream of tartar until stiff. Gradually fold the hot syrup into the egg whites. Beat meringue until cooled to 100°, about 10 minutes.

6. Spread the meringue with a spatula over the cake. Top with glacéed cherries. Bake cake for 30 minutes. (Do not brown meringue.) Serve hot or cool to room temperature.

Serves 4

STRAWBERRY CREAM CAKE
(gâteau de fraises)

Preparation time: 1½ hours   **Baking time:** 10 minutes

France

Ingredients

5	egg yolks
½	cup sugar
1½	ounces hazelnuts, toasted and ground
1½	ounces pecans, toasted and ground
2	tablespoons cake flour
1	teaspoon vanilla
6	egg whites

	Pinch salt
1	pint fresh strawberries
5	tablespoons sugar
3	tablespoons framboise or kirsch
1	envelope unflavored gelatin
1½	cups heavy cream
½	cup red-currant jelly, melted

1. Preheat oven to 400°. Beat the yolks until pale yellow. Gradually add the sugar, beating until mixture is fluffy. Beat the flour into the yolk mixture, then blend in the nuts and vanilla.

2. In another bowl, beat the egg whites with salt until stiff. Fold the whites into the yolk mixture. Pour into 2 well-buttered and floured 8-inch-round cake pans and bake until done, about 8 to 12 minutes. Cool the cake in the pans for 10 minutes, then turn onto a rack and let stand until cool.

3. Slice ½ pint of the sliced strawberries, then sprinkle with 1 tablespoon of the sugar and 2 tablespoons of the liqueur. Combine the remaining liqueur and 3 tablespoons of water in a small saucepan. Add the gelatin and stir over low heat until it dissolves. Stir in the remaining sugar, then let cool.

4. Whip the cream until stiff. Stir the gelatin mixture into the cream, then blend in the drained strawberries. Refrigerate.

5. Spread the currant glaze over the cooled cake layers. Place one layer on a serving plate and spread ⅓ of the strawberry cream over the top. Cover with the other layer of cake and frost the entire *gâteau* with the remaining strawberry cream. Arrange whole strawberries on the top and brush with the glaze. Refrigerate cake until set, about 2 hours.

Serves 4

ALMOND MACAROONS
(macarons de Saint-Émilion)

France

Preparation time: 30 minutes   **Baking time:** 30 to 35 minutes
Macaroon mixture chills—½ hour

Ingredients

3 cups sugar	2 tablespoons lemon juice
¾ cup water	¼ teaspoon almond extract
10 ounces blanched almonds, finely chopped	Superfine granulated sugar for sprinkling
4 egg whites, very lightly beaten	

1. In the top section of a double boiler combine the sugar and water. Blend mixture well, then stir in the finely chopped almonds and the lightly beaten egg whites.

2. Using a wire whisk or an electric beater, beat mixture over simmering water until light and fluffy, about 10 minutes.

3. Raise heat slightly and continue beating until mixture is dried out and somewhat lumpy, about 5 minutes. Refrigerate until completely cooled, about ½ hour.

4. Preheat oven to 275°. Line a baking sheet with greaseproof paper. Using 2 teaspoons, shape the macaroon mixture into small mounds and drop onto the paper. Sprinkle with superfine granulated sugar and bake until golden, about 30 to 35 minutes. (Do not open oven door during baking.)

5. When the macaroons are done, transfer (on paper) to a cake rack and allow to cool to room temperature. Remove cooled macaroons from paper by placing the paper on a damp cloth and lifting off the macaroons with a spatula.

Yields about 3 dozen macaroons

PINE NUT MERINGUES
(gâteaux soufflés aux pignons)

Preparation time: 30 minutes   **Baking time:** 45 minutes   *France*

Ingredients

2   *egg whites*
    Pinch salt
    Pinch cream of tartar

⅔   *cup superfine*
    granulated sugar
⅓   *cup pine nuts, slivered*

1. Set oven at 225°.

2. Line a cooking sheet with greaseproof paper and butter generously.

3. In a bowl beat the egg whites until frothy. Add a pinch of salt and a pinch of cream of tartar, then continue beating until very stiff.

4. Gently fold in the sugar and pine nuts.

5. Using a tablespoon, drop little mounds of the mixture onto the buttered paper.

6. Bake meringues until they can be removed from the paper without sticking, about 45 minutes.

Yields about 15 meringues

ALSATIAN CHRISTMAS COOKIES
(schwowebredles)

France

Preparation time: 20 minutes
Dough chills—overnight

Baking time: 10 minutes
per batch

Ingredients

½	pound unsalted butter, at room temperature
1	cup sugar
1¾	cups flour
8	ounces almonds, ground
4½	ounces candied orange peel, finely minced
4	teaspoons ground cinnamon

1	egg
½	teaspoon rose water (optional) or ½ teaspoon lemon juice
½	teaspoon salt
1	egg yolk, beaten, for glazing
	Sugar and ground almonds for garnish

1. In a bowl, cream the butter with the sugar. Blend until fully integrated. Gradually beat in the flour, then add the rest of the ingredients. Mix thoroughly.

2. Knead the dough well, then cover with a damp cloth and refrigerate overnight.

3. Set oven at 400°.

4. Place the chilled dough on waxed paper and roll out to ¼-inch thickness. Using cookie cutters or a knife, cut the dough into various Christmas-shaped cookies. Brush the tops with the beaten egg and sprinkle with sugar and ground almonds.

5. Arrange the cookies on buttered and floured baking sheets and bake for 10 minutes.

Yields about 60 cookies

BRANDY RING TWISTS
(konjakskränsar)

Preparation time: 25 minutes   **Baking time:** 10 minutes   *Sweden*

Ingredients

½ *pound butter, at room*
    temperature

⅔ *cup sugar*

2½ *cups flour, sifted*

4 *tablespoons brandy*

1. Preheat oven to 350°.

2. In a mixing bowl cream the butter well. Gradually blend in the sugar and beat until light and fluffy. Beat in the brandy, a tablespoon at a time, then gradually blend in the flour. Mix thoroughly.

3. Transfer the dough to a lightly floured board. Roll out dough to ¼-inch thickness, then cut into thin 5-inch strips.

4. Assemble the brandy rings: Twist 2 of the dough strips together to form a rope, then join the ends of the rope to form a ring. Repeat process with the remaining strips of dough.

5. Transfer the brandy rings to a buttered baking sheet and bake until golden, about 10 minutes.

Yields about 6 dozen brandy ring twists

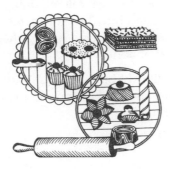

DUTCH SPICE COOKIES *(Speculaas)*

The Netherlands

Preparation time: 30 minutes   **Baking time:** 15 to 20 minutes

Ingredients

4	cups flour
4	teaspoons baking powder
½	teaspoon salt
1	teaspoon cinnamon
1	teaspoon ground cloves
1	teaspoon ground nutmeg
½	teaspoon white pepper
½	pound unsalted butter, at room temperature
1	cup brown sugar
1	tablespoon lemon peel, grated
⅓ to ½	cup milk
6	ounces almonds, slivered

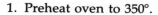

1. Preheat oven to 350°.

2. Sift the flour, baking powder, salt, cinnamon, cloves, nutmeg and white pepper into a mixing bowl. Reserve.

3. In a large mixing bowl, cream the butter well with a wooden spoon. Gradually work in the sugar, then beat mixture until light and fluffy. Blend the spiced flour, a little at a time, into the butter and sugar mixture, and then add the lemon zest. Gradually add ⅓ cup of the milk to the mixture. Blend thoroughly, adding a little more milk, if necessary, to make a soft dough.

4. On a lightly floured surface, roll out dough to ¼-inch thickness, then cut dough into 3-inch squares. Using a spatula, transfer the squares to buttered baking sheets, then sprinkle with the slivered almonds.

5. Bake cookies until light brown, about 15 to 20 minutes. Cool slightly on baking sheets, then transfer to a wire rack and cool to room temperature.

Yields 40 cookies

In the Netherlands, windmill-patterned Speckulaas molds are pressed onto the rolled-out dough. At Christmastime, tree, star, or Santa Claus cookie cutters can be used.

SCANDINAVIAN GINGERSNAPS
(pepparkakor)

Preparation time: 30 minutes
Dough refrigerates—2 hours

Baking time: 8 to 10 minutes
per batch

Sweden

Ingredients

⅔ cup light brown sugar
½ cup granulated sugar
⅓ cup molasses
⅓ cup water
10 tablespoons butter
1½ teaspoons cinnamon

2 teaspoons ground ginger
1 teaspoon ground nutmeg
1½ teaspoons baking powder
2¾ cups unbleached flour, sifted

1. In a saucepan combine the brown sugar, granulated sugar, molasses and water. Bring to a boil.

2. Stirring constantly over moderate heat, add the butter a tablespoon at a time. Continue stirring until butter is melted, then remove pan from heat and cool for 20 minutes.

3. Add the cinnamon, ginger, nutmeg and baking powder to the sugar mixture, then gradually blend in the flour.

4. Cover the cookie dough and refrigerate until firm, about 2 hours.

5. Preheat oven to 350°.

6. Transfer the chilled dough to a lightly floured surface. Knead dough until smooth and even, then roll out to ⅛-inch thickness.

7. Using the rim of a small glass or a 2-inch cookie cutter, cut the dough into rounds. Place on a buttered baking sheet and bake until golden, about 8 to 10 minutes.

Yields about 100 cookies

SHORTBREAD COOKIES

Canada

Preparation time: 15 minutes
Dough chills—1 hour

Baking time: 20 minutes

Ingredients

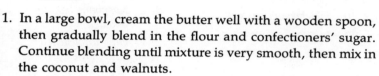

¾ cup butter, softened
3 cups flour
2 cups confectioners' sugar
2 ounces shredded coconut

6 ounces walnuts, finely chopped
Sugar for sprinkling cookies

1. In a large bowl, cream the butter well with a wooden spoon, then gradually blend in the flour and confectioners' sugar. Continue blending until mixture is very smooth, then mix in the coconut and walnuts.

2. Roll dough into a ball, wrap in greaseproof paper and refrigerate for 1 hour.

3. Set oven at 300°.

4. On a lightly floured greaseproof paper, roll out the dough to ½-inch thickness. Using a sharp knife or cookie cutter, cut dough into various shapes.

5. Arrange cookies on an unbuttered cookie sheet and bake for 20 minutes. When the cookies are done, transfer to a cake rack and sprinkle with sugar.

Yields about 4 dozen cookies

CAEN COOKIES *(sablés de Caen)*

Preparation time: 15 minutes   **Baking time:** 8 minutes
Dough chills—1 hour

France

Ingredients

1¾ *cups flour*	*Peel of 1 orange,*
¼ *teaspoon salt*	*grated*
3 *egg yolks, hard-boiled*	½ *pound butter, chilled*
½ *cup sugar*	

1. Sift the flour and salt into a mixing bowl. Make a well in the center of the flour and sieve the egg yolks into the well.

2. Add the sugar and grated orange peel. Mix lightly.

3. Using 2 knives, cut the butter into the flour mixture, cutting the butter down to pea-sized pieces.

4. Using fingertips, lightly work the dough until smooth, then shape into a ball, wrap in greaseproof paper and refrigerate for 1 hour.

5. Set oven to 400°.

6. On lightly floured greaseproof paper, roll out the dough to about ¼-inch thickness. Using cookie cutters, cut dough into desired shapes.

7. Arrange the cookies on a buttered baking sheet, score the tops with a fork and bake 8 minutes.

Yields about 3 dozen cookies

WALNUT DELIGHTS *(koeka)*

Preparation time: 10 minutes   **Baking time:** 25 minutes

Denmark   **Ingredients**

1 cup graham cracker crumbs	3 ounces walnuts, chopped
¾ cup sugar	1 teaspoon vanilla
1 teaspoon baking powder	Salt
2 eggs, separated	Ice cream or whipped cream for garnish

1. Preheat oven to 350°.

2. Combine the graham cracker crumbs, sugar and baking powder in a large mixing bowl.

3. Lightly beat the egg yolks and stir into the dry ingredients. Add the walnuts and vanilla. Mix well.

4. In a separate bowl beat the egg whites with a pinch of salt until stiff. Fold carefully into the graham cracker mixture, then pour the batter into an 8 × 8-inch buttered and floured pan.

5. Bake until golden, about 25 minutes. Cool in the pan, then cut into bars. Top with ice cream or whipped cream.

Serves 6

HONEY AND NUT PASTRY *(baklava)*

Preparation time: 30 minutes

Baking time: 45 minutes

Turkey

Ingredients

Syrup:

   1 *cup sugar*
  ½ *cup water*
   1 *tablespoon lemon juice*
   1 *tablespoon orange-blossom or rose water*

20 *prepared phyllo pastry sheets*
 ½ *pound butter, melted*
  8 *ounces shelled walnuts or almonds, chopped*
  3 *tablespoons sugar*

1. Preheat oven to 350°.

2. Combine the sugar and water in a saucepan. Stir over low heat until sugar dissolves, then add the lemon juice. Bring to a gentle boil and simmer until thickened. Stir in the orange blossom water and simmer briefly, then refrigerate.

3. Lay a sheet of phyllo pastry in a well-buttered rectangular baking dish. Brush some of the melted butter over the pastry. Add another sheet of pastry, then brush with butter. Continue until ½ the pastry and ½ the butter have been used.

4. Top the stacked pastry sheets with the chopped walnuts (or almonds), then sprinkle with the sugar. Cover the nuts and sugar with a layer of phyllo, then brush with butter. Repeat until all the phyllo and all the butter have been used.

5. Using a very sharp knife, cut through the baklava to make strips about 3 inches wide, then cut diagonally at 5-inch intervals making a diamond pattern.

6. Bake for 30 minutes, then raise oven temperature to 450° and continue baking until the pastry has puffed and colored slightly, about 15 minutes more. Remove from oven and cover with the chilled syrup. Cool to room temperature. To serve, slice baklava along original incisions and top each piece with some of the syrup.

Yields about 2 dozen pastries

PEACH COBBLER

Preparation time: 30 minutes   **Baking time:** 45 minutes

USA

Ingredients

8	*large fresh peaches, peeled and sliced*
3	*ounces shelled walnuts, chopped*
½	*cup light brown sugar*
1	*tablespoon lemon juice*
½	*teaspoon cinnamon*
1	*cup flour*
2	*teaspoons baking powder*

¼	*teaspoon salt*
¼	*pound unsalted butter, at room temperature*
½	*cup granulated sugar*
2	*eggs, beaten*
	Rind of 1 lemon, grated

1. Preheat oven to 375°.

2. Toss the peaches and walnuts in a deep ovenproof dish with 6 tablespoons of the brown sugar, the lemon juice and the cinnamon. Reserve.

3. Sift the flour, baking powder and salt into a bowl. Reserve.

4. In a mixing bowl, cream the butter well with a wooden spoon, then gradually blend in the sugar. Beat mixture until light and fluffy.

5. Beat the eggs into the butter and sugar mixture, then blend in the lemon rind.

6. Gradually beat the flour mixture into the butter and sugar mixture. Stir until batter is thoroughly blended.

7. Spread the batter over the reserved fruit. Top with the remaining brown sugar. Bake until crust is golden, about 45 minutes. Serve piping hot from the baking dish.

Serves 4

Top each portion of cobbler with a generous dollop of whipped cream, vanilla ice cream or hard sauce.

APPLE TART *(tarte aux pommes)*

Preparation time: 45 minutes   **Baking time:** 25 minutes
Pastry chills—1 hour

France

Ingredients

Sweet Short-Crust Pastry:

 1¾ cups presifted flour
   5 ounces unsalted butter
   3 tablespoons shortening
  ¼ teaspoon salt
   3 tablespoons sugar
  ½ cup iced water
   1 egg yolk

Filling:

   5 pounds cooking apples,
      peeled and sliced

  ⅓ cup apricot jam
  ½ cup plus 2 tablespoons
      sugar
  ½ cup Calvados
   3 tablespoons butter
   1 tablespoon lemon juice

Glaze:

  ½ cup apricot jam, melted

1. Using the above-listed ingredients, prepare the sweet short-crust pastry (page 481). Chill for 1 hour.

2. Set oven at 375°.

3. Roll out the pastry to ⅛-inch thickness and line a buttered 11-inch pie pan. Prick and partially bake shell for 10 minutes.

4. Place 3 pounds of the apples in a saucepan, cover pan and cook apples over low heat until very soft, about 15 minutes. Beat in the apricot jam, sugar, Calvados and butter. Stirring constantly, bring to a boil and cook until applesauce is very thick, about 5 minutes. Remove from heat.

5. In a bowl, toss the remaining 2 pounds sliced apples with the lemon juice and the remaining 2 tablespoons sugar.

6. Pour the slightly cooled applesauce into the tart shell. Top with the sliced apples. Bake tart until apple slices are tender, about 25 minutes. Remove from oven. Glaze the warm tart with the apricot jam. Serve at room temperature.

Serves 6 to 8

FRENCH APPLE-CUSTARD PIE

(cadet Mathieu)

France

Preparation time: 45 minutes
Pastry chills—1 hour

Baking time: 1 hour

Ingredients

Sweet Short-Crust Pastry:

1¾   *cups presifted flour*
  5   *ounces unsalted butter*
  3   *tablespoons shortening*
  ¼   *teaspoon salt*
  3   *tablespoons sugar*
  ½   *cup iced water*
  1   *egg yolk*

½   *teaspoon ground cinnamon*
½   *cup sugar*
3   *tablespoons flour*
1½   *cups milk, scalded*
1½   *teaspoons orange-flower water (optional)*
4   *egg yolks*
___
1   *egg, beaten, for glazing*

Filling:

1½   *pounds cooking apples, peeled and sliced*

1. Using the above-listed ingredients, prepare the sweet short-crust pastry (page 481). Chill for 1 hour.

2. Toss the apples, cinnamon and half the sugar in a bowl, cover and reserve.

3. Place the flour in a saucepan. Beating constantly, gradually add the scalded milk, then stir in the remaining sugar (and the orange-flower water). Beat over moderate heat for 5 minutes. Remove from heat.

4. In a bowl, beat the yolks with a whisk until pale yellow. Gradually beat in the milk mixture. Cool until needed.

5. Set oven at 350°.

6. Roll out ⅔ of the pastry and line an 11-inch buttered pie pan. Pour the custard mixture into the pie shell. Layer the sliced apples on top. Roll out the remaining pastry and cover the pie. Seal the edges and make 2 or 3 slits on the top. Brush with the beaten egg. Bake until golden, about 1 hour.

Serves 6 to 8

APPLE ENVELOPES
(douillons à la Normande)

Preparation time: 30 minutes
Pastry chills—1 hour

Baking time: 45 minutes

France

Ingredients

Sweet Short-Crust Pastry:

3½	cups presifted flour
10	ounces unsalted butter
5	tablespoons shortening
½	teaspoon salt
5	tablespoons sugar
1	cup iced water
2	egg yolks

6	cooking apples
	Juice of 2 lemons
6	teaspoons cinnamon
6	teaspoons brandy
6	teaspoons butter
1	cup sugar
1	tablespoon cinnamon
	Heavy cream for topping

1. Using the above-listed ingredients, prepare the sweet short-crust pastry (page 481). Refrigerate for 1 hour.

2. Peel and core the apples, leaving a ¼-inch plug of core at the base of each apple. Trim bottoms evenly so that apples will stand. Sprinkle all surfaces of the apples with the lemon juice. Place a teaspoon of cinnamon, brandy and sugar in each core. Refrigerate.

3. Combine sugar and cinnamon in a small bowl. Reserve.

4. Divide pastry into 6 equal pieces. Roll out 1 section of pastry to ⅛-inch thickness between 2 sheets of waxed paper.

5. Using a plate as a guide, carve a 10-inch circle. Cover prepared apple with the dough round. Fold edges around apple and pinch pastry to seal. Sprinkle outsides with cinnamon-sugar. Repeat entire step for remaining apples. Arrange apples on a platter and refrigerate for 30 minutes.

6. Preheat oven to 350°. Bake on a buttered baking sheet for 45 minutes. Serve piping hot, topped with chilled heavy cream.

Serves 6

APPLE STRUDEL *(Äpfelstrudel)*

Preparation time: 1 hour

Baking time: 45 minutes

Germany

Ingredients

2	pounds tart apples, peeled, cored and sliced
	Juice of 1 lemon
½	cup sugar
1	cup raisins
	Rind of 1 lemon
½	teaspoon cinnamon

Dough #1:

2	packages dry yeast
1	teaspoon sugar
½	cup warm water
1	cup presifted flour
2	egg yolks

Dough #2:

¼	pound unsalted butter, chilled
1	cup presifted flour

¼	cup raspberry jam, melted
1	egg yolk, lightly beaten

1. Preheat oven to 400°. Toss the first six ingredients and cover. Prepare Dough #1: Combine the yeast, sugar and warm water. Add ¼ cup of the flour, stirring well. Let rest for 5 minutes. Add the remaining flour, kneading well. Add the egg yolks, then shape dough into a ball, cover and reserve.

2. Prepare Dough #2: With a pastry blender, quickly cut the butter into the flour until mixture is the consistency of cornmeal. Roll into a ball, cover and refrigerate.

3. Roll out each of the doughs separately between pieces of floured wax paper to ⅛-inch thickness. Place Dough #1 on top of Dough #2. Fold in half, roll out to ¼-inch thickness. Repeat the process of folding and rolling the dough 2 more times. Transfer the dough to a floured cloth and roll the dough as thinly as possible into a long rectangle.

4. Trim the edges, then brush with the raspberry jam. Spread the apple mixture on a long edge of the dough. Carefully roll the dough, jelly-roll fashion, into a compact cylinder. Tuck in the edges and seal. Transfer the strudel to a buttered baking sheet. Brush lightly with the egg yolk and bake until golden, about 45 minutes.

Serves 6

PEAR FLAN *(flan de poires Tourangeau)*

Preparation time: 1 hour   **Baking time:** 15 minutes
Pastry chills—1 hour

France

Ingredients

Sweet Short-Crust Pastry:

1¾	cups presifted flour
5	ounces unsalted butter
3	tablespoons shortening
¼	teaspoon salt
3	tablespoons sugar
½	cup iced water
1	egg yolk
——	
2½	cups sugar
2	tablespoons cornstarch

2	egg yolks
1	cup milk
	Pinch salt
½	cup almonds, ground
A	1-inch piece vanilla bean
¼	cup unsalted butter
6	pears, peeled
2	cups water
1	cup apricot jam, melted

1. Using the above-listed ingredients, prepare the pastry (page 481). Chill for 1 hour.

2. Preheat oven to 400°.

3. Roll out the pastry to ⅛-inch thickness and line a 10-inch pie pan. Bake pie shell until golden, about 15 minutes.

4. Combine ½ cup of the sugar and the cornstarch in a mixing bowl. Add the yolks and ¼ cup of the milk, mixing well. Blend in the salt and the almonds. Heat the remaining milk and add the vanilla bean. Bring almost to a boil, then pour a small amount of the hot milk into the yolk mixture. Pour the eggs back into the saucepan, remove the vanilla bean and stir until thickened. Cool to room temperature, then incorporate the butter. Pour the custard into the shell and refrigerate.

5. Combine the remaining sugar and the water and stir until the mixture clears. Poach the pears in the liquid until tender, about 10 minutes. Remove, drain and slice. Arrange the pears in an attractive pattern on top of the custard and glaze with the apricot jam. Refrigerate or serve immediately.

Serves 6

SWISS PLUM TART *(tarte aux quetsches)*

Switzerland

Preparation time: 40 minutes
Pastry chills—1 hour

Baking time: 30 minutes

Ingredients

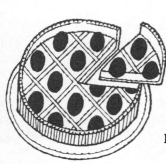

Sweet Short-Crust Pastry:

1¾	cup presifted flour
3	ounces unsalted butter
3	tablespoons shortening
¼	teaspoons salt
3	tablespoons sugar
½	cup iced water
1	egg yolk

Filling:

¾	cup white cake crumbs
4	tablespoons almonds, finely ground

12 to 16	fresh purple plums, pitted and quartered
2	tablespoons sugar
1	tablespoon lemon juice
3	tablespoons unsalted butter, softened
½	cup apricot jam, melted
	Confectioners' sugar

1. Using the above-listed ingredients, prepare the sweet short-crust pastry (page 481). Chill for 1 hour.

2. Preheat oven to 400°.

3. Roll out the pastry to ¼-inch thickness and line a 9-inch pie pan. Spread the cake crumbs and almonds over the dough. Arrange the plums in concentric circles over the crumbs. Sprinkle the sugar and the lemon juice over the plums and dot with the butter. Bake the tart until the plums are soft and the crust is golden brown, about 30 minutes. Brush with the apricot glaze. Cool. Sprinkle with confectioners' sugar just before serving.

Serves 6

PRUNE AND CUSTARD TART
(tarte Albigeoise)

Preparation time: 30 minutes
Pastry chills—1 hour

Baking time: 25 minutes

France

Ingredients

Sweet Short-Crust Pastry:

1¾	cups presifted flour
5	ounces unsalted butter
3	tablespoons shortening
¼	teaspoon salt
3	tablespoons sugar
½	cup iced water
1	egg yolk
1	pound pitted prunes

Custard:

1½	cups milk
½	vanilla bean or ¼ teaspoon vanilla
3	egg yolks
1	egg
⅓	cup sugar

1. Using the above-listed ingredients, prepare the sweet short-crust pastry (page 481). Chill for 1 hour.

2. Set oven at 375°.

3. Soak dried prunes in a bowl of hot water for 10 minutes. Drain and reserve.

4. Roll out pastry and line a 9-inch pie pan. Prick the surface with a fork and partially bake shell for 10 minutes. Reserve.

5. In a small saucepan, combine the milk and the vanilla. Bring to a boil, then immediately remove pan from heat. Discard vanilla bean (if used) and let milk cool.

6. In a bowl beat the egg yolks and whole egg. Beating constantly, slowly add the sugar. Continue beating until mixture is light and fluffy, then gradually beat in the scalded milk.

7. Arrange prunes in the shell and cover with the custard. Bake until the custard sets, about 25 minutes. Serve cold.

Serves 6

VERMONT PUMPKIN PIE

USA

Preparation time: 1½ hours
Pastry chills—1 hour

Baking time: 1 hour

Ingredients

Flaky Pastry:

2	cups flour
1	teaspoon salt
¾	cup butter
⅓	cup iced water

A	3-pound pumpkin or a 1-pound can pumpkin purée

⅔	cup grated maple sugar or brown sugar
1	teaspoon cinnamon
½	teaspoon ginger
⅛	teaspoon nutmeg
⅛	teaspoon ground cloves
½	teaspoon salt
1½	cups heavy cream
2	eggs, slightly beaten
¼	cup rum
	Whipped cream

1. Using the above-listed ingredients prepare the pastry (page 474). Chill for 1 hour.

2. Preheat oven to 325°. Halve the pumpkin and remove the seeds and strings. Place cut sides down on a baking sheet and bake until soft, about 1 hour.

3. Roll out the dough to ¼-inch thickness on a lightly floured surface. Line a 9-inch pie pan.

4. Remove the cooked pumpkin from the oven. Purée the pulp in a food mill or ricer. Combine 2 cups of the purée (or canned pumpkin) with the maple sugar, cinnamon, ginger, nutmeg, cloves and salt. Mix thoroughly. Beat the cream into the mixture, then thoroughly beat in the eggs. Add the rum.

5. Pour the mixture into the shell and bake until a knife inserted in the center of pie comes out clean, about 1 hour. Serve at room temperature or chilled, either plain or topped with whipped cream.

Serves 6 to 8

Sweet Dishes

GLAZED APPLES *(la sze ping kuo)*

Preparation time: 15 minutes   **Cooking time:** 10 minutes

China

Ingredients

¼ cup peanut oil	2 tablespoons peanut oil
4 apples, peeled, cored and cut in pieces	1 tablespoon sesame seeds

Syrup:

1 cup sugar
½ cup water

Bowl of iced water

1. Heat the oil in a large skillet over moderately high heat.

2. Add the apple pieces and stir-fry over moderately high heat for 3 minutes. Using a slotted spoon, transfer apples to absorbent paper and drain thoroughly.

3. Prepare the syrup: Combine the sugar and water in a saucepan and bring to a boil over moderate heat. Stir in the peanut oil, then lower heat slightly and simmer until syrup turns golden brown, about 10 minutes. Stir in the sesame seeds, then remove pan from heat.

4. Add the fried apples to the syrup mixture, stirring gently so that each piece is thoroughly coated.

5. Plunge the coated apples into the iced water until the syrup hardens, a few seconds, then transfer to a platter and serve immediately.

Serves 4

Some cooks arrange the glazed fruit on an oiled platter, and guests dip individual portions into the iced water at the table.

BAKED APPLES MARZIPAN
(fyllda stekta äpplen)

Preparation time: 15 minutes   **Baking time:** 20 to 25 minutes

Sweden

Ingredients

Almond Paste Filling:

3   ounces blanched
    almonds, ground

¼   cup sugar

2   tablespoons water

2   tablespoons fine dry
    bread crumbs

2   tablespoons sugar

8   firm apples

Lemon juice

2   tablespoons butter,
    melted

**Sugar-Almond Whipped
   Cream:**

1½   cups heavy cream,
     whipped

Pinch sugar

½   teaspoon almond
    extract

1. Set oven at 425°.

2. Work the almonds, sugar and water to a paste in a mortar or
   blender. Reserve.

3. In a bowl, combine the bread crumbs and sugar. Reserve.

4. Peel and core the apples, sprinkling each apple with lemon
   juice to prevent browning.

5. Coat the apples with the butter, then roll in the bread crumb
   and sugar mixture.

6. Arrange the apples on a buttered baking dish, then fill the
   cores with the reserved almond mixture.

7. Bake until apples are tender but still hold their shape, about
   20 to 25 minutes. Serve piping hot, accompanied by chilled
   whipped cream flavored with sugar and almond extract.

Serves 8

WITCHES' FROTH *(boszorkány hab)*

Hungary

Preparation time: 30 minutes　　　**Refrigeration time:** 1 hour

Ingredients

6　*firm cooking apples,*
　peeled and quartered
　Juice of 2 lemons

1¾　*cups superfine*
　granulated sugar

　Rind of 2 lemons,
　grated

2　*tablespoons brandy*
　Pinch freshly grated
　nutmeg

3　*egg whites*
　Pinch salt
　Pinch cream of tartar

1. Combine the apples and the juice of 1 lemon in a saucepan. Place over low heat, cover and cook until apples are tender, about 30 minutes.

2. Press apples through a sieve into a large bowl. Beating vigorously with a wire whisk, gradually add the sugar, remaining lemon juice, lemon rind, brandy and nutmeg. Continue beating until mixture is very frothy. Adjust flavoring. Cover bowl and refrigerate for 1 hour.

3. In another bowl, beat the egg whites until frothy. Add the salt and cream of tartar. Continue beating until stiff.

4. Carefully fold the egg whites into the chilled apple mixture. Pour the froth into a glass serving bowl or individual dessert dishes. Serve chilled.

Serves 4

APPLE OMELET *(omelette Normande)*

Preparation time: 15 minutes

Apples simmer—5 minutes

Cooking time: 5 minutes

France

Ingredients

1½	pounds firm cooking apples
6	tablespoons butter
3	tablespoons Calvados, warmed

6	eggs
	Pinch salt
	Sugar
3	tablespoons water

1. Peel and core the apples, then slice thinly.

2. Heat ½ the butter in a frying pan. Add the apple slices and 1 tablespoon of the Calvados. Stir briefly to coat with the butter, then cover pan and cook over low heat until barely tender, about 5 minutes.

3. In a mixing bowl, combine the eggs, salt, a pinch of sugar and water. Beat lightly.

4. Place a large omelet pan or skillet over high heat for 1 or 2 minutes, then swirl in the remaining butter. When the butter foam subsides, quickly pour in the eggs and stir briskly until eggs begins to set.

5. Using a slotted spoon, transfer the apples to the eggs and cook until omelet is set. (Lift the edge of the omelet and tilt the pan as the omelet cooks to allow all egg liquid to cook.) Fold the omelet in half. Sprinkle with a little sugar and the remaining Calvados. Flambé and serve immediately.

Serves 3 to 4

BEVERLOO APPLE SOUFFLÉ

(Applelschoteltje)

The Netherlands

Preparation time: 35 minutes   **Baking time:** 45 minutes

Ingredients

8	tart apples		*Rind of 1 lemon, grated*
	Juice of 1 lemon		
12	*tablespoons butter*		*Pinch salt*
⅔	*cup sugar*	4	*eggs, separated*
½	*cup flour*	8	*zwieback, crumbled*
1	*cup hot milk*		

1. Peel, core and slice the apples. Toss with the lemon juice. Set oven at 325°.

2. In a saucepan, melt 3 tablespoons of the butter. Add the apples and ½ cup of the sugar. Stir briefly over low heat, then cover and cook for 15 minutes.

3. Melt the remaining butter. Beat in the flour, then stir over moderate heat for 2 minutes. Slowly add the milk, stirring constantly. When thoroughly blended, stir in the lemon rind, the remaining sugar and a little salt. Continue stirring until smooth and thick. Remove from heat.

4. Beat the egg yolks, one by one, into the milk mixture. Stir in the apples.

5. Beat the egg whites with a pinch of salt until stiff, then carefully fold into the apple mixture.

6. Fill a buttered and floured 1½-quart baking pan with alternating layers of the apple mixture and the crumbled zwieback. Bake for 45 minutes. Serve hot.

Serves 6

CHILLED APRICOT PURÉE
(mishmishieh)

Preparation time: 15 minutes
Apricots soak—15 minutes

Cooking time: 40 minutes
Prepared dish chills—1 hour

Lebanon

Ingredients

1½	pounds dried apricots
1¼	cups sugar
7½	cups water
1½	teaspoons cornstarch, dissolved in ½ cup water

2	teaspoons lemon juice
	Whipped cream flavored with sugar for garnish
	Chopped almonds for garnish

1. Soak the apricots in a bowl of hot water for 15 minutes. Drain and reserve.

2. Combine the sugar and water in a large saucepan, and bring to a boil. Stirring constantly, cook over moderate heat until liquid is clear. Add the drained apricots and cook over moderate heat until fruit is very tender, about 20 minutes. (Stir occasionally while apricots cook.)

3. Purée the apricot mixture in a food mill or blender.

4. Return mixture to saucepan. Stirring briskly over moderate heat, add the cornstarch mixture and cook until purée thickens, about 3 minutes. Remove from heat. Stir in the lemon juice, then taste and adjust seasoning.

5. Spoon the purée into a large serving bowl or into individual dessert dishes. Refrigerate for 1 hour. Serve chilled, topped with sugared whipped cream and chopped almonds.

Serves 4

DATE AND BANANA COMPOTE
(nakhil wa mooz)

Jordan

Preparation time: 20 minutes

Cooking time: 3 to 4 minutes
Compote chills—3 hours

Ingredients

6   bananas, peeled and
    thinly sliced
1   pound pitted dates,
    halved
6   ounces almonds,
    halved

1   cup light cream
    Brown sugar for
    glazing

1. Layer the sliced bananas in deep ovenproof dish, covering each layer of bananas with date halves and almonds.

2. Pour in the cream. The cream should barely cover the last layer of fruit. Refrigerate for at least 3 hours.

3. Just before serving, sprinkle a very thin layer of brown sugar on the fruit. Glaze for 3 or 4 minutes under broiler and serve immediately.

Serves 4

BANANA WHIP WITH ORANGE CREAM

Preparation time: 15 minutes   **Cooking time:** 5 minutes   *Jamaica*
Banana mixture chills—2 hours **Orange cream chills**—2 hours

Ingredients

6	bananas
3	tablespoons sugar
¼	cup almonds, coarsely chopped
¼	cup orange juice
	Pinch ground cinnamon
3	tablespoons light rum

¼	cup coconut, shredded
3	egg whites
	Salt

Orange Cream:

3	egg yolks
3	tablespoons sugar
1	cup orange juice

1. Mash the bananas in a non-metallic bowl. Add the sugar, almonds, orange juice, cinnamon, rum and coconut, mixing well.

2. In a separate bowl, beat the egg whites with a pinch of salt until stiff.

3. Carefully fold banana mixture and egg whites together. Do not overmix. Pour into a serving bowl and chill for at least 2 hours.

4. Prepare the orange cream topping: Beat the egg yolks with the sugar until lemon-colored. Pour the eggs into a small saucepan, then add the orange juice, whisking constantly until foamy. (Do not boil.)

5. Chill the topping for 2 hours, then serve with the banana whip.

Serves 6

AVIGNON FIG ROLL

(saucisson de figues)

France

Preparation time: 10 minutes

Refrigeration time: 3 hours

Ingredients

> 1   *pound dried figs, chopped*
>
> 4   *ounces blanched almonds, coarsely chopped*

> ¼   *cup confectioners' sugar*

1. In a mortar or blender, crush together the figs and almonds.

2. Form the mixture into a sausage shape and roll in the confectioners' sugar. Wrap in aluminum foil and refrigerate for at least 3 hours.

3. To serve, unwrap, place on a serving plate and slice thinly.

Serves 6

FRESH FIGS IN HONEY AND WINE

Preparation time: 10 minutes

Cooking time: 20 minutes
Compote chills—1 hour

Tunisia

Ingredients

1½	*pounds underripe green figs*
2	*cups dry white wine*
¾	*cup honey*

Vanilla-flavored whipped cream for topping

1. Wash figs and trim stems. Place in a saucepan and cover with the white wine. Bring to a boil over low heat, then stir in the honey. Cover pan and simmer until figs are tender, about 15 minutes.

2. Using a slotted spoon, transfer the figs to a serving bowl. Reserve.

3. Reduce fig syrup slightly over high heat, then pour over the fruit. Cover bowl and refrigerate for at least 1 hour. Serve chilled, topped with vanilla-flavored whipped cream.

Serves 6

ORANGE FLOWERS *(naranjas pili)*

Preparation time: 10 minutes   **Cooking time:** 20 minutes

Spain

Ingredients

6 *navel oranges*
2 *cups sugar*
2 *cups water*

2 *tablespoons orange-blossom water*
1 *quart vanilla ice cream*

1. Using a vegetable peeler, peel the oranges, then cut the peel into julienne strips. Carefully remove the pith from the oranges, leaving the orange sections intact.

2. Blanch the oranges and peel into a large saucepan of boiling water for 5 minutes, then drain and reserve.

3. In the same saucepan, combine the sugar, water and orange-blossom water. Stir over moderately high heat until mixture reaches a slow boil. Add the blanched oranges and peel, then lower heat and poach fruit gently until oranges are tender, about 10 minutes. Transfer the oranges with a slotted spoon to a wire rack and cool.

4. Reduce the orange-peel syrup over moderately high heat until it reaches the soft-ball stage (234° F. on a candy thermometer).

5. Assemble the orange flowers while the syrup reduces: Partially separate the sections of the oranges, then transfer to individual dessert dishes and place a scoop of vanilla ice cream in the center of each orange.

6. Pour the reduced syrup over the orange flowers and serve immediately.

Serves 6

ORANGE PUFFS *(oranges surprises)*

Preparation time: 30 minutes   **Baking time:** 20 minutes

Ingredients

France

4	*large navel oranges*	2	*egg yolks*
3	*tablespoons sugar*	3	*tablespoons sugar*
1	*tablespoon kirsch*	¼	*cup flour*

Custard: 2   *egg whites*

1   *cup milk*

1. Set oven at 250°. Cut the top third off the oranges. Carefully carve out the flesh from the oranges. Reserve both the top sections (caps) and the bottom sections (cups) of the shells.

2. Remove the membrane and the seeds from the orange sections, then arrange pulp on a greased baking sheet. Sprinkle lightly with sugar and place in the oven until slightly dried out, about 10 minutes. Reset oven to 325°.

3. While the orange sections are drying, remove the peel with a vegetable peeler; cut into julienne strips, then place in a small saucepan. Add the kirsch and place over low heat until the kirsch has evaporated, about 2 minutes.

4. Prepare the custard: Pour the milk into a saucepan; bring to a boil, then remove from heat. In a bowl, beat the egg yolks until pale yellow, then gradually add the sugar and the flour. Pour in the scalded milk and transfer mixture to a saucepan, then beat over moderate heat until custard thickens. Combine ⅔ of the custard in a bowl with the orange sections and mix well. Reserve the remaining custard.

5. In another bowl, beat the egg whites until stiff, then fold in the reserved custard. Spoon the custard-orange mixture into the orange cups. Add the orange peels, then top with the egg-white mixture. Arrange the orange puffs in a shallow dish containing ½ cup water. Bake for 20 minutes and serve.

Serves 4

SICILIAN STUFFED PEACHES
(pesche imbottite alla Siciliana)

Italy

Preparation time: 25 minutes

Baking time: 20 minutes

Ingredients

6	*large peaches*
2	*egg yolks*
¼	*cup sugar*
¼	*pound stale macaroons, finely crushed*
¼	*teaspoon almond extract*
2	*pinches freshly grated nutmeg*

2	*tablespoons unsalted butter, at room temperature*
	Heavy cream or whipped cream flavored with sugar and almond extract
	Fresh mint sprigs for garnish

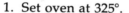

1. Set oven at 325°.

2. Blanch the peaches in a pot of boiling water and drain. Peel, halve and pit the peaches. Reserve.

3. In a small bowl beat the egg yolks well. Gradually beat in the sugar. Continue beating until mixture is light and fluffy.

4. Add the crushed macaroons, almond extract and nutmeg to the egg-sugar mixture. Blend thoroughly, then work in the butter until well incorporated.

5. Fill 6 of the reserved peach halves with the macaroon mixture. Top with the remaining peach halves.

6. Arrange the stuffed peaches in a buttered ovenproof dish and bake until tender, about 20 minutes. (The peaches should not lose their shape.)

7. Serve hot or cold with heavy cream or with whipped cream flavored to taste with sugar and almond extract. Garnish baked peaches with mint sprigs.

Serves 6

PEACHES WITH STRAWBERRY CREAM *(pêches Juliette)*

Preparation time: 20 minutes   **Refrigeration time:** 2 hours   *France*

Ingredients

8 peaches, peeled and sliced	¼ cup confectioners' sugar
Juice of ½ lemon	1 tablespoon crème de cassis
½ cup brown sugar	¾ cup heavy cream, whipped
3 tablespoons water	
2 pints strawberries	

1. Toss the peaches with the lemon juice in a serving bowl.

2. In a small saucepan, combine the brown sugar and water. Bring to a boil over moderate heat and swirl until the liquid starts to thicken, about 2 minutes. Stir the syrup into the peaches. Cover and refrigerate.

3. In a food mill or blender, purée the strawberries with the sugar and crème de cassis. Fold the whipped cream into the purée and refrigerate 2 hours. Just before serving, spoon strawberry cream over the peaches.

Serves 6

CARMELIZED BAKED PEARS
(poires à la Savoyarde)

France

Preparation time: 10 minutes   **Baking time:** 1 hour

Ingredients

2   *pounds pears, peeled and quartered*

⅓   *cup sugar*

6   *tablespoons butter*

2   *tablespoons water*

½   *cup heavy cream*

1. Set oven at 400°.

2. Arrange the pears in a buttered ovenproof dish. Sprinkle on the sugar, then dot with the butter. Moisten slightly with the water.

3. Bake, uncovered, until the pears are tender and the sugar becomes caramel-colored, about 1 hour.

4. Remove dish from the oven, pour in the cream and serve immediately.

Serves 4

PINEAPPLE PAVLOVA

Preparation time: 10 minutes   **Baking time:** 1 hour

Ingredients

New Zealand

6	*egg whites*
1¼	*teaspoons cream of tartar*
¼	*teaspoon salt*
¾	*cup sugar*

1	*teaspoon vanilla extract*
3	*cups sliced pineapple*
1½	*cups heavy cream, whipped*

1. Preheat the oven to 250°.

2. Beat the egg whites, cream of tartar and salt until frothy. Add the sugar and vanilla and continue beating until stiff and glossy.

3. Line a 9-inch round pan with waxed paper. Lightly grease and flour the pan, then pour in the egg white mixture. Make a slight indentation in the center. Bake until cream-colored and firm, about 50 minutes to 1 hour. Cool the meringue in the pan.

4. Transfer the meringue to a serving platter. Arrange the pineapple slices on the top and cover with the whipped cream.

Serves 6

RHUBARB FOOL

Great Britain

Preparation time: 15 minutes

Cooking time: 5 minutes
Rhubarb purée chills—1 hour

Ingredients

1 pound rhubarb	2 pinches ground cloves
½ cup light brown or white sugar	½ pint heavy cream, chilled
Rind of 1 lemon, grated	Toasted almonds for topping
Rind of ½ orange, grated	

1. Wash the rhubarb and trim stalks. Discard the leaves (they are poisonous). Cut the stalks into 2-inch sections.

2. Place the rhubarb in a saucepan and cover with cold water. Add the sugar, grated lemon, orange rinds and the cloves. Mix briefly. Bring to a boil, then lower heat and simmer until the rhubarb is just tender, about 5 minutes.

3. Using a slotted spoon, transfer the rhubarb to a blender or food mill. Add a little of the cooking liquid and purée. Transfer purée to a bowl and refrigerate for 1 hour.

4. Whip the cream lightly, then stir in the purée. Serve cold, topped with toasted almonds and accompanied by shortbread cookies (page 402).

Serves 4

SUMMER PUDDING

Preparation time: 30 minutes

Cooking time: 10 minutes
Pudding chills—12 to 24 hours

Great Britain

Ingredients

½ *pound fresh raspberries*
½ *pound fresh cherries, pitted*
½ *pound red currants*

¼ *cup light brown or granulated sugar*
10 *slices white bread, crusts trimmed*
Whipped cream

1. In a heavy saucepan, combine the fruit and sugar. Cover and cook gently over low heat until fruit is soft, about 10 minutes. (Stir fruit once or twice during cooking to prevent sticking.)

2. Drain the hot fruit in a sieve, reserving the cooking juices.

3. Line all sides of a glass bowl or dish with trimmed bread slices. Patch any gaps between the slices with smaller pieces of bread.

4. Pour the fruit into the bread case. Sprinkle with the reserved fruit juice, then top with a lid of bread slices.

5. Cover with a double thickness of waxed paper and weight with a heavy plate. Chill for 12 to 24 hours.

6. Before serving, discard the waxed paper and unmold the pudding onto a serving dish. Serve with whipped cream.

Serves 6

CHOCOLATE MOUSSE
(mousse au chocolat)

France   **Preparation time:** 10 minutes   **Cooking time:** 10 minutes
Mousse chills—2 hours

Ingredients

6 ounces semisweet chocolate	1 cup heavy cream
5 eggs, separated	3 tablespoons rum or brandy
1 teaspoon vanilla	½ cup sugar
2 teaspoons coffee	

1. Melt the chocolate in a double boiler.

2. Beat egg yolks to lemon color and gradually stir into the chocolate. Add the vanilla and coffee.

3. In a mixing bowl, beat the cream until thick. Stir in the rum or brandy and fold into the chocolate.

4. In another mixing bowl, beat the egg whites and the sugar until stiff and carefully fold into the chocolate mixture a little at a time.

5. Pour mousse into a large bowl or individual serving dishes. Chill for 2 hours.

Serves 4 to 6

LEMON MOUSSE *(mousse au citron)*

Preparation time: 25 minutes

Cooking time: 10 minutes
Mousse chills—1 hour

France

Ingredients

5 egg yolks	3 egg whites
½ cup superfine granulated sugar	Pinch salt
Juice of 2 lemons	½ cup heavy cream
Rind of 2 lemons, grated	

1. In a mixing bowl, beat the egg yolks with a wire whisk until pale yellow. Beating constantly, gradually add the sugar. Continue beating until mixture is light and fluffy, then blend in the lemon juice and rind.

2. Transfer mixture to the top section of a double boiler. Using a wire whisk, beat over simmering water until mixture is the consistency of soft custard, about 10 minutes. Remove from heat and reserve.

3. In a bowl, beat the egg whites with a pinch of salt until stiff.

4. Beat 2 tablespoons of the egg whites into the custard to lighten mixture, then fold in the remaining egg whites. Pour into a bowl and refrigerate for 1 hour.

5. Whip the cream in a bowl and gently fold into the chilled mousse. Pour into a serving bowl or individual dessert dishes. Serve chilled.

Serves 3 to 4

For a tarter lemon mousse, omit the cream in Step 5.

LEMON SNOW

Canada

Preparation time: 15 minutes   **Dessert chills**—2 hours

Ingredients

1	*package lemon gelatin*
⅓	*cup honey*
⅛	*teaspoon salt*
1¼	*cups boiling water*
3	*tablespoons lemon juice*

1	*large can condensed milk, chilled overnight*
2½	*cups vanilla wafer crumbs*

1. Dissolve the gelatin, honey and salt in the boiling water. Stir in the lemon juice, then refrigerate until the mixture is syrupy, about 20 minutes. Whip until frothy.

2. Whip the condensed milk until stiff, then lightly fold it into the lemon mixture.

3. Line an 8 × 10-inch dish with half the cookie crumbs. Pour in the mixture and top with the remaining crumbs. Chill until firm, about 2 hours.

Serves 6 to 8

CRANBERRY PURÉE
(kissel)

Preparation time: 5 minutes   **Cooking time:** 15 minutes   *USSR*

Ingredients

2 cups cranberries, uncooked	3 tablespoons cornstarch
1½ cups water	*Light or heavy cream flavored with sugar and vanilla extract*
½ cup sugar	

1. Place the cranberries in a saucepan and cover with the water. Bring to a boil, then lower the heat and simmer for 10 minutes.

2. Purée the fruit in a blender or food mill, then return the mixture to the saucepan. Add the sugar and bring to a boil.

3. Dissolve the cornstarch in a little water. Blend into the fruit mixture, stirring constantly, and cook until thickened. Pour into a large serving dish and chill for 3 hours. Serve with cream.

Serves 4

ESPRESSO ICE CREAM (gelato al caffè)

Italy

Preparation time: 30 minutes

Cooking time: 3 minutes
Ice cream freezes—6 hours

Ingredients

1½ cups milk, scalded	½ cup superfine granulated sugar
⅔ cup espresso coffee grounds	½ pint heavy cream
4 egg yolks	¼ teaspoon cinnamon

1. Combine the scalded milk and the coffee grounds in a saucepan. Place over very low heat and steep for 15 minutes.

2. Using a fine sieve lined with cheesecloth, strain the coffeed milk into a bowl and reserve. (Discard grounds.)

3. In a mixing bowl, beat the egg yolks with a wire whisk until pale yellow, then gradually beat in the sugar. Continue beating until mixture is light and fluffy. Gradually beat the coffeed milk into the egg and sugar mixture, then slowly beat in the cream.

4. Transfer the ice cream mixture to a large saucepan. Stir in the cinnamon. Using a wooden spoon, stir mixture over low heat until nearly doubled in volume, about 2 to 3 minutes, then immediately remove from heat.

5. Pour mixture into a metallic container. Cool to room temperature. Freeze for 6 hours, beating thoroughly with a wooden spoon every ½ hour to break down ice crystals.

Serves 4

MOLDED VANILLA CREAM
(coeur à la crème d'Angers)

Preparation time: 20 minutes   **Refrigeration time:** 24 hours   *France*

Ingredients

6   ounces creamed cottage
cheese

6   tablespoons heavy
cream

¼   cup superfine
granulated sugar

2   egg whites
Pinch salt
Crème fraîche for
topping (page 473)
Vanilla sugar for
topping (page 481)

1. Put the cottage cheese in a sieve. Drain off the excess liquid, then sieve the curds into a large mixing bowl.

2. Add the cream and beat vigorously until thickened, then beat in the sugar.

3. In another bowl, beat the egg whites with a pinch of salt until stiff. Gently fold the egg whites into the cottage cheese mixture.

4. Spoon the mixture into small heart-shaped pierced molds lined with cheesecloth. Place molds on a plate and refrigerate for 24 hours. (If molds are unavailable, spoon the mixture onto cheesecloth. Tie up the cheesecloth and hang in the refrigerator for 24 hours. Place a bowl under the cheesecloth bag to catch any liquid that drips out.)

5. To serve, unmold the vanilla cream (or remove from the cheesecloth), transfer to a serving dish and top with *crème fraîche* and vanilla sugar.

Serves 4

MARSALA CREAM *(sabayon)*

Preparation time: 10 minutes   **Cooking time:** 20 minutes

France

Prepared dessert chills—1 hour

Ingredients

½	cup Marsala wine	4	egg yolks
1	piece lemon peel	¼	cup sugar
A	3-inch stick cinnamon	¼	cup kirsch or rum
1	clove		Ladyfingers for garnish

1. In a small saucepan, combine the Marsala, lemon peel, cinnamon stick and clove. Bring to a boil and simmer for 3 minutes, then remove from heat, strain and reserve.

2. In a mixing bowl, beat the egg yolks with a wire whisk until pale yellow. Beating constantly, gradually add the sugar. Continue beating until mixture is very light and fluffy.

3. Beat in the strained Marsala, then transfer mixture to the top section of a double boiler.

4. Beat over hot water until mixture clings to a wooden spoon, about 10 minutes. (Do not let the water in the bottom section of the pan come to a boil as the mixture cooks.)

5. Beating constantly, very slowly add the kirsch (or rum) and cook for 5 more minutes. Remove from heat.

6. When the Marsala cream has cooled to room temperature, pour into a serving bowl and refrigerate for at least 1 hour. Serve chilled, garnished with ladyfingers.

Serves 4

For a delicious hot variation, gently fold 4 stiffly beaten egg whites into the Marsala cream at the end of Step 5 and serve immediately.

CHAMPAGNE CREAM

(crème Champenoise)

Preparation time: 10 minutes

Cooking time: 10 minutes
Prepared dish chills—1 hour

France

Ingredients

20	*small sugar cubes*
1	*lemon, washed*

1	*cup champagne or dry white wine, heated*
4	*eggs, separated*

1. Rub each sugar cube over the rind of the lemon to absorb the oil, then place cubes in a bowl.

2. Pour the hot champagne (or wine) over the sugar cubes. Stir until the sugar dissolves.

3. In another bowl, beat the egg yolks until pale yellow. Beating constantly, gradually add the sugar mixture.

4. Transfer mixture to the top section of a double boiler and place over low heat. (The water in the bottom section of the double boiler should not boil.) Beat with a wire whisk until mixture thickens. Remove from heat.

5. Cool mixture slightly, then refrigerate for 1 hour.

6. Just before serving, beat the egg whites until very stiff and fold into the chilled champagne cream.

Serves 2 to 3

PISTACHIO DELIGHT
(crème de pistaches)

France   **Preparation time:** 10 minutes   **Cooking time:** 10 minutes
                                                    Prepared dish chills—1 hour

Ingredients

3   *egg yolks*
½   *cup sugar*
2   *tablespoons kirsch*
1   *pint heavy cream*

5½   *ounces pistachio nuts,*
      coarsely ground
      Halved shelled
      pistachios for
      decoration

1. In a mixing bowl, beat the egg yolks until pale yellow. Beating constantly, gradually add the sugar. Continue beating until mixture is light and fluffy, then gradually beat in the kirsch and heavy cream.

2. Transfer egg yolk mixture to the top section of a double boiler. Blend in the ground pistachios.

3. Place pan over barely simmering water and beat mixture with a wire whisk until very thick and fluffy, about 10 minutes. Remove from heat.

4. Pour into a serving bowl and decorate with halved pistachios. Refrigerate for at least 1 hour. Serve chilled.

Serves 4 to 6

CARAMEL CUSTARD *(crème renversée)*

Preparation time: 15 minutes   **Baking time:** 40 to 45 minutes

France

Ingredients

Caramel Glaze for Mold:

½   *cup sugar*
2   *tablespoons water*
───
4   *whole eggs*

4   *egg yolks*
⅔   *cup sugar*
3⅓   *cups milk, scalded*
3   *tablespoons cognac*

1. Set oven at 350°.

2. Using the ingredients listed above, caramelize (page 472) a 1½-quart fluted metal mold. Reserve.

3. In a mixing bowl, beat the whole eggs and extra egg yolks with a wire whisk or an electric beater until pale yellow. Beating constantly, gradually add the sugar. Continue beating until mixture is very light and fluffy.

4. Beating constantly, gradually add the scalded milk and cognac to the egg and sugar mixture. Continue beating until very smooth and light.

5. Strain the custard mixture into the caramelized mold. Place in a shallow pan of hot water and bake until a knife inserted into the center of the custard comes out clean, about 40 to 45 minutes.

6. When the custard is done, remove mold from the oven. Cool to room temperature in the mold, then unmold by running a knife around the edge of the mold and quickly inverting onto a platter.

Serves 6

COFFEE CUSTARD *(crème de cafe)*

Brazil

Preparation time: 20 minutes

Baking time: 45 minutes to 1 hour

Ingredients

1½	*cups milk*
A	*1-inch piece vanilla bean*
4	*whole coffee beans*

½	*cup very strong coffee*
5	*egg yolks*
½	*cup sugar*
1	*teaspoon cornstarch*

1. Set oven to 325°.

2. Combine the milk, vanilla bean and coffee beans in a saucepan. Bring rapidly to a boil, then remove pan from heat.

3. Stir in the strong coffee. Reserve.

4. In a bowl, beat the egg yolks, then gradually blend in the sugar and cornstarch. Mix well.

5. Strain the cooled milk, a little at a time, through a fine sieve lined with cheesecloth into the egg and sugar mixture.

6. Pour the mixture into a buttered baking dish or into individual ovenproof custard cups.

7. Cover the baking dish, set in a pan of hot water and bake until a knife inserted into the center of the custard comes out clean, about 45 minutes to 1 hour.

8. Cool custard to room temperature, then chill until needed. Before serving, run a knife around the inside edge of the baking dish and invert custard onto a serving dish.

Serves 4

RAISIN CUSTARD *(far Breton)*

Preparation time: 15 minutes   **Baking time:** 45 minutes
Raisins soak—1 hour

France

Ingredients

3	ounces seedless raisins	1¾	cups flour
¼	cup rum	4	cups milk, warmed
4	eggs	2	tablespoons vanilla sugar (page 481)
¾	cup sugar		

1. Soak the raisins in the rum for 1 hour, then drain and reserve.

2. Set oven at 325°.

3. In a mixing bowl, beat the eggs until pale yellow. Beating constantly, gradually add the sugar. Continue beating until mixture is light and fluffy, then gradually beat in the flour and the warm milk.

4. Pour ¼ of the milk mixture into a buttered and floured 2-quart ovenproof dish. Bake for 10 minutes, then remove from oven.

5. Reset oven at 425°.

6. Sprinkle the raisins into the baking dish, then cover with the remaining milk mixture and bake until set, about 35 minutes.

7. Sprinkle the baked raisin custard with the vanilla sugar and serve piping hot.

Serves 4

BASQUE BROWN SUGAR
CUSTARD *(milhassou)*

France   **Preparation time:** 20 minutes   **Baking time:** 1 hour

Ingredients

4½ *cups milk*
1½ *cups cornstarch*
10 *tablespoons butter, at room temperature*
8 *eggs*

10 *ounces dark brown sugar*
1 *tablespoon orange flower water (optional)*

1. Set oven at 275°.

2. Pour the milk into a large saucepan. Bring rapidly to a boil, then immediately remove pan from heat.

3. Beating constantly, gradually add the cornstarch to the milk. Continue beating until the mixture is smooth.

4. Allow mixture to cool slightly, then beat in the butter, a tablespoon at a time. Beat in the eggs, incorporating each one well before adding the next, then gradually beat in the sugar. (When the mixture is thoroughly blended, stir in the orange flower water.)

5. Pour custard into a buttered 2-quart ovenproof dish and bake until set, about 1 hour. Serve hot.

Serves 6

PENANG COCONUT CUSTARD

(sarikauja)

Preparation time: 40 minutes   **Refrigeration time:** 2 hours

Malaysia

Ingredients

Coconut Cream:

6	cups coconut meat, grated
2	cups scalded milk
½	cup sugar
⅛	teaspoon salt

1	teaspoon vanilla extract
2	tablespoons cornstarch
¼	cup cold water
½	cup pineapple, crushed
8	teaspoons shredded coconut

1. Steep the coconut meat in the hot milk for 20 minutes. Strain through a double thickness of cheesecloth, squeezing all the liquid out of the coconut.

2. In a saucepan, heat the coconut milk over a low flame to the boiling point. Add the sugar, salt, vanilla and the cornstarch dissolved in the water. Stir constantly until thickened, about 5 minutes. Pour into individual custard cups and refrigerate for about 2 hours.

3. To serve, top each custard with 1 tablespoon crushed pineapple and 1 teaspoon shredded coconut.

Serves 8

NOTE: *Canned coconut milk or coconut cream can be substituted for the fresh, if necessary.*

SWEET MILK CLOUDS
(doce de claras e ovos moles)

Portugal

Preparation time: 15 minutes   **Cooking time:** 8 minutes
Ingredients

Custard: **Sweet Milk "Clouds":**

2 cups milk	4 egg whites
½ cup sugar	2 tablespoons sugar
4 egg yolks	1 cup milk

1. Boil the milk in a saucepan and stir in the sugar until dissolved. Cool slightly.

2. Beat the egg yolks to a lemon color. Add a small amount of the syrup to the yolks, beating constantly, then stir mixture into remaining syrup. Cook over low heat until mixture thickens. Do not boil.

3. Pour the custard into a serving dish or individual bowls and chill.

4. In a mixing bowl, whip the egg whites and sugar until stiff.

5. Boil the milk in a large saucepan. Drop a large tablespoonful of the egg whites into the hot milk. Poach each "cloud" for 4 minutes. Remove and drain. Float the "clouds" on the custard and serve.

Serves 4

GLAZED FRUIT PUDDING
(crème Bourdaloue)

Preparation time: 30 minutes   **Cooking time:** 10 minutes   *France*

Ingredients

5	tablespoons sugar		7	tablespoons sugar
1	cup water		6	eggs, separated
4	pears, peeled and quartered		¼	cup flour
1	banana, sliced		2	tablespoons butter
⅓	cup seedless raisins		½	cup almond macaroons, crushed
⅓	cup currants			Confectioners' sugar

Custard:

1⅓ cups milk

1. Combine the sugar and water in a saucepan and boil until clear, about 5 minutes. Add the pears to the syrup and poach gently until tender, about 10 minutes. Remove with a slotted spoon and reserve.

2. Keeping the syrup over low heat, add the banana, raisins and currants. Remove from heat and let stand for 2 minutes, then drain and arrange in a deep ovenproof dish. Strain the syrup back into the saucepan and reduce over moderate heat to about 3 tablespoons. Pour over fruit and refrigerate.

3. Prepare the custard: a) Boil the milk and sugar; b) beat the egg yolks in a bowl and blend in the flour; c) gradually beat in the heated milk; d) return mixture to pan and cook over low heat, beating until mixture is thickened; e) remove from heat and stir in butter a bit at a time; f) beat the egg whites until stiff and fold into the custard; g) add the macaroons.

4. Pour custard over cooled fruit. Sprinkle with confectioners' sugar and glaze under broiler until light brown. Cool and serve.

Serves 4 to 6

SURREY SUMMER TRIFLE

Great Britain

Preparation time: 15 minutes

Ingredients

2 ½ to 3   *cups raspberries
            (fresh or frozen)*
        1   *cup red currants*
       ½   *cup sugar*
        4   *spongecake shells,
            split in half*

Custard:

        6   *egg yolks*

       ¼   *cup sugar*
        2   *teaspoons cornstarch*
        2   *cups heavy cream*
        1   *teaspoon vanilla
            extract*
        1   *ounce almond flakes,
            toasted*

1. Combine the raspberries, red currants and sugar in a saucepan. Stir over low heat to dissolve the sugar, then simmer for 5 minutes. Remove from the heat and allow to cool.

2. Arrange the spongecakes in a glass serving bowl and cover with the fruit and the juices.

3. Prepare the custard: Beat the egg yolks well; then add the sugar and cornstarch and whisk thoroughly to blend. Heat the cream to the simmering point. Pour the cream into the egg mixture, a little at a time, blending well. Strain the custard back into the saucepan and stir over low heat until thickened. (Do not boil.) Add the vanilla and cool slightly.

4. Pour the custard over the fruit. Cool and chill until firm. Sprinkle with the almond flakes just before serving.

Serves 4

BLUEBERRY PUDDING

Preparation time: 15 minutes   **Baking time:** 45 minutes
Blueberries stand—30 minutes

Canada

Ingredients

1 *quart blueberries*	2 *cups dry bread crumbs*
¼ *cup flour*	2 *cups milk, heated*
½ *cup brown sugar*	1 *egg, lightly beaten*
2 *tablespoons white wine vinegar*	2 *tablespoons butter*
Juice of 1 lemon	*Light cream for topping*
Pinch salt	

1. Preheat oven to 350°.

2. Place the blueberries in a buttered baking dish. Sprinkle on the flour, brown sugar, vinegar, lemon juice and salt. Toss lightly, then let stand for ½ hour.

3. Put 1½ cups of the bread crumbs in a mixing bowl. Cover with the milk. Stir until well blended, then incorporate the beaten egg.

4. Spoon the bread-crumb mixture into the baking dish with the blueberries. Stir gently, then sprinkle on the remaining bread crumbs and dot with the butter.

5. Bake pudding for 45 minutes. Serve warm with cream.

Serves 6

YOGHURT PUDDING *(shrikhand)*

India

Preparation time: 10 minutes
Yoghurt drains—overnight

Refrigeration time: 2 hours

Ingredients

2 *pints yoghurt*	¼ *teaspoon freshly grated nutmeg*
6 *tablespoons sugar*	¼ *teaspoon ground cinnamon*
¾ *teaspoon ground cardamom*	*Salt*
¼ *teaspoon saffron, soaked in 1 tablespoon warm milk*	2 *ounces pistachio nuts, sliced, for garnish*

1. Place yoghurt in cheesecloth bag and suspend over a bowl in the refrigerator overnight so the liquid drips out.

2. The next day add the sugar, cardamom, saffron, nutmeg, cinnamon and salt to the yoghurt curds remaining in the cheesecloth. Mix well and chill for 2 hours in a serving bowl.

3. Serve the pudding cold, garnished with the pistachio slices.

Serves 4

SWEET MILK TREAT
(dulce de leche)

Preparation time: 10 minutes   **Cooking time:** 45 minutes   *Argentina*

Ingredients

6 cups milk	1 stick cinnamon
2½ cups sugar	1 ounce almonds, ground
A 1-inch piece vanilla bean	Lemon peel

1. Combine all ingredients in a heavy saucepan and cook over low heat until pudding thickens, about 45 minutes.

2. Pour into a large serving dish or individual soufflé dishes and chill thoroughly before serving.

Serves 4

Dulce de leche *is used in Honduras and Argentina as a snack, as a topping for many desserts or as a filling for cookies.*

BUTTERMILK LEMON MOLD
(Karnemelk Pudding)

The Netherlands

Preparation time: 15 minutes   **Refrigeration time:** 1 hour

Ingredients

½   *cup cold water*

2   *ounces powdered unflavored gelatin*

1   *cup fresh lemon juice, heated*

2   *cups sugar*

2½ *cups buttermilk*

Sugared whipped cream for topping

1. Pour the water into a saucepan. Sprinkle the gelatin on top, then let stand for 5 minutes.

2. Place the saucepan over low heat and stir gently until gelatin is completely dissolved. Reserve.

3. In a bowl, combine the sugar and lemon juice. Stir until sugar is completely dissolved, then pour in the buttermilk. Mix thoroughly.

4. Pour the buttermilk mixture into the gelatin mixture. Stir until well blended.

5. Pour the mixture into a lightly oiled 1-quart mold. Refrigerate until firm, about 1 hour.

6. Unmold the chilled dessert onto a serving plate. Serve chilled, topped with sugared whipped cream.

Serves 6

CHERRY PUDDING *(clafoutis)*

Preparation time: 10 minutes

Ingredients

1 pound fresh black
   cherries or canned
   Bing cherries
1½ cups flour
   Pinch salt

Baking time: 45 minutes

3 eggs
3 tablespoons sugar
3 cups milk
¼ cup confectioners'
   sugar

France

1. Preheat oven to 375°.

2. Prepare the cherries: If fresh cherries used, wash and dry, then remove pits and stems. Reserve. (If canned cherries used, drain thoroughly and reserve.)

3. In a mixing bowl, combine the flour and salt. Beat in the eggs, one at a time, thoroughly incorporating each egg before adding the next. Beat in the sugar. Gradually pour in the milk, stirring until batter is smooth.

4. Pour a ¼-inch layer of batter into a buttered ovenproof dish. Spread the cherries over the batter and then cover with the remaining batter.

5. Bake until the pudding begins to set, about 25 minutes, then dust with the confectioners' sugar and continue baking until golden, about 20 minutes. Serve hot.

Serves 4 to 6

PARSONAGE PUDDING
(pappilau pudding)

Finland

Preparation time: 10 minutes

Cooking time: 1½ hours

Ingredients

2   *cups dry bread cubes*
1   *cup buttermilk*
1   *teaspoon baking soda*
½   *cup sugar*
½   *teaspoon ground cinnamon*
¼   *teaspoon freshly grated nutmeg*

1   *egg, beaten*
    Lingonberry preserves for garnish
    Light cream for topping

1. In a mixing bowl, combine the bread cubes and buttermilk. Let stand until the buttermilk is completely absorbed, about 15 minutes.

2. Add the baking soda, sugar, cinnamon and nutmeg to the soaked bread cubes. Mix thoroughly, then incorporate the beaten egg.

3. Transfer the pudding mixture to a well-buttered pudding mold. (The mold should be ⅔ full). Cover tightly with a buttered lid or foil.

4. Rest the mold on a rack in a kettle of boiling water. Cover and steam the pudding over moderately low heat for 1½ hours. (If necessary, add more water to the kettle during steaming.)

5. Serve pudding piping hot, topped with lingonberry preserves and cream.

Serves 4

NOODLE PUDDING *(Nudelspeise)*

Preparation time: 30 minutes   **Baking time:** 1 hour

Germany

Ingredients

½ *pound egg noodles*	*Juice of 1 lemon*
¼ *pound unsalted butter, at room temperature*	5 *ounces raisins*
1½ *cups sugar*	4 *ounces blanched almonds, slivered*
6 *egg yolks*	6 *egg whites*
Rind of 1 lemon, grated	*Pinch salt*

1. Preheat oven to 350°.

2. Plunge the noodles into a large pot of boiling water and cook until noodles are *al dente* (page 470), about 12 minutes. Drain, rinse under cold water, then drain thoroughly. Reserve.

3. While the noodles cook, cream the butter in a large mixing bowl, then gradually blend in the sugar and beat until light and fluffy. Beat the egg yolks into sugar mixture, incorporating each yolk before adding the next. Stir in lemon rind, lemon juice, raisins and almonds. Combine the noodles with the sugar mixture. Blend thoroughly, then reserve.

4. In another large bowl, beat the egg whites with a pinch of salt until stiff. Carefully fold the egg whites into the noodle mixture. Pour pudding into a buttered soufflé dish and bake until browned, about 1 hour. Serve hot from the dish.

Serves 6

For variety, top each portion with raspberry sauce or sabayon.

SEMOLINA PUDDING WITH RASPBERRY SAUCE

(flamri à la purée de framboise)

France

Preparation time: 20 minutes   **Cooking time:** 25 minutes

Ingredients

2½ cups white wine	½ cup sugar
2½ cups water	2 egg whites
⅔ cup semolina	Pinch salt
1 egg	2 pints fresh raspberries

1. Pour the wine and water into a saucepan. Bring rapidly to a boil, then remove from heat and gradually beat in the semolina. Cover pan and simmer over low heat for 20 minutes, stirring occasionally. Remove pan from heat.

2. In a bowl, beat the egg well, then gradually stir in the sugar. Reserve.

3. In another bowl, beat the egg whites with a pinch of salt until stiff. Gently fold the egg whites into the sugar mixture, then fold this mixture into the semolina.

4. Pour the pudding into a 2-quart buttered ring mold. Place the mold in a pot filled with enough hot water to reach halfway up the sides of the mold. Cover the pot and steam pudding over low heat until set, about 25 minutes. (The water should barely simmer while the pudding cooks.)

5. When the pudding has set, remove from pot and cool to room temperature. Chill until needed.

6. While the pudding chills, prepare the raspberry purée by pressing the berries through a sieve, then adding sugar to taste. To serve, turn the pudding onto a plate and cover with the purée.

Serves 4 to 6

RICE PUDDING *(kheer)*

Preparation time: 10 minutes

Cooking time: 1¼ hours

Pakistan

Ingredients

- 6 cups milk
- 2 tablespoons long-grain rice
- 3 tablespoons seedless raisins
- ½ cup sugar
- 4 whole pods or ¼ teaspoon ground cardamom
- ¼ teaspoon ground cinnamon
- 10 unsalted pistachio nuts, slivered

1. Bring the milk to a boil in a saucepan, then lower the heat and add the rice. Cook, stirring frequently, until the rice is done, about 1 hour.

2. Add the raisins and sugar. Cook for 10 minutes over very low heat.

3. Stir in the cardamom and cinnamon. Pour mixture into a serving bowl.

4. Serve at room temperature, sprinkled with pistachio slivers.

Serves 6

RICE MOLD WITH CUSTARD SAUCE *(gâteau de riz)*

France

Preparation time: 1½ hours

Baking time: 40 minutes

Ingredients

1¼ cups sugar
¼ cup water
2¼ cups milk
2 tablespoons butter
1 vanilla bean
1 cup long-grain rice
2 ounces glacéed fruits
1 ounce raisins
2 tablespoons cognac
3 egg whites

Pinch salt and cream of tartar
Glacéed cherries and angelica for decoration

Custard Sauce:

3 egg yolks
⅓ cup sugar
1½ cups milk, scalded
1 teaspoon vanilla

1. Caramelize (page 472) a 2-quart ring mold with 1 cup sugar and the water. Soak the fruits and raisins in the cognac.

2. Combine the milk, ¼ cup sugar, butter and vanilla bean in a saucepan. Bring to a boil, then stir in the rice and simmer until milk is absorbed, about 45 minutes. Discard the vanilla bean, then stir in the cognac and fruit.

3. Preheat oven to 375°. Beat the egg whites with the salt and cream of tartar until stiff. Gently fold into the rice, then pour into the mold. Cover with buttered waxed paper and bake until set, about 40 minutes. Remove from oven and invert onto a platter. Decorate with the cherries and angelica. Serve warm or refrigerate for 2 hours.

4. About 20 minutes before serving, prepare the custard: In a small saucepan, beat the yolks until pale yellow, then beat in the sugar until mixture is fluffy. Slowly stir in the milk and cook over low heat until thickened. Beat in the vanilla and serve in a heated sauceboat.

Serves 6

CHILLED CHOCOLATE-ALMOND PUDDING *(tort czekóladowy niepieczony)*

Preparation time: 30 minutes   **Refrigeration time:** 2 hours   *Poland*

Ingredients

½ *pound unsalted butter*	*Juice of 1 lemon*
1¾ *cups sugar*	**Topping:**
8 *ounces semisweet chocolate, melted*	2 *ounces semisweet chocolate, melted*
1 *tablespoon vanilla*	1 *pint heavy cream*
4 *ounces almonds, ground*	

1. Cream the butter in a mixing bowl. Gradually beat in ¾ cup of the sugar. Continue beating until smooth, then blend in the vanilla.

2. Beating constantly, slowly pour in the melted chocolate. Blend until creamy.

3. Pour mixture into small soufflé dishes or *pots de crème* and refrigerate.

4. In another bowl, combine the almonds, the remaining sugar and the lemon juice.

5. Cover the chocolate mixture with the almond mixture, then refrigerate again.

6. Combine the chocolate and cream for the topping. Mix well, then spread over the chocolate-almond layers. Return to refrigerator and chill for at least 2 hours before serving.

Serves 6 to 8

COTTBUS STEAMED CHOCOLATE PUDDING
(Cottbus Schokoladenpudding)

Germany

Preparation time: 25 minutes   **Cooking time:** 1 hour

Ingredients

¾ cup unsalted butter, softened	2 tablespoons Grand Marnier (optional)
⅔ cup sugar	6 ounces almonds, grated
6 eggs, separated	¾ cup dry bread crumbs
2 egg yolks	Pinch salt
2 ounces semisweet chocolate, melted	

1. Cream the butter in a large mixing bowl. Beating constantly, gradually add the sugar.

2. Lightly beat the 8 egg yolks in a separate bowl, then gradually add to the butter and sugar mixture. Beat until fluffy, about 10 minutes. Stir in the chocolate, (Grand Marnier), almonds and bread crumbs. Mix well.

3. In another bowl, beat the egg whites with a pinch of salt until stiff. Gently fold the egg whites into the chocolate mixture.

4. Pour the pudding into a well-buttered steamed pudding mold. Cover tightly. Set the mold in a pot of boiling water and steam over moderate heat for 1 hour. (During steaming the level of water in the pot should remain near the top of the mold. Add more boiling water when necessary.)

5. When the steamed pudding is done, unmold by running a knife around the inside edge of the mold. Quickly invert the mold over a serving platter. Serve hot.

Serves 6

CHOCOLATE TRUFFLES
(truffetes Dauphinoises)

Preparation time: 15 minutes   **Cooking time:** 15 minutes   *France*
Chocolate mixture chills—3 hours

Ingredients

8 ounces semisweet chocolate, slivered	2 tablespoons rum or cognac or 1 teaspoon vanilla powder
½ cup milk	2 egg yolks, well beaten Unsweetened cocoa for coating truffles
3 tablespoons unsalted butter, at room temperature	

1. Combine the slivered chocolate and milk in the top half of a double boiler. Place over gently simmering water until the chocolate melts. (Do not boil.)

2. When the chocolate has melted, beat in the butter, a tablespoon at a time. Continue beating over the simmering water until mixture is very smooth, then remove from heat and stir in the rum (or cognac or vanilla powder).

3. Cool the mixture slightly, then beat in the egg yolks.

4. Transfer the mixture to a small bowl. Cover with greaseproof paper and refrigerate until chocolate is firm enough to be molded, about 3 hours.

5. Form the chocolate into small balls, then roll in unsweetened cocoa until well coated.

Yields about 30 truffles

FLANDERS RAISIN CRÊPES
(bouquettes aux raisins)

Preparation time: 20 minutes
Batter chills—2 hours

Cooking time: 3 minutes
per crêpe

Ingredients

1	cup presifted flour		Rind of 1 orange, grated
1½	cups milk		
2	tablespoons sugar	4½	ounces raisins
3	tablespoons butter, melted	¾	cup kirsch or brandy
			Oil for coating pan
4	eggs		Sugar for sprinkling crêpes
¼	teaspoon salt		

1. Combine the first 7 ingredients in a large mixing bowl and beat thoroughly until smooth. (This can also be done in a blender.) The batter should be the consistency of cream. Refrigerate for 2 hours.

2. Soak the raisins in ½ cup of the kirsch for ½ hour. Stir the raisins into the batter.

3. Brush a crêpe pan or skillet with oil. Heat to the smoking point, then pour in approximately ¼ cup of batter. Swirl quickly to lightly coat the pan and cook until golden. Turn the crêpe over and cook lightly for another minute. Reserve. Re-grease the pan and repeat until all the batter is used.

4. Fold the crêpes in thirds and arrange on a heated serving dish. Lightly sprinkle with sugar and the remaining kirsch. Flambé and serve.

Serves 4

APRICOT CRÊPE CAKE
(gâteau de crêpes aux abricots)

Preparation time: 20 minutes
Batter chills—2 hours

Cooking time: 3 minutes
per crêpe

France

Ingredients

1	cup presifted flour
1½	cups milk
2	tablespoons sugar
3	tablespoons butter, melted
4	eggs

¼	teaspoon salt
	Oil for coating pan
1¼	cups apricot jam, melted
¾	cup almonds or walnuts, ground

1. Combine the first 6 ingredients in a large mixing bowl and beat thoroughly until smooth. (This can also be done in a blender.) The batter should be the consistency of cream. Refrigerate for 2 hours.

2. Brush a 6-inch crêpe pan or skillet with oil. Heat to the smoking point, then pour in approximately ¼ cup of batter. Swirl quickly to lightly coat the pan and cook until golden. Turn the crêpe over and cook lightly for another minute. Reserve. Re-grease the pan and repeat until all the batter is used, preparing a dozen crêpes.

3. To prepate the *gâteau,* glaze each crêpe with the apricot jam. Sprinkle lightly with the nuts and stack the crêpes one upon the other. Cover with a cloth to keep warm. Slice the *gâteau* like a cake when serving.

Serves 4

LEMON FRITTERS *(bugnes de Lyon)*

France

Preparation time: 15 minutes
Batter stands—40 minutes

Cooking time: 3 to 4 minutes
per fritter

Ingredients

2   *cups flour*
1   *egg*
1¼ *cups milk*
1   *tablespoon sugar*
¼   *teaspoon salt*

Grated rind of ½ lemon
Peanut or vegetable oil for deep-frying
Confectioners' sugar for dusting

1. In a large mixing bowl, combine the flour, egg, milk, sugar and salt. Mix thoroughly, then add the lemon rind. Cover and let stand for 40 minutes.

2. Pour enough peanut (or vegetable) oil into a large saucepan to reach a depth of 4 inches. Place pan over high heat.

3. When the oil begins to sizzle, dip a long-handled rosette mold (or a long-handled deep-well gravy ladle) into the oil. Coat mold thoroughly in oil.

4. Pour the excess oil off the coated mold, then dip into the batter, filling the ladle about ¾ full.

5. Plunge filled ladle into the hot oil (the fritter will detach itself). Fry until golden brown, about 3 to 4 minutes, then remove with a slotted spoon and drain on absorbent paper. Repeat Steps 4 and 5 until all the batter has been used.

6. Dust the fritters with confectioners' sugar. Serve hot or cold.

Yields about 20 fritters

PILAR PUFFS *(buñelos de viento)*

Preparation time: 15 minutes   **Cooking time:** 3 to 5 minutes per batch

Spain

Ingredients

¼ pound unsalted butter
2 tablespoons sugar
⅛ teaspoon salt
1 cup water
1 cup flour
4 eggs
1 tablespoon brandy

Rind of 1 lemon, grated
Vegetable oil for deep frying
1 pound apricot jam
Confectioners' sugar

1. In a large saucepan, melt the butter. Over moderate heat blend in the sugar, salt and water. Bring to a boil.

2. Remove saucepan from heat and beat in the flour, a tablespoon at a time. Add the eggs (one at a time), beating well after each addition.

3. Stir mixture over moderate heat until batter pulls away from sides of saucepan.

4. Remove saucepan from heat. Blend in the brandy and lemon rind. Reserve.

5. Pour enough vegetable oil into a large saucepan to reach a depth of 4 inches. Heat almost to smoking point (385° to 390°).

6. Using 2 teaspoons dipped in water, shape batter into small balls. Drop balls into the hot oil and deep fry until golden, about 3 to 5 minutes, then remove with a slotted spoon and drain thoroughly on a wire rack or absorbent paper.

7. Split the fried puffs. Fill each with apricot jam and dust with confectioners' sugar.

Yields about 3 dozen puffs

PLUM SURPRISES *(svestkove knedlíky)*

Preparation time: 30 minutes   **Cooking time:** 12 minutes

Czechoslovakia

Ingredients

3 *cups all-purpose flour*	¼ *cup sugar*
1 *teaspoon salt*	1 *teaspoon cinnamon*
7 *tablespoons butter*	*Pinch freshly grated*
2 *eggs, lightly beaten*	*nutmeg*
½ to ¾ *cup milk*	16 *blue plums, pitted*

1. Sift the flour and salt into a bowl. Reserve.

2. In a large mixing bowl, cream well 4 tablespoons of the butter, softened, with a wooden spoon or beater, then gradually beat in the eggs. Blend thoroughly.

3. Stir the salted flour into the butter-egg mixture, then blend in enough of the milk to make a stiff dough.

4. Transfer the dough to a lightly floured board and roll out to ¼-inch thickness. Using a lightly floured 3½-inch cookie cutter or glass, cut dough into 32 rounds.

5. Combine the sugar, cinnamon and nutmeg in a small bowl. Mix thoroughly. Reserve.

6. Top ½ the dough rounds with plums and sprinkle with some of the spiced sugar, then cover plums with the remaining dough rounds. Firmly seal edges.

7. Drop the dumplings into a kettle of salted boiling water, cover and simmer until tender, about 12 minutes.

8. Using a slotted spoon, transfer the cooked dumplings to a serving dish. Dot with the butter and sprinkle with the remaining sugar mixture. Serve hot or cold.

Yields 16 dumplings

Apricots, cherries or peaches can be substituted for the plums.

Fundamentals

al dente:

An Italian cookery term most often used to describe the cooking of pasta. It means that the spaghetti, noodle, macaroni, etc. should be cooked until barely tender (it should retain a "bite")— anywhere from 5 to 6 minutes for thin pasta to 12 to 15 minutes for broad noodles. Check package instructions if in doubt. Other foods that are also cooked *al dente* are rice and certain vegetables.

bard:

To tie strips of pork fat or bacon around a piece of meat, fowl or fish before cooking to improve the flavor and to protect the delicate portions of the flesh during cooking.

baste:

To moisten foods with a marinade, butter, pan drippings or water during cooking. Basting prevents drying and adds to the flavor.

béarnaise sauce:

¼ cup vinegar
¼ cup white wine
2 teaspoons dried tarragon
1 tablespoon shallots, finely minced
  Salt
  Freshly ground pepper
4 egg yolks
½ pound butter, at room temperature
1 to 2 tablespoons water, boiling

A rich, creamy sauce served with grilled or broiled red meats, fish and poultry. A *béarnaise* sauce is prepared in the same way as a hollandaise, but the lemon of the hollandaise is replaced by a reduced mixture of vinegar, wine, tarragon, shallots and seasonings.

1. Combine the vinegar, wine, tarragon, shallots, salt and pepper in a saucepan and reduce to 2 tablespoons over moderately high heat. Cool.

2. Melt the butter and add the reduced vinegar. Bring nearly to the boiling point.

3. Beat the egg yolks with the salt and pepper in a small saucepan. Beat the hot butter mixture into the yolks until thickened. If the sauce curdles, beat in a little boiling water until smooth.

bean curd (tofu):

A white, 3-inch square cake made from ground, softened soy beans and water. It is available canned or fresh in Chinese or Japanese markets and large metropolitan supermarkets. *Tofu* may be refrigerated for up to 2 weeks if kept in a bowl of water. Change the water daily.

béchamel sauce:

3   tablespoons butter
3   tablespoons flour
2   cups milk, scalded
    Salt
    Freshly ground pepper

A basic thick white sauce prepared by adding hot milk, salt and pepper to a *roux*. Used in cream dishes or in the preparation of more complex white sauces.

1. In a small saucepan, prepare a *roux* with the butter and flour. Remove pan from the heat, pour in the scalded milk and beat briskly with a whisk until well blended. Beating constantly with the whisk, return to moderate heat, bring to a boil and cook for 3 minutes. Season to taste with salt and pepper.

Variation: Add a finely minced onion to the melted butter before adding the flour. Proceed as above, then strain the sauce before serving.

beurre manié:

French cookery term (literally "kneaded butter") for a mixture of softened butter and flour that is used to thicken sauces, soups and stews. To prepare a *beurre manié*: combine 1 tablespoon butter and 1 tablespoon flour in a bowl. Knead the mixture thoroughly, then shape into tiny balls. Stir the prepared *beurre manié* into the sauce, soup or stew a few minutes before serving and beat briskly over low heat for 1 to 2 minutes. Do not boil.

bind:

To use beaten eggs or a sauce to hold other ingredients together—i.e., if a stuffing calls for bread crumbs, onion, celery, sausage, etc., beaten eggs are used to "bind" these ingredients together.

blanch:

To briefly heat foods in a large quantity of boiling water before cooking. Blanching is done for several reasons: to remove the excess salt or bitter taste of a food; to firm white meats such as brains, sweetbreads, chicken or veal; to make some fruits or vegetables easier to peel, or as a preliminary step in freezing, preserving and canning.

boil:

To heat a liquid until bubbles form rapidly on the surface.

bok choy:

The Chinese cabbage that looks like a common celery but has large, dark green leaves and white stalks. In an emergency, a firm green cabbage may be substituted.

braise:

To sear meat over high heat in oil or fat and then cook slowly in the oven in a covered dish with a small quantity of liquid.

caramelize:

To heat sugar until it forms a golden brown syrup or to coat a mold or food with caramelized sugar. To caramelize a 1½-quart metal mold, combine ½ cup sugar and 2 tablespoons water in the mold. Place the mold over moderate heat and boil the mixture until the syrup turns golden-brown, about 3 to 4 minutes. Swirl the mold gently during cooking. When the sugar caramelizes, set mold briefly into a shallow pan of cold water to stop the cooking, then remove and swirl the caramel until all surfaces of the mold are coated and the syrup has cooled. Invert coated mold over a plate.

Chinese parsley:

Very similar to coriander or cilantro but having a more pronounced flavor and pungent aroma. The best substitute is Italian flat-leaved parsley.

chop:

Using a sharp knife, cut off a slice of the meat or vegetable. Hold the slice firmly on the cutting board and cut straight ⅛-inch strips. Turn and cut the strips at ⅛-inch intervals.

court bouillon: A flavorful broth used for poaching fish, chicken or vegetables. A basic court bouillon is prepared by boiling 2 carrots, 2 onions, a celery stalk and an herb bouquet in salted water for at least 30 minutes. When preparing a court bouillon for fish, white wine and a lemon are frequently added.

crème fraîche: A French term for heavy cream that has been allowed to mature and ferment slightly. It is served cold as a topping on sweet dishes, fruits or puddings. *Crème fraîche* is difficult to find but a good substitute can be prepared by combining 2 parts heavy cream to 1 part sour cream or buttermilk. Blend mixture thoroughly, then cover bowl and let stand at room temperature until the mixture thickens, about 4 hours. Refrigerate until needed.

croutons: Small cubes of bread that have been toasted in a 300° oven for 5 minutes, then tossed with melted butter or oil. Another way to make croutons is to pan-fry bread cubes in oil until golden-brown. A good way to use up stale bread. A garlic clove can be added to the oil for variety.

cube: To cut meat or vegetables into pieces 1 inch on all sides.

deglaze: To scrape the drippings and brown particles from a meat cooking utensil by adding water, stock or wine. When a small quantity of flour mixed with water is briskly stirred into the liquid and heated, a simple gravy is formed.

dice: To cut meat or vegetables into regular ½-inch squares—about half the size of cubes.

dredge: To dip foods, especially meats, lightly in flour to provide a coating that helps the foods brown more quickly and evenly.

flaky pastry:

1 ¾ cups flour
8 tablespoons butter, chilled and cut into pieces
4 to 6 tablespoons iced water
½ teaspoon salt

The basic dough used in the preparation of all savory pies such as quiches, flans, flamîches, pissaladières and ramekins.

1. Sift the flour onto a pastry board. Make a well in the center of the flour and add the butter. Using a pastry blender or your fingers, mix the butter and flour together into a stiff granular dough that is the consistency of cornmeal.

2. Make an indentation in the center of the dough and add 4 tablespoons of the iced water and the salt. Mix only until the liquid is absorbed. Do not overhandle. If the dough will not hold together, add up to 2 more tablespoons of water. Form the dough quickly into a ball, wrap in a damp towel and chill for 1 hour.

3. Roll out the dough to the desired thickness (usually ¼ inch) and carefully place in the pie plate. Trim the edges and prick the surface of the pastry. Line the prepared shell with aluminum foil or waxed paper and fill with dried beans to prevent the crust from puffing. Bake in a preheated 350° oven until golden, about 10 to 15 minutes. Allow to cool slightly before adding a filling.

garam masala:

A prepared mixture of ground spices used to flavor the meat and vegetable dishes of India and Pakistan. It consists of black pepper, coriander, black and white cumin, cardamom, cloves, ginger, mace, nutmeg, cassia and fenugreek. It can be bought in the gourmet sections of department stores or in specialty shops. Curry powder can be substituted in an emergency.

garnish:

To decorate a dish just before serving with colorful accents (parsley, watercress, croutons, tomatoes or lemon) or to accompany a main dish with complementary foods such as rice, noodles or beans.

glaze:

1) To put a dish under the broiler to form a golden-brown crust just before serving. 2) To coat with a frosting or syrup when preparing breads, pastries, cakes and pies.

goose fat:

Rendered goose fat from a roast bird can be stored in an earthenware crock for months. Fresh goose fat may be purchased in containers from many German butchers.

Canned goose fat and preserved goose (*q.v.*) may be found in many gourmet markets. Rendered chicken fat may be substituted for goose fat where necessary.

herb bouquet
or
bouquet garni:

A "bunch" of herbs tied together with string or secured in a cheesecloth bag that is used to flavor soups, stews and foods during cooking and then discarded before the dish is served. The traditional herb

bouquet contains a bay leaf, parsley and thyme, but numerous other herbs are also used. Both the quantity and type of herbs chosen will depend on the particular recipe.

hollandaise sauce:

4 *egg yolks*
2 *tablespoons water*
1 *tablespoon lemon juice*
   Salt
   Freshly ground pepper
½ *pound butter, at room temperature*

A rich, thick sauce with a base of egg yolks, butter and lemon juice. Served hot or cold with fish, eggs, chicken and vegetables or used as the basis for other sauces.

1. Place the egg yolks in the top section of a double boiler. Using a wire whisk, beat yolks for 1 minute,

then add the water, lemon juice, salt and pepper. Beat for 1 minute. Place over barely simmering water.

2. Beating constantly with a whisk, gradually incorporate the butter, 1 tablespoon at a time. Stir until thickened.

hoisin sauce:

A thick, sweet brownish sauce made from soybeans, flour, sugar and spices. Possible substitutes are bottled duck sauce (Chinese plum sauce),

available in most supermarkets, or combine equal amounts of catsup and soy sauce and add a little sugar.

lard:

1) Solid pork fat that has been rendered and clarified. Commonly used as a cooking fat and in the preparation of pastries and biscuits. 2) To thread thin pieces of pork fat

or unsmoked bacon through the flesh of uncooked lean meat or fowl to give it additional juiciness and flavor during cooking.

lobster:

To prepare a live lobster, place it shell side up on a cutting board. To kill it humanely, cut its spinal cord (where the tail and body meet) with a sharp heavy knife. Split the undershell lengthwise. Remove and discard the dark vein, the tough sac behind the eyes and the spongy tissue. Do not discard the soft green liver (called "tomalley") or the red roe (known as "coral")—these are great delicacies. Separate the tail from the chest—if the recipe calls for cut-up lobster. Cut off the claws and crack them. Lobsters should be prepared just before using them, not hours in advance.

marinate:

To soak food in a liquid (the marinade) to season and tenderize it before cooking. A marinade is usually made of oil and vinegar (or lemon juice or wine) and appropriate spices for the dish.

marrow:

This ingredient may be cooked in the bone or may be removed from the bone first. Because it is very fatty and disintegrates easily under high heat, marrow should be poached gently in good stock (*q.v.*) for no more than 1½ to 2 minutes, then removed promptly with a slotted spoon.

mayonnaise:

2   *egg yolks, at room temperature*
¼   *teaspoon salt*
     Pinch sugar
½   *teaspoon dry mustard*
½   *teaspoon white wine vinegar (or lemon juice)*
1 to 1¼   *cups olive oil*

A creamy, cold sauce made from egg yolks, oil and lemon juice. Served hot or cold with fish, eggs, chicken and vegetables or used as the basis of other sauces.

1. Place the egg yolks in a warm bowl and beat with a wire whisk for 1 minute. Add the salt, sugar and dry mustard. Beat for 1 minute.

2. Beating constantly, add ¼ cup of the olive oil *a drop at a time*, then blend in the vinegar (if lemon juice is used, add when indicated below). Still beating, very slowly add enough of the remaining olive oil to make a thick and fluffy sauce. Correct the seasonings (and stir in the lemon juice). If the mayonnaise curdles during preparation, place another egg yolk into a clean, warm bowl and very slowly blend the mayonnaise into it.

mince:

To cut an ingredient into very small pieces. Meat or vegetables can be put through a grinder if large quantities are needed.

---

pastry:

See discussions under *flaky pastry* and *sweet short-crust pastry*.

---

portions:

The number of servings yielded in the main-course recipes in this book are based on the assumption that the dish will be served with accompaniments and/or an appetizer, a soup, perhaps a dessert. If served alone, the portions could be increased—e.g., a recipe that "Serves 6" might be served to 4.

---

preserved goose (confit d'oie):

Pieces of a goose (wing, leg and breast sections) rendered in its own fat for storage. Available canned in gourmet sections of department stores or supermarkets. Considered essential for cassoulet and other French provincial stews and soups. To prepare *confit d'oie*:

1. Clean a 10- to 14-pound goose, reserving all the fat. Cover the goose with approximately 2 pounds of kosher (coarse) salt and let stand in a cool place overnight.

2. Render the goose fat with four cloves of crushed garlic in a large skillet.

3. Rinse the salt from the goose and pat the pieces dry. Place the pieces in the fat, cover and cook for 30 minutes. Remove the goose with a slotted spoon and place in a large earthenware crock.

4. Allow the fat to cool, then strain through a double thickness of cheesecloth. Pour over the goose pieces.

5. Melt ½ pound of lard and let cool slightly. Pour over the goose, forming a 1-inch topping. Whenever a piece of goose is removed, melt the lard and pour over the remaining pieces of goose to seal. Can be refrigerated for several months.

reduce:

To decrease the amount of a liquid by boiling, uncovered, over high heat. Reducing is done to intensify the flavor and improve the consistency of the liquid.

refresh:

To stop the cooking process by immediately plunging cooked foods into cold water. Refreshing helps retain flavor and sets the color.

rouille:

1 *slice white bread or 1 medium potato, cooked*
1 *hot red chili pepper or 1 jalapeño pepper*
1 *clove garlic*
½ *cup olive oil*
Salt
Freshly ground pepper
2 *tablespoons hot fish broth*

A thick creamy, cold sauce prepared like a mayonnaise but also incorporating a highly seasoned paste of garlic, hot red peppers and potatoes (or bread crumbs). Served with soups, stews and fish.

1. Soak the bread in water and squeeze dry. In a mortar, pound the bread (or potato) hot pepper and garlic into a smooth paste. Add the oil by drops. Season with salt and pepper, then slowly add the hot soup. Serve in a sauceboat.

roux:

A mixture of equal amounts of butter and flour, cooked gently over low heat. Used to thicken sauces or soups or as the base of a variety of white and brown sauces. To prepare a *roux*: Melt 3 tablespoons of butter over low heat, remove pan from heat and briskly beat in 3 tablespoons of flour with a wire whisk. Return the pan to low heat and beat briskly until the mixture is well blended and the flour is cooked through, about 3 minutes.

sauté:

To fry quickly in a small amount of fat.

score:

To partially gash the surface of foods, e.g. whole hams, steaks and chestnuts.

sesame-seed oil:

A topaz-colored oil made from roasted sesame seeds. It has a special nutty flavor that heightens the taste of any dish. It is available in bottles in Chinese or Japanese markets and many supermarkets with a gourmet or foreign food section.

shred: To cut or pull apart a meat or vegetable into thin strips, especially for Chinese dishes. Raw vegetables are best done by straight slicing, then cutting into narrow strips about 1 inch long and ⅛ to ¼ inch wide. Cooked meats or poultry can be shredded with fingers.

shrimp, dried: Amber-colored small brine shrimp with a strong salty taste. Tiny canned shrimp marinated in a good soy sauce may be substituted.

simmer: To cook foods in a liquid heated to just below the boiling point.

sliver: To chop a food, especially nuts, into thin strips.

sorrel: A green, leafy vegetable that is sometimes called "sourgrass." In recipes calling for sorrel, spinach may be successfully substituted but add a little fresh lemon juice to achieve the best taste. As with spinach, use only enamel or stainless steel cooking utensils.

star anise: A licorice-flavored spice that resembles a tiny 8-pointed star. It is sold only in Chinese markets. Anise powder can be substituted if the whole spice is not available.

steam: To cook a meat, fish, vegetable or pudding in a covered pan placed over boiling water. The food is cooked by the intense steam given off by the water.

stir-fry: To constantly stir or toss foods while cooking in a little oil over fairly high heat. An essential technique in Chinese cooking, stir-frying is most easily done in a wok.

stock:

A liquid base for soups, sauces, stews or gravies made from the slow cooking of the bones and the trimmings of meat, fish or chicken. A stock can simmer between 30 minutes and 5 hours, with the flavors intensifying during the cooking. Stocks can be refrigerated in covered containers for up to 3 weeks or frozen for several months.

meat stock:

2 *pounds shin of beef*
3 *pounds veal or beef bones*
4 *quarts water*
Salt
3 *carrots, chopped*
3 *onions, chopped*
2 *leeks*
2 *celery stalks*
Herb bouquet (thyme, bay leaf, peppercorns, parsley)
1 *clove garlic*

1. Cover the meat and bones with cold water. Bring to a boil and skim the surface. Add the remaining ingredients.

2. Partially cover the pot and simmer over moderate heat for 4 hours. Skim the surface occasionally. Strain the liquid, allow to cool and skim the fat again. Correct the seasonings and refrigerate. Yields about 2½ quarts.

chicken stock:

Substitute a 3-pound whole chicken and any extra giblets available for the beef and bones listed in the meat stock. Remove the chicken when tender, about 1¾ hours, and use for other purposes. Continue to simmer the broth for another hour. Strain, cool and refrigerate.

fish stock:

2 *pounds fish flesh and trimmings*
2 *onions*
1 *carrot*
1 *celery stalk*
Herb bouquet (bay leaf, fennel seed, parsley, peppercorns, thyme)
1 *cup dry white wine*
1 *clove garlic*
Salt

1. Place all the ingredients in a saucepan, cover with cold water and simmer for 45 minutes. Pour the broth through a strainer lined with cheesecloth and cool.

sweet short-crust pastry:

1 ¾   cups presifted flour
5   ounces unsalted butter, cut into bits
3   tablespoons shortening
¼   teaspoon salt
3   tablespoons sugar
½   cup iced water
1   egg yolk

The basic dough used for dessert pastries and pies.

1. Place the flour in a mound on a pastry board.

2. Make a well in the center of the flour. Add the butter bits and shortening. Using a pastry blender or your fingers, mix the fats and the flour together into a stiff granular dough.

3. Make an indentation in the center of the dough and add the salt, sugar, water and egg yolk. Knead until the dough is smooth, about 3 minutes. Do not overhandle. Form dough

into a ball, wrap in a damp towel and chill for 1 hour.

4. Roll out the dough to ¼ inch thickness and place in the pie plate. Trim the edges and use the blunt end of a knife to make a decorative edge. Prick the surface of the pastry and line the shell with aluminum foil or waxed paper. Fill with dried beans to prevent puffing and bake in a preheated 350° oven until golden, about 10 to 15 minutes. Cool slightly before adding the filling.

truffles:

Many fanciful tales have been told about these exotic and expensive fungi, but the facts about them are equally intriguing. Black truffles come from France, where they are hunted for and dug up by trained pigs. White truffles, which are actually beige, come from Italy and are hunted by "truffle hounds." Truffles are available fresh (during certain months of the year at gourmet shops) and canned. To prepare

fresh truffles, wash them at least twice before slicing thinly. Save all the peelings and any small bits for garnishes, sauces and soups. Canned truffles need no advance preparation. Leftover truffles can be refrigerated, soaked in oil or wine to cover, for up to a month. If truffles are not available, mushrooms (perhaps marinated in Madeira for ½ hour) can be substituted in most recipes.

vanilla sugar:

Granulated sugar with a slight vanilla flavor. To prepare, add a vanilla bean to a jar of sugar,

cover tightly and store for at least 1 day. Vanilla sugar may be stored indefinitely.

vinaigrette sauce:

3   tablespoons red wine
     vinegar
9   tablespoons olive oil
¾   teaspoon salt
     Freshly ground pepper
1 to 2 cloves garlic, minced
     (optional)
2   shallots, minced
     (optional)

A basic dressing usually comprised of about 3 parts oil to 1 part vinegar. Served on salads, vegetables, cold meats and fish.

1. Combine all the ingredients listed and beat until thoroughly blended.

Variation: Add 1 tablespoon mixed herbs or ½ tablespoon dry mustard.

---

wok:

The standard Chinese cooking utensil. It is a concave, thin iron pan with a round bottom, resembling a large salad bowl. Woks are available in most hardware and department stores and many Chinese food markets. A well-seasoned iron skillet (12-inch diameter is best) with a tightly fitting lid is a satisfactory substitute.

CHARTS

USA/GREAT BRITAIN EQUIVALENTS TABLE FOR LIQUID MEASUREMENT

USA	GREAT BRITAIN
1 teaspoon = ⅓ tablespoon	1 teaspoon = ½ tablespoon
1 tablespoon = ½ ounce	1 tablespoon = ½ ounce
3 tablespoons	2 tablespoons
4 tablespoons (¼ cup)	3 tablespoons
6 tablespoons	4 tablespoons (2 ounces)
⅓ cup	4 tablespoons (2 ounces)
½ cup (8 tablespoons)	Scant ¼ pint
⅔ cup	¼ pint (1 gill or 5 ounces)
¾ cup (12 tablespoons)	Generous ¼ pint
1 cup (1½ pint or 2 gills)	⅓ pint
1½ cups	Generous ½ pint (10 ounces)
2 cups (1 pint or 16 fluid ounces)	Generous ¾ pint
2½ cups (1¼ pints)	1 Imperial pint (20 ounces)
3 cups	1¼ pints
3½ cups	1½ pints
4 cups (1 quart)	Generous 1½ pints
5 cups	2 pints (1 Imperial quart or 40 ounces)
6 cups	2½ pints
8 cups (2 quarts)	3¼ pints
9 cups (2¼ quarts)	3½ pints
2½ quarts	4 pints
3 quarts	4¾ pints
4 quarts	6½ pints
5 quarts	8 pints (1 gallon)

BASIC FOOD EQUIVALENTS

butter

1 pound	=	2 cups
¼ pound (1 stick)	=	½ cup (8 tablespoons)
2 ounces	=	¼ cup (4 tablespoons)

beans

Great Northern or white	1 pound (1½ cups) =	9 cups cooked
kidney	1 pound (2⅓ cups) =	6 cups cooked

cheese

shredded	½ pound =	2 cups
freshly grated	½ pound =	2½ cups
cottage	½ pound =	1 cup

cream

sour	½ pint =	1 cup
heavy or light	½ pint =	1 cup
whipped	½ pint =	2 cups

flour

all-purpose

	ounces	grams
1 teaspoon	$1/12$	2
1 tablespoon	¼	6
1 cup	3½	100
1 pound	16	454
unsifted = 3½ cups		
sifted = 4 cups		

cake

1 teaspoon	$1/18$	1⅔
1 tablespoon	$1/6$	5
1 cup	2¾	80
1 pound	16	454
unsifted = 4 cups		
sifted = 4½ cups		

lemon and lime

juice	1 medium =	2 to 3 tablespoons
rind, grated	1 medium =	2 teaspoons

mushrooms

sliced, raw	½ pound =	2½ cups

nuts

almonds

shelled, whole	1 pound =	3½ cups
ground	1 pound =	2⅔ cups
slivered	1 pound =	5⅔ cups

pecans and walnuts

shelled, whole	1 pound =	4 cups
ground	1 pound =	2⅔ cups

onions   1 pound (3 large) = 2 to 2½ cups, chopped

orange

juice	1 medium =	⅓ to ½ cup
rind, grated	1 medium =	2 tablespoons

potatoes   1 pound raw = 2 cups mashed
(3 medium)

rice

raw	1 pound =	2½ cups
cooked	1 pound =	7½ cups

sugar

brown	1 pound =	2¼ cups
confectioners'	1 pound =	3½ cups
granulated	1 pound =	2 cups
superfine	1 pound =	2⅓ cups

tomatoes   1 pound = 3 to 4 small

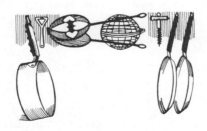

METRIC CONVERSION TABLE

To convert *teaspoons* to *milliliters* multiply by 5

To convert *tablespoons* to *milliliters* multiply by 15

To convert *fluid ounces* to *milliliters* multiply by 30

To convert *cups* to *liters* multiply by .24

To convert *pints* to *liters* multiply by .47

To convert *quarts* to *liters* multiply by .95

To convert *ounces* to *grams* multiply by 28

To convert *pounds* to *kilograms* multiply by .45

WEIGHTS AND MEASURES

Less than ⅛ teaspoon	=	Dash
3 teaspoons	=	1 tablespoon
2 tablespoons	=	1 liquid ounce
3 tablespoons	=	1 jigger
4 tablespoons	=	¼ cup
5 tablespoons plus 1 teaspoon	=	⅓ cup
8 tablespoons	=	½ cup
12 tablespoons	=	¾ cup
16 tablespoons	=	1 cup
1 cup	=	½ liquid pint
2 cups (16 fluid ounces)	=	1 pint
4 cups	=	1 quart
2 pints	=	1 quart
4 quarts	=	1 gallon
8 quarts	=	1 peck
4 pecks	=	1 bushel

RECIPES BY COUNTRY OF ORIGIN

ARGENTINA:
mixed-meats stew (*puchero*), 290
tongue with almond sauce (*lengua con salsa alemendras*), 268

AUSTRALIA:
beefsteak and kidney pie, 226
Canberra lamb fondue, 246
pineapple Pavlova, 431

AUSTRIA:
goulash with sauerkraut (*Szeged goulasch*), 286
Sand cake (*Sandkuchen*), 383
soup with liver meatballs (*Leberklössesuppe*), 83
Tyrolean beef soup (*Rindsuppe*), 84
veal scallops with anchovy butter, breaded (*Schnitzel mit Sardelenbutter*), 230

BELGIUM:
Flanders raisin crêpes (*bouquettes aux raisins*), 464
Flemish fish soup (*waterzooï de poissons*), 97
Gand-style potato casserole (*potée de Gand*), 331
ham and endive rolls au gratin (*Lof, Ham en Kaasaus*), 250

BRAZIL:
Bahia fish soup (*bouquet do mar*), 99
black bean and meat casserole (*feijoada à Brasileira*), 289
coffee custard (*crème de cafe*), 444

BULGARIA:
moussaka, 299
zucchini in sour cream (*tökfäzelék*), 368

CANADA:
blueberry pudding, 451
carrot cake, 390
chicken liver pâté, 58
lemon snow, 436
salmor in aspic, cold, 137
shortbread cookies, 402
split pea soup, 82

CHINA (All the Chinese recipe titles have been rendered in the Mandarin transliteration, the national language of China):
bean curd and pork (*dou fu ru*), 262
beef with bamboo shoots, shredded (*tung sun chao new ru*), 218
bok choy with pork (*bai tsai ru*), 261
chicken
with asparagus (*lu sun chao jee pien*), 189
with bamboo shoots and mushrooms (*jam bao-chee ting*), 187
wings with ginger (*chiang jee yeh*), 190
five spiced cold beef (*wu shiang new ru*), 53
fried rice (*chow fan*), 310
gingered string beans (*chiang pien tou*), 340
glazed apples (*la sze ping kuo*), 416
hot and sour soup (*shran la tong*), 70
noodles with pork or chicken, fried (*tzu ru chao mien*), 308
pineapple chicken (*po lo jee*), 188
roast pork strips (*tsa sow ru*), 259
sesame seed chicken (*jee ma jee*), 174
shrimp, stir-fried (*chao-sha*), 161
spareribs, roast (*tas sow py kua*), 54
spinach, stir-fried (*po tsai*), 362
spring rolls (*chun chuan*), 36–7
steamed ground pork (*tsing tzu ru*), 263
steamed sea bass (*tsing lu yu*), 108
sweet and sour pork (*koo loo ru*), 260
wonton soup (*won ton*), 71

CUBA:
beef with rice and beans, ground (*carne con arroz y frijoles*), 288
kidney bean salad (*ensalada de habichuelas*), 23

CZECHOSLAVAKIA:
plum surprises (*svestkove knedlíky*), 468

DENMARK:
Christmas pickled herring (*sild*), 40
walnut delights (*koeka*), 404

EGYPT:
beef with okra, stewed (*bamia*), 223

ETHIOPIA:
chicken with hot sauce (*doro-weutt*), 183

FINLAND:
lamb, beef and pork hot pot (*karjalanpaisti*), 294
marinated herring with 3 dressings (*suolasilli*), 41
parsonage pudding (*pappilau pudding*), 456
Spring vegetable soup (*kesäkeitto*), 72

FRANCE *(cont.)*

INDEX

512

COLOR PLATES

*Drawings by Christiane Neuville,
Claude Rougeot, Jacques Dehornois.*